The Well of Five Streams
Essays on Celtic Paganism

Praise for *The Well of Five Streams*

Erynn's work expresses a deep feel for, and knowledge of, Celtic text, drawing from these wisdom and insight that will aid any reader in developing a spiritual path rooted in the knowledge of the past, but wholly appropriate for our modern age. For Erynn, Celtic Reconstructionism is not a series of practices rigidly set in a static past but a vital path that is alive and constantly evolving. There is great thought, depth and sensitivity here -- a must for all those who have a passion for keeping the Celtic Spirit alive!

Philip Carr-Gomm
Author of *Druid Mysteries*

Erynn's writing is wide-ranging, laced with ingenuity. Laurie brings forth and synthesizes diverse elements, combining diligent scholarship with a carefully thought out, ethical, and personal Polytheist sensibility. I am delighted to have this extraordinary resource in my possession.

Mael Brigde
Founder of Daughters of the Flame, and blogger at Brigit's Sparkling Flame

Within these pages is a solid foundation of careful historical and cultural research, tempered with a curiosity steadied and strengthened through years of experience. This collection of essays, interviews, and reviews not only gives background to Laurie's previous books, but gives the reader an insider's view into how she became the mature spiritual practitioner and author she is today.

Lupa
Author of *New Paths to Plant Totems*; and *Fungus Totems*

An inspiring work, these essays truly give an understanding of what Celtic Reconstructionist Paganism is all about. Riveting from the first page to the last, this opus is a must read both for those first embarking on their Pagan path, and those who have studied Celtic Paganism for years.

Sean Harbaugh
Priest, Ár nDraíocht Féin

A treasure trove of wisdom, this anthology offers invaluable discussions of concepts that are key to Celtic polytheism, Celtic Reconstructionism, and modern Druidism. Erynn Rowan Laurie takes the reader on a journey through beauty and madness, poetry and truth, the divine and the mundane, weaving them all together into a cohesive and captivating whole. Truly essential reading for anyone interested in understanding the beliefs of the ancient Irish, and how those beliefs can be interpreted and applied today, as well as a fascinating and essential view into one woman's journey along the path.

Morgan Daimler
Author of *By Land, Sea, and Sky*; *Where the Hawthorn Grows*; and *Pagan Portals: The Morrigan*

The Well of Five Streams
Essays on Celtic Paganism

Erynn Rowan Laurie

Megalithica Books
Stafford England

Editor: Taylor Ellwood
Layout: Taylor Ellwood
Cover Design: Erynn Rowan Laurie/Storm Constantine

ISBN: 978-0-9932371-1-9

MB0175

A Megalithica Books Publication
An imprint of Immanion Press

info@immanion-press.com
http://www.immanion-press.com

For my friends, too many to be named,
may you always be blessed as you have blessed me.

Table of Contents

Foreword

Poetry isn't something to be trifled with. Oh, I know, plenty of people these days do trifle with it, treating the endeavor as some sort of relaxing spa therapy, the literary equivalent of a hot soak after a long day. However, those of us who know better know that poets are a fearsome bunch, endowed with frightening powers of gifting ever-lasting infamy through withering satire. In short, you better treat your local poet well, or else you'll soon be on the receiving end of their pen. Further, those of us who've given poetry more than a passing glance know that poetry is one of the last vestiges of real, old magic left in our disenchanted age. Poetry is the go-to thing for when you absolutely, positively, have to walk out of Hel(l) in one piece.

I wax rhapsodic about poets and poetry because my friend Erynn is a real live capital-P Poet. That means she doesn't just write verse in a rustic, romantic European town somewhere (though she does do that from time to time, or so I hear), it means she wades through the trenches of debate, digging through archives and translations to bring more light to a discussion, and uses her knowledge to improve the world around her. Erynn is a Poet who has endured torment, and who understands that her experience brings with it gifts and burdens. Here, in this collection, you'll get to see the process of a real Poet writing, thinking, and sharing about a number of important matters.

Religious debates, academic papers, reviews, and deep-dive explorations about history, ritual, trauma, and poetry are what you'll find here. It is a glimpse into the question of what, exactly, Poets do when they aren't reading and writing poetry. This book is a light into the mind of one of the best people I know, and we are privileged that Erynn has taken the time to collect them into this convenient volume. Much of the writing is formal, but it also gives an intensely personal glimpse into the workings of a particular mind, a mind that has been far more influential in the world than many would know. A now-passed religious leader within modern Paganism once tried to joke that Erynn was an "archdruid," and that was quite incorrect, but I can understand why he would want to say that. Erynn is not a Druid, but she does represent an ideal of mind, vision, and art united in purpose and intent.

I am honored to be able to write a foreword for Erynn, and hope that whatever small sliver of infamy I have earned with my own writings will encourage people to pick up this book and then, so inspired by the quality of writings here, pick up her other works as well. It is well worth your trouble, because I assure you, capital-P Poets don't walk this Earth often, and we should mark the moment when they pass through our lives. I consider myself lucky that Erynn passed through mine, and hope you'll share my luck in the days to come.

Blessings,

Jason Thomas Pitzl (aka Jason Pitzl-Waters)
The Wild Hunt

A Word Against the Wave

For the ancient and medieval Irish, to be a *fili* ("poet," from roots meaning "seer") is not a pointless, marginal, ivory-tower pursuit far removed from the social world, the arena of the political, or even the concerns of the everyday. To be a *fili* is to be one of the supreme power-holders and -wielders of the community. As a result, the poet's profession is not something peaceful, their words uncontested or inconsequential in their impact upon everyday thought, nor the fate of rulers or the reputations of the worthy or unworthy alike.

To be a poet is to be combative, not only in words but in ideas. To take up the poet's mantle is not to express one's self alone in a battle for authenticity amidst a banal world, it is to speak for the people, but also for the land, the legacy of the ancestors, and occasionally for the gods themselves in a struggle which has the entire world as stakes. To be a *fili* is to stand against a wave, and with one's words to turn those waves back when necessary.

How different things are now....

The word "bard" has been adopted by the wider pagan community, in an effort to continue certain aspects of "Celtic" cultures. It is often thought to mean anyone who is a storyteller, a musician, or a poet of any level of skill or education. While recognition of the sacred dimension of entertainment and all of the pleasures that it can provide is certainly a communal benefit, the *fili*'s work is not, and never has been, mere entertainment.

The medieval Irish poetic corpus is known as "bardic poetry" (though not only commonly, but also by academic authors), which would have outraged and demeaned the fully-trained and recognized *filid* of the medieval period. Their skill was not arrived at easily or without years of difficult training. A "bard" to the Irish was someone of perhaps some small amount of natural talent, but who did not have the hereditary tradition and lineage, the training, or the social recognition of the *fili*. In some reckonings of the grades of poetic accomplishment, a *bard* was a poet of the lower grades, an aspirant to greater glories in the future perhaps, but someone without the accomplishment that formal training and personal testing and triumph had yet produced. The modern claimants of the title "bard," though they do not know it, are for the most part accurate reflections of the Irish understanding of the term, since few (if any) are from acknowledged poetic schools or have undergone the ordeals necessary to be recognized as *filid*.

Meanwhile, in academia as well as in certain informed sections of paganism, "druids" are thought to be the end-all and be-all of "Celtic" religiosity, the conveners of rituals, the repositories of lore, and the holders of the tradition. It is often thought, further, that what the medieval Irish *filid* had of the practices of seership, of lore-keeping, and of supernatural contact was inherited or appropriated from what would have been "originally" druidic custom and functions. This seems unlikely for all sorts of reasons — including that the poetic and the druidic functions were separate and distinct from an early period — but this may be the case especially in Ireland, where the evidence for the religious status of druids as anything other than diviners and practitioners of certain varieties of magic is scant, and little is known in general of their status, their functions, or their teachings. To point this out is not to diminish the worthiness of the premodern druids, nor of those who seek to recapture "druidry" in the modern period, but instead to indicate what can and cannot be known with certainty, and to contrast this to what is definitely known about the institutions of *filidecht* in both practical and historical terms.

Too many modern people have been looking for something in druids and druidry which cannot be known. It has been so filled with speculation-become-certainty that far too many people speak of druidic beliefs, mores, and opinions as if they are obvious, plain, and commonplace rather than a palimpsest of such various accretions as environmentalism, Freemasonry, and ideas drawn from (largely discredited) Indo-European structuralist assumptions that may have little or no bearing on the ancient realities, insofar as these can be known at all.

These matters are well-understood by modern practitioners of the methodology of Celtic Reconstructionism, who have spent their days delving into the actual historical sources and literate texts of the medieval Irish and other Celtic cultures, and have steeped themselves in the scholarship interpreting these sources — while being aware of academia's limitations and biases as well. Rather than offering certainties, CR practitioners present options drawn from the premodern Irish as well as other Celtic cultural heritages, which are often far more nuanced, rich, and interesting than any modern notions related to these subjects, no matter how well cherished or commonly thought these modern notions might be.

It is standing against such a wave of misconceptions, of romantic flights of fancy, and often of willful and deliberate ignorance in preference to the realities (both bleak and blissful) of the known and extant tradition that the writings of Erynn Rowan Laurie have emerged over the past few decades. The books emblazoned with titles about "Celtic" this and "Druidic" that can be a morass of subjectivity lightly glazed with assurances of "the Old Ways" being faithfully transmitted by them. If one wades into that morass, one cannot easily avoid becoming mired in fabrications and falsities. There is no danger of this in anything Erynn has written, because what comes from legitimate sources is marked as such, and what comes from experienced speculation, comparative evaluation, spiritual experimentation, and experiential gnosis is likewise indicated plainly so that only deliberate obfuscation on the part of the reader can explain (though not excuse) someone not knowing which is which.

Erynn Rowan Laurie emerged as one of the early visionaries (in several senses!) of the Celtic Reconstructionist movement, and became one of the better-known such pioneers on the West Coast of the U.S. The dedication of resources — time, attention, energy, and money, with the latter resulting in a dedication of shelf-space in an extensive library — in order to have properly prepared for this role is not to be minimized in the case of Erynn, and many other CR practitioners. Indeed, the knowledge and familiarity many of them have with these materials rivals some academics, and even surpasses many of them in breadth or depth. This is due in no small part due to the ever-increasing specialization encouraged and even demanded in modern doctoral programs, which have sacrificed comprehensiveness in general knowledge for a specificity often so narrow as to be useless even amongst disciplinary peers.

In general, all those who use a reconstructionist methodology in modern pagan and polytheist religions, attempt (with whatever level of success) to bridge the erudition of the scholarly edifice of knowledge with the spark of inspiration that is at the heart of every devoted spiritual practice's pursuit. The success of Erynn in doing this for those interested in *filidecht* and in the Irish and Scottish dimensions of ancient polytheist practices is and remains a paradigmatic one which all future aspirants can hope to emulate, and from which any future practitioner can benefit.

Writings contained in this volume range across a variety of topics, but several themes come up consistently. It is often said that someone who sets out to seek a vision from the gods in Irish tradition will end up receiving poetry, madness, or death, and we see a bit of each in what follows. Poetry, certainly, is the thread that weaves all of these pursuits together — it is the denominator of the Irish tradition, which is never the lowest nor common — and which has brought cohesiveness to Erynn's corpus of works herein. Madness is dealt with in what the Irish called the *geilt*, the "insane-person" who takes refuge in wild nature after trauma of some sort, and who sometimes becomes a poetic martyr in their attempts at re-integration into society after this trauma. To find the poetry in madness is to find redemption, and Erynn's life and circumstances have often been a modern retelling of these tales of trial and transformation. Death is never final nor simple in Irish tradition, and one area in which it makes its appearance several times in this collection is in relation to healing herbs and the deities associated with them in premodern Ireland, with whom Erynn has had ongoing devotional relationships for decades. You will find these subjects and many others touched upon as well as greatly elaborated in the pages which remain in this book.

To understand Erynn as a person, read the interviews she has given that are included in this volume as the necessary background to all else that comes after. To do so will be insightful into the context that produces a poet and leads someone to pursue the rivulets from the fountain of wisdom back to their source. To understand Erynn as an important and innovative theorist and founder of modern CR practice, read the longer pieces she has written for their comprehensive framework-building and precedent-setting. To understand Erynn as an engaged practitioner, read the shorter pieces that apply her personal experiences and her foundational thinking to particular matters of interest.

According to an Irish Triad, the Three Things Required of a Poet are *imbas forosnai, teinm laedo,* and *dichetal do chennaib.* While the exact meanings of two of these phrases are still argued over, my own alliterative suggestion — appropriate, in any case, for the Irish poetic tradition, which used alliteration extensively — is inspiration, interpretation, and improvisation respectively. *Dichetal do chennaib,* "speaking from heads," is the unexpected word at the right moment, whether that moment is quotidian or more historically significant, which a *fili* can produce due to their ability to read the signs of the times and to act upon them with the light of their inspiration. *Teinm laedo,* "cracking the marrow," is the ability to penetrate to the heart of any matter presented to the poet in the inspired light of the attested tradition and how this continually refracts through every permutation of what may present itself to the poet's senses and intelligences. *Imbas forosnai*, "great knowledge which illuminates," is the binding force without which useful interpretations or meaningful improvisations cannot be created, and which relies directly on the *fili*'s ability to tap into the divine worlds—of nature, of deities, of the Otherworlds, of ancestral wisdom, of ancestors as people, and of Poetry Itself—and to be the window, the vessel, and the vehicle of that illuminating spark in their words and compositions. With these three items in the Triad as both goals and gateways, products and processes, ideals and itineraries, any student of *filidecht* can begin to gain purchase in their climb toward becoming an accomplished poet.

The words of Erynn Rowan Laurie herein are what she has brought thus far to this all-important project. In a sea of apathy, amidst a storm of illusions, and against waves of meaninglessness, Erynn's words are a sturdy bulwark in which many may be able to seek protection, find solace, and begin to build their own foundations to stem the tides of confusion that buffet us now, not only as polytheists, pagans, poets, and spiritual practitioners, but as humans living in a troubled world. The waves will not be turned back by the words of a single poet, but the fire of poetry that can be kindled in others from such words will surely provide illumination for all who wish to see through the illusions of the storm that is already upon us.

Dr. Phillip A. Bernhardt-House

Preface

I've been writing about Celtic polytheisms and Paganism for over twenty years – online for blogs, in print magazines and newsletters, in anthologies, and in my own books. I've written articles, essays, reviews, poetry, and more. I've given interviews on a number of topics of interest to these communities, and I've talked about other parts of my life that, in most cases, have had a profound impact on my spirituality and my writing about these topics. Some of this material has been easily available with a quick web search, while other pieces have appeared in obscure or difficult to find print anthologies.

Many of my readers have, over the years, expressed a desire for a collection of my work under one cover. I hope that what I've brought together will satisfy that want, allowing access to the more obscure material, while offering a convenient way to bring together works that are more easily found, as well. There are also a couple of entirely new pieces here, never previously published, which I hope you will enjoy, or at least find thought-provoking.

This volume, like its author, is idiosyncratic, opinionated, and wider-ranging than one might expect at first glance. I make no claims to any sort of authority beyond a love of research and a deep devotion to my deities of choice. I'm not an academic, nor am I formally affiliated with any particular Pagan or polytheist organization. I speak as and for myself, and myself alone, and I note here that any problems or errors in the text are my own, and not those of the people who have offered edits or comments during the process of compilation – most notably Dr. Phillip A. Bernhardt-House, a Celtic studies scholar and a dear friend of mine for many years now. Without Phil's input, several of the articles herein would not even exist in their current form.

Because this collection brings together work from a period of a little over twenty years, it traces an evolution of thought that would not be visible from a look at any individual piece. Beneath the writing lies a life in motion, rife with immense changes in circumstance and situation. The communities for whom I have written have changed as much, or more than I have myself over the years; I think there is a reflection of that in this collection as well.

There have been entirely too many people involved in the creation of these works over the years to mention everyone by name. It would be impossible to list everyone, which I think is a sign of having lived a good and fruitful life. Yet, there are those who do need to be recognized by name. First, I would like to thank Timothy White for his kind permission to reprint our jointly-authored article, *Speckled Snake, Brother of Birch*, from Shaman's Drum magazine, which he edited for many years. The late Alexei Kondratiev and Francine Nicholson were both invaluable for their conversation and contributions to the direction of my study and my work; they are still missed. Casey June Wolf, founder of Daughters of the Flame, introduced me to the practice of flamekeeping as a devotional practice for Brigid; my flamekeeping continues to be a solid bedrock for my spiritual life.

To all of my friends, colleagues, and collaborators who are not mentioned in this short list, it's not because I don't appreciate you and your work, or acknowledge your influence. Your conversation, inspiration, and support over the years have been and will always be important to me. I'm delighted that you have touched my life in so many profound ways, and you have my deepest thanks and affection. *Ad-rae búaid ocus bennachtain!*

Erynn Rowan Laurie
Trieste, Italy
March 2015

Technical Note

A technical note is necessary here, in that the spelling of some names and terms shifts from place to place in the book. Their spellings aren't consistent in the early sources, and I was usually using the spelling that agreed with whatever source I was using at the time. One thing that is consistent throughout the Gaelic language corpus is the idea that "other sources say..."[1] and that things vary from region to region and era to era.

In earlier pieces, particularly, the word "Celtic" is used in a more generic way than I would use it now. Most of the Pagan community hears "Celtic" and thinks of Ireland, Scotland, or Wales. It is a much broader term that deals with linguistic history and some cultural similarities, but it should be pointed out that "Celtic" is not a race, regardless of what the Celtic Twilight writers would have you believe. In some of these pieces, "Celtic" is used to refer to the Insular Celts, while in other pieces it is more intended as that far wider, more accurate term.

---

[1] I was introduced to this concept by Dr. Bernhardt-House, who has consistently made use of this phrase for many years.

Chapter 1
Articles and Essays

Themes and Evolutions

The articles and essays in this chapter span more than twenty years of my writing life. They are largely, but not entirely, about Celtic cultures, Gaelic poetics, and Celtic deities. A few are more personal accounts that explore my history, where I came from, and other paths that I follow. They are included primarily as context for much of the rest of the work.

The Truth Against the World originated on the Nemeton email list in 1994, at a time when most of the visible Pagan world was Wiccan, and ethics in the Pagan community was assumed to mean the Wiccan Rede. It is a very basic exploration of other types of ethical theory, founded in what I then understood of Celtic mythologies and cultures.

Goddess of the Growing Green was my first paid, professional publication, in the Spring 1994 issue of *SageWoman* magazine. I framed a photocopy of the check I got, and it hung on the wall near my computer for years as an inspiration and a reminder that I could do this; I could write things people wanted to read, enough to pay me to do so. I wrote about Airmed, an Irish goddess of healing herbs and springs, at a time when little was known about her in the Pagan community. I am delighted and heartened that her name is better-known today, and that she has devotees around the world.

One of the most well-known of my works is *The Cauldron of Poesy*, a translation of the Middle Irish poem and some of its notes, originally published in the Spring 1996 issue of *Obsidian* magazine. It has been reprinted several times in different magazines, and a new version of this translation will soon be published in an anthology of "Outsider poets" edited by Jerome Rothenberg in early 2015. Rothenberg is the editor of the groundbreaking anthology of indigenous and ethnic poetry, *Technicians of the Sacred*, and its poetic sensibilities deeply influenced aspects of my own work.

My translation of this poem has been controversial for a variety of reasons, many of which are addressed in Christopher Scott Thompson's excellent book on the poem, *A God Who Makes Fire*.[2] Despite the various issues expressed regarding my translation and commentary, it is still widely read and referred to, and Thompson's general defense of my translation was encouraging.

---

[2] *A God Who Makes Fire: The Bardic Mysticism of Amergin*, Christopher Scott Thompson, Lulu, 2013

The Preserving Shrine essay was published in Philip Carr-Gomm's anthology, *The Druid Renaissance,* in 1996 and again in its reissue under the name *The Rebirth of Druidry* in 2003. As I recall, it took me only a few hours to write, and required little editing between the draft and the final version. It explicates a modern Druidic rather than a reconstructionist sensibility, but this was precisely what the anthology called for.

Another controversial work, *Speckled Snake, Brother of Birch,* was written with Timothy White and published in *Shaman's Drum* 44, in 1997. Written about the potential use of entheogenic mushrooms among the insular Celts, it originated as a response to an article on "Irish Soma" by Peter Lamborn Wilson in a 1995 issue of *Psychedelic Illuminations;* Wilson's article later became the basis for his book, *Ploughing the Clouds,* on the same topic, wherein he cited some of our analysis in his footnotes.

Because *Speckled Snake* was written for a magazine on shamanism, and White was the editor of that magazine, the article asserted the existence of a Celtic shamanism in ways that I would not advocate had I been the sole author of the piece. Still, White's work on the material I sent to him was excellent and enriched the article greatly. It would not be what it is without him and would have been much less complete and complex. We focused narrowly on the use of *Amanita muscaria,* though I believe it is also, or perhaps even more likely, that various species of *Psilocybe* were used. As it was, the article was pushing the size limits usually allowed in *Shaman's Drum,* so inclusion of other materials expanding the argument was impossible.

It was over ten years before I was writing and publishing regularly again. I still maintained an online presence, but my health had taken a severe turn for the worse in the late 1990s. I ended up in the Veterans hospital in Seattle, dealing with post-traumatic stress resulting from my time in the Navy, and then went on disability. I got divorced in 2002, sold my house, and moved to Everett from Seattle in 2004 before I was once again settled and stable enough to write for publication.

2008 saw the publication of Lupa's anthology on cultural appropriation in the Pagan community, *Talking About the Elephant.* Both *Dead Religions, Living Cultures,* and *Work and Fear* appeared in that anthology. *Dead Religions* addresses who owns religions that the original culture discarded, or religions whose original cultures have long been gone. *Work and Fear* tackles problematic attitudes in Celtic Reconstructionist communities online that inhibit exploration and new growth, hoping to explain why it's so hard to find material on people's actual practices, rather than arguments about language and theory.

Gramma, I Want to Be a Witch is an autobiographical piece, written after a long conversation with my mom about my initial explorations of the Pagan community and her reactions to these changes. It was published in Arin Murphy Hiscock's 2009 anthology *Out of the Broom Closet*, exploring the "coming out" stories of fifty modern Pagans.

His Mother's Whole Body Heals takes us in an entirely different direction, exploring my experiences within the Greco-Roman-Egyptian syncretist group Ekklesía Antínoou, for Brandy Williams's 2009 anthology *Women's Voices in Magic*. This group has been both useful and important to me, and it is one of the few places where I have never felt objectified, nor had my gender turned into a "polarity" to which I have never genuinely related, as a person in a female body.

The essay *Becoming Poetry*, from the gorgeous 2010 anthology of esoteric poesis, *Datura*, edited by Ruby Sara, explores the traditions of *filidecht* and Celtic poetic craft. It offers thoughts on poetry as a healing path and the work of the sacred poet.

Since Feathers Have Grown on My Body, published in 2011 in the academic anthology *Disability and Religious Diversity* edited by Darla Schumm and Michael Stoltzfus, returns to this theme in a much deeper and more detailed way. The figure of the *geilt* or mad poet of Celtic literature, from Myrddin to Suibhne Geilt and beyond, is addressed as a method of understanding post-traumatic stress in mythic and spiritual terms. This is one of the pieces that gives me the most pride in its publication, as I was the only non-academic included in the anthology.

Ruby Sara published a second anthology of esoteric poesis, *Mandragora*, which included my work *Burying the Poet*, in 2012. This piece explores the use of incubation and sensory deprivation as initiatory rituals in Welsh and Gaelic poetcraft.

A Word Among Letters is the final previously published piece in this section, from Lupa's 2013 anthology *Engaging the Spirit World*. It addresses animism as expressed in Celtic literatures, and ways in which some in the Celtic Reconstructionist movement engage with the spirits and their worlds.

The next piece, *Building the Perfect Beast*, was intended for an anthology on theories and practices of sacrifice in modern Pagan religions that never materialized. It was based on a post from the

Nemeton list, back in 1995 or so, that deserved expansion and a much more in-depth treatment.

Queering the Flame, the final piece in this section, was written in response to a controversy in the Celtic Reconstructionist community some years ago regarding whether or not men should be "allowed" to tend Brigid's flame. The article examines arguments on both sides, as well as exploring the histories of perpetual flames in Ireland and other countries. I hope that the article will serve to open a few eyes to information that is not well known in the Pagan communities, and further the honoring of Brigid by all who are called to her service.

It should be noted that some of the articles and essays in this chapter are heavily footnoted, while others have minimal footnoting, or none at all. This is due to the original publication venues. Some publishers prefer works without them while others will use them, but only very sparingly. Academic publishers, obviously, go in for footnotes in a big way, insisting on documentation for everything. I'm rather fond of footnotes myself and tend to prefer them so that I can see where the writer is getting their information if I wish to do further exploration on my own. I hope that you will find the ones included here useful to your own work.

Several of the essays and articles in this chapter have been translated into other languages. I am deeply grateful to the people who have been interested enough in my writing to do the work of translation, and who have shared that information with others around the world.

The Truth Against the World:
Ethics in Modern Celtic Paganism

Three things of ill repute: inertness, grudging, close-fistedness
from *The Triads of Ireland*[3]

One of the most important things that defines a people as a distinct social and cultural group is how they act toward one another; what they expect from each other socially, what their rules of conduct are, and how they deal with those who step outside the boundaries of what their culture considers "proper behavior." These social rules, whether "don't stare at strangers" or "thou shalt not kill," are among the cultural guidelines to ethical behavior within any given group. Ethics govern not only these social interactions, but also what is acceptable in religious ritual, and the whys and whens of the appropriate use of magic.

Without an ethical structure of some sort, religion and magic become self-serving, meaningless beyond the single individual. Magic can easily become manipulative rather than transformative, serving only the needs of this moment rather than the needs of a lifetime, or of an individual rather than a community. Religion and social interaction become a minefield where killing your neighbor because you want tomatoes from her garden is as valid a method of obtaining your dinner as trading for them. Within many public Neopagan organizations there are no agreed upon ethics, no generally accepted rules of conduct. While individual freedoms are a good thing, and one which should be supported and striven for, it is also useful to have a groundwork upon which we can assume that one person will not lie to or about another, that oaths will not be falsely sworn, and that the organization's land fund won't be used to buy the group treasurer a new pickup truck. These things may indeed be generally deplored by individuals in the group, but without stated guidelines, objections become irrelevant and the cause of the objection is often lost in the ensuing muck-throwing contest, while the group debates what actually constitutes a lie, whether or not theft is actually theft, and whether any act is ever legally or ethically actionable. Where there are no standards of behavior, it is difficult for community and trust to develop.

---

3. Meyer, Kuno, *The Triads of Ireland*, Royal Irish Academy, Todd Lecture Series vol XIII, Hodges, Figes & Co., Dublin 1906, p. 27

Without trust between individuals, there can be no tribe. Groups with known and expressed ethical guidelines seem to be spared the worst aspects of this kind of struggle. People know where they stand and what the boundaries of interpretation are. Trust develops more easily, and community becomes more than a group of people who claim they believe similar things. Known guidelines don't guarantee absolute compatibility and social cohesion, but they certainly make it easier to determine the boundaries of acceptable behavior, make it possible for minor and major breaches of those codes of conduct to be pointed out, and create a starting point for dealing with those situations when they inevitably arise. Clear group ethical models also offer something for people to build their individual ethics upon. Ethics can be based upon ancient or modern models, derived from some philosophical source or created by mutual agreement and discussion. Celtic Reconstructionist Paganism recognizes the need for a set of ethical guidelines and bases its structure upon that of the ancient Celts. This is not to say that our ethical structure is identical to that of the early Celts, or directly derived from early Irish or Welsh laws. Many things laid out in those laws and illustrated in the tales are distasteful to us as moderns, no longer either acceptable or legal within the overculture under which we must all live. Trial by ordeal, death by exposure in pits, and slavery for forfeiture of contracts are some of the more blatant examples of things that our Celtic forbears did which we would find abhorrent. Knowing our ethical history allows us to intelligently modify those beliefs into modern applications for Celtic Reconstructionist Pagans.

Ethics Among the Celts

The people should worship the Gods, do no evil, and exercise courage.
Gaulish Druids to Diogenes Laertius[4]

There is a great deal of romantic folklore surrounding the Celtic peoples and their Gods. Some starry-eyed folk believe that the Celts were noble knights, others that they were a pure, matriarchal society suppressed by the Pale Patriarchal Penis People, or by the early Christian church. Richly attired faerie rides from Victorian illustrations, and billowy Celtic Revival poetry contribute to an

---

4. Ellis, Peter Berresford, *The Druids*, William B. Eerdmans Publishing Company, Grand Rapids, 1994, p. 168

image of an impossibly pure and upright people with sage philosophers and Arthurian kings of great moral depth and mythically perfect stature. I have even heard it asserted that the Celts were a peaceful people, and that they and their Gods never fought battles or participated in any violence. Although it may be nice to think so, none of these "noble savage" or "lost golden age" visions are accurate. In truth, the Celts were Indo-Europeans, a violent and warlike people who were related to the Norse, the Greeks, the Romans, the Persians and the Vedic Indians among others. They were a patriarchal people, part of the waves of mobile cultures that either conquered or absorbed the native Neolithic (stone age) cultures that they encountered.[5] They were, in fact, the very same warrior culture that the more radical feminist scholars so deplore.

Celtic society did show some signs of being matrilineal (reckoning descent through the mother's line), particularly in the islands. This matrilineality may be an aspect of their culture inherited or absorbed from the earlier inhabitants of the islands. Warriors were honored members of Celtic society, and were part of the nobility. Kings frequently came to power, as in so many other cultures around the world, through the overthrow of the previous ruler, although election seemed to have occurred on a regular basis. The ancient Celts also indulged in ritual headhunting, as well as offering animal and the occasional human sacrifices to their deities and land spirits. Certainly none of this fits with an image of a particularly chivalrous or gentle people, nor with the ideal of a peaceful matriarchal society. This fantasy wishfulness has not been applied to the Celts alone; it is also commonly seen about Native American cultures, particularly among those who study New Age versions of shamanism. Both the pre-Columbian Native Americans and the pre-Christian Celts were diverse societies of human beings just like us, capable of fault, cruelty, ignoble behavior and mean-spiritedness, along with their better and more noble qualities. If we wish to follow a Celtic Reconstructionist path with integrity and honesty, we must own this history, for it becomes our history. We should also attempt to understand the current state of Celtic-speaking peoples. If we choose to ignore these facts and indulge in fantasy, we do so at our own risk. Fantasy can be blinding, and this can lead us to call upon powers and deities that we do not truly

---

5. Mallory, J.P., *In Search of the Indo-Europeans: Language, Archaeology and Myth*, Thames & Hudson, London 1989, p. 105

understand. This, in turn, can cause great harm to individuals or groups who are suddenly confronted with an unexpected and primal energy of violence or blood-lust.

Owning this history does not mean that we, as the spiritual descendants of the Celts, must follow the ancient Celtic paths precisely, in all their ways and with all their faults. For one thing, we cannot know everything about what the various Celtic peoples did and believed. But accepting it does mean that we need to understand the ethical frameworks of the Celts so that we can modify them intelligently and call them our own. With this understanding, we can safely call upon the Celtic deities in full knowledge of who and what we invoke. We can also live lives of honor in a modern society without a great deal of conflict with the overculture.

Among the Celtic peoples a person's word was binding through this life and into future lives. Oaths were sworn by the Gods, within the three realms of land, sea and sky[6], and they were taken very seriously. When the Gods are real, their displeasure is as real as their favor, and they do not like their names being taken lightly. Calling upon them in swearing oaths brought their attention to you, and they watched to be certain that sworn oaths were not violated. Death was considered preferable to the breaking of oath, for without the honor of individuals and the trust between members of the *tuath* ("people, children, tribe"), the entire tribe could collapse, and who would want to be responsible for the destruction of the tribe?

Loyalty to the *tuath* was also important, for without this trust and cohesiveness it would be all too easy for any individual to perish, alone and without aid. The *tuath* depended upon mutual assistance and collective labor, for the survival tasks of herding, farming and gathering were beyond the means of any one "nuclear" family. Loyalty to one's *tuath* ensured a continuance of shelter, clothing, food, love, companionship, fuel, and protection from the dangers of man and beast. Contracts were sometimes composed with provision for payment in future lives, and there was full expectation of payment, for the Celts were firm believers in reincarnation of some sort. Reincarnation as descendants in the family line seems to have been a Celtic belief, and so your grandchildren (who may well be you reborn) might pay back your neighbor's grandchildren at the completion of a contract's term of

---

6. Ellis, 1994, p. 131

agreement. Most contracts were also sealed with a material forfeiture in the event of failure to fulfill the contract. The loyalty and trust of family was essential in the making of any contracts, because failure to fulfill a contract obligated your *tuath* to pay your debts if you could not. If the *tuath* did not trust you, you would never be able to borrow or loan property, make contracts, or advance in social status. One unfortunate side effect of forfeiture was slavery for the forfeiter, and so you obviously would only allow kin that you firmly trusted to enter into contracts. This trust follows naturally upon the ethical foundation that required honesty in swearing oaths, and which was demonstrated on a daily basis as you lived within the constraints of the oaths you had previously sworn.

Truth was of utmost importance to the Celts, and the discernment of truth is a theme that is touched upon in many of the traditional tales. In "Cormac's Cup" for instance, the object of the tale was a cup that would shatter when three lies were told and mend again when three truths were uttered. This implies that some actions are not and cannot be "relative," but instead are considered absolute and have value as being true. One either has or has not put water in the bucket. It cannot be both full and empty at the same time, at least within ordinary, mundane reality. The state of the bucket is a truth. Truth is one basis of proper judgment, and offering false judgments was believed to be one of the things that destroyed a *tuath*.

Many modern Pagans, particularly Wiccans, follow the rede Harm None as their guiding principle. There is certainly a need for this in the modern world, but it is not, nor has it ever been a Celtic ideal. Instead, honor and "face" or social perception were very important to the Celtic peoples. Honor consists largely of the *tuath*'s perception of each individual's level of truthfulness, right action and loyalty. Honor had to be upheld at any cost, and the tales are full of stories of warriors brought to their deaths because they had to uphold the honor of self, *tuath* or king. A person's honor had a specific monetary value in Celtic culture, and if one's honor was damaged, the person who had done the damage could be made to pay a price in cattle or goods equal to the amount of damage done[7].

Strength was also greatly valued. Games such as lifting stones or tossing the caber showed a person's physical strength, which

---

7. All legal references are to Kelly, Fergus, *A Guide to Early Irish Law*, Dublin Institute for Advanced Studies, Dublin 1991

reflected on their capability as a farmer, herd-keeper or warrior. Strength was also found in family and emotional bonds, and one's honor was a kind of strength as well. If an enemy tried to harm a Celt, they would likely lose body parts for the trouble. Should one of the *tuath* be killed or wounded, the person's relatives would be honor-bound to avenge the death or injury, and a severe fine would be imposed on the criminal and his family. Clan members were liable for the actions of their kin, and if an individual could not pay the fine, the family was legally bound to make payment in the criminal's stead. For committing some crimes, a person's honor price was revoked, which meant that others could kill or wound them with impunity, and the family could not ask for compensation. War was fought according to particular rules, and individual combat between heroes and champions was not uncommon. Honor kept others from interfering in battle between champions. Social status was an important aspect of life, but the status of one's birth was not the sole factor that determined a person's life path. One maxim of the Irish Celts was that every person is better than their birth. The Irish laws clearly lay out the paths that can be taken by an individual to increase personal or family status. Many of these paths involved risk and responsibility, and most of them took several generations to come to fruition. This type of farsightedness is uncommon in our culture, but was well known among the early Celts.

Celtic society was very legalistic, and the Irish and Welsh have a stunning and complex array of law codes that the society's lawgivers were expected to memorize and be able to recite. An Irish lawgiver or judge was called a *breitheamh* or brehon. These law texts take up dozens of volumes of tiny print in modern libraries. Many of the traditional Irish tales are taken from the law texts, and illustrate the way in which law operated in Celtic society. Precedent, or giving a legal ruling based on the fact that previous lawgivers had made similar decisions in similar cases, is clearly shown in the Irish tales and reflected in many of the Irish triads. A brehon was expected to be an honorable, truthful and trustworthy person, not because a false judgment would be considered "unjust," but because the honor, health and safety of the entire tribe was embodied in the accuracy of the brehon's judgment. Several of the Irish triads address this issue.

Three ruins of a tribe: a lying chief, a false judge, an offending religious official.

Three ranks that ruin tribes in their falsehood: the falsehood of a king, an historian, a judge.

Three doors of falsehood: an angry pleading, a shifting foundation of knowledge, giving information without memory.

The importance of precedent in Celtic law is also addressed in similar style.

The four deaths of judgment: to give it in falsehood, to give it without forfeiture, to give it without precedent, to give it without knowledge. [8]

Irish law addresses concepts of honor and social perception through the *dire* fine or "honor-price." When a crime was committed against a person or against personal or tribal property, a fine would be assessed against the criminal and his *tuath*. This is similar to modern law, in cases where a criminal must make restitution to a victim through payment, or to society through community service sentences. The fine's size and the severity of punishment for crimes varied according to the rank and station of the victim or the person aggrieved, as well as the severity of the crime itself. Causing a bruise on a person's face would be grounds for a fine, as would a crime of property, like allowing your cattle to graze on a neighbor's pastureland. Of course, bruising the face of a noble would result in a considerably greater fine than bruising the face of a slave. Honor and face were taken so seriously that teasing someone with a nickname that stuck was considered a slight to one's honor and worth recompense.

Even serious crimes like murder were often resolved with a fine being assessed on the criminal and his family, which was then given to the family of the victim. Each life had a particular socially determined value, and although the Celts might impose a death penalty for some particularly heinous crime, under most circumstances fines were the preferred method of redress. Banishment by setting a person adrift in a boat, or outlawry and banishment from the tribal territory were some options for dealing with serious crimes. When a death penalty was mandated, one of a number of types of death sentences might be imposed. These included things like stabbing with swords or spears, exposure in a pit, or hanging, among others. Burning is one death penalty that is

---

8. Meyer, 1906

never mentioned, however. Even the Celts seemed to have their limits. As for the "lesser" penalties, a person set adrift for crimes could be taken into slavery by anyone who found them, and those banished from a territory could be killed without penalty, as a wolf that raids the flocks. The outlaw's family was not entitled to a fine or an honor price for their kin's death.

Along with a high value on honor, truth and orderly society, the practice of offering hospitality or *aíocht* was considered one of the cornerstones of Irish Celtic civilization. Indeed, hospitality was "the favorite virtue of the Irish," according to one French chronicler of the 18th century. It was looked upon as a sacred duty, not to be neglected by anyone. A traveler who came to the door was to be offered whatever food and drink that might be available according to their rank, even if the family was poor and had little to give. Everyone, from the king on down to the poorest peasant, was expected to practice *aíocht*. The Irish tales show that refusal of proper *aíocht* could even cause the downfall of a king. The first satire in Ireland was created to punish a king for offering a high-ranking poet only a dry crust of bread as his *aíocht*. Within weeks, the king's rule had come to an end. The Gods, too, were sometimes known to walk abroad, and one never knew if the ragged stranger at the door was human or *aes sídhe*. It was undoubtedly better to be safe, and give the stranger hospitable treatment. Poets, druids, smiths and artisans were treated with reverence and courtesy, for one of these might create good fortune for a family, or curse it to oblivion with a deadly satire or a raw bolt of magical power.

Likewise, the land spirits were spoken of kindly, and offerings of milk, oats, mead, or other food and drink were left outside the cottage door each night by the household. In the minds of many Celts, there was but a fine line between the Gods of the *sídhe* mounds and the human *aes dána* or "people of art."

Family and fostering were an important part of Celtic social structure as well. Children were often fostered at an early age to other families to establish affectional and social links between groups. A child was the responsibility of the community, and not merely of its blood parents. The bond of fosterlings or *comhaltai* with foster siblings and parents was considered in many cases to be even more powerful than the link of blood. Fostering was arranged for either "affection" or for payment. Being able to afford to foster your child with a higher-ranking family often brought status for the child, which then reflected on the birth family. But fostering for affection did not cost either party anything beyond the basic necessities for food and clothing, and was done to strengthen the bonds between two groups who were already friendly. Foster parents taught their charges the duties of a clan member, and their responsibilities according to their rank. The children worked in the fields and pastures, just like everyone else, to help assure the group's survival. For Celtic Reconstructionists, this practice can be seen as a powerful incentive to create chosen families that are drawn together by love, mutual interest and respect, rather than the vagaries of biology and chance.

The ancient Celts were not particularly peaceful or benign in their religious practices and beliefs. Many Celtic deities were known for their ferocity and their links with war and death. Animal sacrifice was a common practice, and human sacrifice was known as well, often as a foundation sacrifice at the construction of a large building. Occasionally human sacrifices took place at the funerals of very high-ranking individuals, probably of slaves or relatives intended to accompany the deceased into the Otherworld. We can only speculate on the actual purpose of animal and human sacrifices, but it is known that individual deities had their preferences for different ritual victims. In studying Celtic religion, it pays to remember that popular Celtic tales were considered a ripping success if most of the characters had died by the end of the story. Tragedies were a favorite mythic and folkloric theme.

It is apparent from Celtic texts and statuary that the Celtic peoples believed in the actual existence of their deities. The Gods were thought to have a real, worldly influence in the lives of individuals, in the workings of the *tuath*, and over the fate of nobles and kings. Divination was done to ascertain the will of these deities, and sacrifices were dedicated to the Gods, not to a set of internal psychological concepts or abstract archetypes. These deities could and would hold a person to their oaths, ensure victory or defeat for a warrior, or validate the sovereignty and right of the king to rule over the territory. The king's right was known by the physical fertility of the land and herds, and the prosperity of the people he ruled. If the people suffered, the king could, and often would be overthrown by someone who had a better connection with the Gods, as proved in the field of battle.

Pride and boasting were a part of Celtic philosophy as well. Most modern westerners are taught the value of humility and self-effacement, and through the less reputable branches of the Christian church, are taught that all pride is a grave sin. There was no discernible Celtic doctrine of "original sin" or any inherent evil in humanity. Rather than dwelling on their personal faults, Celts reveled in taking credit where it was due, and often boasted of their rank and abilities. Being able to back these boasts was necessary, however. The tales imply that the Celts often carried these boasts to extremes, falling into battles at the dinner table over who was the most accomplished warrior, and who would win the "champion's portion" of the feast. If these tales are to be believed, we can envision the Welsh or Irish sitting down to dinner, getting up to argue and fight, killing each other, and the survivors sitting down again as though nothing had happened. Undoubtedly, the truth was not quite so colorful.

One popular fiction that touches on the ethical practices of the Celtic people offers us a view of the Celts as a matriarchal society, peacefully ruled by women. The status of women in Celtic lands was certainly higher than that of women in Greece or Rome, or many other civilizations of the time, but the society was far from the peaceful matriarchal realm of easy equality that some feminist authors portray. Women could and did fight as warriors, but they could also be forced into battle against their will. Among the Irish Celts a female slave or *cumhal* was one of the standard units of trade value. A slave woman was worth three cows.

These facts should not cloud our appreciation of other realities, however. Women did have some status, and could often make their own choices in marriage. Under many circumstances they could own and transfer property, or make contracts, particularly if the husband was of a lesser social status or was from outside the *tuath*. Women could divorce their husbands, provided they had cause. Wealthy women owned their own herds and had their own servants, which they could take with them in most kinds of divorce. Women could be poets, druids, seers, judges, treaty negotiators, and even rulers, but these women were the exceptions rather than the rule, and this is reflected in Celtic law texts and Roman accounts. Despite the numerous problems of women in Celtic society, the Romans often commented on the respect in which women were held in Celtic countries.

Among the Celts, sexual roles were not as strictly defined as they are in modern society. Where moderns might identify as heterosexual, homosexual or bisexual, the Celts did not appear to have categories and classifications of sexuality. Warriors in the field slept with one another without comment. Even the Greeks, whose penchant for same-sex love was well known in the ancient world, commented on the fact that Celtic warriors slept so often with other men. We know less about the sexuality of women, as they were less often discussed by ancient authors, but we can guess that they may have had a similar range of choices in their affections. Hints in the tales show the powerful presence of female sexuality, and it was often equated with the land itself. From this it can be seen that gay, lesbian, bisexual and transgendered Celts would be more than welcome as fellow mystics and worshippers.

Much is made of the ecological sensibilities of the Celts. While it is true that their tales and poetry show a sensitivity to the land around them, and the personification of the land as Goddess, it is also true that they practiced slash and burn agriculture, and that they deforested most of Ireland by early in the Christian era. They were, as we too often are, people who put human needs before the needs of nature. This is a mentality that we all need to break free from, in order that everyone can survive.

The Irish Celts themselves tell us what they thought best, when king Cormac instructs Cairbre on the proper attributes for a chief in *The Instructions of King Cormac Mac Airt*.[9] These qualities include having good *geasa* or ritual taboos, pride and humbleness, steadfastness, poetry, being versed in legal lore, wisdom, generosity, sociability, decorousness, gentleness and hardness, love, mercy, perseverance, true judgments, raising up the weak by the strong, feeding orphans, being brilliant in company, and loving truth. Patience, affability without haughtiness, caring for ancient lore, attending to the sick, worship of the deities, fostering science and consolidating peace were valued as well.

Modern Ethical Applications for Celtic Reconstructionists

"What was it that maintained you so in your life?" Patrick enquired; and Caeilte answered: "truth that was in our hearts, and strength in our arms, and fulfillment in our tongues."
The Colloquy of the Ancients[10]

The ancient Celts had a different sense of ethics than modern Pagans. Their views were the result of the violent age in which they lived. While we live in a very different world, if the mere idea of violence is offensive to you, you are not likely to be comfortable

9. Meyer, Kuno, *The Instructions of King Cormac Mac Airt*, Royal Irish Academy, Todd Lecture Series vol XV, Hodges, Figes & Co., Dublin 1909
10. O'Grady, Standish H., *Silva Gadelica: Translations and Notes*, Williams & Norgate, London, 1892, p. 104

living within a Celtic Reconstructionist worldview. But with creativity and flexibility, we can adapt the ideals and the worldviews of the ancient Celts into a Celtic Reconstructionist Pagan reality for our own, still violent age. Celtic Reconstructionists can take many concepts from the older Celtic cultures, like honor, truth, loyalty, fostering and hospitality, and attempt to build a better culture for our time than that offered to us by Hollywood, the White House, and Madison Avenue.

Some Celtic Reconstructionist Pagans have proposed an ethical model based on the Ásatrú or Norse reconstructionist concept of the nine noble virtues. Several lists have been proposed, and many of these virtues have already been mentioned in this essay. The list that I keep consists of these virtues: honor, justice, loyalty, courage, community, hospitality, gentleness, wisdom and eloquence. Above these nine stand the three great virtues that sustained Fionn and the Fianna, quoted from *The Colloquy of the Ancients*: truth, strength and fulfillment, and the Gaulish exhortation to worship the Gods.

Private worship and public ritual played a central role in early Celtic life, and for Celtic Reconstructionists they are also important. When we are connected to our deities, they can guide and teach us through dreams and visions, as well as through the ancient tales and traditions. Creating and maintaining healthy relationships with our Gods and Goddesses gives us firm ground to stand upon as we create the ethical basis of our lives.

Celtic Reconstructionist practitioners can come together in clans and chosen families where each individual has a place, and where each person is loyal to every other, working to create the healthy relationships that many people in our society are deprived of in their birth families. Current social movements offer us useful models such as neo-tribalism, group relationships, and co-housing, which can be a fertile ground for those who want to create alternatives to the "traditional" western nuclear family groups. Common interests and goals, common religious beliefs or magical practices, emotional support, or the cooperative raising of children can be valid reasons to come together in clans or tribes. Children are a valued part of the *tuath*. By reviving some of the practical aspects of the Celtic practice of fostering, we may be able to avoid some of the difficulties of having children raised in homes with abusive, or simply poorly prepared parents. A modern tradition of fostering that combines cooperative child care and participating in local foster-parenting programs could derail the problems of Pagan children being removed from their homes and placed in non-Pagan foster homes, or of social workers who refuse to allow Pagan children to participate in Pagan community activities and rituals due to misunderstandings of our non-mainstream cultures.

Groups of cooperatively living adults, extended families of several households in the same neighborhood, or a few Pagan families living in the same apartment building may be able to give more attention to a small group of young children than harried single parents, or partnered parents who work all day, come home too exhausted to do anything more than throw dinner together, then collapse into bed. Adults can share the burden of caring for and educating Pagan kids, making things easier for everyone involved. Taking care of the children in a more effective way may also begin to provide some answers to the terrible problems of crime, drug abuse and poor education that are rampant in our society.

The Celts valued their communities and supported one another in their herding and harvesting, and in the production of the things they needed to survive. They worked to send their children to the religious schools of the druids and *filidh*, where they could learn to read, commune with the Gods, work magic, and support their communities when they returned home. By consciously working to create Pagan communities, we can provide ourselves with the support that the overculture often fails to give. Pagan communities can support Pagan businesses, Pagan private schools, food banks, clothing exchanges, college or research scholarships and grants, or other services that many mainstream religions offer to their adherents as a matter of course. With a mature and cohesive Pagan community, we could expect to be able to help each other with counseling, divination, legal aid, western and alternative medical care, and even with coordinated ecological or political action for the preservation of our planet and our civil rights.

At the heart of every community are the individuals that create it. As people practice and become confident in their Pagan path, they can become contributing members in a vital and interesting local Pagan community, no matter where they live. Celtic Reconstructionists can take some of the boasting and delight in accomplishment of the Celts to heart, taking pride in our works, believing that each of us is the best at something, and offering our unique and valuable talents and skills to our communities.

The Pagan movement as a whole needs intelligent people who are willing to think deeply, and confident enough to act from the heart. We can each, no matter what the station of our birth or our current circumstances, create honor and respect within our lives by acting in an honorable and respectable fashion. Through work, inspiration and the creation of relationships, we can make our lives more interesting, more inspired, more full than they would otherwise have been. This is a path of wisdom. Even if we are solitary practitioners, this work does not stop at our doorstep, or at the boundaries of our neighborhood. As members of a local community, we can reach out to other communities and work toward the creation and maintenance of national and international networks in the service of the Old Gods and the earth.

Sexual discrimination and inequality is a social attitude that should be alien to Celtic Reconstructionists. Too often in the modern world respect is only given to social equals or superiors. Without equality of the genders, respect between men and women is effectively impossible in our society. The relatively high status of women in the Celtic world gives us a vision of a society where everyone is valued for their individual contributions. When we can view each person as a manifestation of deity, we are that much closer to bringing equality to our corner of the world.

Likewise, a Celtic Reconstructionist ethic should advocate active understanding, equality and communication between races and peoples. Inequities of race and gender have identical roots in the belief that "we" are superior to "them." This kind of alienation endangers not just the American inner cities, but the world as a whole. While our ancestors may have been content to work with their own *tuath* and treat outsiders as the enemy, our world is much smaller and more fragile. Ethnic wars shatter the fabric of societies all over the planet. We have a responsibility to our community, but our community is affected by everything outside it and around it as well as what originates within it. Each person who becomes a friend expands our world by that much experience and knowledge. We also reduce the number of potential enemies in the world by one person. Discrimination, whether gender, religious, racial, or any other kind, destroys lives and reduces the world's options in a time where all constructive views and ideas are essential to our planet's survival.

The destruction of Celtic civilizations by the invading Romans, and by the infiltration and conquest of the early Christian church should give Celtic Reconstructionists a certain amount of sympathy for minority cultures and viewpoints. The highland Scots and the Irish were driven from their ancestral lands by famine and war. Thousands of peasants from Ireland were sold into slavery in the Caribbean by Cromwell after the English conquest. And when Irish immigrants came to the US, they were treated as subhuman by those already in residence. Signs in shops with job openings often stated "No Irish need apply." The Scots were forcibly removed from their farms by absentee landlords and resettled to make room for sheep. The Gauls were displaced and finally absorbed by the Romans. Our spiritual ancestors have had common experiences with Africans and Native Americans, and many other ethnic groups, knowing slavery and genocide, the loss of ancestral lands, and the destruction of ancestral religions. They felt the pains and problems of discrimination, just as many other immigrants, whatever their religion or national origin. Modern Celtic peoples are still suffering social and economic discrimination in their own lands, their languages dying, their customs being forgotten or turned into watered-down tourist attractions. To forget or deny the past, to participate in discrimination and repression, will only bring us full circle and lead us to destruction.

Even supposedly simple things like our choice of diet are influenced by our ethical decisions. The ancient Celts had to hunt, and to kill herd animals if they were going to eat meat. Their survival through the winter depended on grains and other vegetable foods they had preserved, as well as the meat they preserved, and the hunting they did. As Celtic Reconstructionists, we must acknowledge that meat comes from dead animals if we are going to eat flesh foods. The realization that life must feed on life is a real and ever-present thing. We must live consciously, aware that meat is more than a plastic-wrapped slab of tissue, that grain is more than a hard kernel of organic matter. With each plant and animal that we eat, we need to acknowledge the sacrifice that has occurred.

The word sacrifice frightens many people, and some wish to avoid it entirely. But sacrifice means "to make sacred," and it is this acknowledgement of the sacred that is vitally important in our lives. City dwellers may not kill or harvest their own food, but those living in rural areas should consider the implications and practice of sacrifice as they slaughter their own food animals and harvest their crops. Animal life should only be taken when necessary for food, and with keen attention to both the life of the animal and the presence of the Gods. In many cultures, sacrifice recreates the origins of the universe and it is considered a generative, life-giving act that restores order to the chaos of the world.

Celtic concepts of honor, generosity, truth and justice need to be adopted into our personal lives. When we speak, we should speak eloquently, and mean what we say. When we offer oaths, we should keep them. When we offer hospitality to someone, we should give it without grudging or cheapness. Only when we demand honesty and honor from ourselves are we truly able to demand it of those around us. And only when we as individuals act with honesty and honor will others respect our demands for this behavior from society. We are obligated to act with honor out of respect to our deities, and held to the truth because each of us is an example to the larger society. The things that we say and do reflect not only on ourselves, but on each and every other person in our *tuath*, and in our Pagan community.

When we speak out before the community at large as Pagans, we have an obligation to speak with wisdom, honesty and eloquence. In the eyes of those who see us, we represent all Pagans, whether we claim to do so or not. Remembering that false judgments and lies are two of the things that bring a *tuath* to downfall, we are all equally responsible for the community in which we live. What we say can bring either honor or humiliation to the people we value most. It takes courage to speak with honesty in our society. Modern western values have made it much easier to lie and cheat than to act and speak with honest intent. Our eloquence and wisdom can be persuasive. Our words and actions can heal or they can destroy. The choice is ours.

Goddess of the Growing Green:
Airmed of Ireland

The Celtic peoples honored hundreds of deities throughout the British Isles and Western Europe. A few are known through tales and poetry, but of most, little is known beyond the names, taken from inscriptions in stone. When thinking of Irish healing Goddesses, most minds turn immediately to Brigid, but she is not the only healing Goddess of the Irish. The stories of Airmed are few. She is mentioned only two or three times in all the translated Irish tales. Airmed is an herbal healer, part of a family of healers among the Tuatha Dé Danann, one of the groups of Gods and Goddesses of Pagan Ireland. Together with her father Dian Cécht and her brother Miach, a God of surgery, she tended a sacred spring that brought the dead back to life. The tales tell us:

> The slain and mortally wounded were cast into a healing well over which Dian Cécht, his sons Miach and Octriuil, and his daughter Airmed sang incantations, and all were restored to full vigor.[11]

As a healer, Airmed surpassed her father in power, for while Dian Cécht replaced the severed arm of the Dé Danann king Nuadha with one of silver, she and Miach regenerated the flesh arm to perfect health. The healing charm they recited remains in Celtic folk use even today.

Bone to bone
Vein to vein
Balm to Balm

Sap to Sap
Skin to skin
Tissue to tissue

Blood to blood
Flesh to flesh
Sinew to sinew

---

11. *The Healing Gods of Ancient Civilizations,* p. 514. Walter Addison Jayne, MD, Univeersity Books, New Hyde Park, NY 1962

Marrow to marrow
Pith to pith
Fat to fat

Membrane to membrane
Fibre to fibre
Moisture to moisture[12]

Folk tradition is powerful, remaining in the memory of the people for generations after the reason for the traditions die away. There may be no explanation, only that "this is the way it has always been done." Such is the power of the growing green. Cut down a rowan tree and a dozen young saplings arise from the stump to take its place.

As the origin of the charm was lost from memory, so the secret of the healing herbs was lost to the people as well. Dian Cécht, jealous because he could not compete with Miach's surgical skills or Airmed's powers of regeneration, killed his son and confused the herbs that grew from his grave so that mortal humans would not share in the power and immortality of the Gods.

> After that, Miach was buried by Dian Cécht, and three hundred and sixty-five herbs grew through the grave, corresponding to the number of his joints and sinews. Then Airmed spread her cloak and uprooted those herbs according to the770ir properties. Dian Cécht came to her and mixed the herbs, so that no one knows their proper healing qualities unless [she] taught them afterwards. And Dian Cécht said "Though Miach no longer lives, Airmed shall remain."[13]

Airmed's herbs, spread upon her cloak, were scattered by her father. Yet Airmed still remembers the powers of the herbs, and can teach us their secrets. Through her, we may learn to use and appreciate the sacred power of plants and healing waters. Her medicinal herbs were powerful, offering cures for every part of the body. The symbolic number 365 tells us that, with time, Airmed's herbs can

---

12. *Carmina Gadelica, volume IV,* pp. 215-217, Alexander Carmichael, Scottish Academic Press, Edinburgh 1970
13. *Cath Maige Tuired: The Second Battle of Mag Tuired,* p. 33, ed. Elizabeth A. Gray, Irish Texts Society, Naas 1982

heal all wounds. Airmed's herbs have power throughout the solar year, whether in seed and root, bud and stem, or flower and leaf. Fresh in spring or dried in the dead of winter, the herbs have effect. She works through nature's cycles, and through the energy that connects the body's joints and sinews in lines of power.

Is Airmed, the Goddess of medicinal plants, only a healer of the body? The simple answer is no; the healing power of every green place looms palpably within it. We have but to stand in a grove of trees or listen to the rush of a fern-circled waterfall to feel the weight of our spiritual and emotional wounds begin to lift from our shoulders. The healing power of plants goes far beyond their physical effect on human biochemistry. When we delight in the color and scent of blooming flowers, the heady green scent of pines and cedars, the healing power of Airmed is there. In our cup of honeyed tea, she resides. She dwells in forest and field, and for those of us living in cities, she dwells in the potted herbs of garden shops, the apartment window box, and the stubborn yellow dandelion pushing out of a crack in the sidewalk. The essence of Celtic religion is found in contradictory states, in the neither/nor, the liminal fringe. Airmed is that Celticly odd balance of toughness and delicacy that manifests in the blackberry -- bright, fragile blossom and tangling thorn. She creates life from death, bringing healing from the grave of Miach. Three kinds of medicine were recognized in Brehon law:[14] surgery, dietary control, and herbal healing. Herbalists were greatly respected and had a fairly high status in Celtic society. The "woman-physician of the *tuath*" or tribe (*banliaig túaithe*) was considered independent of her husband and commanded her own honor-price,[15] unlike many other women in Celtic society. The *banliaig túaithe* was most likely an herbal healer and midwife. Herbalism was considered a very important part of Irish medicine, and this would have made Airmed a Goddess of some stature, despite the few mentions of her in the Irish mythological texts.

---

14. The Brehon laws are a traditional body of religious and secular law whose source texts are largely in the Old Irish language. Preserved by Druids and Brehons (law-givers), they were eventually absorbed and modified by the Celtic Christians, who added a great deal of Biblical material to them. Despite this, the law texts are a rich source of information on the social context of Celtic Paganism and the status of women in Celtic Ireland.

15. *A Guide to Early Irish Law*, p. 77, Fergus Kelly, Dublin Institute for Advanced Studies, Dublin 1988

The sagas and law-texts agree in stressing the medical importance of herbs. *Táin Bó Cualigne* describes how a poultice of healing herbs was placed in Cú Chulainn's wounds. *Bretha Crolige* states that the purpose of herb-gardens is the care of the sick, and refers to the great service given by garden herbs in nursing.[16]

Our window boxes and backyard herb gardens can be shrines to Airmed. The groves and all wild places where plants grow are her natural temples. Rites of healing, trance induction, and meditation are all appropriate devotional work for this Goddess of the Green. Work to preserve wilderness areas is a form of devotion to her as well, for many medicinal plant species are still found only in the wild, or cannot be successfully cultivated.

A home altar for Airmed should be covered with a cloth, symbolizing the cloak on which she laid out the healing herbs. It can be scattered with dried or fresh plants of all types. Flowers in vases, bunches of herbs, potted plants, wreaths of branches or piles of berries could all be placed on its surface. A bowl or cauldron of spring or rainwater can symbolize her well of healing and regeneration. Incenses for her should be floral or earthy scents redolent of growth and verdant green, pine or fir resins, or the elegant sweetness of amber. If you use candles, they should be of beeswax to symbolize the fertilizing work of the bees and the curative powers of honey. If you feel a need for a blade on the altar, consider using a sickle for its close association with agricultural work, rather than an athame. Bronze, silver, stone or wood are preferable to iron, for the folklore tells us that the Dé Danann dislike iron. Your indoor temple can be decorated with bunches of drying herbs hanging from the ceiling, herbal wreaths on the walls, baskets of dried flowers, with indoor herb gardens in pots and under sunlamps, with bottles filled with your dried herbs, and mortars and pestles for their preparation.

If you have space in your yard for a garden, it would be highly appropriate for you to devote an area to be her special shrine and ask her blessings for the growth and preparation of your herbs. Celtic deities were often represented by a rough-hewn face in a log or by a small standing stone. With a little inspiration and some care you can create a similar stone or wooden icon for yourself. A bowl or birdbath set into the ground before the image can serve as her healing spring. Scrying and healing meditations can be done by gazing into the reflective surface of the water. For those with some

---

16. Ibid, pp. 58-59

money available and a taste for something unusual, small fountains of rough natural stone can sometimes be found in garden shops. The initial cost may be a few hundred dollars, but a fountain pump runs on less electricity than it takes to run a fish tank air purifier. The musical sound of moving water can deepen meditation and provide a refuge from the distraction of everyday activities. If you are not fortunate enough to live close to a river or waterfall, this might be a useful alternative. Inspiration is one of the roots of Celtic worship. No scripted rites are necessary for the worship of Celtic Goddesses. Poetry is their preferred form of invocation. Time spent in an herb garden or among the wildflowers could easily inspire you, as it has many poets over the centuries. Even if you are not feeling particularly inspired, there are a number of books available with samples of Celtic poetry that can be used or modified for your rituals.

I will pluck the yarrow fair,
That more benign shall be my face,
That more warm shall be my lips,
That more chaste shall be my speech,
Be my speech the beams of the sun,
Be my lips the sap of the strawberry.[17]

Many Celtic poems exist which are centered around the harvest of particular herbs for healing or magical purposes. The *Carmina Gadelica*, originally a compilation containing poetic material in both Scottish Gaelic and English translations, was recently re-released in an all-English format,[18] and is a rich source that contains many plant charms and folk-beliefs concerning plants, from late 19th-century Scotland. Other folk poems use herbs and plants as a part of their symbolism, even if they are not directly related to the use and cultivation of healing plants. These can also be modified for use in rituals. The triad is a traditional form of wisdom text in Celtic Ireland. One of the Irish triads speaks of the attributes of a healer, saying "Three things that constitute a physician: a complete cure, leaving no blemish behind, a painless examination."[19] Through our work in ritual with Airmed, we can strive to fulfill these conditions.

---

17. *Carmina Gadelica, Voume II,* P. 95, Alexander Carmichael, Scottish Academic Press, Edinburgh 1972
18. *Carmina Gadelica,* Alexander Carmichael, Lindisfarne Press, 1992
19. *The Triads of Ireland,* Todd Lecture Series vol XIII, Kuno Meyer, Royal Irish Academy, Dublin 1906

In devotion to her, we can work to heal ourselves, and through the knowledge of her herbs, those close to us as well. Through our gardens and our devotion to the green world of plants, we can move the circle outward and work to heal our planet.

The Cauldron of Poesy

During the 7th century CE, an Irish *fili* or sacred poet composed a poem on one of the mysteries of the Irish wisdom tradition. This poem is preserved in a 16th century manuscript,[20] along with the glosses in 11th century language explaining some of its more obscure references. When it was finally "discovered" by modern scholars, it was named "The Cauldron of Poesy" for its references to poetry being created in three internal cauldrons.

Three translations of this text exist, published by the Celtic scholars P.L. Henry[21] and Liam Breatnach,[22] and by the well-known occultist Caitlin Matthews.[23] I am aware of two other discussions of the text in the Pagan press, one by the Canadian druid Sean O'Tuathail[24] and the other in my own work under the name Erynn Darkstar.[25] In this article, I offer my own translation of the poem and commentary, along with some theories and suggestions for working with the internal cauldrons as a path to poetic and magical achievement.

There is some debate in the scholarly community about whether the *filidh* were a subclass of druid, or an independent order of poets and magicians. The highest ranking *filidh* were called *ollamh*. The word *fili* probably means "seer."[26] The word derives from the Archaic Irish **weis* by way of the Insular Celtic word **wel-* which had the original imperative meaning "see!" or "look at!" and is related to the Irish verb to be.[27] Their work included divination, blessing and blasting magic, creating praise poetry for their patrons, the preservation of lore and genealogies, and occasionally the

---

20. Legal codex H.3.18, dated to c. 1500 CE.
21. Henry, P.L., "The Cauldron of Poesy," Studia Celtica #14/15, 1979/1980, pp. 114-128.
22. Breatnach, Liam, "The Cauldron of Poesy," Ériu #32, 1981, pp. 45-93.
23. Matthews, Caitlin and John, *The Encyclopedia of Celtic Wisdom: A Celtic Shaman's Sourcebook*, (Rockport, MA: Element Books, 1994).
24. "Cainteanna na Luise," a privately published Canadian Druidic periodical, issues #7 (1985), #17 (1988), and #26 (1990).
25. Darkstar, Erynn, *The Cauldron of Poesy: Lectures on Irish Magick, Cosmology and Poetry based on the Irish Text called The Cauldron of Poesy*, (Seattle: Preppie Biker Press, 1992).
26. Chadwick, N. Kershaw, *Poetry & Prophecy*, (Cambridge: Cambridge University Press, 1952).
27. Meyer, Kuno, *Sanas Cormaic (Cormac's Glossary)*, (Felinfach: Llanerch Publishers, 1994). This is an untranslated edition.

rendering of judgments. *Cormac's Glossary* derives *fili* from *"fi,* 'poison' in satire, and *li* 'splendor' in praise, and it is variously that the poet proclaims."[28]

The early Irish *filidh* wore cloaks of birds' feathers called *tugen* and were sometimes ecstatic hermits known as *geilta*,[29] composing their poetry and seeking mantic visions through various techniques involving incubatory darkness, liminal times or places such as dawn and dusk or doorways, and the ingestion of raw substances such as the meat of sacrificed animals.[30] The chewing or eating of raw flesh is apparently a link to the Otherworld, for spirits and the inhabitants of the *sídhe* mounds are said to eat raw foods.[31] By the 14th century, the *filidh* were divided into seven grades of achievement, requiring at least twelve years of study to attain the highest grades. During the eighth year of study, mantic and divinatory techniques began to be taught, and those capable of practicing them were known as *ollamh*.[32] This title is still in use in Ireland to denote a university professor.

During the time of the Christianization of Ireland, the druids were repressed or absorbed, and the *filidh* subsumed many of their social functions and status in Irish society. *Filidh* were often associated with monasteries, and this association was maintained until at least the 17th century, when the English began earnest attempts to destroy Irish Catholicism.[33]

My translation of this *fili* text is offered with the understanding that my command of the Old Irish language is not perfect. I render some lines and words very loosely and others with a stubborn literality, choosing that which suits me and attempting to make the whole understandable as an important magical text. It should be understood that every translator has biases, whether or not they are spoken. For the most complete understanding of the text, I can only recommend that you undertake to make your own translations.

---

28. McCone, Kim, *Stair na Gaeilge*, (Maigh Nuad, Ireland: Coláiste Phádraig, 1994).
29. Chadwick, Nora K., "Geilt," Scottish Gaelic Studies, vol V, part II, 1942, pp. 106-153.
30. Chadwick, 1952.
31. Chadwick, Nora K. "Imbas Forosnai," Scottish Gaelic Studies , vol IV, Part II, 1935, pp. 97-135.
32. Calder, George, *Auraicept na n-Éces: The Scholar's Primer*, (Edinburgh: John Grant, 1917).
33. Ford, Patrick K., "From Orality to Literacy: The Route of the Táin," lecture at CSANA conference, Seattle, 1993.

The commentary that I offer on the poem is based not only on research, but also on personal intuitions and practical workings. Some of it will be quite subjective, and your own experiences may lead you to other conclusions. I encourage every would-be modern *fili* to study and work with this material from many angles and in its several translations in an ongoing search for enlightenment.

The Cauldron of Poesy Text

> *Moí coire coir goiriath*
> *gor rond n-ír Día dam a dúile dnemrib;*
> *dliucht sóir sóerna broinn*
> *bélrae mbil brúchtas úad.*
> *Os mé Amargen glúngel garrglas gréliath,*
> *gním mo goriath crothaib condelgib indethar*
> *-- dath nád inonn airlethar Día do cach dóen,*
> *de thoíb, ís toíb, úas toíb --*
> *nemshós, lethshós, lánshós,*
> *do h-Ébiur Dunn dénum do uath aidbsib ilib ollmaribh;*
> *i moth, i toth, i tráeth,*
> *i n-arnin, i forsail, i ndínin-díshail,*
> *sliucht as-indethar altmod mo choiri.*

My perfect cauldron of warming
    has been taken by the Gods[34] from the mysterious abyss of
the elements;
    a perfect truth that ennobles from the center of being,
    that pours forth a terrifying stream of speech.

I am Amirgen White-knee,
    with pale substance and grey hair,
    accomplishing my poetic incubation in proper forms,
    in diverse colors.

The Gods do not give the same wisdom to everyone,
    tipped, inverted, right-side-up;
    no knowledge, half-knowledge, full knowledge --
    for Eber and Donn,[35] the making of fearful poetry,

---

34. In the text, I have pluralized deity where I found reference to God. This is a bias on my part, and not reflective of the original Christian writer's words.
35. The original text says "Eber Donn" but it is obvious that these are two individuals mentioned in the Invasions texts.

of vast, mighty draughts death-spells, of great chanting;

in active voice, in passive silence, in the neutral balance between,

in rhythm and form and rhyme,

in this way is spoken the path and function of my cauldrons.

Ciarm i tá bunadus ind airchetail i nduiniu; in i curp fa i n-anmain? As-berat araili bid i nanmain ar ní dénai in corp ní cen anmain. As-berat araili bid i curp in tan dano fo-glen oc cundu chorpthai .i. ó athair nó shenathair, ol shodain as fíru ara-thá bunad ind airchetail & int shois i cach duiniu chorpthu, acht cach la duine adtuíthi and; alailiu atuídi.

Where is the root of poetry in a person; in the body or in the soul? Some say it is in the soul, for the body does nothing without the soul. Some say it is in the body where the arts are learned, passed through the bodies of our ancestors. It is said that this is the truth remaining over the root of poetry, and the wisdom in every person's ancestry does not come from the northern sky into everyone, but into every other person.

Caite didiu bunad ind archetail & cach sois olchenae? Ní ansae; gainitir tri coiri i cach duiniu .i. coire goriath & coire érmai & coire sois.

What then is the root of poetry and every other wisdom? Not hard; three cauldrons are born in every person -- the cauldron of warming, the cauldron of motion and the cauldron of wisdom.

Coire goiriath, is é-side gainethar fóen i nduiniu fo chétóir. Is as fo dálter soas do doínib i n-ógoítu.

The cauldron of warming is born upright in people from the beginning. It distributes wisdom to people in their youth.

Coire érmai, immurgu, iarmo-bí impúd moigid; is é-side gainethar do thoib i nduiniu.

The cauldron of motion, however, increases after turning; that is to say it is born tipped on its side, growing within.

Coire sois, is é-side gainethar fora béolu & is as fo-dáilter soes cach dáno olchenae cenmo-thá airchetal.

The cauldron of wisdom is born on its lips and distributes wisdom in poetry and every other art.

Coire érmai dano, cach la duine is fora béolu atá and .i. n-áes dois. Lethchlóen i n-áer bairdne & rand. Is fóen atá i n-ánshruithaib sofhis & airchetail. Conid airi didiu ní dénai cach óeneret, di h-ág is fora béolu atá coire érmai and coinid n-impoí brón nó fáilte.

The cauldron of motion then, in all artless people is on its lips. It is side-slanting in people of bardcraft and small poetic talent. It is upright in the greatest of poets, who are great streams of wisdom. Not every poet has it on its back, for the cauldron of motion must be turned by sorrow or joy.

Ceist, cis lir foldai fil forsin mbrón imid-suí? Ní ansae; a cethair: éolchaire, cumae & brón éoit & ailithre ar dia & is medón ata-tairberat inna cethair-se cíasu anechtair fo-fertar.

Question: How many divisions of sorrow turn the cauldrons of sages? Not hard; four: longing and grief, the sorrows of jealousy, and the discipline of pilgrimage to holy places. These four are endured internally, turning the cauldrons, although the cause is from outside.

Atáat dano dí fhodail for fáilte ó n-impoíther i coire sofhis, .i. fáilte déodea & fáilte dóendae.

There are two divisions of joy that turn the cauldron of wisdom; divine joy and human joy.

Ind fháilte dóendae, atáat cethéoir fodlai for suidi .i. luud éoit fuichechtae & fáilte sláne & nemimnedche, imbid bruit & biid co feca in duine for bairdni & fáilte fri dliged n-écse iarna dagfhrithgnum & fáilte fri tascor n-imbias do-fuaircet noí cuill cainmeso for Segais i sídaib, conda thochrathar méit motchnaí iar ndruimniu Bóinde frithroisc luaithiu euch aige i mmedón mís mithime dia secht mbliadnae beos.

There are four divisions of human joy among the wise -- sexual intimacy, the joy of health and prosperity after the difficult years of studying poetry, the joy of wisdom after the harmonious creation of poems, and the joy of ecstasy from eating the fair nuts of the nine hazels of the Well of Segais in the *sídhe* realm. They cast themselves in multitudes, like a ram's fleece upon the ridges of the Boyne, moving upstream swifter than racehorses driven on midsummer's day every seven years.

Fáilte déoldae, immurugu, tórumae ind raith déodai dochum in choiri érmai conid n-impoí fóen, conid de biit fáidi déodai & dóendai & tráchtairi raith & frithgnamo imale, conid íarum labrait inna labarthu raith & dogniat inna firthu, condat fásaige & bretha a mbríathar, condat desimrecht do cach cobrai. Acht is anechtair ata-tairberat inna hí-siu in coire cíasu medón fo-fertar.

The Gods touch people through divine and human joys so that they are able to speak prophetic poems and dispense wisdom and perform miracles, giving wise judgment with precedents, and blessings in answer to every wish. The source of these joys is outside the person and added to their cauldrons to cause them to turn, although the cause of the joy is internal.

> *Ara-caun coire sofhis*
> *sernar dliged cach dáno*
> *dia moiget moín*
> *móras cach ceird coitchiunn*
> *con-utaing duine dán.*

> I sing of the cauldron of wisdom
> which bestows the nature of every art,
> through which treasure increases,
> which magnifies every artisan,
> which builds up a person through their gift.

> *Ar-caun coire n-érmai*
> *intlechtaib raith*
> *rethaib sofhis*
> *srethaib imbais*
> *indber n-ecnai*
> *ellach suíthi*
> *srúnaim n-ordan*
> *indocbáil dóer*
> *domnad insce*
> *intlecht ruirthech*
> *rómnae roiscni*
> *sáer comgni*
> *cóemad felmac*
> *fégthar ndliged*

deligter cíalla
cengar sési
sílaigther soƒhis
sonmigter soír
sóerthar nád shóer,
ara-utgatar anmann
ad-fíadatar moltae
modaib dliged
deligthib grád
glanmesaib soíre
soinscib suad
srúamannaib suíthi,
sóernbrud i mberthar
bunad cach soƒhis
sernar iar ndligiud
drengar iar frithgnum
fo-nglúaisi imbas
inme-soí fáilte
faillsigther tri brón;
búan bríg
nád díbdai dín.
Ar-caun coire n-érmai.

I sing of the cauldron of motion
understanding grace,
accumulating wisdom
streaming ecstasy as milk from the breast,
it is the tide-water of knowledge
union of sages
stream of splendor
glory of the lowly
mastery of speech
swift intelligence
reddening satire
craftsman of histories
cherishing pupils
looking after binding principles
distinguishing meanings
moving toward music
propagation of wisdom
enriching nobility
ennobling the commonplace
refreshing souls

relating praises
through the working of law
comparing of ranks
pure weighing of nobility
with fair words of the wise
with streams of sages,
the noble brew in which is boiled
the true root of all knowledge
which bestows according to harmonious principle
which is climbed after diligence
which ecstasy sets in motion
which joy turns
which is revealed through sorrow;
it is enduring fire
undiminishing protection.
I sing of the cauldron of motion.

Coire érmai,
ernid ernair,
mrogaith mrogthair,
bíathaid bíadtair,
máraid márthair,
áilith áiltir,
ar-cain ar-canar,
fo-rig fo-regar,
con-serrn con-serrnar
fo-sernn fo-sernnar.

The cauldron of motion
bestows, is bestowed
extends, is extended
nourishes, is nourished
magnifies, is magnified
invokes, is invoked
sings, is sung
keeps, is kept,
arranges, is arranged,
supports, is supported.

Fó topar tomseo,
fó atrab n-insce,
fó comair coimseo
con-utaing firse.

53

> Good is the well of poetry,
> good is the dwelling of speech,
> good is the union of power and mastery
> which establishes strength.

> *Is mó cach ferunn,*
> *is ferr cach orbu,*
> *berid co h-ecnae,*
> *echtraid fri borbu.*

> It is greater than every domain,
> it is better than every inheritance,
> it bears one to knowledge,
> adventuring away from ignorance.

"I am Amirgen White-Knee"

Amirgen, one of the most powerful Irish *filidh*, is credited with the authorship of the poem. The practice of crediting famous and powerful poets with the creation of poems is common in Irish and Welsh literary practice, as one can see from the immense body of poetry of many periods said to have been composed by the Welsh poets Taliesin and Aneirin, or poems ascribed to Fionn Mac Cumhail. While this may be simply a device to garner honor for the poem, I have to wonder if, in some cases, it was not believed that a poet may have been possessed by the spirit of these great *filidh* during the process of composition.

The poetry is said to be composed for Eber and Donn, both of whom were brothers of Amirgen. Eber was one of the kings of the Milesians, and Donn became a God of the dead. He is said to greet the descendants of Mil at Teach Duinn, the House of Donn, after their deaths. This house is often described as being on or in a rock by the same name that is found off the furthest southwest point of Ireland. I believe that this line refers to the poet's duty of creating praise poetry for kings and patrons, and of making poetry for the Gods and for the dead so that we remember them.

"Three Cauldrons Are Born in Every Person"

In this poem, three cauldrons are described. I have rendered them as the Cauldron of Incubation, the Cauldron of Motion, and the Cauldron of Wisdom. The word used to indicate "incubation" (*goiriath*) may equally mean "warming," "sustenance," or "maintenance." These three cauldrons are said to be born in every person, taken by deific forces from out of a great mystery. The cauldrons are described as bestowing nobility upon people through the process of the creation of poetry, the pouring forth of "a terrifying stream of speech from the mouth."

My own experience, and the comments of others, lead me to place the cauldrons within the body as one might understand the positioning of chakras. It should be understood that the cauldrons are not identical to chakras, and their functioning is different. Rather than "wheels" of energy, they are containers, holding or pouring out different substances. Within these cauldrons one may heat, boil, or brew one's health, talents, emotions, and wisdom or poetry.

The Cauldron of Incubation is in the abdomen, upright in every person. It is upright because it is necessary for maintaining one's health and basic survival needs. This cauldron might spill onto its side in cases of severe illness, and turn "on its lips" or upside down at the point of physical death or during a near-death experience.

The Cauldron of Motion is in the chest. It is said to be born on its side in some people. This is the cauldron which processes and expresses our emotions, and from which the beginnings of the poetic art arise. In its side-slanting position, it holds only a little, and it must be turned through the understanding, expression, and transformation of powerful emotions in order to attain a fully upright position. I believe that this central, pivotal cauldron is the one that determines access to the next cauldron according to our inborn talents.

The Cauldron of Wisdom is in the head, and is born "on its lips" in all people. This cauldron is turned through training and through deific inspiration. Its gifts are not limited to poetry, but are said to be "every art besides." In the imagery of the Well of Wisdom as described by Manannán,[36] the people with this cauldron active are those who have drunk from both the well and all of the streams of the senses issuing from the well. This cauldron "magnifies every common artisan," taking them beyond human capacity into a semi-divine level of functioning, and "builds up a person through their gift." The early Irish believed that every person was capable of exceeding the limitations of their initial station in life, saying "a man

36. "Cormac's Adventure in the Land of Promise" in Cross, Tom Peete and Clark Harris Slover, *Ancient Irish Tales*, (Totowa, NJ: Barnes & Noble, 1988).

is better than his birth,"[37] and this philosophy is clearly shown throughout the poem and its commentary.

The qualities of these cauldrons can be thought of as similar to a triad of yogic concepts[38] in the same way that the cauldrons themselves bear a passing resemblance to chakras. This may point to a common Indo-European heritage for these concepts of internal energy structures and their workings.

The first of these yogic concepts, *tamas*, meaning obscurity or heaviness, could be related to the qualities found in the Cauldron of Incubation. Physicality is conceptually "heavier" and denser than thought, motion or inspiration. In yogic thought it "obscures" the spirit or soul, hiding it within a veil of flesh and mortal weakness. The Irish Celts dealt with this dichotomy by announcing that the seat of poetry was in both the body and the spirit.

Rajas is the concept of energy. Motion and transformation are ways that energy is transmitted into or through objects. The Cauldron of Motion moves and transforms our emotions, and our emotions are said to "move" us in many ways. Energy is found at liminal points between this realm and the Otherworld, between day and night, summer and winter. The Cauldron of Motion is at a significant, liminal point between the body and the illumination of pure wisdom. It is the gateway between.

Sattva is the concept of illumination or purity. The Cauldron of Wisdom provides illumination and enlightenment through the processes of poetic composition and creativity, ennobling a person, "purifying" them of their baser components.

The poetry that results from the activation of the cauldrons is described as "a terrifying stream of speech," "fearful," and "vast, mighty draughts of death-spells." These are no mere rhymes. They are words and images of immense magical power, truth summoned from the Otherworlds and named by the *fili*, who is acting with passion and intensity. Through our poetry, we reach into the liquid fires of creation, the fire that arises from the Well of Wisdom. The fire fills us until we can hold no more, and then fills us even further. The creation of this true, fearful poetry is inherently ennobling, raising the poet from the basest of conditions into enlightenment.

We can see from these phrases that the translation of the word *imbas* as "poetic frenzy" is not an overstatement of the

---

37. MacNeill, Eoin, *Early Irish Laws and Institutions*, (Dublin: Burns, Oates & Washburn, 1934).
38. Eliade, Mircea, *Yoga: Immortality and Freedom*, (Princeton: Princeton University Press, 1969).

condition. This Celtic form of enlightenment is no gentle melding with the oneness of the universe. Instead, it is a passionate, sometimes uncontrollable engagement with the fabric of reality. The energies accessed when all the cauldrons are turned into their upright positions does indeed feel like fire flowing through the head, expanding, quickening, and burning, as when Amirgen proclaimed "I am a God who shapes fire for a head."

The tilted condition of the cauldrons is equated with the state of knowledge of the poetic practitioner: "no knowledge, half-knowledge, full-knowledge." It is stated outright that not everyone has the same capacity and talent, but also implied that what we have can be worked with and improved, whatever our initial state. We each have gifts that are given to us, and it is our sacred duty to take those gifts and hone them to a fine edge. In doing this, we show our divine origin as children of the Gods, becoming *aes dána*, or "people of art."

"In the Proper Construction of Rhyme"

There are several references in the poem to poetic forms and grammatical construction. The line that I rendered "in active voice, in passive silence, in the neutral balance between" is more literally a reference to the grammatical gender of words in the Irish language. Since English does not have these distinctions of word gender, it seemed necessary to phrase this concept in more easily understandable imagery. Traditional Irish poetry is a mix of grammatical rules, metre, voice, and silence, and a certain balance is necessary for the entire composition to hold together in a powerful and pleasing manner. Irish magic was largely a matter of poetry, composed and chanted for particular purposes. The rules of grammar, therefore, might be thought of as the building blocks of magic. The proper creation of poetry, and of magic, is "the path and function of my cauldron."

Along with the grammar and metre, proper breathing was considered important. The *Auraicept* tells us "proper to bard poetry, i.e., its measure to suit the ear, and proper adjustment of breathing," and "five words are adjudged to be the breath of a poet."[39] These are probably references to breath control techniques. Some discussions of bardic training refer to a technique called "stone upon their belly" that may describe one way for ensuring that proper breathing was

---

39. Henry, P.L., 1979/1980.

maintained.[40] I believe that breath control was a part of the process of learning to turn the cauldrons, just as it is a part of the practice of yoga.

"The Root of Poetry"

The *filidh* debated whether poetry was at root a thing of spirit, sparked by the Gods, or whether it was a characteristic inherited from one's ancestors. The phrase that I have given as "ancestors" actually refers to one's father and grandfather, but in Irish society women were also known to be poets. Brigid, one of the most popular and powerful of the Celtic Goddesses, was a poet and the patron of *filidh*. These powerful Irish women have long been ignored, just as many women poets through the ages in many civilizations have been left in obscurity. I believe this was, and continues to be, an injustice to the many inspired women poets of the world. Socially speaking, the highest ranking poets were those whose parents or grandparents had been *filidh*, but without the spark of *imbas*, or poetic inspiration, even the best genealogy was not enough.

An interesting feature of the question regarding the "root of poetry" is that the word indicating the origin of poetry (*adtuithi, atuidi*) may imply "from the north (*atúaid*)." Mythologically the north is the place in which the Tuatha Dé Danann learned their druidic and magical arts. In the tale of the *Second Battle of Magh Tuired*, it is said that they were "in the northern islands of the world, studying occult lore and sorcery, druidic arts and witchcraft and magical skill, until they surpassed the sages of the pagan arts. They studied occult lore and secret knowledge and diabolic arts in four cities: Falias, Gorias, Murias and Findias."[41] Note that all of these cities are in the north, not scattered to the four directions as many occult authors insist.

"Turned by Joy or Sorrow"

For the turning of our cauldrons, joy and sorrow are specifically mentioned as necessary, with subdivisions of both emotions. Where some modern philosophies encourage the banishment of sorrow

---

40. Calder, 1917.
41. Gray, Elizabeth A., *Cath Maige Tuired: The Second Battle of Mag Tuired*, (Naas: Irish Texts Society, 1982).

and other so-called "negative" emotions, the Irish magical tradition insists that we must embrace the entire range of our emotions and experience them to the fullest possible extent. Through the transformation of these emotions we are able to create poetry and magic of immense power.

Longing, grief, and jealousy are explicitly named as emotions that turn the cauldrons of sages. Some of the greatest songs of the Irish musical tradition are based around these emotions, and this musical tradition arose directly from the earlier poetic tradition, where poets were often accompanied by instrumentalists.[42] Much popular music is still written around these emotional themes.

The discipline inherent in pilgrimages to holy places is also mentioned. Such disciplines often included restricted diets and particular rituals to be performed when the holy site was reached. Many still-active holy wells in the islands are associated with neolithic megaliths, and have never been linked to Christian saints.[43] These sites and the rituals associated with them may be a direct, if very diluted, survival from the earliest Pagan past. To travel to one of these sites implied the proper observation of times and rituals, which might be a hardship upon the pilgrim. Some pilgrimages were best, or only, to be undertaken at particular times of year. Modern Pagans are often driven by a desire to make pilgrimages to the old holy sites in response to this need generated by the cauldrons and the subsequent burst of creativity.

Joy is divided into two types, human and divine. Divine joy is not described in the text, but I believe that the joy one feels welling up within at the sights and sounds of nature can be considered divine joy. The joy sometimes felt when meditating upon the Gods and their manifestations is also a form of divine joy. And those moments of pure bliss that arise out of nowhere unexpectedly are also joy of divine origin.

Human joy is found in four categories. The first is the joy of sexual union. This elation needs no explanation for those who have experienced it. This category of human joy could give rise to unfounded speculations about secret Celtic techniques of sexual magic. It should be noted that there does not appear to be much evidence to suggest that the Pagan Celts were advocates of celibacy. In the tales of many Celtic traditions, sexual unions with the

---

42. Breathnach, Breandán, *Folk Music and Dances of Ireland*, (Dublin: Mercier Press, 1971).
43. Brenneman, Walter L. Jr. and Mary G. Brenneman, *Crossing the Circle at the Holy Wells of Ireland*, (Charlottesville: University Press of Virginia, 1995).

territorial Goddess or the personification of sovereignty are common, and often signal significant transformations in the hero.

Good health is the second category of human joy. This state of health does not imply physical perfection, but rather refers to being free from illness and reasonably hale. Many famous *filidh* and musicians were said to be blind or blemished in some way. There are a number of tales about poets who were hideous in form but perfect in poetic knowledge.[44] Their deformation may be evidence of a link to the Otherworld, for many Otherworldly beings of great power are described as having a single arm, eye, or leg. Cú Chulainn in his battle frenzy of *ferg* displays the same deformations. Bóann, in bringing the power of the Well of Wisdom into this world, loses an eye, an arm, and a leg, and it should not be forgotten that parallels are found in Norse mythology, where Odhinn sacrifices an eye in exchanges for wisdom at a well. It could be said that those with "second sight" have one eye in this world and one in the Other.

This lack of a requirement for perfection opens up the basics of poetic craft to nearly everyone, regardless of their physical condition. The only substantive qualifier is the potential for the development or possession of the spark of *imbas*. We can contrast this to the Celtic institution of kingship, which required absolute physical perfection as a necessity of the king's right to rule.

The third joy is the joy of good poetic construction, and probably refers to the ability to follow the proper rules of grammar, rhyme, and structure to compose poetry. Well-wrought poetry can be a joy to the ear in addition to being a powerful verbal spell, and the ability to construct such poetry brings many of its own satisfactions.

Fourth, and most esoteric, is the "joy of fitting poetic frenzy" which results from "grinding away at" or eating the hazels of wisdom. These nuts are found in the *sídhe* realm, at the center of the worlds. They fall into the Well of Wisdom, which is said to be the source of the Boyne, and of every other river. The well itself is found under the sea. The nuts of wisdom swim up the river, possibly in the form of salmon, every year, or every seven years, during the 'middle-month' of the year carrying wisdom with them. Their movement is 'swifter than racehorses," reflecting the lightning flash

---

44. Ford, Patrick K., "The Blind, the Dumb, and the Ugly: Aspects of Poets and their Craft in Early Ireland and Wales," Cambridge Medieval Celtic Studies , #19, Summer 1990, pp. 27-40.

of poetic inspiration and frenzy, and the silver lightning of the quick flashing salmon. In many tales, *filidh* wait on the banks of the river for years awaiting the passage of the salmon so that they may catch and consume it to obtain knowledge.

The Cosmic Mill and the World Tree

There is fascinating unstated imagery here that bears mentioning. In the book *Hamlet's Mill*,[45] a conceptual bridge is built between the themes of well, cauldron, whirlpool, and the cosmic mill or *sampo* that grinds the stuff of reality. In Finnish mythology, the *sampo* was a mill created by the smith-God Ilmarrinen[46] that ground prosperity and happiness, later grinding salt. This mill deteriorated and now is said to grind sand and stone, generating a vast whirlpool at the bottom of the sea. The mill had a many-colored lid that was the vault of the sky, and its central post was the world-tree.

Next to the Well of Wisdom stand the hazel trees that can be seen as an Irish world-tree image. The ogham tracts of the *Book of Ballymote*[47] describe the ogham alphabet as a tree that is "climbed" by the poet, and in the poem we are examining, we are told that within the Cauldron of Motion is "the true root of all knowledge... which is climbed after diligence, which poetic ecstasy sets in motion."

Poets of different grades are described as being part of the tree, with the lower grades of poets at the roots, and the highest grades sitting at the top of the tree in the "seat of Baiscne." Baiscne is the grandfather of Fionn Mac Cumhail, the Irish hero, and his name means "a great tree.[48] The grade of poet two grades below the highest rank, or *ollamh*, is known as the *druimclí*, a name which means "the top of the ridgepole of knowledge,"[49] or simply as the *clí*, implying that the poet was the tree itself.

---

45. de Santillana, Giorgio and Hertha von Dechend, *Hamlet's Mill: An Essay on Myth and the Frame of Time*, (Boston: Gambit, 1969).
46. Lönnrot, Elias, *The Kalevala or Poems of the Kaleva District*, trans. Francis Peabody Magoun, Jr., (Cambridge: Harvard University Press, 1963).
47. Calder, 1917.
48. Nagy, Joseph Falaky, *The Wisdom of the Outlaw: The Boyhood Deeds of Finn in Gaelic Narrative Tradition*, (Berkeley: University of California Press, 1985).
49. O'Curry, Eugene, *Lectures on the Manuscript Materials of Ancient Irish History*, (Dublin, 1878). "*Druimclí*, i.e., he who has (or knows) the top-ridge (or highest range) of learning; a word compounded of *druim*, the ridge of a hill or the back of a person, or the ridge of the roof of a house; and *clí*, a form of *cleith*, the column or tree which in ancient times supported the house; and the man who was a

Féige Find

The ogham glyph called the *Féige Find*, from the *Auraicept* [figure 1], illustrates what I believe to be the ogham as world-tree, arrayed as stars in the vault of heaven. The phrase is often translated as "Fionn's Window," but *féige* means "ridgepole" or "rooftree," and is the tree which supports the house, and therefore the personal cosmos. Each ogham letter has a color assigned to it in *dath* or color ogham, and this may be a later echo of the many-colored cover of the Finnish *sampo*. It would seem that the hazel nuts of wisdom must be ground in the mill of our internal cauldrons in order for poetic wisdom to find its true outlet.

In Irish, the word *coire* means both "cauldron" and "whirlpool." It is fascinating to see the implication of motion and turning in this wordplay. Our cauldrons must turn like whirlpools, tilt from their lips to an upright position in order to contain what is ground in the mill of the cosmos. The results of this process are announced in detail; the poet will speak in mantic verse and prophetic poems, dispense wisdom, perform great feats of magic, have "mastery of words," harm with "reddening satire," and offer wise judgment.

"I Sing of the Cauldron of Motion"

The Cauldron of Motion in its action is "streaming poetic inspiration as milk from the breast." This bounty is offered up by Bóann, who

---

druimclí was supposed to have climbed up the pillar or tree of learning to its very ridge or top, and was thus qualified to be a *ferleiginn* -- a professor, or man qualified to teach or superintend the teaching of the whole course of a college education."

brings the rivers from the Otherworld into the physical realm through her act at the Well of Wisdom, circling the well three times counterclockwise.[50] F. Marian McNeill says "the hazel was associated with the milk-yielding goddess because of the milk contained in the green nut."[51] Bóann's name means "white cow," and in the tale of the *Táin Bó Fráich*, she gives birth to the three harp strains which are capable of producing joy (*gentraige* or "joy strain"), sorrow (*goltraige* or "crying strain"), and sleep (*suantraige* or "sleep strain").[52] Joy and sorrow have already been specifically named as the mechanisms for turning the cauldrons within; the poem tells us that the "noble brew" of our cauldrons is that "which joy turns, which is revealed through sorrow." The cauldrons are even described as "moving toward music."

Sleep, the third harp strain, can be a metaphor for the act of mantic trance itself. In the ritual of *imbas forosnai*, the *fili* enters into a three- or nine-day (*nómaide*) period of incubatory sleep to seek visions after offering the appropriate sacrifices.[53] We can speculate that the *fili* who undertook this process was one whose cauldrons were all in their proper upright positions, giving "swift understanding."

These talents and rewards were not dispensed without effort. Both duty and diligence are mentioned as necessary ingredients in the cauldrons. Regulation, at least in the *filidh* associated with the courts, is implied with "looking after binding principles... through the working of the law." The *filidh* had long and arduous programs of study lasting for many years, involving the memorization of incredible numbers of poems, cryptic oghams, and texts. The Cauldron of Motion gives the *fili* the capacity of "distinguishing the intricacies of language," which may refer not only to the complex rules of grammar and poetic composition, but to the riddling languages used by the wise.[54]

The goal of these studies was promised as "lasting power, undiminishing protection." In fact, the person of the *fili* was generally held to be inviolate. *Filidh* could cross borders with

---

50. Stokes, Whitley, "The Bodleian Dinnshenchas," Folklore III , 1892, pp. 467-516.
51. MacNeill, F. Marian, *The Silver Bough*, (Edinburgh: Cannongate, 1989).
52. Byrne, M.E. and Myles Dillon, *Táin Bó Fráich*, (Dublin, Medieval and Modern Irish Series 5, 1937).
53. Chadwick, 1935.
54. MacAlister, R.A. Stewart, *The Secret Languages of Ireland with Special Reference to the Origin and Nature of the Shelta Language*, (Cambridge: Cambridge University Press, 1937).

impunity and confer protection and the privilege of border crossing on others by giving them the *bunsach comairce* or "rod of safe conduct."[55] In a more metaphoric sense, the *fili* provides "safe conduct" for poetry and images from the Otherworld realms into mortal time and space.

"What is This Motion?"

The motion of the cauldrons is described as "an artistic journey" that "bestows good wisdom and nobility and honor after turning." Gathering knowledge from Otherworldly sources is sometimes described in tales through the image of journeying. The *fili* must strive to artfully examine and relate the journey in order to utilize this knowledge and wisdom in the mortal realms. This "turning" does not always seem to refer to journeying, but may refer to "turning" toward the Otherworlds to be receptive to visions and dreams that proceed from places and entities that dwell there. *Aisling* or dream tales are common in the literature, and once again, this would bring us back to the sleep strain of the harp that "turns" the Cauldron of Wisdom.

The Nine Virtues

The final segment of the poem gives us a list of the nine virtues of the cauldrons. The virtues seem obscure, but taken in conjunction with the glosses (not given in this article) they begin to become clear.

The cauldron "bestows, is bestowed." This refers to praise that is given by the *fili* and which is then bestowed upon the poet for the proper practice of the craft of praise poetry. It "extends, is extended," which refers to extending, in the same manner as territory, its influence covering great distances. The cauldron "nourishes, is nourished" through the telling of tales and the making of poetry for those who have come to hear the *fili*. It "magnifies, is magnified" by providing a high honor-price for the poet, greater than that of an ordinary craftsman.

The cauldron "invokes, is invoked" by the requests of the people for knowledge from the *fili* through her contact with spirits and Gods who provide wisdom and answers to questions. It "sings, is sung" through the singing of spells and poetry for various

---

55. O'Curry, Eugene, *Ancient Laws of Ireland*, (Dublin, 1865).

purposes, which might include blessings, healing, satire, divination, or other desires of the poet and those who have employed her.

The cauldron "preserves, is preserved" through the making of binding spells, or through the laws which bind a person in a judicial sense. Another rendering of this line is "delays, is delayed," which refers more specifically to the legal aspects of binding a person to appear before judges. These bindings were apparently believed to work on both the person bound and upon the one doing the binding, linking both persons together for the duration of the litigation.

Caitlin Matthews makes some interesting comparisons of these virtues of the cauldrons with the "genealogy" of Nede mac Adne from the tale of *The Colloquy of the Two Sages*. She says, however, that "no part of either text has been reordered to form this poetic riddle,"[56] which is not the case. She rearranges her translation of the virtues of the cauldron to better suit the order of Nede's genealogy. Still, these connections seem to offer a good way to make sense of this part of the poem, and they are certainly worth time and meditation.

"Good is the Well of Measuring"

The cauldrons are described as "the source of measuring" of poetic verse and metres. The "dwelling of speech" is found in the cauldron "in which is the fire of knowledge."[57] The cauldrons are a "confluence of power which builds up strength" in both a social and a spiritual sense.

The knowledge and activation of these cauldrons is "greater than any domain, it is better than every inheritance, it brings one to knowledge." The power, prestige, and knowledge available to one who could access all three cauldrons was unequaled within early Irish society.

The word "adventuring" (*echtraid*) is the same word used to describe the genre of Irish tales that tell of adventures into the *sídhe* mounds. This takes us back to the "artistic journey" that we make when we begin to turn and activate our cauldrons. It seems to be a significant word choice, and one that is apparently missed by the other translators.

---

56. Matthews and Matthews, 1994.
57. Breatnach, 1981.

* * *

In working with the cauldrons, there are several things to consider. The first is that not everyone will achieve the same results because not everyone's cauldrons are in the same starting positions. It is implied that few will be able to achieve the activation of all three cauldrons. Also, once a cauldron is turned, there is no reason to believe that it will stay permanently in one position. The cauldrons are always in motion, their processes dynamic. Entering a new emotional state may turn a cauldron upright, or it may tip it back onto its side or its lips.

In my own practice, I have developed two "cauldron breathing" patterns that I use to activate or to examine and meditate upon the contents of the cauldrons. The first pattern, the "breath of fire," is used to activate the cauldrons that are upright. This method is to inhale slowly for a three-count, hold for a three-count, exhale for a three-count and hold for a one-count. This should be repeated nine times for each cauldron, and produces a feeling of energy movement.

The second pattern is the "breath of introspection," and is used to examine the contents of the cauldron and to meditate upon their symbolism and significance. It produces a much calmer, internalized, and meditative feeling. This pattern is to inhale slowly for a three-count, hold for a three-count, exhale for a three-count and hold for a five-count.

Neither of these breathing patterns is particularly suited for the chanting of poetry, which was apparently at least part of the intent of the Irish tradition. They are intended as more passive methods of opening and examination. I would add, however, that the breath of introspection can be used to gain information and examine images, which can then be spoken and explicated in chants and rhythmic speech. This may feel awkward at first, and may require some practice to get into the spirit of the working. At other times, you may feel as though you cannot control the speech, that it bursts from you in torrents and that you could not hold it in if you wanted to. I believe that this is the state that the *filidh* strove to inhabit in their creation of poetry.

In using the "cauldron breathing" patterns to examine and meditate upon the contents of the cauldrons, you may find yourself experiencing various sensations. The cauldrons may vary in temperature, which can be an indication of their state of activity.

Cooler cauldrons are less active, while warmer cauldrons are usually processing something.

The contents of the cauldrons may be solids, liquids, objects, or symbols. You may perceive these things as having various colors. I have found the color ogham to be a useful tool in helping to interpret the meaning of colors found within the cauldrons. The colors of the twelve *airts* or winds of the directions[58] can sometimes also provide clues. Symbols or objects that appear may have their source in the literary tradition, or you may find pictures of similar objects in books of Celtic artwork. For this reason it is necessary to be fairly knowledgeable about the symbolism in tales and poetry. You may see herbs or animals reflected in the cauldrons that may be able to give you information through conversation.

With some practice, you will find that you can sense the positions and contents of the cauldrons within others. You may find this useful in doing magical workings, divinations, or healing for them. While my experience and divination does not suggest that we can turn or fill the cauldrons of others, the contents of their cauldrons can be interpreted, cleared of intrusions and various kinds of contaminations, or clarified to help with the other person's understanding of their own internal processes. We can also place images into the cauldrons of others for them to work with and assimilate.

In working with others, as for yourself, the creation of poetry is important. Being able to state what you perceive in poetic form is an important part of the process of working with the cauldrons and transforming their contents. The poetry itself generates a certain amount of magical power that should never be discounted. Poetry provides a context for information and power, and a matrix within which to work. It ritualizes the information and becomes the ritual through which power flows.

I have found that the filling of our cauldrons is a joint process. It is possible to put things into our cauldrons to be heated through intense meditation and visualization, cooked by breaking down and interpreting the contents and symbols, bringing them from their "raw" Otherworldly state into a "cooked" condition of being understandable in this realm, and brewed through deliberate work toward inner and outer transformation. It seems, however, to be the Gods who have the active role in providing the majority of the

---

58. Matthews, Caitlin, *The Elements of the Celtic Tradition*, (Longmead: Element Books, 1989) is the most easily available source for these colors.

contents. Our task is primarily to process the contents through heating, cooking, and brewing them into useful poetry and magic, containing or dispensing the images and energies according to need.

The keys to the cauldrons are experiencing, working through, and transforming the emotions, a deep and detailed study of the tales and lore of the Irish corpus, and constant practice in the use and composition of poetry as a path for working magic. Without all three of these keys, the process of turning the cauldrons and using the wisdom and energy generated through them cannot be accomplished.

The Preserving Shrine

Three perfect immovable rocks on which are supported all the judgments of
the world:
poet, letter, nature.
Senchus Mór

In Seattle, we live with the trees. They line our streets and shelter
our yards. They stand in parks and urban groves, filling the city
with a thousand shades of green. Hidden in a corner of West Seattle
is a pocket of old growth forest, with towering cedars wider than a
man is tall. A Druid learns from the trees: patience, strength,
serenity, perseverance. A tree doesn't complain about the boulder
beside it. It grows around the stone, gaining grace and beauty with
the years, developing personality through the quirks imposed by
the circumstances of its growth. The tree is a teacher. It is an
embodiment of deity.

The early Celts had a deep and visceral connection with
nature. They honored and revered the world around them. The
Gods themselves were identified with nature, as voices in the wind,
the brightness of the sun, or the black feathers of a raven. For the
Celts, the world was wilderness and wilderness was the embodied
sacred. *Wilderness.* For most westerners, the word evokes a tangled
wasteland fraught with the danger of lurking carnivores; bears and
wolves, biting insects, poisonous snakes, deep and hazardous
waters. The wilderness is experienced as dark and foreboding. How
different is our grasp from the understanding of the Celts.

In the law text called the *Senchus Mór*[59] there is a haunting
passage. "What is the preserving shrine?" it asks. "Not hard," the
answer comes, "the preserving shrine is memory and what is
preserved in it." Again, the question is asked. "What is the
preserving shrine?" This answer is slightly different: "Not hard; the
preserving shrine is nature and what is preserved in it." How can
we appreciate the subtle message this gives? Nature and memory
are one. They are the places where all things remain, luminous and
intact, for future generations. They are linked in Celtic lore by tales
of transformation, the hidden art of ogam letters, and the connecting
thread that moves between all things.

---

59. The *Senchus Mór* is a collection of early Irish law texts that include tales and
lore which illustrate legal points.

The Irish sage Tuan preserves the memory of mythic time by living as stag, eagle, and salmon, inhabiting all three of the sacred realms of land, sea, and sky. His cycles of life and death in animal form provide one of the most beautiful stories in Celtic myth. Tuan is nature, and he serves as history, continuity, memory, and the transmission of lore from past generations into the 'mythic' present. Through his many lives, the genealogy of ancestors is kept so that they may be honored by subsequent generations.

The Filidh, or poets, Amargen and Taliesin, identify themselves completely with their wilderness, becoming wind and water, sound and sunshine, the crest of the ninth wave that separates this world from *an saol eile*, the Otherworld. These transformations speak of the wilderness that is within each of us, waiting to be called forth. Wisdom is hidden in nature; ways of relating and ways of coping with adversity, paths leading to strength of character and creativity. This same wisdom is hidden in each of us. Taliesin tells us:

> I was in many shapes before I was released. I was raindrops in the air, I was stars' beam; I was a path, I was an eagle, I was a coracle in seas. As for creation, I was created from nine forms of elements. From the essence of soils was I made, from the bloom of nettles, from water of the ninth wave.[60]

The poet Amargen offers the same sense of identity:

> I am a wind on the sea, I am a hawk on a cliff, I am the most delicate of herbs, I am a lake in a plain.[61]

Because of their identification with nature, both of them know deep secrets. "In what place lies the setting of the sun?" asks Amargen, and it is apparent that he knows the answer. "I can put in song what the tongue can utter," says Taliesin, daring to put into words the mysteries that cannot be spoken by lesser poets.

Taliesin's expression of mystery reaches into the Otherworld and brings forth song. Poetry is revealed as the only fit language for

---

60. Ford, Patrick K., *The Mabonogi and Other Welsh Medieval Tales*, Univeristy of California Press, Berkeley 1977
61. Amargen quote is the author's translation of an early Irish poem.

speaking the deepest of riddles. The *Auraicept na n-Éces*[62] calls this "the great darkness or obscurity of poetry." Taliesin's words and metaphors lead glowing fragments of truth from the Otherworld, through the interplay of darkness and light; the "great darkness" of poetry, and the brilliant fire of *imbas*, poetic frenzy. The ancient techniques of *imbas forosnai* required the isolation of the poet in darkness, a way to insulate and create sensory deprivation that allowed intense contact with the inner wilderness. Emerging from this inner forest, we re-enter the outer world and experience dark poetry as a blinding flash of light. This darkness of incubation produced Taliesin himself, whose name means "radiant brow." At the moment of stepping over the threshold from one world into another, from darkness to light, poetry explodes from the poet in torrential streams.

In silence and darkness we find the inner wilderness, and so the outer wilderness must likewise be approached in silence. Cormac Mac Art[63] explains this in precise terms: "I was a listener in woods, I was a gazer at stars, I was blind where secrets were concerned, I was silent in a wilderness."[64] The poet deliberately closes her eyes, seals her lips, and places herself in darkness so that the inner senses may reveal wonders. The human silence of the wilderness is contrasted with the human sounds of culture in early Irish poetry. Fionn Mac Cumhail and his warriors cherished this wilderness, as did the mad poet Suibhne Geilt.[65] Again and again, the belling of stags and the calling of blackbirds, the shriek of eagles or the quack of a duck are compared with the call of a church bell, and the civilized tones of bronze and iron are consistently found lacking.

Our culture imposes its civility upon us. Its urbanity stifles and conceals our inner wilderness. It gives us no silence. It

---

62. The *Auraicept na n-Éces* is a collection of texts from early manuscripts that concern the training of the filid or poets.
63. Cormac Mac Art was a legendary Irish High King who was known for his wisdom and excellent judgments.
64. Meyer, Kuno, *The Instructions of King Cormac Mac Airt*, Royal Irish Academy, Todd Lecture Series, vol XV, Dublin 1909
65. Fionn Mac Cumhail was the leader of a roving band of warriors called the Fianna. Fionn was famous for his wisdom and generosity. There is a great body of mythology surrounding Fionn and his Fianna. Suibhne Geilt was the King of Dal Araidhe, an early Irish kingdom with territory in Scotland. Suibhne was cursed by a saint and went mad in battle. This madness caused him to live naked in the forest, eating only plants and flying like a bird from tree to tree. He was a famous nature poet.

substitutes rationality for intuition and believes that this is no loss. As we grow older, we forget the wilderness of childhood, forget that we are one with our world. We grow civilized and insist that we are separate from nature. But our deepest mind remembers that we are cedar, starfish, and wren. It is written in our genes. Should civilization vanish, our bodies would still remember how to tell nourishing plants from poisons, and find shelter under the trees. When we begin to dissolve the artificial boundaries between human and nature, we gain a glimpse of what the poets knew. Our world is transformed. We become shape-shifters.

Modern Druids seek this wilderness within and without. We look for it in our back yards and parks, in forests, and amid the stones of the mountains. We pursue it with meditation and divination. We ask our Gods to break down the barriers that civilization has set between us and our birthright. Through the perfect immovable rock of the letter, we seek connections in the tales of Celtic tradition, and in the mnemonic device of the ogam alphabet.

For some, the ogam consists of a list of trees with their associated lore. This is but a fragment of the vast body of information associated with the letters. All the natural world is represented in these enigmatic scratches on wood and stone. The ogham alphabet is a forest of trees and poetry, populated by creatures of flesh and metaphor. Each letter is a world of its own. H-úath, for instance, is the whitethorn, but it is also a pack of wolves, a raven, an ox, a color called 'terrible', and is 'fearsome' as the monsters lurking within the deep caverns of the psyche.

This forest of words was created by the God Ogma to serve as a carrier of wisdom for Druids and poets. The letters of the ogam make the stave of words wielded by poets for blessing, for satire, and for the transmission of knowledge from one generation to the next. In this way, nature serves as a literal memory, for each plant, animal, river, and bird has its own fragment of poetry residing within. Each color in a stone has its own tale to tell. A complex web of meaning can be read by making a journey into the wilderness and looking for the story that each thing must tell by its very existence. The task of the Druid is to separate out the disparate threads of the tale and combine them into a coherent order.

To truly understand the preserving shrine of nature, we must seek it out. Because I live in North America, my wilderness is not that of the Irish Iron Age, or of the forests and mountains of modern Wales. My wilderness lies on Puget Sound. It shares many things with the wild lands of my European ancestors; wolf and salmon, oak and eagle. But it holds many different things as well. I live with cedars and dog-tooth violets, with banana slugs, and Steller's jays. I live with the Duwamish river and the mountain called Tahoma. These things have as much to teach us as the rowan or the Shannon or Mount Snowdon. Because they are here, now, they speak more clearly to me and with greater power than places half a world away. They come to embody the Gods for me.

All my life, I have been a wanderer, with no native place to call my own. But the great cedar and fir forests of the Northwest have laid their claim on me. I can no more refuse them than I can refuse my own death in the hour of its approach. The poetry of this place is implacable, inexorable. It is awe-full in its wildness. And yet between the time I write this, and the moment of your reading, more salmon runs will become extinct and more wild forest will disappear forever under the kind "care" of the US Forest Service.

The early Celts were wanderers too, and they understood the power of place. Wherever they settled, they opened themselves to the spirits of the land there, and became one with them. And we, as modern Celts by blood or by spirit, would do well to follow in those footsteps. We can honor the spirits of whatever place we live in, whether that place is a cottage on a Scottish moor, an apartment in Singapore, a tract house in Seattle, or a farm on the steppes of Russia. Each place is sacred in its own right, with history and with memory. Each has its own tales to tell if we know how to listen. Each place has its own ogam of trees, animals, and birds. The lapwing is the letter A of the Irish bird ogam, but what can this mean for me when I know no lapwings? How can I read the tale of my wilderness if it is phrased in words that do not exist here?

If we listen to the spirits of our own place, we need not follow a human calendar to tell us when it is Samhain or Beltain, Imbolc or Lughnasadh.[66] Nature preserves the memory of the holy days for us. The calendar of nature speaks volumes, even in the city of

---

66. Samhain (also Samain, Samhuinn) is the festival of the dead and the time of the Celtic new year, generally celebrated around November 1st.
Beltain (also Beltane, Beltaine) is the festival of the beginning of summer, celebrated around May 1st.
Imbolc is the festival of the triple Goddess Brighid, the deity of poets, smiths and healers, celebrated around February 1st.
Lughnassadh (also Lugnasad, Lughnasad, Lughnasadh) is the harvest festival of the God Lugh, whom the Romans described as "the Celtic Mercury", celebrated around August 1st.

Seattle. When does the hawthorn bloom? That is the time of Beltain. The crocus and the cherry blossom speak of Imbolc. The first frost marks Samhain, and the blackberry season brings Lughnasadh. The sun itself marks the days of solstice and equinox, circling in its eternal dance.

The Irish law texts tell us that all things are "connected by a thread of poetry." It is through this connecting thread that we begin to touch the sense of the sacred in wilderness and in ourselves. In the preserving shrine of nature is kept the liquid fire of music, the poetry of a beating bird's wing, the scarlet law of wolf and hare, the genealogy of life from stone to star. Within our bodies are the pounding surf of our blood and the spinning moon of our menses. Our flesh is the flesh of every living creature. When we dissolve the artificial boundaries between human and nature, we are nature, and we become poetry. Its poetry is ours. We reflect both nature's austerity and its excesses.

This connecting thread of poetry does not exist as words on paper. It is not, and cannot be, what we write. Analysis, like dissection, kills the beast. This poetry is instead the memory of motion and stillness. It exists in the stuttering fall of leaf to loam or the recursive eddying of a stream. It is the force of gravity that binds us to earth, and the unbearable lightness within us that happens when the sun pierces the clouds and illuminates the rolling green hills below. Poetry is the terror of the whirlwind and the sudden stillness of death. The connecting thread exists in the tension and resolution between the inner wilderness of the Druid and the external wilderness of the whirling planet.

We can perceive poetry through our senses. Sound, touch, taste, sight, and scent are spoken of as streams arising from the well of wisdom located in the heart of a hazel grove. Wisdom precedes and is the source of our senses. Without wisdom, we cannot truly see or hear, we merely go through the motions. We sleep-walk through our lives, thinking ourselves separate from wilderness. We do not understand that what we do to the world, we do to ourselves. We cannot read the connecting thread that links us to our ancestors and our children, to the stones in the garden or the snow that falls soft on our skin.

With wisdom, we act in right relationship to the wilderness. The poet becomes the world-tree. We consume the salmon of wisdom, and the spark of *imbas* strikes a bonfire in our soul. The Celtic tales and poems speak consistently of wisdom in images of nature. Wisdom is a stream, a well. It is the tide-water point where river and ocean meet and become a single turbulent, fertile estuary. It is the sweet meat of the hazel nut, and the swift, flashing salmon. Wisdom illuminates us from within until we are consumed in its fire, eaten by inspiration as the salmon is consumed by the waiting poet. We are one with nature, eaten and eater, hunter and prey.

The Tale of Cormac[67] in the Land of Promise describes the well and the streams. Manannán tells him:

> ...the well which you saw with the five streams flowing from it is the well of knowledge. And the streams of the five senses, through which knowledge is obtained; and no one will have artistic ability who does not drink from the well itself, and from the streams. The people of many skills are those who drink from them both.[68]

Wisdom is preserved in nature. The comfrey root does not forget its medicinal powers. The Goddess Airmed[69] has the knowledge of the healing properties of herbs, and teaches them to the careful student. The bee knows the place of the sun and the secrets of making honey. Ogma Honey-Mouth, the God of eloquence, creates sweet, persuasive words that can bind the hearer. Whenever we seek diligently for wisdom, we can find it.

A Druid finds the Gods embodied in nature. The sacred tree is called a *bile* in Irish, and the name of their ancestor-God is also Bile. He has his epiphanies in birch, stag, sun, and ram-horned serpent. He is the world-tree that links the sky above with the land, and the waters below. A description in the tale 'The Sickbed of Cú Chulainn[70] can give us an idea of how this God may have been seen: 'there is a tree at the entrance of the inclosure – it were well to match its music – a silver tree on which the sun shines, brilliant as gold.'[71]

---

67. In the tale of Cormac's Cup, king Cormac finds himself in the Otherworld at the palace of Manannán Mac Lir, the sea God, where he encounters the well of wisdom and is gifted with a cup that breaks if three lies are told and repairs itself when three truths are told. It is from this well of wisdom that the five streams of the senses issue.

68. Stokes, Whitley, *The Irish Ordeals*

69. Airmed is the Irish Goddess of healing herbs. When her father, Dian Cécht the physician, killed her brother Miach the surgeon, 365 herbs grew up from Miach's grave. Airmed arranged them all on her cloak according to their healing powers.

70. Cú Chulainn is the central hero of the Ulster Cycle of tales.

71. Dillon, Myles, *Early Irish Literature*, University of Chicago Press, Chicago 1948

The Goddess Danu[72] is ancient beyond memory. Her name is preserved from India to Ireland in the names of rivers, and she is called Mórrígan, the Great Queen. In Ireland, two hills called the Paps of Anu are her breasts. She is creator and destroyer, a Goddess of life and death. Manannán Mac Lir[73] is seen in the rolling waves, and the sea-foam is the hair of his wife, Fand. The tears of Manannán created three Irish lakes and, in the Isle of Man, rushes are offered to him at midsummer as rent for his sacred island. In Ireland, it is lucky if it rains on Lughanasadh, because the rain is the presence of the God Lugh at the festival. Caer Ibormeith and Oengus Mac ind Óg[74] became swans, and four birds were the kisses of Oengus. In the oral tradition of Scotland, the green land of spring is the cloak of the Goddess Brigid.

Each deity is identified with, or brings into being, some aspect of the natural world. With this as a basis for understanding nature it is impossible to treat wilderness as an impersonal other. The Gods are vitally involved in the lives of those who worship them, and their epiphanies are sacred. We cannot cut down the great ancient tree that embodies a God, nor can we dump sewage or poisonous chemicals into a river that holds our image of a Goddess. We are brought into an understanding that nothing lives outside of nature. The living world becomes a being rather than a thing, and we realize that we cannot treat this being, which is our body, with disrespect.

Heroes and poets are one with nature through *geas*, a word that means a binding spell or ritual stricture, through poetic or literal identification. It was *geas* for Cú Chulainn to eat dogs, because he was himself a dog. Cú Chulainn means "hound of

---

72. Danu is the primordial mother Goddess who gave her name to the Gods of Ireland, the Tuatha Dé Danann, which means Children of Danu. She was originally a river Goddess, and her names is found as an element in river names all over Europe, such as the Danube, the Donn, and the Dnieper.
73. Manannán Mac Lir is the sea God of the Irish Celts. He is a shape-shifter and possesses a cloak of mists, a crane bag containing myserious secrets, and many other magical objects. Manannán rules Tír na mBan, the Land of Women, and Tír Tairngiri, the Land of Promise in the Otherworld. At the center of his kingdom lies the well of wisdom.
74. Oengus Mac ind Óg is the young son of the Irish father God Dagda and his wife Bóann, who is the Goddess of the river Boyne. He is often called the Irish God of love. One night Oengus had a dream in which he saw Caer Ibormeith, and he fell into a deep love-sickness. Oengus searched the world for her, and found her at Samhain in the shape of a swan among one hundred fifty swans on a lake.

Culann." The name was given to him when the young boy Setanta killed the watchdog of the smith Culann. Setanta volunteered to serve as the smith's hound until a puppy could be raised to take his place. His fierceness ultimately led to him being called the Hound of Ulster, guardian of the province. There was no shame in identifying with the animal. In fact, this identity satisfied the demands of honor. Canine and human become one in word and deed. The hound is the emblem of a fierce and loyal companion. For Diarmuid[75] the *geas* was against killing the Boar of Ben Bulben, his half-brother. Boar and man shared one flesh in blood relationship. When Diarmuid violated his *geas* and killed the boar, he was himself slain on its tusks. To violate nature is a deadly business. Our own civilization is learning this lesson in myriad lethal ways.

In early Ireland, poets were identified with the sacred tree and with the stream of wisdom issuing from the hidden well at the bottom of the sea. Their ranks were seen as places within the tree, with the highest ranks becoming the crowning branches. Taliesin claims the region of the summer stars as his place, sitting at the top of the tree.

The Irish called their poets *ansruith*, "great stream." The poet issues from the well of wisdom just as the streams of the senses do. Through *Filidecht*, the making of poetry, we regain our senses and express the mysteries. We take liquid language and give form to the elemental forces of emotion and epiphany. The Irish said that we need not be born into a family of poets to learn the ways of *Filidecht*. The great stream of *imbas* will wash over those who must walk the path, taking them up and carrying them, swifter than racehorses, to the well of wisdom itself.

As we reach into the darkness seeking *imbas*, we are possessed by the spirit of poetry. The poet finds depth and true perception of the senses in the darkness of ecstatic trance. This is not the extraordinary control of spirits, as in shamanic trance, but rather the blinding and paradoxical loss of self found in the Welsh *awenithon*, or the loa-ridden horse of modern Voudon.[76] Giraldus

---

75. Diarmuid was one of the men of the Fíanna of Fionn Mac Cumhail and foster son of Oengus Mac ind Óg. His half-brotehr was killed as an infant, but brought back to life as the boar of Ben Bulben. A curse, or *geas*, was placed on the boar that he would bring Diarmuid to his death. Diarmuid likewise had a *geas* placed on him, that he should never hunt the boar of Ben Bulben, or he would die.

76. Voudon is an Afro-Carribean religion. One of its major features is the deep ecstatic trance of the practitioners, who are 'ridden' or possessed by a deity or powerful spirit known as a loa. The one who is ridden is called the 'horse'.

Cambrensis[77] tells us that the *awenithon* spoke from a trance "as if possessed," and that they uttered poetry of such intensity and powerful expression that it seemed nonsense. The *awenithon* did not remember what was said, but the inquirers found their answers nonetheless in the images brought forth from the inner wilderness.

The flash of *imbas* can be so bright that at times we are drowned in its fiery stream and cannot remember what we see. Poetry comes and is gone like echoes of a hawk's scree. We are dismembered, like Bóann[78] as she ran before the rising waters of Nechtan's well. In this loss of control, we are touched by the Gods. We are subsumed by nature. We return from the experience profoundly changed.

The *Filidh* were also called *druimcli*, "the top of the ridge-pole of knowledge." This ridge-pole is also called the roof-tree, which supports the house, bringing the forest inside the human dwelling. It is every person's world tree, central to their daily life. Fionn, himself a master poet, was raised in a tree by three Goddesses. From his earliest days, he dwells in the midst of wilderness, sheltered and clothed in the wild.

The poem on the Yew of Ross[79] expresses the spiritual significance of trees. It calls this *bile*, or sacred tree, 'best of creatures, a firm-strong God, door of heaven, strength of a building, light of sages, spell of knowledge.'[80] Beneath trees like this, judgments were given by Druids and poets. The tree stood as silent witness to the proceedings, and all of nature was expected to respond if the judgment were false. Lugaid Mac Con gave a false judgment that Cormac Mac Art corrected. "At that, one side of the house, the side in which the false judgment was given, fell down the slope. It will remain thus forever, the Crooked Mound of Tara. For a year

---

Horses, like the Welsh *awenithon*, rarely recall the details of their trances, and they may pass on messages from the spirit world.

77. Giraldus Cambrensis was a medieval Welsh traveler and scholar who collected folklore and observations from his travels in Wales and Ireland.

78. Bóann's husband Nechtán guarded the well of wisdom. One day Bóann decided that she would get wisdom from the well, and she went to it and circled it three times counterclockwise. The waters of the well rose up and pursued her down the course of the river Boyne, tearing from her one eye, one arm, and one leg before they drowned her. This theme is similar to Odin's giving an eye in exchange for wisdom at Mimir's well in Norse mythology.

79. The Yew of Ross was one of the five ancient sacred trees of Ireland. The poem of the Yew of Ross is found in the *Dindshenchas* or place-name tales, explaining the sacredness of this tree.

80. Stokes, Whitley, *The Prose Tales XVI*

afterward, Lugaid was king in Tara, and no grass came out of the ground or leaves on the trees or grain in the corn."[81]

The Féige Find is symbolic of a number of fivefold patterns in Irish mythology and may hold some clues to early Celtic cosmology.

The circular ogam glyph called the *Féige Find*,[82] usually translated as Fionn's Window, is actually a graphic representation of the world tree. The word *féige* means "roof-tree" or "ridge-pole". Its five rings are the five groups of ogam letters, the five invasions of Ireland, and her five provinces. In the tale *Scéla Éogain*, five rings of protection were drawn around the infant Cormac. "When Cormac was born, the Druid smith Olc Aiche, put five protective circles about him, against wounding, against drowning, against fire, against enchantment, against wolves, that is to say, against every kind of evil."[83]

The concentric rings may be seen as the circling stars in the branches of the world-tree, which Taliesin claims for his own. The *Auraicept na n-Éces* tells us that "five words are adjudged to be the breath of a poet," and it is likely that techniques of breath control were taught as the poet began to climb the tree. "Proper to bard

---

81 Dillon, 1948

82. The Féige Find is found in the 14th century manuscript, the *Book of Ballymote*. It is an arrangement of ogham letters. This five-ringed pattern is found at a number of early Celtic sites, including the ritual site at Emhain Macha. The pattern may have some ritual significance, and its five rings may be symbolic of a number of fivefold patterns in Irish myhthology.

83. O'Daly, Mairin, ed. 'Scéla Éogain' in *Cath Maige Mucrama: The Battle of Mag Mucrama*, Irish Texts Society, vol L, Dublin 1975

poetry, i.e., its measure to suit the ear, and proper adjustment of breathing."[84]

With breath control comes the ability to alter consciousness, to identify fully with the tree and with the natural world. The ogam is here compared to a tree. The first set of ogam letters are scores made to the right of the trunk-line, the second to the left, and so on. The poet is encouraged go climb the "tree" of ogham by using the letters, right hand first, left hand after, all the way up the tree.

Where the poets climb up, the Gods also climb down. The tale concerning the making of Cú Chulainn's shield[85] has the deific craftsman Dubdetha climbing down the ridge-pole through the smoke hole in a roof, to trace a pattern in the ashes for the craftsman Mac Endge. Somewhere in the middle of this great world-tree, at a silent place in the wilderness, Gods and mortals meet.

The preserving shrine of nature holds all of these memories and stories within it. The Druid studies each of them carefully, piecing together the ancient wisdom of lichen and stone, listening to the speech of boar and raven. The poet snatches fragments from the darkness and, with the spark of *imbas*, builds these keen-edged shards into song. But how much longer will we have this store of treasure?

In this time, the preserving shrine itself stands in need of protection. The memory of the earth is lost, day by day, through the extinction of species. Poet and letter are not enough. No poem's magic will recall the salmon when the last one dies. No book will fully describe the great old growth forest once it has gone. We must be able to see these things for ourselves, to touch rough bark, hear the moan of the cougar, taste wild blackberries, and smell the wet scent of cedar in the air, so that the wilderness within can be complete. We must have the perfect immovable rock on which to lean if we and our sibling species are to survive the next century.

---

84. Calder, George, *Auraicept na n-Éces: The Scholar's Primer*, John Grant, Edinburgh 1917
85. Best, R.I., 'Cuchulainn's Shield', Ériu 5, 1911

Speckled Snake, Brother of Birch:
Amanita Muscaria Motifs in Celtic Legends

Erynn Rowan Laurie and Timothy White

References to magical brews and foods abound in Celtic legends dealing with journeys to *Tír Tairngire* (Land of Promise) or into the *sidhe* (faery mounds). In the Welsh *Hanes Taliesin*, the young Gwion Bach imbibes three drops of magical brew simmering in Cerridwen's cauldron; he is immediately gifted with inspiration, and then he is launched on a magical journey that entails shapeshifting into various animal forms, being eaten and rebirthed by Cerridwen, and then being set adrift in a dark skin bag on an endless sea for forty years. In the Irish *Adventures of Cormac*, Manannán, king of the Land of Promise, gives Cormac a magical, sleep-inducing silver branch with three golden apples and, before long, Cormac travels to the otherworld where he discovers a marvelous fountain containing salmon, hazelnuts, and the waters of knowledge. Considering that the old Celtic legends of Ireland and Wales are filled with motifs of sleep-inducing apples, berries of immortality, and hazelnuts of wisdom, it is remarkable that Celtic scholars have largely ignored the possible shamanic use of psychoactives and entheogens in the British Isles.[86]

---

86. Except for the early linguistic inquiries of R. Gordon Wasson, *Soma: Divine Mushroom of Immortality* (New York: Harcourt Brace Jovanovich, 1968), and the mythopoeic studies of Robert Graves, *The White Goddess* (Toronto: McGraw-Hill Ryerson, 1948/1966), there was, until recently, little scholastic interest in the historic use of psychoactive mushrooms in Celtic Europe.

Since the 1960s, numerous cross-cultural studies have established that shamanic use of psychoactive substances to induce altered states of consciousness is much more prevalent in all parts of the world than once thought. See for example Peter Furst, ed., *Flesh of the Gods: The Ritual Use of Hallucinogens* (New York: Praeger, 1972); Michael Harner, ed., *Hallucinogens and Shamanism* (New York: Oxford University Press, 1973); Michael Ripinski-Naxon, *The Nature of Shamanism: Substance and Function of a Religious Metaphor* (Albany, NY: State University of New York, 1993); Richard Evans Schultes and Albert Hofman, *Plants of the Gods: Their Sacred, Healing, and Hallucinogenic Powers* (Rochester, VT: Healing Arts Press, 1992); and R. Gordon Wasson, *The Wondrous Mushroom: Mycolatry in Mesoamerica* (New York: McGraw-Hill, 1980).

Ripinski-Naxon 153-166 provides a good summary of the evidence that Indo-European peoples have, at various times, used psychoactive substances in their shamanic rituals. Historical and archaeological evidence indicates that the

There are several sound reasons why Celtic scholars have feared to tread where amateurs now dare to venture. First, due to the prohibition on writing that surrounded the ancient Celtic druids and Irish *filidh* (poet-seers), we know few specifics about the religious practices of the ancient Celts. Second, there are no direct references in the early histories to the Celts using psychoactives other than meads and wines in their ceremonial rituals and practices. Third, there is no irrefutable archaeological evidence — such as the discovery of an archaic medicine bag filled with psychoactive mushrooms — to prove the Celts actually used psychotropic substances capable of inducing ecstatic, visionary experiences.

Nevertheless, the abundance of Celtic legends about crimson foods that induce mystical experiences, inspire extraordinary knowledge, and impart the gift of prophecy, is highly suggestive. To our knowledge, no one has adequately explained why apples, berries, hazelnuts, and salmon were selected by the *filidh* as magical foods, or why they were associated with otherworldly journeys, and with the training of poets. None of these foods are inherently psychotropic.[87]

Even if one assumes that the frequent Celtic literary references to magical brews of knowledge indicate that the Celts utilized some type of psychotropic substance, several questions remain — most notably, exactly what was used and how was it used? Given the paucity of reliable information on Celtic religious practices, the answers to these questions may remain forever speculative. However, the absence of direct evidence is not proof that evidence is nonexistent.

---

ancient Scythians burned *cannabis* in their sweat tents, the Greeks used opium poppies and other psychoactives in their mystery religions, and the Voguls (Khanti) of western Siberia used *A. muscaria* in shamanic rituals.

Although there is still no direct evidence indicating *A. muscaria* usage among the Irish Celts, there is growing evidence suggesting its possible use in other parts of Europe. Ripinski-Naxon 154-165 summarizes evidence for the prehistoric use of *A. muscaria* in Europe and includes the interesting research of Italian entho-botanist Giorgio Samorini. Based on the appearance of mushroom-like motifs in the rock carvings of Valcamonica, and one naturalistic image of a spotted mushroom (*A. muscaria*?) depicted in association with an individual or effigy, it is conceivable that the Celts, who once inhabited the region, might have practiced a ritual mushroom complex.

87. It is likely that the apples, berries, and hazelnuts were sometimes made into alcoholic brews, for there are references to hazel mead in Celtic texts. However, alcoholic inebriation tends to produce drunken fools, not instantaneous wise men.

The Celtic druids and bards had a definite penchant for poetic metaphors — for always speaking in "riddles and dark sayings," as the Roman historian Diogenes Laertius observed.[88] It can be assumed that if the druids and *filidh* did use a psychotropic substance to access knowledge, healing, and wisdom, they would have carefully protected its identity from Roman invaders and Christian missionaries. We contend that the motifs of magical foods can best be explained as metaphoric references to *Amanita muscaria*, the highly valued, red-capped mushroom that was once used shamanicly throughout much of northern Eurasia.[89]

Wasson's Findings on Celtic Toadstools

One reason the possible role of a psychoactive mushroom in Celtic mythology has been overlooked is that *A. muscaria* is difficult to find in Ireland today. *A. muscaria* grows only in a symbiotic, mycorrhizal relationship with the roots of birch, spruce, and some conifers — and Ireland has been almost totally deforested over the last thousand years. However, there were once great forests of birch and pine in Ireland, so the red-capped mushroom could easily have grown there, as it still does in the forests of England and Scotland, and on the Isle of Man (located between Ireland and England).[90]

---

88. As quoted in Stuart Piggot, *The Druids* (New York: Thames and Hudson, 1968/1987) 117.

89. For information on the widespread use of *A. muscaria* in northern Eurasia, see R. Gordon Wasson, "Fly Agaric and Man," *Ethnopharmacologic Search for Psychoactive Drugs*, ed. Daniel H. Efron (Washington D.C.: U.S. Department of Health, Education, and Welfare, 1967) 405-414; Wasson, *Soma*; and Maret Saar, "Ethnomycological Data from Siberia and Northeast Asia on the Effect of Amanita Muscaria," *Journal of Ethnopharmacology* 31 (1991): 157-173.

A. *muscaria* was known to the Khanti and Mansi of western Siberia as *panx*, to the Ket as *hango*, to the Mordvinians and Heremis (Mari) of eastern Europe as *pango*, to the Yurak Sammoyed as *ponka*, to the Chukchi of eastern Siberia as *pon* or *pónmpo*, and — if Wasson is right — to the ancestors of India's vedic priests as *soma*. Wasson, "Fly Agaric" 408-413 argues — based on the widespread appearance of the panx-ponka-ponmpo word pattern among Siberian tribes, as well as on certain linguistic links between Magyar *bolond gomba* (fool's mushroom), Slavic *gomba* (sponge), Greek *(s)póngos* (touchwood) — that Indo-European usage of *A. muscaria* could date back to 3,500 years.

90. Contemporary nature guides indicate that *A. muscaria* is still relatively common in the woods of England and Scotland. In 1995, the Isle of Man's Philatelic Bureau issued a 20-penny stamp depicting *A. muscaria*, indicating it is still found there.

British naturalist Oliver Rackham notes that renowned birch forests were once found throughout the British Isles. It is quite probable that *A. muscaria* was

Furthermore, even if *A. muscaria* never grew in Ireland, the *filidh* could have easily obtained supplies of dried mushrooms from their Celtic neighbors.

The mere availability of *A. muscaria* does not prove its use, however. Even ethnomycologist R. Gordon Wasson—the most enthusiastic proponent of the theory that *A. muscaria* was used by the ancient Indo-European peoples—once admitted that, in all his research, he had found little evidence suggesting the shamanic use of fly-agaric (*A. muscaria*) among the Celts, Germans, or Anglo-Saxons. He stated explicitly that he could find no direct evidence that psychoactive mushrooms had been used either by the "shadowy Druids," or medieval witches.[91]

Despite the lack of hard evidence, Wasson never totally dismissed the possibility of *A. muscaria* use in Europe. Based on his studies into why most European languages are filled with mycophobic references toward mushrooms in general and fly-agaric in particular, Wasson arrived at a very interesting conclusion:

> I suggest that the 'toadstool' was originally the fly-agaric in the Celtic world; that the 'toadstool' in its shamanic role had aroused such awe and fear and adoration that it came under a powerful tabu, perhaps like the Vogul tabu where the shamans and their apprentices alone could eat it and others did so only under pain of death...This tabu was a pagan injunction belonging to the Celtic world. The shamanic use of the fly-agaric disappeared in time, perhaps long before the Christian dispensation. But in any case the fly-agaric could expect no quarter from the missionaries, for whom toad and toadstool were alike the Enemy.[92]

---

once abundant in Ireland, at least until the Irish forests were cleared. Interestingly, as Rackham observes, the last well-wooded remnants of forests in Ireland were typically found on islands or on the ancient earth mounds known as *raths*—the very places said to hold the underground homes of fairies. Oliver Rackham, *The History of the Countryside* (London: Dent & sons, 1986) 112.

91. See Wasson, *Soma* 176. For a thorough discussion on how the mycophobic attitudes of Europeans are reflected in their names, for *A. muscaria*, see Wasson, *Soma* 172-203.

92. Wasson, *Soma* 191.

The absence of evidence led Wasson to conclude that Indo-European usage of the sacred mushroom may have disappeared early during their migrations into Europe. He hypothesized that, as the Indo-Aryans migrated into warm, dry climates, they were forced to adopt various local psychoactive plants as substitutes for *A. muscaria*. Although historical evidence in India, Turkey, and the Mediterranean may support his theory, the proto-Celts would not have needed to find substitutes for *A. muscaria* in their new homelands — the red-capped mushroom flourished throughout much of northwestern Europe.

Did the Irish Practice a *Soma* Cult?

Peter Lamborn Wilson suggests that — in light of the "well-known affinity between Celtic and Vedic cultures," and the fact that "entheogenic cults can thrive under the very nose of 'civilization' and not be noticed" — it should be considered whether the Irish may have once had a "*soma* cult."[93] Although Wilson seems reluctant to draw definitive conclusions, he argues that if the Irish did use soma, the evidence should be encoded in early Irish literature and folklore. "I think we can take for granted," he states, "that whatever we find in Ireland that looks like soma, and smells like soma, so to speak, might very well be soma, although we may never be able to prove the identity."

Although Wilson does not conclusively identify the Vedic soma, he seems to accept R. Gordon Wasson's theory that it was probably *A. muscaria* or — if not that — another psychoactive mushroom.[94] Whatever its source, soma was clearly an ecstasy-

---

93. Peter Lamborn Wilson, "Irish Soma," *Psychedelic Illuminations* VIII (1995): 42-48.

94. The hymns of the *Rig Veda* never directly identify the main ingredient of soma, but they are filled with numerous descriptive references to the mysterious plant. Based on these descriptions, Vedic scholars have proposed various psychoactive plants — including *Peganum harmana* and even *Cannabis sativa* — as possible candidates for soma. A few scholars still favor alternate candidates, but many scholars now endorse Wasson's persuasive proposal that soma was probably *A. muscaria*.

Terence McKenna, *Food of the Gods: The Search for the Original Tree of Knowledge* (New York: Bantam, 1993) 97-120 argues, based largely on two negative personal trials, that *A. muscaria* could not have been responsible for the rapturous visionary ecstasy of the Vedas. He suggests instead that soma is more likely to have been a psilocybin mushroom, possibly *Stropharia cubensis*, but he has not established the availability of *Stropharia sp.* in ancient India.

inducing drink once used by the ancestors of India's Vedic priests, who recorded hundreds of hymns praising its miraculous powers in the 3,500-year-old *Rig Veda*, the oldest extant Indo-European text. Utilizing Wasson's research on soma and *A. muscaria*, Wilson focuses primarily on identifying soma motifs—such as one-eyed, one-legged beings—that also appear in Celtic mythology.[95] Wilson suggests that the Greek legends of one-eyed, one-legged Hyperboreans may be connected to the Irish legends of the Fomorians (the mythic primordial inhabitants of Ireland), who are sometimes depicted as one-eyed, one-legged giants.

The theme of one eye, arm, and leg certainly appears prominently in several Celtic legends about the Fomorians, but the most fascinating reference occurs in the *Second Battle of Magh Tuired*, when the Irish sky god Lugh performs a curious shamanic ritual. During the battle, Lugh adopts a strange posture, standing on one leg, one arm behind his back, and closing an eye in order to cast spells on his opponents, the Fomorians. Working magic in this posture is called *corrguinecht* or "crane sorcery," and Lugh's practice

---

There is substantial evidence that *A. muscaria* can produce ecstatic, euphoric visions. Francesco Festi and Antonio Bianchi, "Amanita Muscaria," *Integration* 2-3 (1992): 79-89 note that it can produce "colorful bright dreams with a particular sense of 'lucidity' as well as dreamlike states in which reality is experienced "as an inner world with a strong feeling of introspection." Clark Heinrich, *Strange Fruit* (London: Bloomsbury Publishing, 1995), who has worked extensively with *A. muscaria*, notes that it is quite capable of inducing euphoric, ecstatic states. While Heinrich's suggestion that biblical prophets used *A. muscaria* is highly speculative, he provides some excellent evidence from the Vedas and other Hindu traditions supporting Wasson's original soma thesis.

95. Although Wasson was primarily interested in proving that *A. muscaria* was the most promising candidate for soma, many of his observations and comments may be extended to support links between *A. muscaria* and the wondrous Celtic brews of knowledge. For example Wasson, *Persephone's Quest: Entheogens and the Origin of Religion* (New Haven, CT: Yale University Press, 1986) 60-67 argues that Vedic references to soma as "single-eyed" and "not-born single-foot" may have the same roots as the one-eyed and one-legged mushroom beings of Siberia. Wilson, "Irish Soma," examines soma motifs found in the saga of Diarmuid and Gráinne from the Fionn Cycle, and he suggests that Searbhán the Surly—the one-eyed Formorian giant who guards the magical scarlet rowan berries of the Tuatha Dé Danaan—could be a mushroom being. In addition, based on the observation in Wasson, *Soma* 44 that soma was pounded to extract a divine inebriant, Wilson suggests that the act of Diarmuid clubbing Searbhán to death could be a symbolic reference to the ritual sacrifice and pressing of soma.

of *corrguinecht* is a clear indication of his shamanic associations.[96] Lugh is well renowned as a shamanic magician who used his magical weapons and spells to win battles. As a deity associated with thunderbolts and magic healing as well, Lugh may also qualify as a god of *A. muscaria* – suggesting a possible link between shamanism and *A. muscaria* in early Irish legends.[97]

As Wilson ultimately admits, the mere existence of soma motifs in Celtic literature does not prove the use of soma by the insular Celts. It is possible, given their conservative nature, that they preserved soma motifs in their myths without actually continuing the use of soma – just as Christians still cherish many ancient pagan religious symbols, such as Yule logs and decorated trees at Christmas, and fertility bunnies and eggs at Easter, without understanding their original pagan context.

While we believe that Wilson is essentially correct in his identification of soma-like motifs in Celtic literature, our quest into the roots of Celtic religion has further convinced us that Celtic legends dealing with foods of knowledge point directly to the use of *A. muscaria* in Celtic shamanism. Of course, even if we can demonstrate the presence of psychoactive mushroom metaphors and motifs in Celtic legends, that still does not prove that the druids or *filidh* used the red-capped mushroom. As in the case of Wilson's soma motifs, the veiled references to *A. muscaria* could theoretically be faded memories of earlier pre-migration Indo-European practices, preserved in oral legends passed down from generation to generation.

Dreams of Paradise

The first hint that the Celts may have used *A. muscaria* can be found in the Irish descriptions of the beautiful, magical Land of Promise and the *sidhe* realms of the Tuatha Dé Danann, the old Celtic gods of Ireland. Celtic otherworlds are almost always exquisitely beautiful places endowed with many attributes typical of psychotropic experiences. Brilliant colors abound, and humans and animals shift from shape to shape. Time and space are typically distorted, faery

---

96. The crane is often associated in Celtic legends with druidic magic, and the magical objects of both the otherworld god Manannán and the hero Fionn Mac Cumhaill were stored in crane-skin bags.

97. As Wasson, *The Wondrous Mushroom* 229 points out, soma is associated with thunderbolts, and many cultures associate thunderbolts with *A. muscaria*, which typically fruits after the first thunderstorms of fall. Lugh's association with thunderbolts could link him to *A. muscaria*.

music is often heard on the wind, and foods tend to taste particularly delicious. Some of these otherworld motifs could theoretically have been inspired by various psychotropic plants, by other forms of spiritual journeying, or even by hunger-induced hallucinations. However, when considered as a whole, the Celtic legends paint pictures that look remarkably similar to dream-visions experienced under the influence of *A. muscaria.*

Consider the following description of the Land of Promise in *The Adventures of Art Mac Conn.* In the middle of the story, the father, Conn, embarks in a magical, oarless coracle (skin boat) that takes him wandering over the sea for a month and a fortnight until he comes to a fair, strange isle:

> And it was thus the island was: having fair fragrant apple-trees, and many wells of wine most beautiful, and a fair bright wood adorned with clustering hazel trees surrounding those wells, with lovely golden-yellow nuts, and little bees ever beautiful humming over the fruits, which were dropping their blossoms and their leaves into the wells. Then he saw nearby a shapely hostel thatched with bird's wings, white, and yellow, and blue. And he went up to the hostel. 'Tis thus it was: with doorposts of bronze and doors of crystal, and a few generous inhabitants within. He saw the queen with her large eyes, whose name was Rigru Rosclethan, daughter of Lodan from the Land of Promise...[98]

Now compare the above scene to a description of an *A. muscaria* experience translated by Wasson from the journal of Joseph Kopec, a Polish brigadier who tried the mushrooms while visiting Russia's Kamchatka Peninsula in 1797.[99] Once, while very ill with a fever, Kopec sought medical help from a local Russian Orthodox priest, who recommended that he take some "miraculous mushrooms." Because Kopec's description of his dream-visions is fairly typical of accounts of *A. muscaria* experiences, it is worth quoting here:

98. For the complete text see Tom Peete Cross and Clark Harris Slover, *Ancient Irish Tales* (Totowa: Barnes & Noble, 1936/1988).
99. Wasson, *Soma* 244-245.

I ate half my medicine and at once stretched out, for a deep sleep overtook me. Dreams came one after the other. I found myself as though magnetized by the most attractive gardens where only pleasure and beauty seemed to rule. Flowers of different colors and shapes and odors appeared before my eyes; a group of most beautiful women dressed in white going to and fro seemed to be occupied with the hospitality of this earthly paradise. As if pleased with my coming, they offered me different fruits, berries, and flowers. This delight lasted during my whole sleep, which was a couple of hours longer than my usual rest. After having awakened from such a sweet dream, I discovered that this delight was an illusion.

Delighted by the results of his first experience, Kopec took an additional dose of dried mushrooms and had a series of new visions, which he unfortunately did not describe. He did, however, volunteer some intriguing observations about their nature:

I can only mention that from the period when I was first aware of the notions of life, all that I had seen in front of me from my fifth or sixth year, all objects and people that I knew as time went on, and with whom I had some relations, all my games, occupations, actions, one following the other, day after day, year after year, in one word the picture of my whole past became present in my sight. Concerning the future, different pictures followed each other which will not occupy a special place here since they are dreams. I should add only that as if inspired by magnetism I came across some blunders of my evangelist [the priest] and I noticed that he took these warnings almost as the voice of Revelation.

The parallels between Kopec's *A. muscaria* dream-visions and the chronicles of Celtic journeys to the Land of Promise are noteworthy. Kopec visits a land "where only pleasure and beauty seemed to rule," encounters beautiful women dressed in white, and comes back with visionary insights—not unlike the gift of inspired sight found frequently in Irish myths. By themselves, such parallels might seem to be coincidental and inconsequential. After all, beautiful people and magical objects are the building blocks of many myths and legends. However, as we shall soon show, Celtic myths of the otherworld are filled with motifs of magical, wisdom-inducing foods and brews that closely parallel what we know about the use of red-capped mushrooms in Siberian shamanism. But first, let us see if there is any historical evidence that could have involved the use of *A. muscaria*.

Traces of Celtic Shamanism

So little is known about the spiritual practices of the druids that some scholars have questioned whether it is appropriate to even speak of Celtic shamanism per se. However, based on comments scattered throughout the early records of Roman historians as well as later accounts recorded by Christian monks, we can conclude that the druids performed shamanic functions comparable to those performed by Siberian shamans.[100] Celtic legends mention that the druids practiced battle magic, invoked storms, conducted healings, used enchantments to put crowds of people to sleep, and performed oracles to predict the future.[101] We also know that the *filidh* were not

---

100. The earliest written records of Druidic and Celtic religion were, for the most part, based on secondhand reports, which were then filtered through the personal prejudices of the Roman authors. For a discussion on the information and misinformation contained in Roman histories, see Piggot 91-120.

    Christian penitentials occasionally condemned prevailing pagan practices, but they gave little substantive information about the practices, and they didn't directly mention any shamanic use of psychotropics. The seventh-century *Liber Penitentialis* of S. Theodore, seventh Archbishop of Canterbury, condemned various magical practices and ceremonies, in particular the idolatry of "soothsayers, poisoners, charmers, diviners." Theodore also threatened to expel from the church anyone who acted as a wizard, invoked demons, raised storms by evil craft, or conducted sexual magic. See Montague Summers, *The Geography of Witchcraft* (New York: A. A. Knoph, 1927) 65-6.

101. The Old Gaelic legends—preserved orally for centuries by Irish *filidh* and bards—often mention pagan and druidic practices in passing. Although the written versions of the Gaelic legends were recorded much later by Christian clerics, these legends contain remarkably sympathetic, insightful comments about druidic practices. Unfortunately, the stories seldom provide detailed descriptions of the rituals, so the best we can do is piece together Celtic practices form various sources. For a sampling of passages dealing with the shamanistic practices of the Celts, see John Matthews, *Taliesin: Shamanism and the Bardic Mysteries in Britain and Ireland* (London: Harper Collins/Aquarian Press, 1991);

only inspired poets but also visionary prophets, healers, and workers of magic.[102]

Working knowledge of druidic shamanic practices may have vanished with the druids, but Irish histories and commentaries have preserved many short descriptions and notes about the divinatory practices of the *filidh*. Through statements made in the tenth-century book *Cormac's Glossary* and elsewhere, we know that the pre-Christian druids and *filidh* practiced three oracles, at least one of which could be considered shamanic: *imbas forosnai*, which can be translated as "manifestation that enlightens" or "kindling of poetic frenzy;" *teinm laída*, or "illumination of song;" and *dichetal do chennaib*, or "extempore incantation."

Nora Chadwick has compiled an informative study of the many historical references to these three methods of divination.[103] Unfortunately, the extant historical notes are usually brief and occasionally contradictory, and they deal primarily with the external forms of the oracles, so we can only speculate on how these divinatory practices actually worked. Nevertheless, because documentation is available on these oracles, any evidence linking them to the use of *A. muscaria* would add historical flesh and bones to the *A. muscaria* metaphors found in Gaelic legends.

According to *Cormac's Glossary*, the imbas forosnai ritual involved chewing a substance described as the "red flesh" of a pig, cat, or dog; chanting incantations; and invoking and making offerings to idols of the gods.[104] After this the *fili* (singular of *filidh*)

---

and Caitlin Matthews and John Matthews, *The Encyclopedia of Celtic Wisdom* (Rockport, MA: Element Books, 1994).

102. The functions of the *filidh* are documented in great detail throughout the literature of the early Irish, although no one source compiles all this information into one place. As Joseph Falasky Nagy, *The Wisdom of the Outlaw: The Boyhood Deeds of Finn in Gaelic Narrative Tradition* (Berkeley: University of California, 1985) notes, Fionn MacCumhail is an archetypal shamanic *fili*, composing poetry, healing by offering a draught of water from his hands, journeying into the *sidhe* mounds, and conducting rituals of divination.

103. Nora Chadwick, "Imbas Forosnai," *Scottish Gaelic Studies* Vol. VI, part II (1935): 97-135.

104. *Cormac's Glossary* is a tenth-century Old Irish text found in the *Yellow Book of Lecan*. Because the glossator was commenting from a time several centuries after the practice of *imbas forosnai* had been outlawed, he was presumably speaking from historical tradition rather than direct experience. However, it is conceivable that the practice of *imbas forosnai* continued underground.

We know that Scottish descendants of the *filidh* practiced two oracles — the *tarbhfeis* and *taghairm* — which bear certain similarities to *imbas forosnai*. Seventeenth-century Scots practiced a rite called the *tarbhfeis*, or "bull-feast," covered his cheeks with his palms or went to sleep in a dark place for a three- or nine-day period of incubatory sleep called a *nómaide*. During that time, several other *filidh* usually stood watch to make sure that the sleeping *fili* was not disturbed and did not move. The seer was expected to experience visions of the gods and the future, and to receive answers to questions being asked. This oracle would qualify as a shamanic ritual under the most stringent definitions of shamanism.

None of the extant accounts of *imbas forosnai* adequately explain how the divinatory visions were induced, but they all indicate that the ritual involved eating "red" flesh and being confined in darkness. Perhaps the *filidh* were natural psychics or lucid dreamers, and chewing the red flesh was merely incidental to the ritual. However, if they were chewing on pieces of dried red-capped mushrooms, that would explain how the ritual induced prophetic dreams. As Wasson and Saar note, *A. muscaria* is often used in Siberian shamanism for the incubation of prophetic dreams.[105] The idea that the red flesh used in the *imbas forosnai* ritual could be a veiled reference to *A. muscaria* may seem farfetched at this point, but it should make sense after we examine other motifs of magical crimson foods found in Celtic legends.

Accounts of the other two divinatory traditions — *teinm laída* and *dichetal do chennaib* — are less consistent, perhaps because those practices were less formal and could be conducted extemporaneously, without specific ceremony.[106] *Dichetal do chennaib*

---

which also involved chewing or consuming red flesh. According to one account by the historian Geoffrey Keating, a bull was sacrificed and then the seer consumed some of its flesh and broth, wrapped himself in the fresh hide of a bull, and waited for a dream or vision (cited in Matthew and Matthews 243). In an eighteenth-century book, *Description of the Western Isles of Scotland*, Marin Martin describes another divination ritual, known there as *taghairm*. "A party of men, who first retired to solitary places, remote from any house…singled out one of their number, and wrapp'd him in a big cow's hide, which they folded about him, his whole body was covered with it except his head, and so left in this posture all night until…[he gave] the proper answer to the question at hand," (cited in Matthews and Matthews 334). No mention is made in Martin's account of chewing on red flesh, but such a detail could easily have been overlooked.
105. Wasson, *Soma* 244; Saar.
106. Matthews 184 quotes a passage from the *Senchus Mor*, a collection of law texts from various periods, that appears to confuse the practice of teinm laída with that of dichetal do chennaib: "When the fili sees the person or thing before him, he makes a verse at once with the ends of his fingers, or in his mind without studying, and he composes and repeats at the same time…" However, the passage gives a good description of how, "before Patrick's time," teinm laída was

has been translated variously as "extempore recital," "incantation from the ends (of the fingers)," and "inspired incantation." It appears to have involved the recitation of *dicetla* (spells) or verses in order to find the answers to the questions posed. This was the one form of divination that Saint Patrick tolerated, reportedly because it did not involve the invocation of pagan deities.

The varied accounts of *teinm laída* suggest it involved the chanting of intuitive images received through the psychometric reading of objects. In one of the Fionn stories, the hero Fionn is asked to identify a headless body. Fionn puts his thumb into his mouth and uses a repetitive chant—referred to as *teinm laida*—to divine that the body belongs to Lomna, his fool. Interestingly, Fionn's ability to achieve poetic insight by sucking or chewing on his thumb harks back to his childhood consumption of a magical red and white speckled salmon and, as we will show later, the salmon may be a metaphor for *A. muscaria*.

Other references also suggest metaphorical links between *teinm laida* and *A. muscaria*. As Joseph Nagy points out, the word *teinm* means "cracking or chewing of the pith," and this word is found in the phrase *teinm cnó*, to crack open a nut; thus *teinm laida* can be translated literally as "the chewing (or breaking open) of the pith (or nut)."[107] Chewing the nut could conceivably refer to mulling over poetic images, but if crimson hazelnuts are *A. muscaria* metaphors (as we hope to show), then the *teinm laida* could have been inspired by chewing the red-and-white mushroom.

Vague references to chewing red meat or nuts are hardly conclusive evidence of an underground Irish mushroom cult, but they do suggest that the Irish seers were chewing something "red." In light of the many Celtic legends about magical red foods—red berries, crimson nuts, and apples—which inspired the gift of insight and induce prophetic visions, we do not think the red flesh used in the *imbas forosnai* was incidental. We also do not think it is coincidental that all these red foods happen to exhibit traits reminiscent of *A. muscaria*.

---

done differently: "The poet placed his staff upon the person's body or upon his head, and found out his name, and the name of his father and mother, and discovered every unknown thing that was proposed to him, in a minute or two or three, and this Teinm Laegha [sic] or Imus Forosna [sic], for the same thing used to be revealed by means of them; but they were performed after a different manner, i.e. a different kind of offering was made at each."
107. Nagy 137.

Assuming that the red-capped mushrooms were used in the *imbas forosnai* ritual to induce prophetic dreams, the purpose of covering the eyes and retreating into a dark environment could easily be explained. *A. muscaria* intoxication can cause such a pronounced visual sensitivity to light that the light of a single candle can hurt the eyes. Since the shamanic use of *A. muscaria* has tended to rely on dream-visions rather than waking journeys, the darkness would also have helped secure the trance-sleep necessary to gain prophetic visions.

The Red Berries of Immortality

Various legends mention that the Tuatha Dé Danann ate magical red rowan berries which had the properties of preserving immortality, returning youth, and offering the gift of healing to those who consumed them.[108] In the medieval Irish tale "The Pursuit of Diarmuid and Gráinne," we are told that one of the magical berries fell from the table at one of these feasts and grew into a tree. This tree is guarded by a giant who refuses to allow any mortal access to the berries (could this be a literary relic of a Celtic taboo against commoners using *A. muscaria?*)

Diarmuid's description certainly supports the *A. muscaria* metaphor: "In all the berries that grow upon that tree there are many virtues, that is, there is in every berry of them the exhilaration of wine and the satisfying of old mead; and whoever should eat *three* berries of that tree, had he completed a hundred years he would return to the age of thirty years."[109] Although no known psychoactive reverses aging so dramatically, many Siberian tribes, such as the Koryak, consider *A. muscaria* brews to be rejuvenating, and they say that in moderate dosages — approximately *three* mushrooms — *A. muscaria* produces a mild inebriation comparable to drinking wine or beer.

---

108. Although Siberians don't associate *A. muscaria* directly with immortality, Salzman et al report that the Koryak of Siberia make a tonic of blueberries and *A. muscaria*, which is drunk for health and longevity. Again, we see parallels to the Vedic soma — just as immortality was promised to Vedic priests who drank soma, immortality is promised to those who eat the foods and drink of the rowan berries of the Dé Danann. Emanuel Salzman, Jason Salzman, Joanne Salzman and Gary Lincoff, "In Search of Mukhomor, the Mushroom of Immortality," *Shaman's Drum* 41 (1996): 36-47.

109. The English translations of quotations from "The Pursuit of Diarmuid and Gráinne" are based on Cross and Slover.

The Voyage of Máel Dúin provides a description of some other magical berries found on a tree on an otherworldly island. They are as large as an apple but have a tough rind. When their juice is squeezed out and consumed by Máel Dúin, he falls into a deep intoxication and sleeps for an entire day. His companions cannot tell whether he is dead or alive, but when he awakens he tells them to gather as much of the fruit as they can, for the intoxication that it produces is wondrous.

Máel Dúin's magical berries sound suspiciously like soma and the red-capped *A. muscaria*. The *Rig Veda* describes soma as being pressed out as a juice, and *A. muscaria*, when consumed in large doses, can result in an intoxicating sleep associated with wondrous visions. Assuming Celtic druids wanted to maintain a veil of secrecy around their use of *A. muscaria*, the image of large, red rowan berries would make a fair substitute for red-capped mushrooms. There are other reasons besides their shape and color why rowan berries would make a useful metaphor for *A. muscaria*.

Throughout northern Europe, the red rowan (*Sorbus aucuparia*) commonly grows in association with the birch (*Betula sp.*), one of the primary hosts of *A. muscaria* mycelia. In many parts of the Eurasian tundra—the primary habitat of *A. muscaria*—the fruiting season of the mushroom follows the early fall rains and coincides fairly closely with the peak of the berry season. Thus, forests in which red rowan berries grow would make excellent places to look for red-capped mushrooms.

There is another less obvious yet vital connection between berries and *A. muscaria*. Many Siberian cultures drink psychoactive brews made from *A. muscaria* mixed with berries. The Khanti believe that mixing *A. muscaria* with bog bilberry (*Vacciunum uliginosum*) strengthens the effect of the mushroom.[110] If adding

---

110. Wasson, *Soma* 246, 324 cites statements made by Georg H. Langsdorf, in 1809, and Carl Hartwich, in 1911, that it was fairly common for Siberians to consume a drink made from *A. muscaria* mixed with bog bilberries (*Vaccinium ulignosum*) or the leaves of the narrow-leafed willow (*Epilobium augustifolium*). Like Wasson, Saar 168 also cites Langsdorf as stating the Khanty believe berries strengthen the brew. Neither source provides any pharmacological explanation for the belief.

Wasson, *Soma* 153-155 notes that there is clear consensus among the Siberians that it is vital to dry the mushrooms before use. Some Siberian tribes say that eating fresh mushrooms is dangerous; others say that fresh mushrooms are more nauseating. Wasson, *Soma* 155 describes how he and his friends discovered that toasting the mushrooms enhances their psychoactive strength.

acidic berries helps make the *A. muscaria* brew not only more palatable but more psychoactive, then large red rowan berries could have made an instructive metaphor for the sacred mushroom.

Journeys to the Land of Apples

Diarmuid's descriptions of magical red berries "as large as apples" may help explain the frequent association between magical apples and the Celtic otherworld. Apples are so commonly associated with the Land of Promise, ruled over by Manannán Mac Lír, lord of the mists, that his kingdom is sometimes called *Emain Ablach*, the Land of Apples.

Anne Ross quotes a passage in *The Sickbed of Cú Chulainn*, translated by Myles Dillon, where the motif of magical apple trees appears: *"There are at the great eastern door / Three trees of crimson crystal, / From which sings the bird-flock enduring, gentle / To the youth from out the royal rath."*[111]

In the twelfth-century Irish tale known as *Tochmarc Emire*, a figure variously identified as Lugh, Eochaid Bairche, or Manannán gives a wheel and a magical apple to Cú Chulainn when the young warrior goes to seek out the martial school of Scáthach in the Otherworld. The wheel and apple miraculously guide Cú Chulainn on his quest to the gates of the woman warrior's domain.[112]

In one *immrama* (vision voyage), when Teigue MacCian reached the shores of the Otherworld, he noticed "a wide-spreading apple-tree that bore both blossoms and fruit at once." When Teigue meets a fair youth holding a fragrant golden apple, he asks, "what is that apple tree yonder?" the answer he receives is revealing: "That

---

Jonathan Ott, *Pharmacotheon: Entheogenic Drugs, Their Plant Sources and History* (Kennewick, WA: Natural Products Co., 1993) 339 cites pharmacological studies by Repke that drying the mushrooms causes decarboxylation of ibotenic acid into the more potent psychoactive muscimol. Ott 328 also suggests that stomach acid may convert ibotenic acid into muscimol. The mixing of acidic berries and *A. muscaria* may catalyze a similar synergistic biochemical interaction. On the basis of personal use, White has observed a synergistic relationship between blueberries and *A. muscaria*.

111. Anne Ross, *Pagan Celtic Britain* (New York: Columbia University Press, 1967) 269.

112. Kuno Meyer, "The Oldest Version of *Tochmarc Emire*." *Revue Celtique* 11 (1890): 433-57

apple tree's fruit it is that for meat shall serve the congregation which is to be in this mansion..."[113]

Magical red apples would make a good visual metaphor for the fresh red-capped mushroom. Furthermore, one well-known trait of *A. muscaria* is that the dried mushrooms are more psychoactive than the fresh red caps, and dried *A. muscaria* caps tend to look a bit like dried red-brown apples. But how does one explain the fairly frequent references to golden apples in Celtic legends? Some varieties of the mushroom turn a metallic golden color when dried.[114]

It is not hard to see that red rowan berries and apples might make effective visual substitutes for *A. muscaria*. But why would the Celts have used hazelnuts and salmon as magical foods of knowledge? Could they be less obvious metaphors for the red-and-white mushroom? As we shall soon demonstrate, there is ample circumstantial evidence linking those foods to *A. muscaria*.

The Crimson Nuts of Wisdom

At first glance, it might appear difficult to explain the many references in Celtic legends to hazelnuts that impart instantaneous knowledge and foresight. There is no evidence that eating hazelnuts is likely to induce visions, wisdom, or precognition. However, there is evidence that the nuts could have served as useful metaphors for *A. muscaria*. First, let us examine some of the linguistic evidence linking hazelnuts and mushrooms.

In Celtic legends, hazelnuts are variously called *cuill crimaind*, the hazels of knowledge; *bolg fis*, bubbles of wisdom; *bolg gréine*, sun bubbles; and *imbas gréine*, sun of inspiration. These terms refer not only to the nuts but also to the bubbles caused by the nuts falling into the waters of the well of wisdom. Significantly, *bolg* is a word frequently found in both Irish and Scots Gaelic names of mushrooms. Wasson and Wasson offer this analysis on the use of the word *bolg*:

---

113. Quotations from Standish H. O'Grady, *Silva Gaelica* Volume 2 (London & Edinburgh: Williams & Norgate, 1892) 394.

114. The references in Celtic literature to golden apples remained a riddle until, while working on this article, White came across a photo of a dried *A. muscaria* specimen with a metallic white sheen. In light of this discovery, it should be considered whether the Greek and Indo-European legends involving sacred golden apples may also be teaching stories about the use of dried *A. muscaria* — designed to remind initiates of useful esoteric knowledge.

"In Irish there are two words for a bag or a pouch, *bolg,* which is related to the Latin *bulga,* and *púca,* which was probably borrowed between AD 800 and 1050 from Scandinavian sources...In Irish one way to refer to a wild fungus is *bolg losgainn,* literally "frog's pouch," and another ways is *púca beireach,* "heifer's pouch." If the "heifer's pouch" refers to the udder, as we suppose, the same figure of speech that in Albanian means "toad" turns up in Irish meaning "toadstool." In Irish, *bolg seidete,* "blown-up bag," is a term for the puffball. It is easy to see why the fungi figure in all these metaphors; puffballs, toadstools, all the wild fungi of the forest and field, impress the visual sense as creatures that quickly swell up."[115]

Colloquial Gaelic preserves other links between mushrooms and the traditional hazelnuts of wisdom, even today. In Irish, we find the phrase *caochóg cnó,* literally a "blind nut" — which means a nut without a kernel. Scottish Gaelic, which often preserves older uses of the language than does Irish Gaelic, gives us the words *caochag,* which means either a nut without a kernel or a mushroom, and *caochagach,* the state of being full of nuts without kernels or full of mushrooms. Colloquially, the word *caochóg* is also used in phrases referring to shyness or to winking. To wink is to close one eye and, as we have seen, Celtic sorcery is often performed one-eyed. The linguistic links between nuts, mushrooms, and the one-eyed winking state are intriguing but there is even more definitive evidence.

In the seventh-century Old Irish text known as "The Cauldron of Poesy," there is a direct statement that the *filidh* found inspiration by chewing on the hazelnuts of wisdom. The text explains that poetic inspiration and the gift of poetry originate in three full cauldrons found within the body of the *fili.* Poetry is said to arise from the experience of sorrow and joy, and one of the divisions of joy experienced by the *fili* — which leads to *imbas,* the gift of prophetic vision — is the "joy of fitting poetic frenzy from grinding away at the fair nuts of the nine hazels on the Well of Segais in the *sídhe* realm."[116]

---

115. R. Gordon Wasson and Valentina P. Wasson, *Mushrooms, Russia, and History* (New York: Pantheon, 1957) 93.

116. For a more detailed discussion see Erynn Rowan Laurie, "The Cauldron of Poesy," *Obsidian* vol. 1, no. 2, Spring 1996.

The Middle Irish gloss on this passage offers a very tantalizing item—the phrase *bolcc imba fuilgne,* "the bubble which sustains or supports *imbas.*" One possible translation of the gloss on this phrase is: "The bubble that sustains *imbas* is formed by the sun among the plants, and whoever consumes them will have poetry." In short we have a direct statement that consuming *bolcc* produces the gift of prophetic vision.

In light of the linguistic link between *bolcc, bolg,* and mushrooms, it is not hard to read these phrases as statements that some type of mushroom was chewed to sustain poetic inspiration. The fact that *imbas,* the poetic inspiration or poetic frenzy of the Irish, is frequently described as a "fire in the head" also suggests that the most likely mushroom would be *A. muscaria.* "Fire in the head" is an excellent term for a signature symptom of *A. muscaria* inebriation—a pronounced heating of the head, apparently caused by blood rushing to that area.[117]

The Sacred Trees of Knowledge

From numerous sources, including the ogam alphabet, we know that the Celts, like other Indo-European cultures, once venerated the birch. According to Celtic myths, the ogam was given to druids and *filidh* by the god Ogma as a secret language for the preservation of their wisdom. The ogam alphabet begins with *beith,* the letter for "birch." This tree is given primacy of place in the alphabet because it was the first letter created by Ogma, who carved seven *beith* strokes on a birch branch. This reference alone suggests that the Celts held great reverence for the birch tree.

As Wasson points out in his book *Soma: Divine Mushroom of Immortality,* most cultures that use *A. muscaria* as a sacred psychoactive have adopted the birch as the sacred world tree. He attributes this association to the symbiotic relationship between the birch and the mushroom. As noted before, the mycelia of *A.*

---

117. Wasson, *Soma* 248 quotes an observation by Langsdorf: "The face becomes red, bloated, and full of blood, and the intoxicated person begins to do and say many things involuntarily." Conrad H. Eugster, "Isolation, Structure, and Synthesis of Central-Active compounds from Amanita Muscaria," *Ethnopharmacologic Search for Psychoactive Drugs,* ed. D. H. Efron (Washington D.C.: U. S. Department of Health, Education, and Welfare, 1991) 435 notes that the warming and flushing of the face is caused by ibotenic acid. While the reddened face is most visible to observers, users experience a pronounced heating of the head.

muscaria can grow only in symbiotic relationship with the roots of a few types of trees—primarily the birch, the spruce, and certain conifers.

Wasson suggests that the motif of sacred world trees found in many Mediterranean cultures originated in the birch forests of Eurasia at a time when Indo-European cultures were still using *A. muscaria*:

> The Peoples who emigrated from the forest belt to the southern latitudes took with them vivid memories of the Herb of Immortality and the Tree of Life spread also by word of mouth far and wide, and in the South where the birch and the fly-agaric were little more than cherished tales generations and a thousand miles removed from the source of inspiration, the concepts were still stirring the imaginations of poets, story-tellers, and sages. In these alien lands far from the birch forests of Siberia, botanical substitutions were made for Herb and Tree.[118]

Wasson's theory may accurately describe what took place in the drier lands of Iran, India, and the Mediterranean. However, the birch has always grown well throughout northwestern Europe, so the insular Celts would not have needed to substitute the hazel for the birch, (the scarcity of birch in many parts of Ireland and Scotland today is due not to warming trends but the relentless overgrazing of sheep and cattle).

Assuming that the Celts never abandoned their use of *A. muscaria*, why would they have bypassed the sacred birch and chose the hazel as their tree of knowledge? As far as we know, *A. muscaria* does not grow under hazel trees. However, the hazel (*Corylus avellana*) is a member of the *Betulaceae* family, and its leaves and catkin flowers resemble those of the birch. Thus, the image of crimson nuts appearing under the hazel tree would make an apt occult metaphor for the birch and the *A. muscaria* that grows at its roots. It would also make a good teaching tool for reminding initiates how to identify the tree beneath which the crimson nuts of knowledge can be found.

---

118. Wasson, *Soma* 215.

The Red-Speckled Brother of Birch

The ogam alphabet may contain another most interesting veiled reference to *A. muscaria*. The ogam alphabet is not unlike the Norse runic alphabet in that the letters are named after various objects starting with the particular letter in question. Although the original names of most ogam letters have known meanings—such as *h-úath* (terror), *tinne* (a bar of metal), and *sraiph* (sulfur)—one letter, *edad*, is a nonsense word with no known meaning.[119] Fortunately, each letter in the ogam has a color, bird, tree, and other objects, as well as kenning phrases called "word ogams," associated with it.

According to Damian McManus and Howard Meroney, the color for *edad* is *erc*, or "red-speckled," and its word ogams are "discerning tree" and "brother of birch."[120] This association of "red-speckled" and "brother of birch" is very suggestive, and the often white-speckled, red-capped *A. muscaria* grows best at the roots of the birch tree. Is it possible that *edad* was one of the names of the mushroom? We may never know, but the notion is intriguing.

The association of "brother of birch" with *erc* or "red-speckled" provides a vital clue linking several potential *A. muscaria* motifs. According to the *Dictionary of the Irish Language*, the word *erc* can refer to speckled fish, particularly the salmon and the trout, and to speckled or red-eared cattle.[121] Significantly, *erc* can also refer to "a reptile of some kind"—for instance, a "viper." In fact, the phrase "red-speckled" is often used in Celtic legends to identify liminal objects and creatures that come from the Otherworld.

---

119. Popular understanding of the ogam makes the names of the letters out to be solely names of trees. The tree ogam is but one of some 150 different ogam lists. According to Damian McManus, *A Guide to Ogam* (Maynooth: An Sagart, 1991), the strong identification of the ogam with trees was popularized by fourteenth-century antiquarians who were working with a tradition several centuries old and only partially understood. McManus suggests that the original names of the ogam letters included words, varied objects, and concepts. McManus, and Meroney (1949) before him, offer translations of the known ogam letter names, but a few of the names are obscure and not amenable to translation. Edad is one of these.

120. McManus 43; Howard Meroney, "Early Irish Letter Names," *Speculum* vol. XXIV, no. 1 (1949): 19-43.

121. E. G. Quin, ed., *Dictionary of the Irish Language Based Mainly on Old and Middle Irish Materials* (Dublin: Royal Irish Academy, 1990) 278.

Red-Speckled Salmon

There are a number of Celtic legends in which eating salmon instantaneously imparts miraculous powers of knowledge. In "The Boyhood Exploits of Fionn," a boy named Demne went to learn poetry from Fionn Éices, or Fionn the Poet.[122] Fionn Éices had spent seven years watching for the salmon of Féc's pool, because it had been prophesied that nothing would remain unknown to whoever ate the salmon of Féc. When the salmon was found, Fionn Éices told Demne to cook it but not to eat any of it. While turning the fish over in the pan, the lad accidentally burnt his thumb on the fish and, without thinking, stuck his thumb into his mouth. Honoring this quirk of fate, Fionn Éices renamed the lad Fionn and gave him the salmon of knowledge to eat. From then on, whenever Fionn "put his thumb in his mouth, and sang through *teinm laida*, that which he did not know would be revealed to him."

Is there any reason the Celts might have selected salmon as a source of instantaneous wisdom? In some of the stories, we are told that salmon gain their miraculous powers by nibbling on the bubbles of knowledge or the hazelnuts floating in the fountains of knowledge, but as far as we know, consuming salmon — even those that have eaten hazelnuts — does not lead to instantaneous enlightenment or poetic insight. However, assuming that the druids used occult metaphors for their miraculous inebriant, the salmon — which is silver and white, speckled with red spots — would make a fair metaphor for *A. muscaria*. Pieces of dried *A. muscaria* could be discretely referred to as pieces of dried salmon — and, in some cases, students may have inadvertently eaten them as salmon. Suddenly the legends about eating the salmon of knowledge begin to make more sense.

The Speckled Snake

Alexei Kondratiev, former president of the Celtic League American Branch, has encountered folk references to *A. muscaria* being called *an náthair bhreac*, the speckled snake, in Scotland and Ireland.[123] This

---

122. Story based on Nagy, 214.
123. Kondratiev notes that the use of the name *an náthair bhreac* in widely separated locations suggests that the name is not a new invention. The use of the term "speckled snake" in thirteenth century Welsh pseudo-Taliesin poetry could be significant.

direct linguistic link between speckled snakes and *A. muscaria* is certainly intriguing, particularly in light of folk legends that Saint Patrick exiled all serpents from Ireland. As we have already noted, *Cormac's Glossary* claims that Saint Patrick banned the oracular practices of *teinm laida* and *imbas forosnai* because those rituals invoked pagan gods. Is it possible that Saint Patrick was waging war against a sacred mushroom cult that involved the invocation of snake deities? If so, post-Christian *filidh* might have had good reasons to adopt the speckled salmon, crimson hazelnuts, or red rowan berries as new metaphors for the most potent *A. muscaria* metaphor — the speckled serpent.

The serpent is certainly an important figure in Celtic mythology, particularly on the continent but also on the islands. Serpents are associated with a number of Celtic deities — especially Brigid, the goddess of poets, and Cernunnos, the god of shamans.

The Dé Danann goddess Brigid — whose mythology was later transferred to the fifth-century Saint Brigid (Saint Bride) of Kildare — was originally a triple-aspected goddess, the patroness of smithcraft, medicine, and poetry. Brigid, whose name means "high or exalted one," was associated with the sun and fire, and she was invoked as a guardian of the home and the hearth fire. As a goddess of healing, Brigid was also closely linked with healing springs. However, Brigid is best known as the goddess of poets, and *Cormac's Glossary* praises her foremost as the archetypal female sage and woman of wisdom. Given the tradition of poets seeking inspiration at wells of wisdom, Brigid may have been one of the pagan deities invoked in the shamanic divinatory ritual of *imbas forosnai*.

In "The Life of Brigid," recorded in the fifteenth-century *Book of Lismore*, Saint Brigid is portrayed as a dutiful virgin of Christ, but her metaphoric links to the liminal Otherworld are well preserved, even there.[124] Saint Brigid was born at sunrise on the threshold of a house — neither within nor without the house. She was raised in the house of a "wizard," who instructed her to drink only the milk from

---

Wasson and Wasson demonstrated the Indo-European link between the serpent and the mushroom but noted that "the snake-mushroom association of Greece and the Indic world, with all its baggage of associations, becomes the toad and toadstool glyph of the West." In the face of "the speckled serpent" associations, however, it appears that the conservative Irish may have preserved the ancient association of the snake with the mushroom.

124. The Whitley Stokes (1890) translation of the "Life of Brigid" is reprinted in Iain MacDonald, ed., *Saint Bride* (Edinburgh: Floris Books, 1992).

a white, red-eared cow. Once, when her nurse was ill, Brigid went to a well and fetched some water, which tasted like ale and also healed the nurse. Later, as a nun, she reportedly turned water into milk, which she used to heal one of her sister nuns. Fiery pillars often appeared over Brigid's head, and in one story, sun rays supported and dried her wet cloak.

Brigid's numerous associations with possible *A. muscaria* themes — red-eared cows, fiery pillars over her head, and healing waters — are highly suggestive. Her ability to transform water into healing wine and milk could hark back to the New Testament miracle, but it could also refer to the healing, rejuvenating powers of *A. muscaria*. Ultimately, it is Saint Brigid's close link to snakes that reveals her essentially pagan nature. Long after Patrick reportedly banned snakes in Ireland, the Scots continued to believe serpents came out of their lairs on Saint Brigid's Day, originally a pagan holy day called Imbolc or Oimelc, celebrated in early February. Significantly, Ó Catháin notes that the feast day of Brigid is associated with two colors — "the Eve of Brigit's Feast, speckled — the Day of Brigid's Feast, white."[125]

While the cult of Brigid was tolerated in subverted form under the Celtic Church, the cult of the antlered god was forced underground — or into the forests. In Gaul, the antlered lord of the animals — known there as Cernunnos — was closely associated with ram-horned serpents of wisdom, and with the world tree through his connection with the stag.[126] It doesn't take a theologian to explain why Christians incorporated the shamanic horned god with his serpents into their imagery of the devil.

One of the earliest European images of the stag-antlered deity may be the so-called "dancing sorcerer" painting, at Les Trois Frères, in France. Some of the most interesting petroglyphs depicting the antlered lord of shamans are found in the Valcamonica (Camonica Valley) of northern Italy — an area inhabited by early proto-Celtic and Celtic cultures. Michael

---

125. Ripinski-Naxon 155-157.
126. The symbology and functions of the stags, trees, and ram-horned serpents of Cernunnos are discussed in some detail in Miranda Green, *Symbol and Image in Celtic Religious Art* (New York: Routledge, 1989) 86-96; and Miranda Green, *Dictionary of Celtic Myth and Legend* (London: Thames & Hudson, 1992) 39-61.

On some Gaulish coins, the stag bears the quartered circle of the solar wheel between its antlers, clearly linking the Gaulish Cernunnos with solar attributes — a trait he shares with the Gaulish Belenos, who is related to the Welsh Beli and the Irish ancestor god Bile, whose name means "a great sacred tree."

Ripinski-Naxon points out that the rock carvings in the Valcamonica depict several classic Indo-European shamanic motifs, including stylized sun disks and representations of antlered "shamans," and "shamans" dancing around or over small trees.[127] Noting that a prehistoric rock carving of a naturalistic spotted mushroom has been found near Monte Bego—also in northern Italy—Ripinski-Naxon cautiously concludes that Indo-Europeans In the region were familiar with *A. muscaria.* If more evidence can be found in those regions directly linking antlered shamans to the use of spotted mushrooms, it would support our speculations about the use of *A. muscaria* in Celtic Ireland. For now, we must wait.

Probably the most familiar image of the stag-antlered figure is that depicted on the Gundestrup Cauldron, a marvelous work of mythic art undoubtedly inspired by Celts, though most likely crafted by Thracian artists.[128] One panel shows a man, crowned with seven-tined stag antlers which branch like tree limbs, who is holding a speckled, ram-horned serpent. Other panels on the cauldron may portray other Celtic gods or scenes from Celtic legends. Although there is no evidence how the cauldron was used, numerous scholars have assumed that it probably had ritual significance. Could the cauldron have been used in a shamanic cult of the speckled serpent? Could it have been used to serve a brew of *A. muscaria?* The idea is certainly provocative.

The Red-Peaked One

A tale from the *Senchas Mór,* a collection of early Irish law texts, called *Fionn and the Man in the Tree,*[129] directly links the primary magical food motifs of the shamanic lord of the animals and to the world tree. In this story, Fionn is hunting in the forest for Derg Corra, a version of the lord of the animals. The epithet *Derg Corra* means "red-peaked" or "red-pointed," and "red-peaked" would make an excellent metaphor for the red-capped *A. muscaria.* Coincidentally, Derg Corra—like several other heroes of the Celtic

---

127. Ripinski-Naxon.

128. For a discussion on the origin of the Gundestrup Cauldron, see Timothy Taylor, "The Gundestrup Cauldron," *Scientific American* March 1992: 84-89.

129. Kuno Meyer, "Finn and the Man in the Tree," Revue Celtique 25: 344-349

otherworld—is famed for his power of leaping, a trait which is associated in Siberia with *A. muscaria*.[130]

While searching through the forest, Fionn beholds a strange sight—a man perched at the top of a tree. A blackbird sits on the man's right shoulder. In his left hand is a bronze vessel in which a salmon leaps. Below him, at the base of the tree, is a stag. This peculiar figure, who is really Derg Corra in disguise, cracks a nut (*teinm cnó*), giving half to the blackbird and eating half himself. He splits an apple in two and shares it with the stag at the base of the tree. Then, he shares the water of wisdom with the salmon, the blackbird, and the stag.

The story is highly significant because we know that druidic apprentices gathered in sacred groves hidden deep in the forests in order to learn their poetic arts. We can infer from other sources that the ranks of the *filidh* were viewed as positions on the world tree.[131] Minor or student *filidh* were the roots, experienced *filidh* were the trunk, and the most powerful *filidh* were the uppermost branches. In this story, Fionn is considered to be a powerful *fili*—having consumed the red-speckled salmon of wisdom in his youth—but now he stands at the root of the tree below the figure of Derg Corra, who holds and eats not one but several wisdom-inducing substances.

In short, this legend weaves together several *A. muscaria* metaphors into an unmistakable tapestry. Fionn has come to study with Derg Corra—the red-peaked lord of the animals, who in many cultures is the lord of shamans. Each of the magical items—the apples, waters of wisdom, and sacred hazelnuts—shared with the animals by Derg Corra is closely linked in Celtic literature with the otherworld and with the imparting of poetic inspiration and

---

130. Wasson, *Soma* 249, 273-4 cites statements by Langsdorf and Bogoraz that *A. muscaria* users are sometimes prone to leaping and may exhibit unusual physical stamina. See also Sarr and Salzman et al.

131. Laurie notes that the "Cauldron of Poesy" text describes *imbas* as a tree that is "climbed through diligence," implying that the more training and inspiration the *filidh* have, the higher up the tree they advance. Nagy 281 notes the word *taman* "trunk of a tree, stock, stem" is used in some Irish bardic and legal texts to describe a lower order of poet. One of the higher orders of *filidh* is called the *druimclí*, the top of the ridgepole or roof-tree of knowledge. Eugene O'Curry, *Lectures on the Manuscript Materials of Ancient Irish History* (Dublin: William Hinch & Patrick Traynor, 1878) 9 says, "the man who was a *druimclí* was supposed to have climbed the pillar or tree or learning to its very ridge or top." Taken together, these nuggets of information suggest a picture of *filidh* inhabiting levels of the world tree according to their rank and station.

prophetic knowledge. Based on this story — and the other evidence we have presented — we will climb out onto the limb of that sacred tree and suggest that the use of *A. muscaria* could have played a prominent teaching or initiatory role in the ancient druidic sanctuaries.

Kindling Poetic Inspiration

Some Celtic scholars may rise up in arms at our suggestion that the druids and *filidh* used *A. muscaria* as a source of poetic inspiration. However, given what we know about soma's role in inspiring the *Rig Veda*, it is certainly conceivable that *A. muscaria* could have inspired the visions and verses of Celtic poets. In Siberian shamanism, *A. muscaria* is definitely associated not only with ecstatic visions, but also with the inspiration of poetry and songs.[132] We know from historical accounts that the *filidh* had to memorize great tracts of legends and poems, but they were much more than just versifiers. In addition to being epic poets, they were inspired philosophers and powerful enchanters. If we are correct that crimson hazelnuts and spotted salmon are metaphors for *A. muscaria*, then we can assume that the ancient *filidh* used the red-and-white mushrooms as a significant source of poetic inspiration and prophecy.

In the Old Irish poem known as "The Song of Amairgen," the primal *fili* of the Milesian invaders announces himself as he sets foot in Ireland: "I am a wind of the sea, I am a wave of the sea, I am a sound of the sea, I am a stag of seven tines, I am a hawk on a cliff, I am a tear of the sun, I am fair among flowers, I am a salmon in a pool, I am a lake on a plain, I am a hill of poetry, I am a god who gives inspiration (literally: forms fire for a head)."[133]

Could the god who gives inspiration — who forms "fire in the head" — refer to a god connected with *A. muscaria*, or to the mushroom itself? We have already noted that Brigid, the goddess of poets, was associated with fires around her head and that *A. muscaria* intoxication can produce a pronounced heating of the head. Moreover, we know from many sources that *imbas forosnai* and *teinm*

---

132. Saar 164 cites an observation by Langsdorf that the heroic epic singers of the Khanty used to consume several mushrooms and then sing inspired songs all night long. Salzman et al 42 indicate that *mukhomor* (*A. muscaria*) continues to inspire songs and singing among the Koryak of Kamchatka.

133. *Lebor Gábala Érenn* (*The Book of the Taking of Ireland*) translation quoted in Matthews and Matthews 11.

laida were both associated with light and the fire of illumination itself.[134]

In the twelfth-century *Hanes Taliesin* (*Romance of Taliesin*), the Welsh poet Gwion announces himself with a similar list of associations, plus a few additions: "I have been a fierce bull and a yellow buck. I have been a boat on the sea...I have been a blue salmon. I have been a spotted snake on a hill...I have been a wave breaking on the beach. On a boundless sea I was set adrift."[135]

A commoner without a broad background in Celtic myth would have found it hard to catch the many metaphors woven into these poems. On one level, the phrases undoubtedly refer to key themes of Celtic legends. However, it is intriguing that many of the phrases could refer to the motifs that we have linked to *A. muscaria*: the stag of seven tines to the stag at the base of Derg Corra's tree; the salmon in pools to the salmon that eat the hazelnuts of wisdom; the boat on the sea to the magical coracles that carry poets to and from the Land of Promise; and the spotted snake on the hill directly to the red-and-white mushroom that grows on the *sídhe* mounds.

Judging from the manner in which poems similar to "The Song of Amairgen" are repeated by various Irish and Welsh poets, these poems may have served as the oral calling cards of the *filidh* entrusted with Celtic legends. In the text known as "*Immacallam in do Thuarad*" (*Colloquy of the Two Sages*), two bards meet and politely test each other's knowledge.[136] In the opening salvo, the aged Ferchertne asks: "A question, wise lad, whence have you come?" The young Nede answers:

> *Not hard: from the heel of a sage,*
> *From a confluence of wisdom,*
> *From perfection of goodness,*
> *From the nine hazels of poetic art,*
> *From the splendid circuits in a land*
> *Where truth is measured by excellence,*
> *Where there is no falsehood,*
> *Where there are many colors,*

---

134. Chadwick records several stories in which *teinm laída* is associated with songs being chanted by severed heads placed near fires. Chadwick observes that the word *teinm* is generally regarded as being derived from the word *tep-* ("heat").

135. *Hanes Taliesin*, translation by Macalister, quoted Graves 211.

136. *Immacallam in do Thuarad* (*Colloquy of the Two Sages*), translation by Whitley Stokes (1905), glossed in Matthews and Matthews 203-218.

Where poets are refreshed.

In short, Nede appears to be saying that he has learned the poetic arts by eating the hazelnuts of wisdom. After a lengthy exchange of poetic metaphors, Ferchertne and Nede acknowledge and honor each other's poetic wisdom. Then Nede asks: "And you, O aged one, have you tidings?" Ferchertne launches into a long list of oracular predictions for the future.

If hazels are metaphors for *A. muscaria*, then we can assume that Nede and other *filidh* probably chewed on inspirational mushrooms during their training, perhaps in a ritual form similar to *imbas forosnai*.[137] Ferchertne's long list of predictions certainly suggests that he also could have been engaging in some type of prophetic divination practice on a regular basis.

While the early historic references to the schools of the druids and *filidh* offer few details about their training practices — beyond mentioning the long lists of verses that had to be memorized and the subjects of grammar, law, mathematics, and natural philosophy — we know from the legends and poems that the training ultimately culminated in the kindling of poetic inspiration. Descriptions of eighteenth-century bardic schools indicate that their initiates — the descendants of the *filidh* — spent long hours practicing and composing poetry in small, dimly lit cells.[138] Although sensory deprivation may be conducive to the practice of poetry and the kindling of prophetic insight, the darkness may have served a more immediate purpose.

If *A. muscaria* was used in the training of the *filidh*, its tendency to increase sensitivity to light would have necessitated the use of dark environments. This pronounced sensitivity to light could also explain the initiatory account of Taliesin being sewn into

---

137. According to early Irish law texts, the rituals of *imbas forosnai, teinm laída,* and *dichetal do chennaib* were taught during the eighth year of study, after the *fili* was already considered an *ollamh*, the highest rank of poet (Calder 1997: xxi). If our contention that *A. muscaria* was the "red flesh" chewed during the *imbas forosnai* ritual is correct, the students may have begun their training with the mushrooms at some earlier point in their course of study so that they would be prepared to take on the role of diviner during this ritual.

138. Matthews 123 quotes an interesting account of bardic training found in the *Memoirs of the Marquis of Clanricarde,* a text written in 1722. The text tells how the training of bards — at that time — took place in "a snug, low hut" located somewhere in a solitary setting. Each student had a small, windowless apartment, or cell, without much furniture beyond a bed, and they spent days and nights in the dark practicing their art on subjects assigned by a professor.

a skin and set adrift on the seas. Based on the many references linking *A. muscaria* metaphors to poetic inspiration, we hypothesize that the training of *filidh* probably included visionary journeys undertaken in darkened rooms or inside bull skins, under the watchful eyes of trained *filidh* — and probably under the influence of *A. muscaria*.

Ethnographic studies of other shamanic cultures show that folk stories are often used to inculcate esoteric shamanic teachings, particularly in oral cultures.[139] If we are correct in identifying the presence of *A. muscaria* motifs in Celtic legends and literature, we should fully expect to find traditional teaching about its use woven into those same legends. Indeed, as we have already seen, Celtic stories may include useful information and teachings relevant to the identification and use of *A. muscaria*.

Is it possible that many of the legends of magical voyages into the otherworld were teaching stories based on the *A. muscaria* experiences of previous generations, refined and polished through the art of poetry? If so, that would explain why new initiates started their training by learning the legends of the past: the legends would provide metaphoric maps and teachings for novices preparing to embark on journeys into the waters of inspiration.

The Wells of Inspiration

Celtic legends are filled with heroes drinking from wells of wisdom or from streams that flow from those wells, and the well of wisdom is often referred to as the ultimate source of the *fili's* art. One of the highest grades of *fili* is even called *ansruith*, or "great stream," referring directly to this flowing of watery wisdom. Although the motif of cosmic wells of wisdom is found in many parts of the world, the Celtic legends contain numerous elements linking these wells fairly directly to the shamanic use of *A. muscaria*.

---

139. Franz Boaz, Ronald and Catherine Berndt, Dennis Tedlock, and numerous other ethnographers have emphasized the role of myth in carrying the teachings of indigenous cultures. Nootka shaman and storyteller Johnny Moses often speaks about how traditional stories are used both as teaching tales and as transformative shamanic healing tools. Daniel Merkur, *Becoming Half-Hidden: Shamanism and Initiation Among the Inuit* (Stockholm: Almquist & Wiksell, 1985) provides an in-depth study of how esoteric information about Inuit shamanic practices is woven into their songs, stories, and legends through the use of archaic symbols and other circumlocutions.

Cormac's Adventures in the Land of Promise, also called "Cormac's Cup," mentions several key *A. muscaria* motifs in direct association with the well of knowledge. For brevity, we will offer only a very abridged version of the story here.

One day at dawn, Cormac encounters a grey-haired warrior carrying a silver branch with three golden apples. Cormac is fascinated by the branch, which makes such wonderful music that when it is shaken it puts to sleep sore-wounded men, women in childbed, and folk in sickness. The mysterious warrior—who is Manannán in disguise—explains that he comes "from a land wherein there is naught save truth, and there is neither age nor decay nor gloom nor sadness nor envy nor jealousy nor hatred nor haughtiness."[140] The two men agree to make an alliance, and Cormac asks for the branch to seal the deal. The warrior agrees, but he asks in return for three unnamed boons to be granted later. Each year afterward, Manannán returns and asks for one of his three boons—first Cormac's daughter, then his son, and then his wife. A man of his word, Cormac grants the boons, but after the third request, he follows the mysterious warrior into a great mist—the *ceo-druidechta* (druid's fog) that appears around him on the plain, and soon he finds himself in a strange fortress in the Land of Promise.

Cormac is shown a silver house, half-thatched with the wings of white birds. Then, he sees a man kindling a voracious fire. Finally, he enters another fortress with a palace that has bronze beams and silver wattling and that is also thatched with the wings of white birds. He sees people drinking from a marvelous fountain with five streams flowing from it. Nine hazel trees grow over the well, dropping their nuts into the water, and "five salmon open the nuts and send their husks floating down the streams."

Cormac is shown Manannán's magical pig, which is cooked in a cauldron by telling four truths. After his hosts tell three truths, cooking three quarters of the pig, Cormac reveals his truth—that he is saddened by the loss of his daughter, son, and wife. When his hosts give him a portion of the pig to eat, Cormac declines, saying he never eats without fifty in his company. Manannán puts Cormac to sleep, and when he awakens he is accompanied by fifty warriors—and by his wife, son, and daughter. During the banquet, Cormac becomes intrigued by a marvelously crafted gold cup. Manannán explains that whenever three falsehoods are spoken

---

140. "Cormac's Cup" quotations are from Cross & Slover 503.

111

under it, the cup breaks into three, and that the only way to restore the cup is to speak three truths under it. Demonstrating how the cup works, Manannán tells three falsehoods, breaking it, and then three truths to fix it again. Manannán then offers Cormac the magical cup as a gift, promises to let him return home with his family, and interpret the strange visions that Cormac has seen.

Manannán functions as a teacher and guide who helps interpret the meaning of the visions for Cormac—and for any students being told the story. According to Manannán, the fountain is the well of knowledge, and the streams are the five senses through which knowledge is obtained. Manannán explains: "No one will have knowledge who drinketh not a draught out of the fountain itself and out of the streams. The folk of many arts are those who drink of them both."

Drowning in the Waters of Wisdom

By studying the lessons preserved in Celtic legends in the context of what is known about *A. muscaria* and about the training and divinatory practices of the *filidh*, a diligent student could conceivably be able to resurrect what appears to be one of the most viable and best documented Celtic shamanic practices. However, before imbibing large quantities of *A. muscaria* in the hopes of becoming instantly enlightened, enthusiastic students would do well to read and heed the warnings found in some of the Irish legends. For example, new initiates interested in exploring the marvelous otherworlds of *A. muscaria* visions would do well to remember that during the *imbas forosnai*, the *fili* seeking the vision was watched over by other *filidh*, who presumably had experience in dealing with the effects of consuming the mushrooms.

In the Irish *dinnshenchas* (land-name tale) of Siannan, the goddess of the Shannon River, we find a teaching that the wisdom from the nine hazel trees can be overwhelming. In this story, the goddess travels to Conla's well, which is said to be the origin of the Shannon, the Boyne, and a number of other rivers. Siannan goes there seeking wisdom, and the waters of wisdom overwhelm her. She flees before them along the course of the river, drowning in wisdom at the mouth of the Shannon. Significantly, the hazel trees around Conla's well miraculously produce their leaves, flowers, and nuts in the space of a single hour—much like mushrooms appearing suddenly after a rain.

The story provides a warning that eating the hazelnuts at the well of wisdom can involve certain dangers. For one thing, if one is not properly prepared, the intensity of the experience can be overwhelming. It is perhaps possible that Siannan's death could also be a warning that eating the wrong *Amanita*—the highly poisonous, green-white *Amanita phalloides*, appropriately known as "Death-Caps"—can be fatal.

If Celtic legends such as this served as shamanic teaching stories, we should expect some of them to include metaphoric maps aimed at helping new initiates navigate the potentially overwhelming waters of wisdom. Let us examine a *dinnshenchas* that describes the creation of the sacred Boyne River from the waters of Nechtán's well. In this story, the goddess Bóann, whose name means "the white cow," is married to the god Nechtán. While the hazelnuts of wisdom are not mentioned directly in this tale, we can assume they also inspired Nechtán's waters of wisdom. Nechtán—whose name means "clean, pure" or "white, bright"—is a symbol of fire in the water and of the power of poetry that comes from the well of wisdom.

The legend states that Nechtán has three cup-bearers who must accompany anyone seeking wisdom and the well or dire consequences will result. Ignoring the traditional warnings, Bóann went to the well alone and challenged its power by walking counter-clockwise around it three times. In response to this action, the waters of the well rose up and ripped Bóann's right eye, arm, and leg from her. She fled before the stream of water, running down to the sea, only to be drowned at the mouth. The waters became the Boyne River, named after her.

It is noteworthy that when Bóann approached the well of wisdom without assistance and challenged its power, she lost an eye, arm, and leg, and then was drowned in its waters. This legend not only links the motif of one-eyed, one-legged beings with the well of wisdom, but also provides a warning about the inherent dangers of using *A. muscaria* without appropriate guidance. A one-eyed person lacks perspective, and a one-legged person lacks balance—two conditions that can overwhelm a novice.[141]

---

141. The single-eyed motif may have multiple symbolic meanings. In early Norse mythology, Mimir's well of wisdom is located at the roots of the world tree Yggdrasill. At that well, Odhinn sacrificed one of his eyes to the giant Mimir in return for wisdom. "Single-eyed" may indicate that both Odhinn and Bóann have one eye in this world and one eye in the otherworld. The single arm and leg

Many teachings can be conveyed in a single legend. The names of the three cup-bearers at Nechtán's well—*Flesc* (a wand or stave engraved with ogam letters), *Lesc* (which can mean lazy, sluggish, or still), and *Luam* (a steersman or guide)—may convey hidden information about the rituals performed at the well of knowledge. *Flesc* may refer to the *bunsach comairce* or "rod of safe passage" that *filidh* carried during their travels. In a mundane social sense, this rod of safe passage referred to the right of the *filidh* to travel unmolested between tribal territories, but it may have also represented a *fili's* right to partake of the well of wisdom and to commune with the gods and spirits.

Lesc, as stillness, could be a veiled reference to the period of prophetic incubatory sleep experience during the rites of *imbas forosnai* and *tarbhfeis* and to the fact that ingestion of *A. muscaria* sometimes produces a somnambulant state. Lesc, as sluggish, could also refer to the fact that heavy usage of *A. muscaria*—perhaps in intensive initiation rites—can result in post-use depression.

Luam, the guide or steersman, could refer to someone who keeps watch, as during the ritual of *imbas forosnai*. If so, this ritualist, most likely an experienced *fili*, would have made sure that the vision-seeker did not turn over during the ritual sleep. The watcher would have also kept vigil to prevent disturbances and to monitor the experience between the seeker and the spirits.

The one-eyed, one-legged goddess Bóann is associated with another sacred triad. She is the mother of the three sacred harp strains: *Goltraige*, the sorrow strain, *Gentraige*, the laughter strain, and *Suantraige*, the sleep strain. Sorrow and joy are the two emotions that turn the internal cauldrons discussed in the "Cauldron of Poesy" text, while the sleep strain seems to describe the state necessary to access the internal cauldron of wisdom through the trance rites of *imbas forosnai* and *tarbhfeis*. Knowing that sorrow, laughter, and sleep are potential side effects of *A. muscaria* consumption might help to keep vision-seeking poets from being overwhelmed by the waters of inspiration.

It is not hard to identify Nechtán's well with that of Manannán and also with the well of Segais mentioned in the "Cauldron of Poesy" text. They are all the well of knowledge found beneath the sea at the center of the world and at the base of the world tree—the source of all the rivers of the earth, as well as the

---

could easily be metaphors for the ability to move and act both in this world and in the otherworld realms.

source of the five senses. Although there are many methods for crossing the thresholds between the worlds and dipping into the well of knowledge, the ritual ingestion of *A. muscaria* is certainly one ancient and honored way. The warnings and teachings woven into Celtic legends about the wells of knowledge suggest that the Celts treated their magical crimson foods as the sacred food of the gods — to be approached with care and respect. The wisdom of these teachings is still applicable today — if approached with care, entheogens can be enlightening, but, if abused, they can be deadly.

In Search of the Land of Promise

The ultimate question remains: Did the Celtic druids and *filidh* use *A. muscaria* in shamanic rituals? Circumstantial evidence suggests that the druids and *filidh* engaged in shamanic oracles, quite possibly involving the use of a vision-producing substance. Based on the complex of legends linking magical red foods with journeys to the otherworld, we believe that the pre-Christian Celts once used one or more vision-producing substances. We think it is significant that all the red substances happen to look a bit like *A. muscaria,* happen to inspire ecstatic poetry as does *A. muscaria,* and happen to induce prophetic visions as does *A. muscaria.* The ongoing use of *A. muscaria* metaphors in the Celtic corpus, in close association with references to the development of poetic wisdom, suggests that the use of the red-speckled brother of birch could have survived underground, perhaps well into the Christian era.

While hard evidence proving the shamanic use of *A. muscaria* in Ireland and Scotland may have disappeared forever — like the Formorians and Dé Danann into the *sídhe* realms — we believe that the Celtic legends are filled with many veiled and shadowy traces of an ancient secret tradition. Perhaps enough remains to inspire the recreation of a viable, fairly authentic Celtic shamanic practice. For those brave souls ready to explore the otherworlds of the red-speckled brother of birch we offer this advice, once given to Bran as he left on a journey in search of the Land of Women:

"Do not fall into sleeping stillness / nor let your intoxication overcome you / but begin a voyage over the pure, bright sea..."[142]

---

142. Translation by Erynn Rowan Laurie, work in progress.

Dead Religions, Living Cultures:
The Reconstructionist Research
and Visionary Blues

What do you do with a "dead" religion? Aside from turning it into a sea shanty filk, of course.

Outside the so-called mainstream of Paganism — Wicca and eclectic Wiccan-styled Neopaganism — lies a vast and largely underrepresented territory of reconstructionist paths. You won't usually find books about these spiritualities in the occult and New Age section of your local Barnes and Noble. There's not much in most Pagan shops, either. The average Pagan reconstructionist is much more likely to be found haunting the history, anthropology, or mythology sections of the bookshop or library.

For some reconstructionist Pagans, issues of cultural appropriation never arise. It's difficult to "appropriate" the culture of, for instance, the ancient Sumerians, whose living culture disappeared a few thousand years ago. Texts and archaeological remains exist to give guidance and hints but, by and large, no one is going to claim that Sumerian reconstructionists are appropriating anything beyond some musty textbooks.

The issue is more complex for reconstructionists working with religions derived from cultures that were converted to Christianity or Islam and which are still extant. Celtic, Norse, Hellenic and other reconstructionists sometimes find themselves the target of accusations of cultural appropriation even when they are descendants of the ethnic group in question and have some direct family connection to the cultural customs that have survived. But in the case of a living culture that abandoned its polytheistic religion hundreds or even a thousand or more years ago, how accurate can such an accusation really be?

We could start with issues of language. An Irish proverb has it, "ní tír gan teanga" — no nation without a language.[143] It could be argued that there is no religion without a language, either. Language is the carrier of cultural understanding and its nuances offer hints and reveal the depths of differences between modern Western approaches to life and spirituality, and the approaches of pre-Christian cultures.

---

143. Daltaí na Gaeilge website, (unknown). *Seanfhocail archive*, accessed 18 October 2007 from website: http://www.daltai.com/proverbs/cat03.htm

In most reconstructionist communities and groups, learning the language of the people who originally practiced the religion being reconstructed is a priority, at least for liturgical purposes. In many cases, these languages have not been spoken since at least the late middle ages. Old Norse, Old Irish, Ancient Greek, Hieroglyphic Egyptian -- all of these and more are the subject of study by reconstructionists of one stripe or another. Some reconstructionists, in a very valid desire to make a reconstructed religion workable in the modern world, advocate the study of modern languages that are the descendants of these -- Irish, Scots Gaelic, Icelandic, Faeroese, and others.[144] Modern languages are usually much easier to learn, having living native speakers, and there are often textbooks and classes available in most urban areas.

When it comes to language study, no one is going to accuse anyone of cultural appropriation. Learning a second or subsequent language is usually looked upon as an accomplishment and welcomed by native speakers, even if the student is a bit awkward and the grammar isn't always right. Those who can sing in a language like Irish or Scots Gaelic are welcome at cultural events ranging from local *ceilidhs* to the Scottish Royal National Mòd. Student efforts are usually greatly appreciated by older folks who speak that language, and student participation is seen as helping to enliven and preserve both the language and the culture that goes with it.[145]

Moving from language into folk customs and the reconstruction of religion, however, opens the question of appropriation. But the real question to ask is whether a modern Christian culture "owns" a discarded Pagan past. Certainly folk customs still in use are a sensitive area, but many of these customs were public property, enacted by entire villages. Many local festivals are commercialized to the extent that tourism is

144. Kathryn NicDhàna, Erynn Rowan Laurie, C. Lee Vermeers, Kym ní Dhoireann, (2007) *The CR FAQ: An Introduction to Celtic Reconstructionist Paganism*. Leverett: River House Publishing
145. Harper, Christina, *Bringing Gaelic to Seattle's Cultural Curious*, 22 November 2005, retrieved 18 October 2007 from website:
  http://heritage.scotsman.com/traditions.cfm?id=2276822005
Ross, John, *Call for international Celtic festival to replace 'boring, outdated Mòd'*, 23 August 2007, retrieved 18 October 2007 from website:
  http://heritage.scotsman.com/topics.cfm?tid=64&id=1335612007

encouraged and locals hope that outsiders will come and participate respectfully.[146]

Unlike many Native American songs and practices,[147] folk songs and customs in Ireland and Scotland are not "owned" by particular families or individuals. In places where folk practices and festivals are not commercialized, it seems that native Irish and Scots are often uninterested in their native beliefs and customs, seeing them as retrogressive, superstitious, and a mark of poverty and shame.[148] This said, certainly some people will feel that local customs are only appropriate for those who live there, regardless of whether the customs are dying away in the younger generations.

Even in cultures where some songs and rituals are the property of particular families or individuals, gifting these things to others is possible. And within the same tribal group or culture, you will often find disagreement among traditional elders and the younger generations about whether or not outsiders should be allowed to participate in cultural traditions. The tension between preserving a culture by opening it to outsiders and keeping a culture as a private property for only those of certain blood quanta is a bone of great contention in many Native American tribes today.[149]

Under such circumstances, people who learn the language, who come to live in the places where the customs are practiced, and who regard the culture with respect are generally much more likely to be welcomed as participants. They are also more likely to be granted permission by tradition-carriers to perpetuate the tradition themselves by teaching others, whether the tradition in question is a song, a dance, a ritual, or the customs of daily life.

In Ireland and Scotland, a few things of spiritual or magical nature were regarded as the property or responsibility of certain families. This seems to be particularly linked with keeping specific holy or healing wells, where the power of the well can only be

---

146. Day, Brian, (2000). *Chronicle of Celtic Folk Customs: A Day-to-Day Guide to Folk Traditions*. London: Hamlyn

147. Goodman, Linda J., and Swan, Helma, (2003). *Singing the Songs of My Ancestors: The Life and Music of Helma Swan, Makah Elder*. Norman: University of Oklahoma Press

148. MacInnes, John, and Newton, Michael (Ed.), (2006) *Dùthchas Nan Gàidheal: Selected Essays of John MacInnes*. Edinburgh: Birlinn

149. Harney, Corbin, (1995). *The Way It Is*. Nevada City: Blue Dolphin Publishing and Tallman, Valerie (1993) *Article on the "Lakota Declaration of War"*, retrieved 18 October 2007 from website:

http://www.thepeoplespaths.net/articles/warlakot.htm

awakened or passed to the person seeking healing through the agency of a hereditary keeper of the well's ritual or its associated relic.[150] I can think of no case where any Celtic Reconstructionist Pagan has attempted to usurp the role of such a person, even where the hereditary office has been abandoned. That said, the idea of a reconstructionist becoming the keeper of a local spring where they live and developing ritual surrounding that spring as inspired by such a practice is well within the both the goals and practices of reconstructionist religion. I do not believe that such an act can be seen as "cultural appropriation".

In addition to language learning and research, more and more reconstructionist Pagans are making what are essentially pilgrimages to the lands where their paths originated. These journeys are taken out of respect for the people and the cultures, to learn more, and to participate as genuinely as possible in the living cultures that preserve customs from the Pagan religions of those lands. Some go to study at universities, living in the culture for several months or years. In some cases, when it becomes practical, some fortunate individuals go as far as permanently moving to the land where they feel their Gods most closely, just as some sincere students of Native American paths move to the reservations to work with and share in the struggles and daily lives of the tribal people whose spiritual path they wish to walk.

When pushing further into the past and reconstructing the worship of pre-Christian deities, I believe that any accusation of "cultural appropriation" becomes moot. There is no living culture to appropriate from. Certainly no one has been practicing the polytheistic Paganism of the pre-Christian Gaels for several hundred years, though some fragmentary customs survive. The only real objection that could be made is when people claim that reconstructing a Celtic religion makes them "Celtic."

The issue of Celticity is in large part one of identity politics. Laying claim to the label means different things to different people. The problems are compounded by the variety of ways in which "Celtic" is defined. Some people see it as a genetic heritage, but this is not a definition that is accepted by any legitimate Celtic scholar. It is most often defined as a linguistic and cultural marker — if one

---

150. Brenneman, Walter L. and Mary G., (1995). *Crossing the Circle at the Holy Wells of Ireland.* Charlottesville: University Press of Virginia

speaks a Celtic language and lives in a Celtic culture, one is Celtic, regardless of heredity.[151]

In much of modern Paganism, "Celtic" is a label that means alleged Celtic deity and holy day names are used, but most of these groups have little or no connection with genuine Celtic languages or cultures, living or dead. Without an understanding of what "Celtic" means in the first place, it is impossible to situate a religion within any of those cultures and so the label is by definition incorrect. Thus, making claims of Celticity without a linguistic or cultural connection, such as in "Celtic" Wicca or "Celtic" shamanism, would much more accurately be seen as appropriation.[152]

Another difficult aspect of reconstructionist religion is that, by its nature, it requires a certain amount of both modernization and syncretism in order to be a fully functional spiritual path. Most reconstructionists don't have the full texts of rituals to fall back upon and they certainly do not have access to much of the original spiritual and theological underpinnings of dead religions. In order to be functional, a reconstructed religion also requires the sensitive exploration of philosophies and techniques from other neighboring cultures and religions. Practices must be constructed from hints, fragments, and speculations. Yet, by and large, reconstructionist Pagans acknowledge this process and take great pains to source the material they use for their beliefs and practices.[153] The process of incorporation is often one of extended debate and experimentation within the community before anything is accepted as part of the emerging canon. Sources external to the culture are carefully examined to determine whether they will fit into the known and understood matrix, whether that source is a nearby culture or the dream and vision work of an individual reconstructionist. Great emphasis is placed upon credit where it is due.

Because the reconstruction process is intended to produce a viable, living spiritual practice with links to the culture of origin,[154] it will inevitably go through phases of change. Understandings will shift as new scholarship opens previously unavailable texts through translation. Folk practices from the living source cultures may be

151. Hale, Amy, and Payton, Philip, (2000). *Introduction*. In Hale, A. and Payton, P. (Ed.), *New Directions in Celtic Studies* (p. 8). Exeter, University of Exeter Press
152. Bowman, Marion, (2000). *Contemporary Celtic Spirituality*. In Hale, A. and Payton, P. (Ed.), *New Directions in Celtic Studies* (pp. 69-91). Exeter, University of Exeter Press
153. NicDhàna, et al. 2007
154. NicDhàna, et al, 2007

reinterpreted through new understandings gained by scholarship, pilgrimage or residence within the culture, or by mystical means. Increasing linguistic facility might shift how a particular phrase is understood within the community and its practice. Living cultures, even conservative ones, undergo these processes constantly. It would be unreasonable to expect reconstructionist paths to fossilize, fixated on one temporal period without deviation.

These processes of syncretism and modernization might also leave reconstructionist religions open to accusations of cultural appropriation. It would be instructive, though, to consider that both Native American and indigenous Siberian cultures are going through the same processes in rebuilding their own cultural practices after the devastations of Christianity, Soviet and capitalist political repressions, the forced relocation of indigenous peoples, and the push to destroy Native languages as a method of removing people from their traditional cultures. These cultural and spiritual reconstructions are not happening in a vacuum.

In North America, intertribal powwows and dances are a powerful matrix for the spread of ritual and practice to individuals of many different tribes and regions.[155] Desert Southwest peyote practices were combined with Christian ideology and symbolism to form the Native American Church, which then spread throughout North America.[156] In Siberia and Mongolia, Michael Harner and other neoshamanic practitioners teach workshops on "core shamanism" to indigenous practitioners who are attempting to reconstruct their own cultural practices. In addition to the stories of living elders, modern Siberian shamans are turning to Russian ethnographic texts and New Age paradigms to recreate and reconstruct lost practices.[157] Many of their methodologies are very similar to what is happening within Western reconstructionist Paganisms. Yet very few people would argue that these indigenous groups are indulging in cultural appropriation, at least in terms of the usual negative connotations of the phrase.

I suspect that controversy will exist around the issue of reconstructionist religions and cultural appropriation until these

---

155. Beck, Peggy V., Walters, Anna Lee, and Francisco, Nia, (1990). *The Sacred: Ways of Knowledge, Sources of Life*. Flagstaff: Navajo Community College Press/Northland Publishing Co.
156. Anderson, Edward F., (1996). *Peyote: The Divine Cactus*. Tucson: University of Arizona Press
157. Znamenski, Andrei A., (2007) *The Beauty of the Primitive: Shamanism and the Western Imagination*. Oxford: Oxford University Press

paths have been functional for several generations. By then, they'll be distinct cultures of their own.

Work and Fear

I have heard it said recently that anyone who practices any non-Celtic path cannot also be a "real" Celtic Reconstructionist. People who practice more than one path have been described as "confused" or "eclectic." It is claimed that they are not being true to the path of their ancestors, or to Celtic cultures. Yet when we look at the historical record we find evidence of people honoring the deities of more than one society at a time, praying at the temples and shrines of those deities they encounter in their travels, and even bringing those deities home and perpetuating their worship in their own communities.

Others in the Celtic Reconstructionist (CR) movement feel that as long as we are not being exploitive of other cultures, we should be able to honor any deities or spirits who come to us. There are also those who work with people from other spiritualities and traditions to study techniques so they can bring them into their personal CR practice in ways that enhance their contact with Celtic deities. These people feel no conflict in working with other deities or approaching Celtic deities respectfully through techniques that are not described in Celtic texts and extant traditions.

On my LiveJournal, not long before writing this essay, I posted a description of Brigid as a meditative exercise based on ideas from Hindu iconography and related concepts of deity yoga found in Hinduism and Buddhism. Using imagery similar to the way a Hindu deity would be described, I offered a description of Brigid holding different symbolic objects -- a harp, flame, flowing water, a smith's hammer -- conceptualized as a series of snapshots superimposed and producing an effect like that of a deity with multiple arms. The idea is one from Hinduism, but I was in no way suggesting that Brigid is a Hindu deity or that she should be worshipped in a Hindu manner.

My post struck a real chord with a number of people. One of my friends went as far as to call me long-distance and thank me for addressing the concept of deity yoga in a CR context. The person had been doing work of that sort for a while but, as with so many things in CR, didn't dare mention it in public for fear of being taken to task over it.

A stifling atmosphere has been created around CR, where people are afraid to say anything that could possibly be construed as "not Celtic" because they know they are going to be hassled over it. This happens in many reconstructionist communities where issues of authenticity collide with those of cultural appropriation and of inspiration. An example within Heathenry is the controversy surrounding the development of *seidh* trance and Otherworld journeying techniques. Many practitioners of seidhcraft are seen as "not Asatrú" or "not Heathen" when the original sources that discuss the Northern traditions describe this form of visionary work within the original context of Heathen societies.

Part of the idea of reconstruction involves the creation of a fully functional polytheistic and animist spiritual path based on the culture in question and its traditions. In many cases, unless there is innovation there cannot be a claim of full functioning and relevance for people living in today's society for the simple reason that we are not privy to what people in those cultures were originally doing. No overt ritual texts survive in the Gaelic corpus or in any sources discussing pre-Christian Celtic religion. Without a source giving us the words to go with even vaguely described ritual actions we would not able to do ritual at all if we were to depend only on the written sources.

An orthodoxy of fear has already evolved within the CR community and it's not pretty. Yet when people talk privately to me about their own practices, so often I see people doing wonderful, innovative things. I see people whose practices have touched upon shared inspirations without any real discussion of it. These practices and patterns are manifesting in everything from a shared gnosis that Airmed has associations with moss agate, to using the techniques of Umbanda within an established House to horse and work with Celtic deities. Umbanda is an Afro-Carribean diasporic religion based on trance-possession techniques. Others approach the idea of working with iconic images of Celtic deities and using them to understand and embody deity in a manner similar to eastern deity yoga practices.

In each of these cases it could be said that the practices are "not Celtic." This is in fact true. We have no evidence that any Celtic people worked with crystals the way modern Pagans do, though there is some evidence that white quartz was used as a protective object. We don't know how the early Celtic peoples did their trancework, but we do know that they engaged in trace activities. Prior to Roman contact, many of the Celtic peoples did not use deity images at all. Without firm textual sources or actual survivals of ritual, we can never know how they would have handled trancework or the development of symbolism or magical technologies involving different kinds of stones. And this is where innovation must come into reconstructionist paths if they are to be complete and viable modern practices.

It is important to note that much of the conservatism in reconstructionist religions, CR in particular, has been in reaction to the plethora of truly bad books purporting to be about "Celtic" religion and spirituality. Wanting to foster an actual understanding of genuine Celtic spirituality is extremely important, and sorting the wheat from the chaff is a necessary part of the process. But in implementing a sorting process some have gone too far, insisting that nothing about the tradition as we know it from archaeology and history books can be changed. If this is the case, then polytheist Celtic religion truly is dead, because all living religions change and evolve with each passing generation. While history should be respected and the living cultures embraced and worked with, living Celtic cultures are not polytheistic or Pagan and so we need to look to other sources to fulfill our own spiritual needs as we attempt to be respectful of the spirit of the various Celtic cultures and their pre-Christian values.

When people are afraid to talk about what they're doing in private or what they're getting as a result of their practices, there's no reason to believe that CR as a community or even as an individual practice is going to evolve. People are often afraid to write ritual because they're afraid of violating unstated guidelines or offending other practitioners. They're afraid of doing it "wrong" at least in part because no actual "right" way has yet been articulated. People have been hesitant to suggest guidelines because there are so many differences between individual Celtic cultures, and even between tribes and regions in one small area. Each town or settlement would have had its own traditions for most celebrations, so to claim that one specific pattern is "the" right way for CR would be a violation of the very idea of reconstructing a path that acknowledges cultural differences.

The social penalties for disagreement within the community are often harsh. People are subjected to ad hominem attacks on email lists and online communities and, rather than fostering discussion, the situation becomes one of shunning and isolation. Instead of trying to negotiate ways of dealing with innovation and the use of concepts from other cultures to help bring Celtic beliefs and practices into relief, expanding them so that Celtic polytheistic ways can reestablish themselves, we see the closing of doors and of minds and the stagnation of a nascent tradition that is framed in terms of the defense of a fictional "cultural purity". Far too often, such claims of "purity" verge on open racism. This has been a particular problem for Heathenry, which has some fairly sharp distinctions between its more liberal branches and the "folkish" Heathens who carry on blood-based rhetoric and associate with Neo-Nazis.

I see so many innovative, fascinating people being cut out of reconstructionist Pagan communities for not playing along with an increasingly conservative orthodoxy, and it disturbs me profoundly. We need the mystics, the poets, the visionaries. We need the comparativists and the syncretists and the folks working in multiple traditions. We need the people working with the An-déithe as much as we need the ones working with the Déithe. We need the people who are walking the edges, even if they (and I include myself in this) sometimes make false steps — how will we find a path through the darkness if we don't put one foot in front of the other and correct for errors when they happen? Is it only acceptable "to boldly go" on a tv screen with big-budget special effects and a nice, safe script?

We need more experimentation, not less. We should be striving for integration into living community instead of dusting off metaphorical goat bones in some archaeological dig. We need to envision our deities and embody them, to examine the virtues and practice them, to speak poetic words that push the boundaries of our knowledge and leave us gasping at the edge of the abyss. Standing on the bedrock of the past, we must cut new stone and build new temples to our deities. With the seeds of trees lying withered, we must plant new groves on the nurse logs of tradition. My vision and articulation of CR has always been a reconstruction of the path suited to our time and our place, based on the threads and patterns we can find, but woven in colorful new cloth. The deities live and grow and learn even as we do. They are not static, changeless images bypassed by time.

Our community needs both the stability and the history that comes from tradition and the freedom that comes with innovation. This innovation can occur without the appropriation of practices from other cultures, even as it looks to them for inspiration and comparison. Reconstructionist communities also have to recognize that culture and tradition change with each new generation, and they always have. If we try to keep the Gods and the traditions static all we succeed in doing is embalming them.

Within the wider Pagan community the same stifling often occurs. People on one side of the fence fling accusations of fluffiness or cultural appropriation while those on the other claim that everything is valid and that to question any individual's insight or right to do anything they desire is repressive. The truth lies between these extremes. There are ways to decide whether a practice is appropriate or appropriating, just as there are ways to test individual inspiration against the practical concerns of history and culture. To accept inspiration and change does not have to condemn a path to certain doom in a bog of pointless eclecticism. To follow a particular cultural tradition does not have to crush all innovation and comparative research. With respectful discussion, wisdom can be found on a middle road, but discussion can't even begin if no one has the courage to speak out.

One of the virtues in CR is courage. We need to have the courage to bring forth our visions, to speak of our work so that we won't feel so alone with our insights and our challenges. Until we speak, we will never know who else is finding the same path through the forest. I see too many good people stifled by our community's fears of mysticism and direct engagement with deity, of being "wrong", of looking foolish, of being different.

Aisling and archaeology. It's a phrase I've been using since the beginning of my involvement with CR, back when I founded the Nemeton discussion list. Vision and history as equals, as equally necessary. Both must be measured against the other. Without history we have nothing to support our practice. Without vision, history is sterile dust. We are denying ourselves a rich and engaging colloquy about practice and community when we stifle outlying perceptions and voices, and yet so much of the task of the *fili* — the poet-mystic -- is to walk within those mists, to dwell in those boundary places between tribes and perceptions and worlds.

Even the *geilta* met in Gleann Bolcain to ease their loneliness and share their visions. Should we settle for less?

Gramma, I Want To Be A Witch

"Gramma, I want to be a witch when I grow up."

It probably wasn't the best way to broach the topic, but I was about twelve or thirteen and had just read an article in the local paper about a coven of witches. What they said and what they did made so much more sense to me than what I learned in church. Unlike some Pagans, my grandmother didn't initiate me into a secret family tradition.

My grandmother — a faithful, very conservative Christian — naturally didn't think much of this witch idea. I got a rather panicked lecture on Satanists and animal sacrifices and the usual anti-Pagan clichés that outsiders hear about us. I dropped the idea at that point, though I still studied astrology and tarot privately. Back in the mid-70s, there really wasn't much point in trying to do it any other way, given that I lived in rural Western Massachusetts and was significantly under-age.

It wasn't until I was twenty-three that I formally became a Pagan. It was a little after I got out of the Navy, and after a two-year stint with the Nichiren Shoshu Buddhists. I never did tell my grandmother that I had left the church. I felt it would hurt her too much, given the type of beliefs she held, and I loved her very much and wanted to respect her feelings as best I could under the circumstances. Living an entire continent away made the situation easier on both of us, I suspect. I didn't have to hide my day-to-day life from my family because they simply weren't around to see what I did.

My mom, Bette, has always been the one in my family who has known the most about my spiritual life. When she was out visiting me from her home in New England during my stint as a Buddhist, I took her to a Buddhist meeting. She didn't seem to have any problems with it, despite its strangeness to her. I've always talked fairly openly with her. These days, she reads my LiveJournal to keep up on what I'm doing, and that often includes lengthy posts about my spiritual activities, my theologies, and my involvement with interfaith work and different spiritual communities. She says she's learned more about me through my online writing than she ever has in our conversations over the years.

Mom made my brother and I go to church when we were kids. "Because it's good for you," she told us. "When you're old enough, you can make up your own minds about what you want to do." These days, my brother is an alchemist with a fancy for Thoth. I'm a Celtic Reconstructionist polytheist who also follows a number of other non-Christian paths. I'm very thankful for her open attitude about our religious choices.

When I was asked if I'd contribute for *Out of the Broom Closet*, I wrote an email to my mom and asked if I could interview her about the situation. She kindly agreed and so I sent her some questions about how she felt regarding my Paganism, how she found out, and what her views are about the whole thing. Her answers were honest and forthright, expressing both her uneasiness and her acceptance about my spirituality. I appreciate her honesty more than I can say and I think I understand her a little better because of it as well.

My mother grew up Protestant. She married a lapsed Catholic. My father, as far as I can tell, is an atheist these days, with no interest at all in religion of any kind and a serious antipathy for Catholicism specifically. I know that he was upset when our Irish Catholic neighbors once asked if I'd like to attend mass with them, despite my interest and curiosity. Most of my family was either Polish Catholic or some form of conservative Protestant. Mom's younger brother is a very conservative fundamentalist Christian who runs a children's ministry from a website. He used to do things like pass out Jack Chick tracts on street corners. I attended a "nondenominational" Protestant church for some years when I was growing up and spent two years attending their private school as well.

When I was first exploring Paganism through eclectic Wicca, my mother was fairly convinced that this was just another phase I was going through. I had, after all, tried a number of Protestant denominations over the years, and had been a Buddhist for a while. None of them had stuck. There was no reason for her to believe that I would remain a Pagan for more than a few years at most. She feels that it's good to know about other religions and the way they change over hundreds or thousands of years and I absolutely agree. Mom has never felt any particular personal need to seek beyond the religion and traditions in which she was raised, however, and I have complete respect for her choices as well.

There are times, she says, when she still thinks perhaps what I do is an "escape" from some of the things that have happened in my life. I've had my share of difficulties and disappointments, of course. Everyone has challenges they face, and most people find reasons to question the path they follow from time to time. For some, that questioning leads them to return to their path renewed. For others, those questions lead them somewhere entirely new. This was the case for me.

I don't feel, as my mother does, that I left Christianity because its God failed me or abandoned me. When I did believe in the Christianity I was raised in, I was quite serious about it. Yet in exploring other religions, I found that there were different perspectives that often made more sense to me. Asian religions and ancient mythologies drew me strongly, and that newspaper article had sparked something that I couldn't ignore. Despite my mother's hesitations, she has never felt afraid or panicked about my spiritual explorations. I don't believe she's ever succumbed to the hysteria that has occasionally arisen over accusations of "satanism" in Paganism or in any way believes that I worship "the devil." Over the years, she's come to accept both my and my brother's religious and spiritual choices and trusts us to make good decisions for ourselves. She often doesn't really understand what it is we do or why we believe and practice those things, but her acceptance, in and of itself, is a blessing that many other people who become Pagan simply don't get from their families.

Mom admits that she still harbors some hope that my brother and I may someday return to the Christianity we were raised in. I think this is natural for any parent, regardless of the religion they practice. Yet she reads and cheerfully comments on many of my journal entries about my work and she enjoys reading the books and articles I write. I always send her copies of things that I publish and she regards them with pride in my accomplishments. She even reads them!

My relationship with my mother has always had its ups and downs, yet we've remained close through some very hard times. She's always made an effort to understand me and to try to accept me for who I am, even when it makes her a little uncomfortable. She's been there for me in some very bad situations and has always loved me and supported my decisions, even when she hasn't agreed with them. I've been very blessed and extremely lucky to have her. We don't get to choose our blood families, but we do get to decide how to talk to them, how much to tell them, and how open to be with them about the core of who we are.

Coming out to my family as a Pagan has been a gradual process over the years since I understood that this was where I belonged. At this point I think everyone still living does know, though I realize that some don't particularly approve and may even think it's a little scary or wrong. I've talked to some of the cousins I was closest to growing up, and have never particularly tried to hide my Paganism from anyone except my maternal grandmother. These were not easy decisions and have sometimes required long, deep conversations in order to allay deep-seated fears. In many ways it has been a process of reconciliation with a family that I largely abandoned when I joined the Navy back in 1979, feeling alienated and alone.

We've all changed since that time. There has been a softening of some of the fundamentalism in parts of my family, and more openness on my part to the risks of talking to people whose paths and sometimes whose actions left me feeling cold or hurt or angry. I can't imagine returning to Christianity but I can, more and more, see myself as part of my blood family once again. Maybe it's not the years, but the mileage.

Thanks, mom.

His Mother's Whole Body Heals:
Gender and Ritual in the Ekklesía Antínoou

In its inception, the cult of Antinous, the deified lover of the Roman emperor Hadrian, is intentionally and intensely queer. Early Christian theologians and apologists attacked the religion in part because of the homoerotic nature of Hadrian and Antinous's relationship.[158] Even Julian, famously apostate, who embraced a return to Paganism after rejecting the Christianity in which he was raised, attacked the deification and worship of Antinous.[159]

Antinous was one of the last classical deities. His death in the Nile at about the age of nineteen during late 130 CE at the festival of Osiris brought him traditional Egyptian deification and identification with the dead and risen god. This tradition was embraced and spread by Hadrian in his grief at his young lover's drowning. Temples were founded and an entire city, Antinoöpolis, was founded at Besa where the death occurred.[160] The worship of Antinous continued for at least two centuries after Hadrian's own death.

In much of the modern cult of Antinous, he is postulated specifically as a god of male homosexuality. One group presents him as a deity of gay triumphalism, declaring him the singular, monotheistic deity for gay men with no other worshippers or deities encouraged.[161] Such a position can be seen as taking coming out theology -- the idea that "it's okay to be gay" -- to its rather literalist and fundamentalist conclusion. This theological position led to a schism and the formation of the Ekklesía Antínoou: a more open and welcoming organization that encourages membership and activity by people of all sexualities and identities.[162] This history is important in contextualizing issues of gender and sexualities in modern Antinoan practice.

Antinous in his original cultus had a far wider appeal than is suggested by a survey of the modern cult on the web.[163] The

---

158. See examples in Royston Lambert, *Beloved and God: The Story of Hadrian and Antinous* (New York: Viking, 1984), pp. 193-194.
159. Lambert, pp. 192-193.
160. Lambert, pp. 198-208.
161. http://www.antinopolis.org/
162. http://groups.yahoo.com/group/ekklesia_antinoou/
163. The only love spell invoking Antinous from the ancient world yet found does so to bring about a liaison between a man (the invoker) and a woman (the

overwhelming modern presentation of this deity as the sole property of gay men places some high obstacles in the path of any woman (or non-queer person) who might wish to engage with this fascinating and rewarding deity.

The queerness of Antinous is an important aspect of his appeal. Most modern Pagan religions are based in and work from within heteronormative assumptions. Deities and energies are paired off in boy-girl arrangements that, however well intentioned, leave out those of us with non-heterosexual or non-binary gender identities. Sexual polarity is presented as the normative driver for much modern Neopagan worship and magic. The Antinoan cult provides a strong option for those of us who stand outside this mainstream, provided we wrest it away from exclusivist male claims and their accompanying focus on perfect male youth and beauty.

The very queerness of Antinous and Hadrian themselves, both deities within the cult, provides incredible affirmation for non-heteronormative spirituality. It elevates queer relationship and queer identity from second-class citizenship within Paganism to a primacy of place, celebrating love that looks beyond gender. Yet the Ekklesía does not begin and end with coming out theology. In fact, this has very little to do with the ritual life of the group at all.

In the Ekklesía we embrace not just Antinous and Hadrian but also Hadrian's deified wife, Sabina. Her companion and court poet, Julia Balbilla, is a Sancta of the Ekklesía and their close relationship is specifically constructed as Sapphic in the modern theology of many members of the cult. Antinous himself was closely associated with the goddess Diana in one Roman funeral society,[164] providing concrete proof that there is no hostility between queer male and queer female deities within the cult. Many modern Sancti of the cult are queer women and people of other genders, revered as inspirations, artists, and leaders within the queer community throughout history.

Mantinoe, the mother of Antinous, is also an important figure of deific power.[165] The obelisk of Antinous, originally situated at

---

focus of his desire): Mary Beard, John North, and Simon Price (eds./trans.), *Religions of Rome, Volume 2: A Sourcebook* (Cambridge: Cambridge University Press, 1998), pp. 266-267.

164. Beard, North, and Price, pp. 292-294.

165. J. R. Rea (ed./trans.), *The Oxyrynchus Papyri*, Vol. 63 (London: Egypt Exploration Society, 1996), pp. 10-11.

Hadrian's Villa,[166] says on its north face, "...his mother's whole body heals."[167] This female deific power is certainly worthy of worship and admiration, a fitting attribute for the mother of a god and a goddess in her own right. It is also a feminine deific presence that is not expressed solely within the too-often seen context of woman/goddess/earth as depersonalized passive fertile womb. A whole body is more than a uterus -- it has hands and mouth, brain and eyes. A body has speech and thought and active, motive participation where a womb has only receptive gestation and a cataclysmic expulsion of the finished product.

Hadrian also firmly established the reverence of Disciplina, the feminine embodiment of military discipline, within the Roman legions.[168] Ever a man of philosophy, and one who apparently had a great respect for the women in his life, he was not afraid to represent iron discipline and warriorship as a female figure.

This essay is not, however, solely intended as a discussion of the history of the modern cult of Antinous or an analysis of how deity is understood in the Ekklesía. My intention is to describe my own perceptions and participation within the group. My presence is welcomed and encouraged, yet all too often the group's discussions tend inevitably toward male homosexual-exclusive language. Supposedly inclusive and welcoming video work from members offers welcome and inclusion, but only for gay men.[169] Attention called to this exclusivity in one video led to some editing, but the problem remains.

I sometimes find it difficult to achieve visibility within the Ekklesía as a woman, at least in the online discussions. I participate fully in the physical rituals and organization of the group. I engage the group on my own terms as an equal. I have never been overtly dismissed for being female, though when I speak up to widen the

---

166. Zaccaria Mari and Sergio Sgalambro, "The Antinoeion of Hadrian's Villa: Interpretation and Architectural Reconstruction," *American Journal of Archaeology* 111 (2007), pp. 83-104; Thorsten Opper, *Hadrian: Empire and Conflict* (Cambridge: Harvard University Press, 2008), p. 178.

167. P. Sufenas Virius Lupus, *The Phillupic Hymns* (Eugene: Bibliotheca Alexandrina, 2008), p. 21. It should additionally be noted that the other Antinoan group leaves this line out of its reading of the obelisk.

168. Lesley Adkins and Roy A. Adkins, *Dictionary of Roman Religion* (New York: Facts on File, Inc., 1996), p. 63; Anthony R. Birley, *Hadrian the Restless Emperor* (London and New York: Routledge, 2001), pp. 117-120.

169. http://www.youtube.com/watch?v=ErgRKDi2ots&feature=channel. Note that though the video itself does not claim a unique gay male association for Antinous after its edits, the title of the video certainly seems to indicate such.

discussion to include women I do find that new members are often surprised to find a woman in their midst. Several members of the group, including P. Sufenus Virius Lupus, our most prolific scholar and writer of Antinoan poetics, theology, and ritual, are explicitly welcoming of women, the other-gendered, and non-homosexual men. Our discourse however, by sheer overwhelming numbers, is unfortunately exclusionary.

I have been asked why a woman would want to be in a gay male group and my only answer to that question is that the Ekklesía is not "a gay male group." To quote Lupus, the Ekklesía is a "queer, Graeco-Roman-Egyptian syncretist reconstructionist polytheist form of mystical religion"[170] -- nowhere does the group claim to be for gay men only. In fact, the group's identity is specifically stated to be wider than this. There is one mention of gay culture in the group's description and I can only imagine that this is where seekers get the idea that the Ekklesía is just for gay men.

I have been initiated as a Mystes and acted as a ritualist in initiating others into the mysteries of our worship. Many other women have also participated as "Assistai" (non-initiate ritualists in the mysteries) for the Ekklesía. All of us have found the ritual itself both profound and transformative in its concept and execution. The mysteries are not based on gender or perceptions of gender, nor do they collapse our mystery into the showing of masculine seed that sprouts in female, fertile earth, as was my experience of the modern Eleusinian mysteries. Any role in the mystery, with the possible exception of Antinous himself, may be taken on by a person of any gender or identity. I experienced this as one of the great strengths of the ritual.

In our larger public rituals I have participated as a Luperca, running in the traditional race of the Lupercalia as the first woman to do so in the history of the cult, either in ancient times or in its modern reconstruction. My ritual role was as Luperca Secunda, who represents blood in the ritual. Ironically, I was also menstruating heavily at the time, so blood was present in more than theoretical form. Yet this was not a specific intention of the ritual or the role itself. The blood normally implied is the blood of wounding and battle, given that this was a ritual role that traditionally was reserved for young males entering adulthood. In this case my status as a middle-aged menstruating woman served to turn the tradition

---

170. http://groups.yahoo.com/group/ekklesia_antinoou/ - group mission statement

entirely on its head and remake it into a much more inclusive symbolic statement.

In 2009 another woman joined me as a Luperca, running the race before nearly a hundred people at PantheaCon in San Jose, California. Given that so far only two public E.A. Lupercalias have been celebrated, this can be considered normative for our large group celebrations, for which I am intensely grateful. It is the stated intention of the group to continue including women as Luperci in these rituals as part of the renewed tradition.

My participation also extends to writing liturgy for the group, specifically constructing ritual for the Lion Hunt and the epiphany of the Lotus, a paired group of rituals acknowledging failures and overcoming them. I expect to write further liturgy as I continue my association with the group, as well. My approach is one emphasizing equality and participation, though the style of Antinoan ritual tends to be more formal than my usual practices outside of that context.

One of the things I find comforting about participation in the E.A. is the fact that I am extremely unlikely ever to find myself unwillingly sexualized as a ritual participant. The focus is never on my body as a vessel of generative femininity or passive receptivity. Creativity is regarded as a given for all participants, and depersonalizing womb imagery is nonexistent. It is this reduction of women to wombs that profoundly disturbs me about my interactions with some women-only Goddess groups. In looking to such groups I would genuinely have expected them to move beyond gender essentialism to embrace all of women's roles and sexualities. Yet even there the goddesses, at least in my experience with such groups, have tended to be expressed either as castrating warriors or as generative wombs. There is little acknowledgment of the scholar, the poet, the builder, the intellectual. Even in specifically women's space, women are reduced to their reproductive capacity.

The triple goddess of Wicca manifesting as maiden, mother, and crone emphasizes childbirth as a defining aspect of womanhood, and one ordinarily can't get to "crone" without passing "mother". To me, this suggests that women who are infertile or those of us who are childless by choice are somehow seen as immature and forever stuck at the maiden stage. This plays an immense role in my appreciation for the cult of Antinous and its lack of emphasis on woman as fertility symbol. My internalized identity as androgynous/genderqueer and my overt bisexuality are respected and embraced within the Ekklesía, where gender and fertility -- male or female -- are not the focus of theology or ritual. As much as women are not reduced to wombs, neither are men reduced to penises and body hair. I find this a distinct improvement over much of modern gender-based Pagan spirituality and its accompanying fertility mysteries.

One aspect of Antinoan theology that is being developed at the moment is a concept of a triad of goddesses of function. Sabina, Hadrian's wife, is the emblem of fidelity. During their long marriage, Sabina never bore children. Despite Hadrian's great love for Antinous, they never divorced even though it was entirely legal and possible for them. Hadrian deified her when she died -- an act that he did not have to perform.[171] There was certainly respect between them, if not love.

Matidia Augusta, the mother of Sabina, and Hadrian's second cousin, represents philosophy. He performed her funeral oration at her death and she was, in fact, the first person he deified as a part of his imperial prerogative.[172] There is a theological assumption within the E.A. that Hadrian's interest in philosophy was pursued with Matidia on some level, given their close friendship.

Julia Balbilla is regarded as a personification of poetry and four of her poems were preserved, engraved upon the Colossus of Memnon during Hadrian's imperial visit to the site after the death of Antinous.[173] The preservation of Julia's poetry is important because it is a recorded woman's poetic voice, praising another woman, with a known authorship and date of inscription during a time when women were largely silent in public.

These roles of fidelity, philosophy, and poetry tend to turn the Neopagan maiden/mother/crone triad on its ear. Matidia, ostensibly the "crone" in her role as Sabina and Hadrian's elder, died at 51, a younger age than either Sabina or Hadrian did. She would certainly be regarded as no more than middle aged today. Sabina, the wife of Hadrian and the one who would normally be placed in a "mother" role as the "consort" of one of the main male deities, had no children. The "maidenly" younger Julia is, as previously noted, constructed as the lover and companion of Sabina.

---

171. Birley, p. 294. A particularly fine relief of Sabina's apotheosis has survived, which is pictured on p. 293.
172. Birley, pp. 107-113.
173. André and Étienne Bernand (eds.), *Les Inscriptions Grecques et Latines du Colosse de Memnon* (Paris: Institut Francais d'Archéologie Orientale, 1960), pp. 80-98. A further fragment by Sabina herself follows on pp. 99-100.

None of these women is presented as a stage of the fertility cycle but all are in relationship to each other and to Hadrian and Antinous. As personifications of admirable concepts often associated with male agency,[174] this is an extremely important theological position with wide repercussions for the cult and for Paganism generally.

I would love to see more participation by women in E.A. I feel that the group and Antinous himself have something important to offer and that, for bisexual, lesbian, genderqueer, and androgynous women especially, there can be a genuine non-sexualized model that most mainstream Pagan groups are unable to provide.

---

174. Regardless of any cultural attempts to force fidelity upon women, it is considered more of an inborn quality of men. The U.S. Marines motto, "Semper Fidelis" -- "always faithful" -- certainly emphasizes the point.

Becoming Poetry

It bleeds out of us onto the page. The work of a poet is made of blood and breath. Sacred poetry in particular puts soul into sounds, defying the indwelling silence and darkness of our experience with spirit, magic, and deity. To be a sacred poet in the early twenty-first century is to embrace a passion lost on most of the world. We are exiles in our societies, unwanted yet unable to depart from the path of poetry.

No one embraces the path of sacred poetry because it is convenient. Each one of us has a soul-deep longing for it and a love of sound and word that transcends our ability to keep silent. Poetry is the only language in which we can express the depths of our lust for sacred experience, for ritual, for the gods and spirits who live in the center of our existence.

My own poetic experience lives in the context of my spiritual practice as a *fili*, a sacred poet in the Celtic Reconstructionist polytheist community. It grows in the soil of my experience as a Navy veteran, living with the results of trauma in nightmares, flashbacks, and the other symptoms of post-traumatic stress disorder. It is this spiritual cataclysm that forced me into poetry, pushing me to ritualize and express both my pain and my desire to heal. My poetry is deeply influenced by the literary and folk traditions of Ireland and Scotland, drawing imagery from tales and song that are engraved upon my heart as much as the results of my rituals are engraved with ink upon my skin.

The process of *filidecht*, the practice of sacred poetry in the Gaelic tradition, works deep within three cauldrons in the body. These cauldrons turn, spin, brew and boil. They contain and overflow. Their action sparks inspiration, immersed within the language of myth and vision. By reading and reciting Gaelic myths, stories, and poems in ritual and magic, I make myself a part of them, bringing their ethic, their wonder, and their worldviews into my life.

I burn juniper in the small room I have set aside as an incubation chamber, purifying myself for visionary rituals, seeking inspiration for my own work and for my community. I lie on my cushions in the darkness as Scottish poets once lay in darkened huts composing their poems, proving themselves to their communities as seers and singers of tales.

Poetry is at the center of my practice; all the work and ritual I perform, all the vigils and the wilderness retreats, all the study and sacrifice I make are intended to engender poetry. When I am tending a fire by the edge of the sea throughout the night, miles from the nearest civilization, cut off from everything by the tide, and my eyes swim with the aura of flame for hours the next day, it is poetry written in my pupils. It is an engagement with the edge of my physical abilities, pushing myself beyond my endurance in hopes of sparking understanding and, through understanding, a healing.

When those moments of healing magic happen, when those connections are forged between myself and the Otherworlds, poetry expresses my sense of liberation from suffering. The body is still weak, but the soul becomes stronger and, in that strength, pours forth on the page. The tattoos and piercings I have endured are poetry marked out on my body, affirming transformations that cannot be spoken in ordinary prose. Only the patterned, flowing, formalized speech of poetry comes close. Only repetition and alliteration, assonance and consonance, can express some fragment of these realizations. Only poetry draws forth the magic of the ephemeral instant embraced by eternity and vanished within it.

To be a sacred poet is a dedication of the soul to magical and spiritual purpose. It is a seeking of balance between vision and the ability to live a daily life in the same world with cities and pavement and genocide and nuclear waste. Sacred poetry seeks to find words to express the anguish and despair that is inevitable when one's eyes are open and one is truly aware. It is the upwelling of joy in communing with what beauty continues to exist in the midst of chaos and destruction. It is the art of communicating that beauty and desolation to others in ways that transform them.

As a sacred poet, I draw upon the words of generations long gone for inspiration in understanding and living with tragedy, for it is an eternal part of being human. But the human heart insists on survival. It finds ways to draw beauty and meaning out of even the most horrifying situations. It creates music and poetry in the midst of war and starvation. This insistence of the heart is holy. It is a commitment to continuance and the seeking of substance. Poetry is the dialectic of the soul and its result is a deeper understanding, shared with others.

The Irish *Cauldron of Poesy* text describes poetry as the fruit of the deep experience of joy and sorrow. These intense emotions turn the cauldrons within, resulting in divine inspiration, prophecy, and the power to heal and perform miracles. The true poet, in this understanding of the art, cannot help but be sacred, cannot help but make magic by her very practice. This poetic work is more than just focused attention on rhyme and metre. It is a dedication to living emotion and sensation in all its fullness, despite the risks. In a society like ours, where hatred is one of the few emotions allowed full sway, to dare to love, to feel sorrow, to empathize, to have joy – all are radical acts of rebellion.

To relish embodied physicality – enjoyment of sexual pleasure and the sensuality of all the senses, embracing the pain of illness and disability – this also is radical in western society. It is also a part of the art of the sacred poet in the tradition of *filidecht*. To fully live with chronic pain has been a formative part of both my poetry and my spiritual work, following the spirit of the enjoinder that all those things we experience have some value and can be the driving force of art.

Embracing and understanding pain has forced me to encounter my body in ways that healthy people do not, and to challenge myself to transcend that pain while still acknowledging the limitations it can impose. It has impelled me to engage my spiritual life and my poetry in ways that help me understand myself more deeply and to express myself more honestly and openly. It has taught me to value more intensely the results of the spiritual work I do that sometimes expresses itself in poetry.

In truth, the art of the sacred poet is to live wholly and fully. We are, each of us, a poem being composed by the world. When we are able to put words to that intensity of life, we have touched the face of a deity. We have become a conduit of that wildness that drives blood through our veins and desire in our bodies. That deity, like our own human selves, is as much animal as divine.

Sacredness is not perfection. It is not disembodied ideal. The sacred is every thing that is; all that lives and breathes and is inhabited by spirit. It is all that does not breathe; the shuddering earthquake and the tsunami are sacred, the flow of lava and the whispering fall of snow. The sacred poet inhabits all of this, speaks of it, makes love with it. Vermin and disease and death are lovers as surely as the beauty of a sunset and we will all know the kiss of death in time, penetrating our bodies and dissolving them into nothingness.

The early Irish *filid* knew this. So did the Welsh *beirdd*. Taliesin and Amairgen sang of their identities as the sound of waves, a drop of dew in the sun, a salmon in a stream, a word in a book. There is nothing inanimate in the universe of a sacred poet; all things have a measure of experience and wisdom to share and, in our rituals and visionary experiences, we become them and share in that existence as stone or star or stallion. Our task is expressing what we learn in these states of being, generating compassion for the world in all its beauty and its suffering. To do this without drowning in despair or dissolving into ecstasy from which one never returns is the balance that we must constantly find. Both have the potential to drag us to death, our duty unfulfilled.

What happens when we lose, or cannot achieve that balance? Irish tradition has it that we become *geilt* – "wild" or "mad" – damaged enough that we can no longer function in society; yet even in this state, poetry remains. Suibhne, Laikoken, Myrddin and Mís are all examples of those who have fallen to despair, their minds and hearts turning on them, destroying their connections with human community because of trauma and grief that cannot be expressed or understood by those who have not suffered it. In all these tales, poetry or music become the lifeline, the connecting thread that brings the poet back to their senses. Whether through composition or through hearing and becoming one with these arts in the process of listening, poetry and music are healing magic.

Originally, poetry and music were the same. Poets were singers; singers were poets. In Gaelic tradition there were said to be three musical modes that the professional harper must know – the strain of laughter, the strain of weeping, and the strain of sleep. As with the cauldrons in the body, the strong emotions of joy and sorrow are brought out and experienced, and sleep is the trance-state that allows healing integration to happen. Again and again we are returned to these emotions and their deep and necessary role in human life and in enlightenment. It is the poet who marks and expertly manipulates them, creating change in self and society.

But internal change is not the only work of the sacred poet. Praise and satire are equally important in the tradition. What today is accomplished by comedians posing as journalists was once the sworn duty of the poet; calling power and authority to task for its abuses and praising those who are praiseworthy. The satire of a poet was said to bring physical blemishes to the one it was recited against. A leader's name and reputation could be entirely destroyed by a single poem, repeated throughout the land. Such was the magic of the *glam dicend* that it was governed by council and believed to cause the earth itself to open and swallow the offending party, whether that be the one satirized, or the poet cursing under false pretenses.

Words still have this power, and the words of poets are feared in repressive political regimes. Writers and poets are still imprisoned in many countries for the power of their criticism. Salman Rushdie is not the only writer whose works have brought condemnation and threats of death. Western "democracies" suppress free speech by the simple expedient of ignoring anything unapproved by the owners of powerful media and political weight. And so, as sacred poets, we should consider it our continuing duty to follow the traditions of our forebears and call to task unworthy authorities. If our words are magical and have power, we must act to right the wrongs of the societies and cultures within which we live.

When sacred poets work, we are often isolated in our task. We sometimes think that our temples, our desks, our wooded paths, our notebooks in a café are the only real manifestations of import. Yet we have a responsibility to the world around us. We have responsibilities to the deities and spirits with whom we work, and whose stories and powers we call upon. If we see our work as shamanic, then we hold a responsibility to the powers of the land and our words must help create meaningful change to preserve the environment that supports those beings who support us. A spiritual link with wolf or bear or eagle is more than a fleeting dream or a sense of internal presence, it is a reciprocal commitment to keep them alive, to help them to flourish. We work in symbiosis with the powers that inspire us and give us the gift of our words. To take without giving in return is a violation of sacred hospitality. In the Gaelic tradition, it was expressed as "a tale from the host, then tales from the guest until dawn." Metaphorically, we owe those who sponsor us both our time and our most intense effort.

Sacred poetry is more than writing. It is more than music. It is more than healing. It is more than technique, though all these things are tools we must master. It is more than making magic or offering a praise-poem to deity or making journeys into Otherworlds. It is more than singing forth our souls and returning them once again to our place in the world. To be a sacred poet is to fill our lives with profound fullness through practicing the fine art of being human. It is, ultimately, to live each moment awake, to act with wisdom and compassion, to show the world as it is in all its beauty and terror: we must become poetry.

Since Feathers Have Grown On My Body:
Madness, Art, and Healing in Celtic
Reconstructionist Spirituality

I have borne many a fight without cowardice
since feathers have grown on my body;
each night and each day
more and more do I endure ill.

The madman of Glen Bolcain am I,
I shall not hide my gnawing grief;
to-night my vigour has come to an end,
not to me is there no for grief.[175]

Geilta in the Celtic Literary Traditions

Celtic myth is rife with "mad" figures: men and women who abandon society after battle, trauma, or being cursed. Suibhne Geilt, Myrddin Wyllt, Mís, Lí Bán, and others within the tradition fled their homes and social roles after trauma, with symptoms that in modern terms resemble such emotional and psychological disabilities as post-traumatic stress disorder (PTSD), panic, paranoia, schizophrenia, and depression.

These tales and poems are filled with sharp images of suffering, the compassion of friends and family, and the daily struggles of the *geilta* or mad/wild figures. The loneliness and isolation of those who have fled to the wilderness is poignant, but the struggle to become whole again is a strong undercurrent in the literature. Some of these figures succeed, while others die on the edge of society, unable to reintegrate and reclaim those aspects of civilized humanity that have been lost to them.

Though the tradition describes people with what appear to be symptoms of mental illness, most modern scholarship does not touch on this interpretation of the texts, instead choosing to read it as an allegory of some other meaning.[176] Shamanism[177] and

---

175. J. G. O'Keeffe (ed./trans.), *Buile Suibhne: The Frenzy of Sweeney*, Irish Texts Society vol. XII (Dublin and London 1913), pp. 119, 133

176. Angela Partridge, "Wild Men and Wailing Women", *Éigse* 18 (1980), p. 25

177. Joseph. F. Nagy, "The Wisdom of the Geilt", *Éigse* 19 (1983), p. 45

Christian ascetic sainthood[178] are two common angles of approach. Despite this, it is still possible to make useful readings of the texts that include the idea of mental illness or disability without ignoring more metaphorical or allegoric shades of meaning.

The Irish world *geilt* (pl. *geilta*) is defined as "one who goes mad from terror; a panic-stricken fugitive from battle; a crazy person living in the woods and supposed to be endowed with the power of levitation; a lunatic."[179] The etymology of the word is problematic, though several possibilities have been offered, including a derivation from the Old Irish root *gel-*, 'to graze'. A variant of *geilt* is found in Welsh as *gwyllt* or *wyllt*, which has a very similar meaning.[180] The Old Norse language borrows the word quite directly as *gjalti* and attributes it in a derogatory sense to the Irish[181], conflating this madness with cowardice and loss of masculinity. The word calls forth images of wildness or the act of grazing, and Suibhne and other *geilta* are described as having a vegetarian diet. This "wildness" is contrasted with civilization, separating the *geilta* from their communities in ways that include dress, diet, and behavior.

The behavior of the *geilta* outside of settled society is defined as "mad" and regarded with both fear and sympathy by those who are not so affected. Attempts are often made to cure the *geilta* and return them to a productive position. Because it is a multifaceted problem, these attempts are not always, or not wholly, successful.

In the Celtic literary tradition, *geiltacht*, defined as "panic, terror, frenzy," is a specific response to trauma involving violent death or battle, acted out in mythic territory. It separates the *geilta* from their homes and families, leading them to isolate themselves in the wilderness. The hypersensitivity and hyperawareness of the *geilt* makes being around others uncomfortable, generating responses of paranoia and panic that can only be eased by self-imposed isolation. Civilization is experienced as painful, ugly, and horrifying.

---

178. Alexandra Bergholm, *The Saintly Madman: A Study of the Scholarly Reception History of Buile Shuibhne*, unpublished doctoral dissertation, University of Helsinki (2009), pp. 148-152
179. *DIL* s. v. geilt 1
180. Nora Chadwick, "Geilt," *Scottish Gaelic Studies* (1942), p. 106
181. William Sayers, "Deployment of an Irish Loan: ON *veriða at gjalti* 'to go mad with terror,'" *Journal of English and Germanic Philology* 93 (1994), pp. 164-165

Even in the society of others like themselves, human contact is tenuous and easily shattered. An individual *geilt* might be helped or re-triggered by contact with other *geilta*.[182]

Cú Chulainn was famous in the Ulster Cycle of tales for his "battle frenzy." Unlike the condition of *geiltacht*, this was regarded as a positive response to the stresses of battle, imbuing him with heroic strength and the ability to terrorize his enemies.[183] Norse warriors, as well, might enter a state of *berserk*[184] madness that, while not particularly discriminating, was seen as a good thing when pointed at the enemy. *Geiltacht*, on the other hand, was seen as a panic reaction causing flight rather than engagement with the enemy.

In some texts, *geiltacht* was believed to be the result of looking up into the sky during battle and catching sight of the spirits of the battlefield. This sight drove warriors out of their minds. This was particularly seen as a risk to younger warriors, but older, seasoned veterans might also succumb. The sight of these spirits, accompanied by the deafening clamor of battle, could prove a chaotic and devastating combination.[185]

For most veterans, the sight of these spirits and the sound of battle were assumed to encourage their warlike behavior. Song and chant, like the *dord* of the Fianna, were used to enflame the heat of battle that might inure men to its hardships and horrors.[186]

In some cases, however, there is an external influence that complicates the situation. The tale of Suibhne offers a preliminary scene where he interacts with a Christian cleric before going to war. Suibhne was presented as a specifically pagan king who attacked Saint Rónán for his attempt to establish a church in Dal nAraide. This resulted in Rónán placing a curse on Suibhne, prophesying his future as a *geilt* and the manner of his death.[187]

The most famous *geilt* in Irish literature is Suibhne, a fictional king of the Dal nAriad, whose tale is told in the *Buile Suibhne* or

---

182. O'Keeffe (1913), p. 61
183. Thomas Kinsella (trans), *The Tain*, University of Pennsylvania Press (Philadelphia 1985), p. 77
184. Cleasby, R, and Vigfusson (eds), *An Icelandic-English Dictionary*, p. 61, Oxford University Press (London, 1847) The *berserk* warrior is associated with shape-shifting into forms such as bears or wolves, and with battle-fury such as that of Cú Chulainn.
185. Sayers (1994), pp. 161-162 n. 12, pp. 164-164, see also Chadwick (1942), pp. 115-116
186. *DIL* s. v. dord[1]
187. O'Keeffe (1913), pp. 9, 11

"Frenzy of Sweeney." The tale has inspired many literary treatments from the time it appeared. The novel of Flann O'Brien (author Brian O'Nolan), *At Swim Two Birds*,[188] deals with the stories of Finn and Sweeney, two of Ireland's most famous poet-warriors. Seamus Heaney's poetic rendering, *Sweeney Astray*,[189] is a popular and well-known version of the tale. Other modern poets have also treated the work,[190] and it is one of the most influential tales in the Irish corpus.

The Welsh Myrddin Wyllt, more commonly known as Merlin, was likewise regarded as a mad figure, living in the wilderness among the animals, reciting poetry and prophecy. His tale is initially told by Geoffrey of Monmouth in the *Vita Merlini*.[191] Merlin is a figure well enough known that references should come easily to mind, from T. H. White's *The Once and Future King*[192] to John Boorman's film *Excalibur*,[193] though most of the popular material elides his madness in favor of eccentricity.

Another Welsh case, presented explicitly as the result of trauma in battle, is that of Cyledyr the Wild. In the tale *Culhwych ac Olwen*, we are told, "He [Gwyn ap Nudd] killed Nwython, cut out his heart, and forced Cyledyr to eat his father's heart; because of that, Cyledyr went mad."[194]

After long sojourns in the wilderness, the *geilta* were perceived as part-bird or part-animal, ambiguously-gendered, taloned, growing feathers or fur in place of clothing.[195] Yet they are also closely and intricately linked with poetry, prophecy, visionary states, and music. Some were healed through their art and isolation while others died in misery after repeated attempts were made to reincorporate them into society. Their wildness was feared, though it did not appear to be considered contagious.

---

188. Flann O'Brien (Brian Nolan), *At Swim-Two-Birds*, Longman, Green, and Co. (London 1939)

189. Seamus Heany, *Sweeney Astray*, Farrar Straus Giroux (New York 1983)

190. John Ennis, *Near St. Mullins*, Dedalus Press (Dublin 2002), Michael Routery in Jamie Robles (ed.), *f(actions)*, New College of California (San Francisco 2005), "Astray," p. 35

191. Geoffrey of Monmouth, Basil Clarke (ed./trans.), *The Life of Merlin: Vita Merlini*, University of Wales (Cardiff 1973)

192. T. H. White, *The Once and Future King*, Fontana/Collins (London 1958)

193. *Excalibur*, dir. John Boorman, Orion Pictures (1981)

194. Patrick K. Ford (ed./trans.), *The Mabinogi and Other Welsh Medieval Tales*, University of California Press (Berkeley 1977), p. 151

195. Ranke de Vries in Joseph Falaky Nagy (ed.), *Myth in Celtic Literatures*, *CSANA Yearbook 6*, Four Courts Press (Dublin 2007), "The Names of Lí Bán," pp. 42-43, O'Keeffe (1913), p. 17, John T. Koch and John Carey, *The Celtic Heroic Age* 4th ed., Celtic Studies Publications (Aberystwyth 2003), p. 283

Traditional tales offer examples of both male and female *geilta* (*bangeilta*, or madwomen), though men are more commonly portrayed. Both male authorship and the association of *geilt* status with the activity of warriors are likely to be factors in this. Where men lose themselves as a result of their own actions or terrifying visions, or of assaults upon them in battle during wartime, women's loss of self traditionally occurs in the context of the death of loved ones and as the result of profound grief. Witnessing the death or finding the body of a loved one who has died violently triggers this descent into "madness."

The most common generative source of the state of *geiltacht* is the clamor of battle. Both Suibhne and Myrddin become *geilta* during or immediately after being engaged in combat and, at the battles of Magh Rath and of Allen, seven or nine unnamed men became *geilta* on the same day.[196] Norse literature warns against particular actions during battle that may result in *gjalti*. This is contrasted with the *berserk*'s high-status battle-madness among Norse warriors.[197]

Suibhne's initiation into *geilt* is described thus:

> Thereafter, when both battle-hosts had met, the vast army on both sides roared in the manner of a herd of stags so that they raised on high three mighty shouts. Now, when Suibhne heard these great cries together with their sounds and reverberations in the clouds of Heaven and in the vault of the firmament, he looked up, whereupon turbulence (?), and darkness, and fury, and giddiness, and frenzy, and flight, unsteadiness, restlessness, and unquiet filled him, likewise disgust with every place in which he used to be and desire for every place he had not reached. His fingers were palsied, his feet trembled, his heart beat quick, his senses were overcome, his sight was distorted, his weapons fell naked from his hands, so that through Rónán's curse he went, like any bird of the air, in madness and imbecility.

---

196. Bergholm (2009), p. 60
197. H. R. Ellis Davidson, *Myths and Symbols in Pagan Europe: Early Scandiavian and Celtic Religions*, Syracuse University Press (Syracuse 1988), pp. 79-80

Now, however, when he arrived out of the battle, it was seldom that his feet would touch the ground because of the swiftness of his course, and when he did touch it he would not shake the dew from the top of the grass for the lightness and nimbleness of his step. He halted not from that headlong course until he left neither plain, nor field, nor bare mountain, nor bog, nor thicket, nor marsh, nor hill, nor hollow, nor dense-sheltering wood in Ireland that he did not travel that day, until he reached Ros Bearaigh, in Glenn Earcain, where he went into the yew-tree that was in the glen.[198]

Here we see the origins of Suibhne's descent into panic, paranoia, illness, and an animal state after raising his eyes above the field of battle, resulting in his literal flight from society, which he now finds a source of horror and disgust. The Welsh Merlin's grief-stricken flight comes about in the aftermath of battle. Unlike Suibhne, he manages to get through the fray, only to disintegrate as the enormity of the situation overwhelms him:

Merlin called his companions from the battle-field and instructed them to bury the brothers in a richly-decorated chapel.

He mourned for his heroes; his flooding tears had no end. He threw dust upon his hair, tore his clothes and lay prostrate on the ground, rolling to and fro. Peredur and the other princes and commanders offered comfort. He would not take the comfort and rejected their entreaties. So for three long days he wept, refusing food, so great was the grief that consumed him.

Then, when the air was filled with these repeated loud complainings, a strange madness came upon him.
He crept away and fled to the woods, unwilling that any should see his going. Into the forest he went, glad to lie hidden beneath the ash trees. He

---

198. O'Keeffe (1913), p. 15

watched the wild creatures grazing on the pastures of the glades. Sometimes he would follow them, sometimes pass them on his course. He made use of the roots of plants and of grasses, of fruit from the trees and of the blackberries in the thicket. He became a Man of the Woods, as if dedicated to the woods. So for a whole summer he stayed hidden in the woods, discovered by none, forgetful of himself and his own, lurking like a wild thing.[199]

As with the description of Suibhne's descent into madness, we see Merlin assimilated into wildness as horrifying sound echoes in the heavens, and he flees the company of his fellows, now mad with grief and horror.

The story of Mís offers another *geilt* tale, this one of a woman going mad from grief after the death of her father in battle. The *bangeilt* Mís is regarded as a predator, unlike the male *geilta*; she violates the boundaries of femininity in her animal status.[200] Yet even here, there is regard for her condition and the hope that she can be brought back into the human fold.

He [Dáire Dóidgheal] brought her with him as she was his only daughter, and after the battle she came with a multitude searching through the slaughter for her father's body, and having found the severely wounded body, she began to suck and drink the blood from the wounds so that eventually in a fever of lunacy she rose aloft and flew to Sliabh Mís, and remained there for the aforesaid time, and there grew on her whiskers[201] and hair of such length that they used to scour the ground behind her. Moreover, the nails of her feet and hands curved inwards, so much that no man or beast encountered her but was torn apart on the spot.

---

199. Clarke (1973), pp. 55, 57 lines 63-82
200. The resemblance of Mís with her long, unkempt hair to the maenads of Greek tradition, wild and rending humans and animals alike in their frenzy, is notable.
201. Whiskers here refers to pubic hair.

> Furthermore, her lunatic frenzy caused her to move at such speed that she ran like the wind and so used to outstrip whatever she wished. And she did not hesitate to eat each and every animal and person that she killed, and to drink as much as she wanted of their flesh and blood, so much that the region called the Barony of Clanmaurice became a wilderness with scant population for fear of her, because King Feidhlimidh issued a general edict that she was not to be killed on any account.[202]

All of these events can be seen as terrible traumas. Slaughter, bloodshed, and the wounding and death of loved ones and friends often result in post-traumatic stress and depression, along with other mental disturbances.

In the tale of Suibhne, a curse is understood as the instigating force behind his becoming a *geilt*. It has always been a puzzle why some people manage to remain whole in the face of trauma while others react with panic, hypervigilance, depression, nightmares, flashbacks, and other disabling symptoms of post-traumatic stress disorder. It is possible to see the saint's curse as a metaphor for this mysterious mechanism, the tipping point from sanity into horror and unassailable grief.

Stories of male *geilta* include resolutions where the individual's art is highly regarded. Poetry, prophecy, and the capacity for supernatural vision and ability are associated with these men. Their tales and songs are recorded, their visions sought out, and their spiritual discourse is valued.

Women *geilta* are rarely given a voice beyond the narration of their history. We rarely see them associated with creative arts or spiritual mastery. Most often, if a *bangeilt* is returned to society, she vanishes into the traditional role of wife to the man who has "cured" her. Her potential for art and spiritual accomplishment is silenced by the expectation that she will once again become the property of a man, and her independent will is negated.

Beyond the difference in ways that gender was treated in stories of the *geilta*, we also find tales with aspects of gender-transgression. Some figures apparently change gender during their

---

202. Koch and Carey (2003), p. 283

loss of self in the wilderness.[203] Suibhne was at least once regarded as female at the beginning of his madness:

> Thereupon they began describing aloud the madman; one man would say that it was a woman, another that it was a man, until Domnall himself recognized him, whereupon he said: 'It is Suibhne, king of Dal Araidhe, whom Ronan cursed the day the battle was fought.[204]

The earliest known tale of the mad wild-man is the Sumerian account of Enkidu in the *Epic of Gilgamesh*. Enkidu is a forest-dweller, wild and uncontrollable, overgrown with hair and acting as a wild animal. His similarities with Suibhne's wildness and association with animals is unmistakable.[205]

> *But as for him, Enkidu, born in the hills —*
> *With the gazelles he feeds on grass,*
> *With the wild beasts he drinks at the watering-place,*
> *With the creeping creatures his heart delights in water —* [206]

In order to bring Enkidu into the fold of civilization, Gilgamesh instructs a woman to go into the wild and bare herself. She is to tempt him and have him lie with her in sexual embrace. When he has lain with her for six days and seven nights, she offers him civilized food and "strong drink." When he has partaken of these, the animals no longer come to Enkidu but flee from him as they would from any ordinary man.

Now a part of civilization, he anoints himself with oil, sheds his bestial hair, puts on clothing, and takes up weapons. In the words of the text, Enkidu "became human."[207]

The Irish story of Mís echoes this transformation by sexual encounter. She, like Enkidu, is extremely hairy. Her finger and toe

---

203. O'Keeffe (1913), p. 17
204. O'Keeffe (1913), pp. 17-19
205. Both Enkidu and Suibhne bear a great resemblance to the Biblical figure of Nebuchadnezzar (Dan. 4: 31-33), who grew animal fur and fed on grass, fleeing the company of men. While the Irish scribes would not have known of Enkidu, Nebuchadnezzar would have been a very familiar figure to the scholars of the time.
206. James B. Prichard, *The Ancient Near East: An Anthology of Texts and Pictures*, Princeton University Press (Princeton 1958), p. 44
207. Pritchard (1958), p. 48

nails are long and curved like claws, and she eats men like a predator.

Hearing of her, the harper Dubh Rois offers to go out and bring her back. He takes his harp with him, along with gold and silver. He sets himself up in a place in the wild, scattering the metal on his cloak, exposing his genitals, and begins to play the harp. Mís, intrigued by the music, comes down to find him. When he meets her he shows her the metals, which she recognizes. She is curious about his genitalia and asks about his penis and testicles:

> When she gave a side-glance, she caught sight of his fine nakedness, and the sporting pieces. 'What are these?' she asked, of his pouch or nest-eggs. 'That,' he said, 'is a tricking staff.' 'I don't remember that,' said she. 'My father didn't have the like.' 'A tricking staff,' she said again; 'what's the trick?' 'Sit beside me,' said he, 'and I'll do that staff's trick for you.' 'I will,' said she, 'and stay with me.' 'I will,' said he, and he lay with her and made love to her and she said: 'Ah, ha, ba, be, ba! That's a fine trick, do it again!'

He plays the harp for her again and serves her bread, which she remembers from before her madness. She brings Dubh Rois a deer and, instead of allowing her to eat it raw, he cooks it for her, serving it to her with bread. After further conversation where Mís remembers her prior life, he stands her in the cooking pit where the deer was boiled and bathes her in the broth and remains. There are echoes here of the cooling of Cú Chulainn's warrior frenzy in three cauldrons of water when he returns from battle.[208]

The pair stays in the forest for two months, until Mís's long hair falls away and she is returned to sanity and can be safely brought back into society.[209]

Both these tales illustrate the use of human intimacy to restore health and sanity that was lost or never known in the first place. The use of sexuality as a treatment for *geiltacht* is problematic in a modern context. Issues of informed consent arise and, for many people suffering from post-traumatic stress, sexual assault may have been causative in itself. Yet regaining an ability to enter into and

---

208. Kinsella (1985), p. 92
209. Koch and Carey, (2003), pp. 284-285

enjoy consensual acts of sexual pleasure may be a measure of progress in the healing of some individuals who are so afflicted.

Geilt tales often involve the equation of the geilt with animals. Their wildness is symbolically equated with that of beasts. Yet the tales go further than simply asserting that the geilt is like an animal. Suibhne grew feathers. In one Breton tale Merlin is regarded as a bird.[210] Lí Bán, also known as Muirgeilt or "sea-geilt," initially appeared to the narrating saint as a salmon with a woman's head.[211]

Werewolf transformations are common in tales about Irish warriors; foreign warriors and other foreigners are also called cú glas (grey-wolf).[212] The color-word glas has deep and subtle connections with liminal and transformative states, and with penance and asceticism[213] that emphasize the betweenness of the wolf-warrior. That geiltacht was regarded as a function of the failed warrior is significant in its link to this animal transformation.

In the tales of Suibhne and of other geilta, the bird-motif occurs again and again. In both Irish and Norse literature, the geilt is said to grow feathers after spending time in the wilderness. Flight is implied or expressly described in the tales, with the geilta leaping from tree to tree, springing away from the battlefield on the tips of spears, and dwelling among the branches.

Some petroglyphs of warriors in Ireland and Scotland are shown with the heads of birds on human bodies.[214] This is brought into a normative state in the tale of Conaire Mór, a mythological king descended from Otherworldly bird-people. Like the geilta, he is part-avian, but as king he is assumed to be a fully-functional – indeed, flawless – member of human society. His royal tenure was called "the Bird Reign" or énlaith and regarded as one of the golden periods of Irish mythical history.[215]

Among the filid or sacred poets of Irish society, a mark of rank was the tugen, a cloak made of bird feathers. It is described as being made of "the necks of swans above and the necks of drakes

---

210. Mary-Ann Constantine, "Neither Flesh Nor Fowl," Arthurian Literature XXI (2005), p. 96

211. de Vries (2007), pp. 42-43

212. DIL s. v. cú[1] (f)

213. Alfred K. Siewers, "The Bluest-Greyest-Greenest Eye: Colours of Martyrdom and Colours of the Winds as Iconographic Landscape," Cambrian Medieval Studies 50 (2005), pp. 31-66

214. Anne Ross, Pagan Celtic Britain, Cardinal (London 1974), p. 316 fig. 155, crane-headed warriors, Shetland

215. Tom Peete Cross and Clark Harris Slover (eds.), Ancient Irish Tales, Barnes and Noble (Totowa 1981), pp. 96-98

below."[216] This cloak of white and brilliantly colored feathers signified the *fili*'s association with Otherworld sight and, possibly, with the ability to travel into the Otherworlds. The druid Mog Ruith, wearing a bull hide and feathered headdress, is described as flying over a battlefield raining fire down upon the enemies of his people.[217]

Yet while the *filid* earn their feathers by twenty years of painstaking study and practice, the *geilta* grow feathers through their years of suffering and isolation in the wilderness. It seems significant that these feathers grow out of the bodies of the *geilta*, a natural occurrence that accompanies their epiphany of madness. Rather than being able to take on and put off their feathers as a poet in civilized society does, the *geilta* are compelled to feathers, flight, and art. Their feathers, like their madness, cannot be shed at will. They are an inherent part of their being.

Wild, raw food is a common theme in several *geilt* tales. Leafy plants like watercress and fruits such as wild apples or berries are often mentioned. The *Buile Suibhne* offers this description of the diet of the *geilta*:

> For it is thus Glen Bolcain is: it has four gaps to the wind, likewise a wood very beautiful, very pleasant, and clean-banked wells and cool springs, and sandy, clear-water streams, and green-topped watercress and brooklime bent and long on their surface. Many likewise are its sorrels, its wood-sorrels, its *lus-bian* and its *biorragan*, its berries, and its wild garlic, its *melle*, and its *miodhbhun*, its black sloes and its brown acorns. The madmen moreover used to smite each other for the pick of watercress of that glen and for the choice of its couches.[218]

If *geilt* is indeed derived from the Old Irish root *gel-*, "to graze," this origin could signify at least the perception of a vegetarian diet among those so defined. Such a diet would be unusual by the standards of the time, but for an individual living alone in the wilderness, it might be the only practical answer to the problems posed by hunting, trapping, or fishing without tools. That this

---

216. P. W. Joyce, *A Social History of Ancient Ireland*, vol. 1, Longmans, Green, and Co. (London 1903), p. 447
217. Davidson (1988), p. 51
218. O'Keeffe (1913), p. 23

vegetarian diet is noted so often indicates that it was considered remarkable. These cold, vegetarian foods place the *geilt* more strongly into the field of the non-human, grazing or foraging as animals do, rather than hunting, farming, and cooking one's food as the civilized majority would.

Such restricted diets also have a long history of association with ascetic practices and with medicinal or healing regimens.[219] In taking to a vegetarian diet, the *geilta* may have been attempting to regulate their health through herbal simples and purification practices. Beneath all of this, however, is the constant reminder that many of the *geilta* are participating in the community of vulnerable prey animals, eating as they do, sleeping in the trees like birds, and fleeing from the approach of the civilized.

The societal response to someone becoming *geilt* is usually an attempt to bring the individual back to their senses. Most stories include one or more scenes of capture, persuasion, temptation by music, food, or sexual availability, the stories also give the *geilt* the chance to tell their own story in the hope that narration will provide a sort of confessional.[220] The *geilta* may be held against their will,[221] just as someone today might be involuntarily institutionalized by concerned family members who fear self-harm or danger to others by someone who has become seriously mentally or emotionally unbalanced. The distress of the family and friends of the *geilt* is genuine.

If the *geilt* cannot be brought back willingly, a spouse or friend might go into the wilderness to accompany them.[222] There are poignant passages where poetic dialogue is exchanged between the *geilt* and the one who has sought them out, expressing grief, longing, and frustration by both parties.

In the academic discussions of Suibhne and Myrddin, *geiltacht* or madness is rarely addressed as genuine mental illness.[223] It has been viewed as symbolic of a variety of things, from saintly hermitage in "white martyrdom"[224] to shamanic initiation and

---

219. Bergholm (2009), p. 149 for βοσκοί, "grazers," Caroline Walker Bynum, *Holy Feast and Holy Fast: The Religious Significance of Food to Medieval Women*, University of California Press (Berkeley 1988), pp. 33-39

220. The tales of Suibhne, Merlin, Mís, and Lí Bán all have these characteristics.

221. O'Keeffe (1913), p. 59

222. O'Keefe (1913), p.49, Clarke (1973), p. 131, lines 1452-1469

223. Bergholm (2009), p. 8

224. Siewers (2005), p. 33. White martyrdom is described as exile or pilgrimage, red martyrdom as death, and *glas* martyrdom as separation from physical desires in fasting and asceticism.

journeying. While these various readings are valuable in examining the *geilt* figure, the catalogue of the *geilt*'s suffering and mental anguish is downplayed and not regarded as mental or emotional disability. At the same time, many items associated with *geiltacht* match up quite well with actual mental illnesses.

Given that the *geilta* are literary and mythological figures, I will not argue that they are diagnosable individuals suffering from mental illness. I will, however, suggest that many of the symptoms of the *geilta* are very familiar to those suffering from PTSD. The examination and cataloguing of some of these points of similarity is useful for understanding how *geiltacht* can be approached as a model for understanding trauma and resulting disabilities.

The primary motif of the *geilt* is one of isolation and homelessness. Without exception, the *geilta* flee from society, even though they may maintain some distant contact with it. It is one of the defining aspects of the type.[225] This loss of society is intimately connected with perceived loss of humanity. To be outside of the circle of family and culture was to exist as an animal.

The *geilta* are wanderers, unable to stay in one place for long. They must be constantly on the move, fleeing their fears and moving toward the unfamiliar, seeking some respite from their pain. The poems of the *geilta* bemoan this constant motion and lack of any settled place.[226] Even those places where the *geilta* gather are only temporary shelters. They come and go, blown about like feathers on the wind.

Panic is one of the motive forces of the *geilt*. It is an unreasonable fear of people and the trappings of civilization that causes their motion. They cannot abide the sound of bells, of battle, the songs of humanity. A marked preference is expressed for the belling of stags, the songs of birds, the sound of wind through sheltering boughs. Natural sounds are the sounds of safety, free of the conflicts that drove them away in the first place. Human society brings with it war, destruction, and violence, deliberate cruelties inflicted upon one human being by another. The *geilt* seeks peace and freedom from panic in isolation, where violence is most often far away.[227]

Along with panic and isolation comes depression. Many of the poems of the *geilta* are laments, expressing deep sorrow at their

---

225. Partridge (1980), p. 26
226. O'Keeffe (1913), pp. 29-33, § 21
227. O'Keeffe (1913), p. 31, p.71

loss of connections with their previous lives.[228] Yet they cannot relieve the sorrow or heal the damage simply by returning to what has harmed them. Merlin, in particular, comes to his madness through what might be interpreted as depression and survivor guilt after the horrifying slaughter of battle and the burial of so many of his people.[229]

Nothing can be done to restore the lives lost to violence. The rent in the fabric of the *geilt*'s mind is filled with the poetry of loneliness, fueled by an inability to return home. Human love becomes impossible because humanity itself is a deep and abiding source of pain. Even when the *geilta*'s loved ones attempt to join them in their exile, the depression cannot end. Compassion for the suffering the loved one is undergoing on the *geilt*'s behalf leads to further sorrow, aggravating the cycle and deepening it further.[230] The *geilta* cannot be raised from their depression or joined in their exile until they have experienced a psychological and spiritual transformation that reconnects them with those they love and offers them a renewed sense of identity and belonging.

Whenever the *geilt* is near other people, even other *geilta*, they are in a constant state of alert. Suibhne and his compatriot Ealladhan spend a year together in Britain, fearful but attempting to protect one another.

> 'O Suibhne,' said Ealladhan, 'let each of us keep good watch over the other since we have placed trust in each other; that is, he who shall soonest hear the cry of a heron from a blue-watered, green-watered lough or the clear note of a cormorant, or the flight of a woodcock from a branch, the whistle or sound of a plover on being woke from its sleep, or the sound of withered branches being broken, or shall see the shadow of a bird above the wood, let him who first shall hear warn and tell the other; let there be the distance of two trees between us; and if one of us should hear any of the before-mentioned things, or anything resembling them, let us fly quickly away thereafter.'[231]

---

228. O'Keeffe (1913), pp. 25-29, § 19
229. see note 199, *supra*
230. O'Keeffe (1913), p. 43, § 28
231. O'Keeffe (1913), pp. 103, 105

Every out of place sound, every shadow, is potential cause for alarm and for flight. The startle response combines with paranoia and panic to trigger an escape attempt. The rational mind is not engaged in analyzing the actual threat level, rather the *geilta* react instinctively to protect themselves from any potential contact with others.

When Suibhne is roaming Sliabh Mís, he encounters visions of floating, disembodied heads and headless torsos that pursue him vigorously. These heads are of goats and dogs and other indescribable creatures.[232] He flees from them just as he flees from the attentions of the people of Dal nAraide. The disembodied heads are regarded as demonic and may well be some of the same spirits that are said to hover over the battlefield and drive warriors into a state of *geiltacht* when they are seen.[233]

Suibhne's flight from the beastly heads once again takes up the theme of feathers and leaping, birdlike, from tree to tree in an attempt to escape his torments. The heads jabber and shriek, recalling the war-cries of the battlefield and the screams of the dying. He is re-exposed to the experiences that drove him from the field in the first place. In their recurrence, they reinforce and maintain the state of *geiltacht* within which he dwells. These are the echoes of his traumas made manifest.

These moments of horror backed by the appearance of apparitions have the same emotional resonance as flashbacks and nightmares,[234] appearing suddenly with varying degrees of perceived reality. The feeling of pursuit by terrifying monsters or memories is an extremely common nightmare[235] and this panicked feeling may also manifest during waking hours in flashbacks that range from feelings of discomfort to a sense of absolute immersion in the traumatic past as it is relived over and over again.[236]

The tale of Suibhne ends tragically with the death of the protagonist.[237] During the course of Suibhne's madness his people went into the wilderness three times to capture him and bring him

---

232. O'Keeffe, pp. 123-125
233. Chadwick (1942), p. 115-116
234. Aphrodite Matsakis, *I Can't Get Over It: A Handbook for Trauma Survivors*, New Harbinger Publications (Oakland 1996), pp. 22-23
235. Frank Galvin and Ernest Hartmann in Stanley Kripner (ed.), *Dreamtime and Dreamwork: Decoding the Language of the Night*, Tarcher (Los Angeles 1990) "Nightmares: Terrors of the Night," p. 238
236. Matsakis (1996), p. 22
237. O'Keeffe (1913), p. 155

home.[238] During one of these returns to civilization the madness leaves him and he resumes his duties and his position.[239] Even this healing, however, was temporary.

While living with his people, Suibhne is confronted by the Mill Hag, who taunts him about his period of *geiltacht* and urges him to demonstrate his leaping and flight. At first Suibhne refuses, wishing to leave that part of his life behind. With each refusal, the woman's demands grow more insistent, until Suibhne makes a leap from floor to bedpost. She insults him and duplicates the feat, pushing Suibhne until he is unable to maintain his sanity and flies out the window, leaping from treetop to peak, pursued by the woman, whose leaps are as prodigious as his own.

Suibhne's final leap takes him over the cliffs of Dun Sobairce, where the woman falters and is dashed on the rocks below.[240] It is this incident that consigns Suibhne permanently to the wilderness. He never returns to civilization, and the closest he comes to other people is lurking at the boundaries of a hermitage, talking with the cleric there and taking a pittance of milk left for him daily in a dunghill by a sympathetic woman.[241] It is this final association with humanity that leads to his death, murdered by the woman's husband, who believes that Suibhne has seduced her.[242]

In the case of Myrddin, there is a partial but controlled return to civilization. His madness is regulated but, after a time, he wearies of civilized life. Rather than returning to the raw wilderness, he builds an observatory with many doors and windows so that he can practice his arts and make his prophecies but still remain sheltered. He is joined in this semi-exile by his sister and an aide.[243]

Myrddin is no longer seen as mad, though he maintains some characteristics of the *geilt*. His place in society is respected and his wisdom sought out by those wishing to know the future. His life at the periphery is much more managed and manageable than Suibhne's, and his situation is his own choice. Though he is isolated and communes with the wild beasts, he is not bereft of human company or of the benefits of society.

---

238. O'Keeffe (1913), p. 37
239. O'Keeffe (1913), p. 61
240. O'Keeffe (1913), p. 83
241. O'Keeffe (1913), p. 143, § 77
242. O'Keeffe (1913), pp. 143, 145, § 78
243. Clarke (1973), bower p. 81, lines 550-559, companions pp. 131-133, lines 1465-1473

In the tales of Mís and Lí Bán, there is a complete cure and, in the case of Mís, a return to society.[244] Her period of *geiltacht* resulted in no poetry, though her name is attached to Sliabh Mís, a mountain where much of her tale was said to have occurred.[245] Lí Bán was also brought back into the fold of civilization – cured, in a sense – but this resulted in her death and her ascent into heaven, for she had already spent centuries in the shape of a woman-headed salmon and her cure resulted in her return to an extremely aged human form.[246] Both women experienced some amount of erasure as a part of their reintegration; it was their madness, their difference, which had given them their notoriety in the first place. Once the cause of that notoriety was removed, Mís was no longer of interest and vanished from the field without leaving behind a body of poetry, prophecy, or art. Lí Bán disappeared physically, though her legacy remains in the celebration of St. Muirgelt,[247] whose feast day is January 27th.

It is art that marks the *geilta* as useful in their cultures, even when they are unable to join with the majority in ordinary ways. Poetry is its primary manifestation in the tales, and the prophetic aspect of their knowledge is normally presented in this form. Like most prophetic utterance, it may be obscure until the prophecy comes to pass, yet the form itself is often regarded as a thing of beauty.

The poetic laments of the *geilta* are among the most beautiful passages in the Celtic literatures. The articulations of loneliness, suffering, and longing echo even today, able to move people removed from the *geilta* by barriers of culture, language, and time.

The experiences of the *geilta* in their pain, their isolation, and their art, are part of the universal human condition. Their ability to reach through the barriers between the everyday world of society, and the spiritual world of wilderness and the presence of the deities offers a possible route to a non-ordinary form of integration. They hold a mirror to our lives today, particularly when we are suffering, and feeling alone and unable to reach out to join family and friends around us through the experiences of our traumas.

---

244. Koch and Carey (2003), p. 285
245. Whitley Stokes (trans.), "The Bodleian Dinnshenechas," *Folklore* 3 (1892), p. 484
246. de Vries (2007), p. 42
247. de Vries (2007), p. 50

Geilta as healing models in the
Celtic Reconstructionist Pagan community

The spiritual community I inhabit is that of Celtic Reconstructionist (CR) Paganism. It is a modern polytheist, animist spirituality inspired by and based upon the texts, myths, folklore, and spiritual principles of the pre-Christian Celtic peoples of Europe.[248] These sources are not seen as infallible but rather as exemplary texts offering commentary on human behaviors, spiritual principles, and models, both positive and negative, for ritual or daily life.

The movement is amorphous and tends to be localized, with small groups or individuals interpreting and developing the traditions for themselves in ways that connect us to what we know of early Celtic cultures, and the deities and spirits we encounter through our spiritual work and our understandings of the tales and poems. In addition to spiritual connection, there is an emphasis on attempts to reconstruct relevant aspects of pre-Christian spirituality in ways that are supportive and valuable to people living in a global technological culture that is under extreme environmental, economic, and population stresses.

The mythologies, folklore, and folk practices of the Celtic nations are our wisdom-texts, our parables, and the basis of our practices. Within this complex, the role of poet, musician, artist, and walker-between-worlds is highly respected. The positive ideals of the warrior – honor, strength, generosity, justice, defense of the weak – are held in esteem, though much of the movement is also involved with peace and social justice issues. The fact that CR contains a specific place of spiritual experience and authority for the "wounded healer," for a so-called sacred madness, is of profound import and offers a hopeful model for those suffering from mental illness.

The *geilt* is a figure who stands in liminal space between the poet and the warrior, damaged but ultimately valuable as someone potentially capable of interacting with the sacred in ways that can be beneficial to the community and that might not be available to those living more normalized lives. *Geilta* may be perceived as "wounded healer" figures who have learned through their suffering and their difficulties and who may be able to share the knowledge gained to help others. The practice of the arts of the *geilt* can be read as similar

---

248. The CR FAQ http://www.paganachd.com/faq/ accessed February 8, 2010

to modern ecotherapy,[249] art and talking therapies; journaling, poetry, dream analysis, spiritual retreats, and group therapy can all be seen as having predecessors in the techniques of the *geilta* in their search for wholeness.

Personal notes regarding geilt and healing from PTSD

I will not attempt here to define disability. I am not an academic nor am I a medical expert. I have, however, been diagnosed with PTSD, chronic clinical depression, fibromyalgia, and other psychiatric and physical conditions. For the intents and purposes of the United States Government, I am considered a disabled person. My daily life is significantly affected, and I live on a disability pension.

Daily life can be a struggle. Nightmares, flashbacks, depression, side effects of medication, and chronic physical pain all take their toll, yet I continue making efforts to improve my physical and emotional life and to work toward healing to the best of my ability. When I'm able, I have an active social and spiritual life, and a vast network of friends all over the world.

I keep exceedingly irregular hours and days-long bouts of insomnia are not uncommon. The people who regularly associate with me are aware that I have a much greater chance than their other friends of canceling appointments with them. They are aware of my physical limitations and generally make allowances for them.

Socially, I present myself as a "professional madwoman." In claiming this status, I claim the *geilt* identity, deliberately and knowingly challenging the normative assumption of modern Western society that everyone not visibly impaired is whole and able-bodied. Invisible chronic illnesses like PTSD are often disregarded and to call attention to the fact that my own "disabilities" are invisible brings them back into open discourse. I have neither the time nor the energy to deal with people who cannot accept me on my own terms. This has been, for me, part of the lesson of the *geilta*. In claiming the role of *geilt* I carve out for myself an extremely useful and empowering semantic and ontological space within my spiritual community and the larger world.

In my healing work, I have taken Suibhne and other *geilta* as inspirational models and "heroic" figures; not because they were

---

249. Robert Greenway in Linda Buzzell and Craig Chalquist (eds.), *Ecotherapy: Healing With Nature in Mind*, Sierra Club Books (San Francisco 2009) "The Wilderness Experience as Therapy: We've Been Here Before", pp. 132-139

healed, but because they were able to function and bring beauty to the world in some way even though they were broken. Despite their isolation or, perhaps, because of it, they were able to take inspiration from their situation and contribute to society through their art. As a disabled veteran, a poet, and a writer, this is a deeply resonant and appealing model. It suggests very powerfully that I do not have to be "normal" to be creative, generative, inspired, or useful.

Within my spiritual community, the figure of Suibhne is recognized and understood, even if the word *geilt* is not always part of the vocabulary. Myrddin Wyllt is also a well-known figure within the mythology. This role of outsider-poet[250] is accepted as a valued mode of being within our community, as a variant on the seer-poet-magician who acts as an advisor to those seeking knowledge of the Otherworlds.

In following the model of Suibhne, I have engaged in wilderness retreats.[251] These have been taken in the company of one or two other people because of the potential danger to one woman backpacking or wilderness camping alone. Being solitary in the wilderness could be triggering in and of itself for some people, since forests provide cover for any number of real or imagined dangers. My companions are chosen for their understanding of my spiritual goals. Most of my encounters with wildlife have been with herbivores or birds, though in the Pacific Northwest rainforest there is always a possibility of running into a cougar or a bear; another reason for going in company rather than alone.

Silence is often a component of these retreats, with an eye to confronting the numinous in the wilderness and to then express these experiences in poetry or through journaling. Meditation takes the form of physical activity such as hiking, gathering firewood, or purifying immersion in a body of water such as the sea or a river.

Another common activity is sitting vigil overnight, tending a fire as a meditative focus. The necessity of feeding the fire helps maintain a mindful wakefulness throughout the process. The soft sounds of fire, wind, and water aid in detaching from the everyday rhythms of urban life. Part of the purpose is to enter a mental and

---

250. The outsider-poet role is also expressed by other figures in Irish mythology; Finn mac Cumhaill, the leader of the Fíanna and the subject of an entire cycle of stories, is an example of the outsider-poet who does not suffer from *geilt*. Joseph Falaky Nagy, *The Wisdom of the Outlaw: The Boyhood Deeds of Finn in Gaelic Narrative Tradition*, University of California Press (Berkeley 1985).

251. Erynn Rowan Laurie, *Ogam: Weaving Word Wisdom*, Megalithica (Stafford 2007) pp.193-196

emotional space where contact with deity and spirit becomes easier and where the stresses of day to day life are reduced and, potentially, tamed. There is an openness that can be achieved under such conditions that is much more difficult under the unrelenting sound of a 60-cycle hum or the whine and buzz of fluorescent bulbs in a "silent" building.

These methods encourage direct experience of other-than-human powers including animals, plants, and land and water features, as exemplified in the *geilt*'s identification and communion with the natural world. During these times, it may be easier for some individuals to confront the emotional realities of living with the effects of trauma, placing them in a larger context that may help bring healing perspective. The modern field of ecopsychology advocates such practices[252] as methods of connection with something greater than ourselves to restore a sense of balance with the world in which we live; being too immersed in human society, as the *geilt* understands, can be harmful to the soul. To be open and aware in nature can chip away at some of the shielding and distancing mechanisms we use to insulate ourselves.

Eremetic isolation is also a part of my daily life, as it was for the *geilta*. I live alone and avoid using the phone. Most of my interaction when I am feeling unwell is done online, offering both comfortable distance and vital connection at the same time. Quiet is necessary for a feeling of control over my environment and because of the hours I keep. This is much more possible for me than it would have been for a *geilt* in the medieval world. Their isolation was near-complete, encounters with other human individuals being rare and emotionally fraught.

Yet isolation is not a prop for some semblance of sanity; it is a spiritual act, my day bounded by ritual and contemplation to help order my world and remind me of my connection to the sacred. Deliberate isolation is an alembic in which growth and transformation may occur.

This isolation is my primeval forest. This is my Glenn Bolcan. It is a place for the incubation of writing and poetry, for pursuing meditation and self-examination away from the disturbance of the outside world. It is the base from which my peregrinations are made and to which I return when my travels are finished.

---

252. Sara Harris in Buzzell and Chalquist (2009), "Beyond the Lie: How One Therapist Began to Wake Up," pp. 84-91

The possibility of connection and communication without the need to expose myself to physical contact with others creates a safe boundary that the *geilta* of the tales might only experience in meeting someone at the edge of a hermitage or the verges of the forest. The internet creates a liminal space that is neither wilderness nor civilization but partakes of aspects of both. It makes safe isolation possible without requiring the difficult physical work of maintaining a cabin in the woods. I can live in monastic silence when it is needed, yet I am still able to touch the human community if I find myself too ill, exhausted, or fragmented to leave the house.

In the course of working through my PTSD, poetry serves a deeply therapeutic role. Expressing sorrows and traumas creates a way to make sense of these incidents. To name something gives it shape, and shape shows ways to grasp and engage with trauma. It can bring a feeling of control over how one reacts to memories and accompanying physical sensations. To give these forbidden things voice helps moderate their effects and shed light on them.

Poetry, moreover, is regarded as a form of magic in Celtic cultures and within CR spirituality. The shapes and sounds of words are resonant with power, weaving spells and demanding results of the universe. When Suibhne speaks of his torments, he speaks in verse, surrounding his pain and classifying it. This expression is expected and his dialogues with would-be helpers, the cursing cleric, and his fellow *geilta* are all couched in formal quatrains. Turning post-traumatic terror into art helps bleed away its power to harm and allows those who suffer to lance the wound so that it may heal.

My mother sometimes jokes that I was dropped off on her doorstep by the alien armada. While understandably humorous because I am very different from the rest of my family in temperament, there is a small grain of truth in this Othering. My disabilities are only one thing that sets me apart from my family and mainstream society. My religion is different, unrelated to the majority's monotheism. My sexuality is different, for I am not heterosexual, homosexual, or monogamous. Like Suibhne and Lí Bán, I am neither fish nor fowl, yet I bear the images of both salmon and raven on my skin, permanently inscribed to acknowledge my spiritual relationship to both.

Gender fluidity and non-heteronormative sexuality are common in alternative spiritual communities, and CR is no exception. These fluidities are seen as part and parcel of what it can mean for the *geilt* to touch the Otherworlds. The images on my body are a mirror of shapes taken outside mundane realms. They are expressive of who I become in the Otherworlds and of the modes in which I interact with what dwells there. These coded symbols are recognizable as sacred art within CR and the wider Pagan communities.

The moment of embracing a *geilt* identity is transformative. Deep ambiguity is accepted as a part of this process. The *geilt* accepts a liminal state of being that reaches into the healing capacity of wilderness by becoming part of that wilderness. *Geiltacht* is an acceptance of our animal bodies, our living, breathing selves beyond all social markers. It is a redefinition of madness or disability as a state that embraces and encompasses creativity and art as a part of its potential and sacralizes it within a specific spiritual context.

To follow the path of the *geilt* to forest or seaside or wild, open meadow is to take in the potential for peace outside of human society. It offers an expansive inner space for exploration and experimentation, wearing other forms and experiencing other ways of perception. This may appear crazy to people who have no experience of the loss of boundaries that can come with PTSD.

Following the example of the *geilta* who congregate in the glens to speak together and share experiences, I engage in group work at the Veterans hospital, as well as making use of individual therapy. My counselors are aware of my alternative spirituality, the importance within that framework of communications to me from Otherworlds, and my practice of ritual and magic through poetry, art, and writing. These professional contacts help keep me from veering too far from reality, acting as a system of checks and balances that alert me if I am beginning to take a path that may cause harm to myself or others. They acknowledge that my approach is unusual but agree that it has been helpful to me.

Journaling is also a part of this process, allowing me to look back upon and reflect on my work and my progress, much as Christian clerics recorded the words and lives of the *geilta*. To write about my experiences, both in my daily life and regarding the traumas in my past, helps me sort through my emotions and gain a greater understanding of my reactions and my direction. Because I do a great deal of this journaling online, it also allows me to share my life openly with others, who often have useful commentary and suggestions when I find myself in a difficult place. For me, this is the dialogue of Suibhne and Ealladhan, and the astronomical observatory of Myrddin.

In all of this, taking the examples of myth and literature, it must be emphasized that I am not reifying an identification of "madness" with either artistic ability or genius. For many people, to follow this path might result only in further psychological harm, particularly if they undertake this work without the support of a spiritual community. Art may help in healing and in giving voice to torment and transformation, but an inborn spark of talent and a keen desire for this expression must already be present for that art to be realized. Isolation and wilderness practices pursued without forethought and due caution can place the practitioner in situations that may be fatal.

It should also be noted that poetry and writing done for therapeutic purposes may be helpful without being at all "beautiful" or "artistic" in any conventional sense. It may take years before art develops out of the raw materials; wounds must be opened and cleansed before they heal properly, ideas must be cultivated and tended before they come to culmination. In some sense, genuine art might be regarded as a serendipitous side-effect of the process of healing.

In an ideal world, the *geilt* strives for healing through shape-shifting soul-flight, expressed in art, and gifted to the community when they meet at the edge of the world. The community of CR practitioners and the examples of its traditional sources and perspectives offer fruitful soil for the work.

Burying the Poet: Brigid, Poetry, and the Visionary in Gaelic Poetic Traditions

Poetry grows underground. It grows in the dark, amid roots and loam. It grows from the cavernous body of the earth, bursting forth like the brilliance of sacred springs. It grows within the poet like the cold, green fire of plants rising from the grave of a seed. It grows through incubation and through the intensification of the alembic, which is the body of the poet. Through darkness, enclosure, and distillation, we spark creation.

This juxtaposition of darkness and light, silence and speech, loam and heat, water and fire, is central to the Gaelic poetic traditions. Time and again we see examples of the isolation of the poet in gestational darkness, both real and metaphorical, uttering inspired poetry upon release into the light. This initiatory act can be traced from some of the earliest writings in the Insular Celtic corpus to the eighteenth century in the islands of Scotland, a period of nearly a thousand years. The practice itself is likely to be far older.

Burial, enclosure, and submergence are repeated themes wherein the sudden release of the poet into light and human company leads to inspired, visionary speech. Gwion Bach is tied into a leather bag and set adrift on the sea for forty years to become Taliesin. Poets undergoing the incubation of *imbas forosnai* lie in a darkened hut for days with druids chanting truth spells over them. Vision seekers performing the *tarbhfeis* wrap themselves in a raw bull's hide and sit behind a waterfall in darkness and the thundering roar of the waters. Aneirin tells of being entombed in an earthen cell, bound with an iron chain, wherein he sang the famous *Y Gododdin*. Myrddin speaks from a grave, uttering prophecy undefeated by his half-life state of suspension within the Otherworld. Muirgen mac Sencháin sat vigil at the tomb of Fergus mac Róich to bring forth the lost story of the *Táin Bó Cúaligne*. Eighteenth century Scottish poets lay cloistered in darkened chambers, plaids wrapped about their heads, to inspire and deepen their work.

Poetry is found in contact with the dead. It is sparked by their spirits, whispered in the ears of dreamers and vision-seekers, chanted from graves and cairns. Severed heads sing and chant in verse: the head of Donn Bó sang at a feast to fulfill an oath he had made before his death in battle. In Welsh myth, the severed head of Bran sang and recited poetry, entertaining his friends in the

Otherworlds for seven years before they returned to Wales. In the Norse myths, closely related to the Celtic traditions, Odin sacrifices an eye the head of Mímir, who drank from the well of wisdom found at the roots of the World Tree, Yggdrasil. In Gaelic tradition, the poet dies to the world, is buried or isolated, in order to be open to these voices, these images, this flow of *imbas* or *awen* from sources deep underground or in the heart of the wilderness. In this initiatory ordeal, the poet would find one of three things: poetry, madness, or death. Sometimes, we find all three, facing madness and the shades of the dead as we sing what we have seen.

Brigid is herself broken open by the presence of death, singing the first *coineadh* in Ireland, keening the death of her son when he was killed on the battlefield, slain by Goibhniu. Her grief is mirrored in our own when we cry out for our dead, and in the *goltraighe*, the sorrow-strain of the harper that brings its hearers to tears and despair with its sound. She is the Goddess who gives poetry and song to her devotees, holding the bright spark of *imbas* – poetic frenzy or inspiration – within her breast. Her mouth opens and it pours forth into us, overwhelming in its emotional intensity.

Poetry has always been Otherworldly, a gift from places beyond our understanding. It is transmitted like breath by the kiss of a faerie lover, emerging from the *sídhe* mounds in the space between day and night. It flows like water, burns like fire, transforming reality and calling the world into being. This creative power is what traditional poets sought and what poet-magicians still seek. For the poet practicing *filidecht*, the Gaelic tradition of magico-spiritual poetry, Brigid is a totemic figure, burning brilliantly in the darkness of our incubatory isolation. She is the wellspring and the flame. She is the power of words that burns on our tongues.

The power that lies in the well of wisdom is expressed as flame. The waters of the well burn and glow, liquid enlightenment to fill the cauldrons within us. Patrick Ford speaks of this illumination in the waters, drawing parallels between Irish and Indo-Iranian myths regarding brilliant, fiery powers within tightly guarded sacred wells. He says, "Irish tradition knows an essence whose main quality is an illuminating brilliance and whose source is ultimately in the water. It is a quality that characterizes wisdom and the poetic arts, and it is called *imbas forosnai*, 'wisdom that illuminates.'" The word *forosnai* has the meanings 'lights up (or burns -- as a candle), illumines, kindles, shines.' *Imbas*, the poetic fire in the head, finds its source in the watery depths, bringing enlightenment to those who drink from it.

To touch this power has always been dangerous. Bóand and Sianann sought *imbas* at sacred wells, finding death and destruction as they fled before the rising waters. Yet even in death, there is creative power – sacred rivers rose behind them, flowing to the sea as the Boyne and the Shannon. To drink from sacred waters is to taste inspiration; to draw forth the salmon within the well, the salmon that swims up the river, is to consume poetic knowledge and allow it to burst forth in word and song.

To create sacred poetry requires us to delve deeply into our innermost darkness. This delving may take place through dreams or drugs or ritual, through isolation or overwhelming the senses, through fasting, or through any other temporary escape from ordinary consciousness. Arthur Rimbaud wrote that a poet "makes himself a visionary through a long, boundless, and systematized disorganization of all the senses." To dive into darkness, into a relationship with death, into the destroying waters that generate *imbas*, is to engage in that disorganization of the senses with the express purpose of finding creative power and bringing it to expression through the voice or upon the page. To lose oneself in such a way can be a fearful experience for the unprepared, and most people are genuinely unprepared for the chaos found there and lack an understanding of how to navigate those waters and return.

The return, laden with power, is the most difficult part of the process. We must never lose sight of the fact that the disordering of the senses is meant to be temporary – to be of use to our communities, to produce our poetry, we must be able to articulate our insights and share them in a meaningful way. To lose ourselves permanently to the madness is to fail at our task. We must return.

There are deities and spirits who can aid us in our explorations and in our return. Part of the art of *filidecht*, of visionary poetry in the Gaelic tradition, is finding and understanding our allies, their identities, and how to properly approach them. The tradition shows us some of the ways in which we may accomplish this.

In a tale of one of the seventeenth-century women poets of the Hebrides, Nic Iain Fhinn's faery lover was the source of her poetic skill, and she was required to approach him fasting in order to enter the mounds and learn from him. Her stepmother wished to end her liaisons with this spirit and flung a cup at her, striking her as she ran out the door and splashing her with a few drops of what

Erynn Rowan Laurie

remained. The mere touch of the liquid upon her body as she left her home to meet him was enough to sever their connection, and the man from the mounds deserted her that night. Poetic talent – *imbas* – was transferred to her through a kiss before they parted. He had promised to give her song, as well, if she would put her tongue in his mouth. Afraid that he would bite it off, she refused, and so she was able to compose poetry, but not to set it to music. Her fear was a legitimate one, for many of the spirits in these realms are capricious and unpredictable. Their trickster nature is a part of the chaotic force of the Otherworlds into which we must plunge if we seek poetry. We must act with caution even as we abandon the order of the world we know.

Isolation in darkness is described in many of the sources. Whether this is deliberate or accidental, it can result in an unmooring of the senses. It might be done in solitude, as the poet practicing the *tarbhfeis* behind a waterfall, wrapped in a fresh bull's hide, or in company as in the *imbas forosnai* ritual where the poet was chanted over by companions who would keep the ritual focused and the poet undisturbed. It might be guided from outside, as with the student poets who were instructed to enter their darkened chambers as they practiced creating their assigned compositions. It might be enforced through constraint or imprisonment, like the experiences of Taliesin and Aneirin, locked away in isolation and left, achieving their poetry without outside aid or influence, laboring under the most difficult of circumstances.

It is possible that entheogenic substances were used by the *filid*, as we are repeatedly told that certain things were eaten as a part of some rituals, like the *imbas forosnai* rite. Hazel nuts and salmon are frequently mentioned, though raw meat is also specifically noted, and it is possible that these are all heavily disguised references to other substances with the power to distort the temporally-bound mind and open the doors of perception. Raw foods are specifically associated with the denizens of the Otherworlds, and Fionn mac Cumhaill gained his poetic ability, in one version of the tale, from the Otherworldly liquid splashed on his thumb when it was caught in the door of a *sidhe* mound. He placed it in his mouth and was illuminated, and ever thereafter if he wished to have the power of prophecy, he would chew upon his thumb.

In the approach to Nechtan's sacred well where *imbas* could be found, it was necessary to have him as a gatekeeper, and to make use of his three cupbearers, Flesc, Lesc, and Luam, whose names translate to "wand, rod, stick", upon which one might engrave ogam letters for magical purposes, or which might be used in the divinatory ritual of *tenm laida*; "lazy, sluggish," or perhaps a state of trance; and "pilot, steersman," the one who shows the way. These may all point to aspects of ritual to be used by the would-be seeker of visions. It was Bóand's attempt to approach the well seeking *imbas* without these necessary guides that led to her destruction, and to the origin of the Boyne river.

Brigid stands within the chaos at the heart of this complex, the fires of her forge a brilliant beacon. In seeking her, we become the ore that is smelted and transformed, made strong enough to carry our burdens from the Otherworlds. This process may well be agonizing, for transformation is rarely either comfortable or easy. Like giving birth, it is a process that may kill if something goes wrong. It should be no surprise when we are told that madness or death might be our fate if we choose to pursue this path. Brigid creates us as conduits for *imbas*, giving us eyes that see through the mists between worlds. She shapes us and shows us mysteries, feeding our creative fire. As the poet-seer, she gives us clarity and discernment, the ability to translate vision into words that can be shared and shaped into the structures that mark words as poetry. She is the wellspring of *fír filid*, the Poet's Truth, and the ability to interpret that truth.

Inspired by the image and ideal of the incubation techniques practiced by the *filid*, wrapped up in fertile darkness, I created a place in my own home for this work. I have a closet that I emptied, painted in a dark, sage green, and furnished with an altar, useful ritual tools, and a soft place to sit or lie down curled into a ball as I do my work. In this place, I have made poems for deities and covered myself in midnight, burning juniper and reaching out to seek the flow of *imbas*. I offer prayers and praise to Brigid and Ogma, Airmed and Suibhne, to the spirits of creatures who aid me in my work, and to those whose aid I wish to receive. There are bones on my altar, stones and fur and shells, and the flesh of trees transformed into paper for me to record what I see. I work with plants and smoke and shadows, with soft drumbeats and the sounds of moving water, and all these things find their way into my poems.

Brigid is well known as the goddess of poetry, smithcraft and healing. She is revered throughout the western hemisphere by both Pagans and Christians, and is known in far-flung lands as the goddess Brigid, the *loa* Maman Brigitte, who rules the graveyards, and as Saint Brigid. Ogma is the deity who created the ogam alphabet, associated with eloquence and writing; he is called honey-tongued for his powers of persuasion. The goddess Airmed, like Brigid, is another of the healers in Irish myth, particularly concerned with plants and their properties, while also tending a healing well with her father and siblings. While Suibhne is not a deity, he is a figure powerfully associated with poetry in the Irish tradition and is credited with the composition of some of the most beautiful and haunting poems in the literary corpus. Along with these, I call upon the powers of birds and beasts, of plants and places. Their strength and wisdom helps guide me in my work.

At night I cultivate dreams, and sometimes they wake me, speaking words I must write down. Their sensory rush becomes the rhythm of my voice, the color of my verse. The touch of Brigid's hand is here as I am led through dreamscape wilderness. I am feathered like Suibhne in his madness. I have fur and fangs and claws. Stars burn like firefly swarms in my body. I take up my pen and write. I whisper the words in rhythm. I hear the resonance of their sounds, pulling order from the chaos of image. Dream-seeking was a part of the tradition of *filidecht* as much as incubation, and the interpretation of dreams was a part of its prophetic function. Irish and Welsh traditions both offer up dream-tales as a part of their ground of being.

Cautioned by traditional tales about the folly of an improper approach to poetic wisdom, Airmed is my guide when I turn to plants for their aid in my incubations. She knows their secrets, the turnings of their roots and the swirling tendrils of their vines. She opens the green gates of their powers for seekers of vision, making connections between the poet and the plant spirit possible. Hers are moments of entheogenic engagement, the seeds of dreaming and becoming. Her power is immense, as is the danger of its misuse. We are buried like seeds and she nurtures our growth, crafting us into a curative for the ills around us as we speak our poet's words, our own *fír filid*. Truth is a medicine. It cures blindness and complacency. Truth is dangerous to power and corruption, and the cure for our ills can be painful even as it is necessary. To wield this truth with precision is a part of the poet's calling to offer praise and satire, as an act of transformative magic.

When I seek poetic knowledge in the isolation of the wilderness, Suibhne is there, perched above me on the branches, alert and twitching, birdlike. He breathes in pain and panic and breathes out poetry, wild and torrential. Nature here is neither bucolic nor savage; it is simply what it is – untamed and unpredictable. At the heart of the mountains, he waits beside springs, seeking an easing of his madness and terror. He lurks at the edges of civilization, watching but not daring to step within its boundaries. His songs are of fur and feather, of trees and streams, of an aching aloneness that cannot be filled. His is a place where cold winds rend our sense of safety, a place where shelter and the warmth of walls is a distant memory. Suibhne reminds us of what we have to lose, and what we might become if our balance is lost. His battle with pain produces beauty even as it separates him from settled society. He sings fierce songs of trauma and its power to destroy, urging us to find what we love and hold on with all our strength.

The power of Ogma is writing and persuasion. He is the creator of ogam, the earliest Irish alphabet, carved on a birch twig to pass a message secretly. "Sound and matter are the mother and father of ogam," in the words of the *Auraicept na n-Éces*, for writing is sound made into matter, visible to the eye, tangible and able to be passed from hand to hand as parchment or paper or stone. In Gaul, his counterpart Ogmios was portrayed as a strong, elderly man whose followers were bound to him by golden chains that stretched from his tongue to their ears. Poetry is the power of persuasion, of connection, of binding. His aid offers us guidance concerning structure and rhetoric, the art of conveying deep emotion within the constraints of form. While Brigid touches us with fiery, *ex tempore* oration, Ogma gives us the gift of preserving those words to be read by others who may never hear them from our lips. Where memory fails, writing may preserve what is vital.

His is also the power of code and concealment. Poetry encodes information, allowing the poet to obscure detail while bringing meaning into sharp focus. To use poetry for magic it is necessary to compress information to its essence, to divert in order to highlight. This is the art of oblique reference and the use of symbol and sign to convey mysteries. The practitioners of *filidecht* held that the language of poetry, the *bérla na filed*, was different than the language spoken by outsiders. It was called "dark speech" and its complex linguistic facility was meant to communicate within a closed community; sometimes that function is indispensable. Poets were described as speaking in such dense riddles that only another poet could decipher the meaning, and the multiple ogam lists of the *Book of Ballymote*'s ogam tracts offered a series of keys to some of this material. The images and motifs of the literary tradition provide further hints to the depth of the Gaelic poetic mysteries. This coded poetry is the language of the *koan* and the riddle, the myth-laden speech of birds that can only be understood by the initiate. It is the secret held by the salmon whose body is consumed by the one seeking wisdom in order to open the eyes to another reality. To encode knowledge in poetic form ensures that the information is interpretable only by the prepared.

The eleventh century Irish text referred to as *The Cauldron of Poesy* speaks of three cauldrons within the body that turn and spin, boiling and brewing health, power, and wisdom in those who know how to access them. Informed by the texts of the ancient *filid* and fortified by the presence of Otherworldly guides and guardians, I open myself to the turning of the internal cauldrons that process raw emotion into poetic expression. These cauldrons ferment what is placed within them, from internal or external sources. They are the focus of the alchemical process, the *solve et coagula*, of the Gaelic poetic tradition. As the poet is rent asunder, dissolved and dispersed in the crucible of Brigid's forge, so she is brought together again under Brigid's hammer, remade and shaped for the work to be carried out, and quenched in the healing waters of the sacred well. Joy and sorrow turn these three internal cauldrons, urging us to experience our most intense emotions fully and turn them into poetry, as Brigid transformed her grief into song.

Encompassing the entire tradition of incubation and visionary poetry is Brigid's blazing power of transformation and inspiration. She presides over the holy well at the center of being where fire and water meet to produce poetry, prophecy, and magic. She is the mystery at the heart of the hazel, the spots on the sides of the salmon, the smith who creates us anew. While the tradition offers us glimpses of the tools, the methods of their use are largely lost to time and the destruction of the culture in which the tradition arose. The situation is not without hope, for the tools of the *filid* include scholarship, inspiration, and experimentation. Incubatory traditions can be rediscovered and renewed, reconstructed from the hints left in the poetry and tales in the manuscripts. We can lay ourselves down in darkness, call upon those who would aid us, disorder our senses, and open ourselves to poetry.

A Word Among Letters: Animist Practice in Celtic Reconstructionist Paganism

I have been a word among letters,
I have been a book in the origin.
from *Cad Goddeu*, "The Battle of the Trees"[253]

Words are alive. Stones have souls. Swords speak to humans. There is much in Celtic literature and historical sources about the Celts to suggest that the early Celtic peoples practiced animistic, polytheist religions before they were forcibly converted to Christianity. Even after the conversion, source texts are alive with tales and poetry that suggest a sense of soul or spirit dwelling within the non-human.

The most obvious manifestation of this animism is found in the poetry ascribed to Amairgen and Taliesin in the Irish and Welsh traditions respectively, but there is a rich corpus of transformation or transmigration tales as well, describing how the soul of a wise ancient moves from body to body and form to form through thousands of years of existence. Poets declare their forms as books, sunlight, stars, sound, waves of the sea, animals. This declaration of form implies a living spirit within that has intelligence and volition that can be engaged by those who are aware of its presence.

The Irish ancient Tuán mac Cairill passes thousands of years as boar, eagle, stag and salmon before he is reborn as a human to tell the tale of Ireland from its beginnings.[254] The implications of such reincarnatory inhabitation demand respect for the non-human by any compassionate, thinking human being. If any animal might be the embodiment of a person or a deity, our relationship with that creature must, perforce, change from unthinking predator and prey to a considered reciprocal relationship between spiritual equals.

Even without the agency of a poet dying and being reborn in non-human forms, we have tales that describe encounters with animals, fish, and birds who offer counsel to humans in time of need. In the tale of *Culhwch ac Olwen* we find the warriors of Arthur's court consulting the oldest animals in the world to help

---

253. William F. Skene (trans.), *Four Ancient Books of Wales*, trans. William F. Skene, Edmonston & Douglas, Edinburgh 1868, p. 277
254. John T. Koch and John Carey (ed.), "Scél Tuain meic Chairill: The Story of Tuán Son of Cairell," trans. John Carey, *The Celtic Heroic Age, 4th ed.*, ed. John T. Koch and John Carey, Celtic Studies Publications, Aberystwythdd pp. 223-225

them in their search for the lost Mabon, son of Modron.[255] These animals speak with the warriors, giving them advice about who to talk to next, where to find important clues, or aiding them in other ways. The mythic Irish elder Fintan mac Bóchra has a dialogue with the Hawk of Aichill where the two share wisdom as equals and Fintan describes escaping the biblical flood during his series of reincarnations.[256]

In the Finn cycle, Finn is out hunting when he finds Sadb, a woman transformed into a deer. Rather than killing her, he takes her home, where she resumes her human shape. After she has once again been cursed to roam in deer-shape, she gives birth to their son, Oisín; the name means "fawn". In this tale, Oisín is seen to have something of the nature of the deer within him.[257]

There are a number of incidents in the *Táin Bó Cúailgne* that show the Goddess Morrígan taking different shapes as disguises. She appears variously as an eel, a wolf, a raven, and red heifer. She shifts shapes in human forms as well, able to appear as a woman of any age.[258]

In *Togail Bruidne Dá Derga*, Conaire Mór is conceived when his mother receives a bird who transforms himself into a man. When Conaire is out hunting in his youth, he encounters a flock of birds. He pursues them and they turn into warriors, who then tell him that they are his father's people and that he is forbidden to hunt birds because they are his family. These bird-men also instruct him to proceed to the Hill of Tara naked, carrying nothing but a sling, for the druids have predicted that they will find the next king traveling the road in this state. Following the advice of the birds, Conaire becomes king and his rule was known as the *Enlaith* or Bird Reign.[259]

Selkies, seals who can shed their skins and take the shape of humans, are also well-known in Gaelic myth and folklore. Many families in Ireland and Scotland are said to be descended from selkies and there are tales of seal-hunters who were captured by the

---

255. Patrick K. Ford (trans.), *The Mabinogi and Other Medieval Welsh Tales*, trans. Patrick K. Ford, University of California Press, Berkeley 1977, pp. 147-149

256. James MacKillop, *Dictionary of Celtic Mythology*, James MacKillop, Oxford University Press, Oxford 1998, p. 203

257. MacKillop, pp. 313, 332

258. Cecile O'Rahilly (ed./trans.), *Táin Bó Cúailnge, Rescension 1*, Dublin Institute for Advanced Studies, Dublin 1976, pp. 152 (bird) 176-177 (young woman, eel, wolf, heifer) 181 (old woman)

259. Koch and Carey, pp. 168-169

selkies and taken to their land beneath the waves. Tales involving taking a seal-hunter under the waves often revolve around the hunter making compensation to or healing a seal that he has wounded.[260]

Child ballad 113, *The Great Silkie of Sule Skerry*,[261] tells the story of a woman who bears a child to a selkie. When the father comes to claim the seal-child, the woman goes on to marry a hunter, who kills the selkie and her son. In an Irish song, *An Mhaighdean Mhara*,[262] a woman named Mary Kinney takes her sealskin back and deserts her family to return to the sea. The Kinneys are a family said to descend from the selkies.

Even in specifically Christian tales, shape-shifting is seen. Saint Patrick transforms himself and his traveling companions into deer to escape detection by the warriors of Laoghaire, sent to prevent their escape after lighting a forbidden fire to declare their religious supremacy. Eight deer and a fawn passed unremarked, where Patrick and his monks would have been slaughtered. This story is given as the origin of the protective prayer or *lorica* called Saint Patrick's Breastplate. It is also known as the Deer's Cry.[263]

The prayer itself is frequently Paganized and calls upon the powers of stone, snow, lightning, fire, wind and other natural features as protective forces. Even within the heart of Irish Christianity, hints of animism survive and thrive. One version of this prayer features prominently in Madeleine L'Engle's children's novel, *A Swiftly Tilting Planet*.[264]

In *Cath Maige Tuired*, Orna, the sword of Tethra, speaks to Ogma,[265] giving voice to what today most would consider an inanimate object. When Ogma defeats Tethra, Orna recites Tethra's deeds and it is this act that legally entitles a sword to cleaning after

---

260. Entire books have been written on this topic. Two of them, containing many tales, are Duncan Williamson, *Tales of the Seal People: Scottish Folk Tales*, Interlink, NY 1992 and David Thomson, *The People of the Sea: A Journey in Search of the Seal Legend*, Counterpoint, Washington DC 2000 (originally published 1954)

261. Francis James Child (ed.), *The English and Scottish Popular Ballads, vol II*, Dover, NY 1965 p. 494

262. Lyrics and translation available at http://www.lyricszoo.com/orla-fallon/an-mhaighdean-mhara/ retrieved October 29, 2009

263. John Carey, *King of Mysteries: Early Irish Religious Writings*, Four Courts Press, Dublin 2000, pp. 130-135

264. Madeleine L'Engle, *A Swiftly Tilting Planet*, Doubleday, NY 1978, p. 18 and other instances

265. Elizabeth A. Gray (trans.), *Cath Maige Tuired*, Elizabeth A. Gray, Irish Texts Society, Dublin 1983, p. 69

it is taken in battle. Not only swords but trees have rights in the early Irish laws, with some trees having an honor price for cutting equivalent to that of some humans.[266] Considering that many types of trees were regarded as sacred in themselves, this is more than an economic measure of recompense. In the poems of Amairgen the poet declares himself "a spear that wages battle with plunder",[267] again inferring that weapons have spirits. The poem *Cad Goddeu*, attributed to Taliesin, expresses this even more fully, inhabiting trees, weapons, books, bubbles in beer, the strings of harps, coracles and a myriad other "objects" with his living presence.[268] Objects ephemeral as bubbles and lasting as trees are declared sentient with the poet's life force. Indeed, this text can be read as a glorious and joyful declaration that all the world and everything in it is alive, thrumming with consciousness and being.

Independent animal spirits also reside within the bodies of some figures. Meiche, a son of the Morrígan, had three serpents dwelling in his heart. It had been prophesied that, should these serpents grow to maturity, they would destroy all the other animals in Ireland. Dian Cécht, one of the healing Gods of the Tuatha Dé Danann, killed Meiche and burned his heart in order to destroy the reptiles.[269]

While the songs and tales themselves are luminous with animist themes, many modern Pagans appear to consider Celtic Reconstructionist Pagan (CR) paths primarily theistic if they consider them spiritual at all, without any animism in their expression or their practice. Some regard CR practitioners as dry pedants interested only in books and research, who have no genuine spiritual lives at all. A large public focus in CR tends to be on Gods and Goddesses with some elements of ancestor reverence that, in itself, belies the idea that CR is unspiritual at heart. Yet this ignores a third, extremely important focus of CR spiritual practice -- land spirits.[270]

---

266. Fergus Kelly, *A Guide to Early Irish Law*, Fergus Kelly, Dublin Institute for Advanced Studies, Dublin 1988, p. 144

267. *The Celtic Heroic Age: Literary Sources for Ancient Celtic Europe & Early Ireland & Wales, 4th ed.*, ed. John T. Koch and John Carey, Celtic Studies Publications, Aberystwyth 2003, p. 265

268. Ford, 1977, pp. 184-187

269. Whitley Stokes, (ed.) 'The Prose Tales in the Rennes Dindshenchas', *Revue Celtique* 15 (1894) p. 304

270. http://www.paganachd.com/faq/theology.html#ancestors retrieved October 29, 2009

It helps to realize that in a Celtic context the boundary between deity, ancestors and land spirits is very permeable. These categories overlap in a spiritual Venn diagram that gives us both seals and deities as the ancestors of families or individual humans, with various non-"deific" entities like the Fomhoire marrying into the "deific" tribes of the Túatha Dé without so much as a lifted eyebrow on either side of the match. The Old Irish phrase *Dé ocus An-Dé* -- Gods and Non-Gods -- found in several places in the corpus,[271] is telling. Both are considered equally worthy of respect and equally capable of giving blessing.

Who are those Non-Gods? Not hard; any spiritual being one might encounter, including ancestors, animal spirits, land spirits, tree spirits, or the spirits of rivers, stones, mountains and other objects. Or, as John Carey puts it, "The phrase has generally been translated 'gods and un-gods,' and should perhaps be understood to mean 'gods and everyone/everything else.'"[272]

This understanding effects CR practice in a number of ways. We primarily see it in the acknowledgement of deity, ancestors and land spirits in most types of formal CR ritual. Offerings are made to these beings as an integral part of our rituals and acting in this manner is considered the due practice of the virtue of hospitality within the tradition. In addition to this we also see practitioners discussing their relationships with land spirits when they travel or migrate and how they negotiate with the energies and spirits of new places.[273] This is perfectly in keeping with Celtic traditions both in the islands and on the European continent.

Our relationship to the land itself is extremely important and there is an entire class of place-name tales called *dindshenchas* in Irish that narrate the history of the land and its relationship to those who have lived upon it.[274] These tales are often told by an ancient figure of wisdom to a saint in the Irish source texts, but they are also found in legal texts and other sources. Places might be named for a

---

271. Instances include the *Táin Bó CúCuailgne*, the *Cóir Anmann* and the *Tuatha Dé Miscellany*

272. John Carey, "A *Tuatha Dé* Miscellany", John Carey, *Bulletin of the Board of Celtic Studies* 39, 1992, p. 37

273. Raven nic Rhóisín and Kathryn Price NicDhana, *KILLYOUANDEATYOU Or, A Well-Intentioned Celt's Guide to Non-Celtic Bioregions* by Raven nic Rhóisín and Kathryn Price NicDhana, 2007, http://www.paganachd.com/articles/killyouandeatyou.html

274. These include both prose and poetic *Dindshenchas* in several collections. The Wikipedia article at http://en.wikipedia.org/wiki/Dindsenchas offers links to several collections and translations. Retrieved October 29, 2009.

prodigious feat or miraculous happening, a famous death, or the sundered parts of mythic bodies.

Emain Macha, now known as Armagh, has three origin tales. One of these tales, and probably the best known, involves Macha giving birth to twins immediately after a horse race. Another places her historically as a warrior-queen who defeats the sons of Dithorba. The third tale concerns her taking a cloak pin and delineating the boundaries of the sacred site. In all of these cases, the place is strongly associated with Macha as a sovereignty figure who is ultimately seen as personifying the land itself and whom the king must marry in order to rightly rule the area.[275]

Many practitioners of CR paths engage with spirits through dream work. Journeys into the Otherworlds are also made, as the Otherworlds are believed to be present but unseen in all the places we inhabit. By engaging the spirits on their own ground, we hope to find answers, deal with problems, aid in our healing of self or others, learn new ways of working, and elaborate on our current knowledge. Otherworld journeying in search of wisdom from the spirits that dwell there is a deeply animist act for, along with deity, what other than the wise and powerful spirits of creatures and places will we find there to engage with?

Rituals might be done in any place that is convenient, including living rooms and rented halls, but most practitioners tend to find places on their property or outdoors near where they live that they feel are particularly conducive to contact with deity and spirit. With increasing regular use of these places, connection is felt to grow. Offerings to the spirits of that place are made and dialogue develops through ritual action and Otherworldly response.

Some people develop relationships with places that may be at some distance from their homes by traveling there on a regular basis for ritual. These might include particular wilderness or coastal sites where vigils or other multi-day rituals are done. Dedicatory rituals that establish or deepen relationships between a practitioner and a particular deity or spirit, dream incubation or vision-seeking rites, or ordeal and vigil rituals that test individuals prior to an initiatory experience within the community, are also done in places that are felt to be particularly resonant with spirit.

Most CRs see themselves as having some relationship with the Celtic lands that bore the deities they worship. This relationship

---

275. Rosalind Clark, *The Great Queens: Irish Goddesses from the Morrígan to Cathleen ní Houlihan*, Rosalind Clark, Barnes & Noble, Savage MD, 1991 pp. 112-115

is also seen in the respectful and loving pilgrimages that practitioners make to the holy lands of these origins, leaving offerings at places where the tales describe the deeds of deities and heroes. Coins are offered to springs, holy wells are circumambulated, mountains are climbed as part of ancient patterns of worship, and offerings are laid at the feet of standing stones, while ribbons and rags are tied to the branches of sacred trees, all as a prayer to the powerful spirits of place. While we do not regard the ancient tales as literal history, we do regard them as mythic and spiritual truths that resonate through the ages and teach deep lessons to those who can hear and understand. Through the tales, much of this wisdom is embodied in the memory of the landscape where each mountain and river has a holy, numinous presence.

Our lives are lived among spirits. This is not expressed specifically as totemism or in imitation of First Nations practices, for the Celtic traditions have their own ways of framing this experience. Our ideal is to treat the world and those animate and inanimate beings within it as our relations, knowing we are of the same blood as the seals, the birds, the salmon, and the deer. We offer our gratitude to those plants and animals we must consume to live. We take our relationships with them and with the land upon which we live as sacred. We strive to act in a reciprocal manner, as good and mannerly guests of the spirits of the land on which we live. Our offerings and our prayers are given to the complex flow and intertwining of spirit that makes up the continuum between land, animal, human, ancestor, and deity. It is this shimmering knotwork cord that binds us to the world of spirit.

In my own personal practice, I have close relationships with several animal and plant spirits. I honor them in a variety of ways, from the use of furs, feathers, and bones to the engraving of their images on my skin. I keep an altar specifically for the plant and animal spirits I work with, along with altars for several deities that I worship, and for some of my beloved ancestors. When I walk in the mists between worlds, I call upon the aid of all of them, and offerings are made to each. I have had the experience of animal spirits coming to live within my body, sharing that physical space with me at all times. For me, animism is an intense and practical reality that influences my entire spiritual life and practice. It is the same for many others within the CR movement.

Given the rich history of this acknowledgment of the myriad living spirits within the world, and modern attitudes toward spirit and the land, it is difficult to see CR as anything other than an animist spirituality at its very core. The lives and discussions of CR practitioners are full of references to our work with the spirits of land, trees, animals, mountains, rivers and seas. Our poetry is resonant with animism. Our ritual embodies it at every turn. Our divinatory practices rely upon it. Our spiritual healing appeals to it through prayers and offerings to the spirits of plants, water, and fire. We name our cars and computers, our harps and guitars, and deal with machines in ways that express our deeply animist belief that some of these manufactured objects have personalities, likes, and dislikes; a modern expression of an ancient thread of animism that our Celtic ancestors would doubtless understand.

In the end, we can stand with Amairgen and say,

> *I am a lake in a plain.*
> *I am the excellence of art.*
> *I am a spear that wages battle*[276]

We are one with the living world.

---

276. Koch & Carey, p. 265

Building the Perfect Beast: Questions of Sacrifice and Substitution in Celtic Reconstructionist Religions

The world begins in blood. We are born in the flow of our mothers' blood, and the origin myths of Indo-European cultures often give birth to the cosmos in the blood of a sacrificed cosmic being who is sundered and whose body becomes the world. Birth and death are linked in an ever-moving complex dance of destruction becoming creation. These are the tales of cosmogony, the generation of the universe.

Sacrifice is a troubling question among modern Pagans. Many will insist that no Pagans ever commit acts of sacrifice yet among some Reconstructionist Paganisms such sacrifices, while uncommon, do occur for a variety of reasons. There are many ethical arguments made, both for and against sacrifice. Issues of animal cruelty, killing to eat, and the intentions behind such acts are complex and must be dealt with by any individual who contemplates making an animal sacrifice. Ultimately, the decision to offer such a sacrifice or not rests in the hands of each group or individual.

But why would a modern Pagan consider performing a sacrificial rite involving a living being in the first place? Aren't we "past all that"?

There are several reasons such rituals might be considered appropriate in some communities. In almost every case the sacrificed animal would be consumed by the community after the act itself. One of the few exceptions is when the animal in question is used as a curative substitute, symbolically taking on the illness of an individual or a community in the role of a scapegoat and being killed to expiate misfortune. Under such circumstances the substitute embodies ritual pollution and would be considered unfit to consume.

Generally, though, sacrifice has been historically seen as a positive or constructive act in the communities and religions in which it is found. The animals used in such rituals are raised in the community or purchased specially for the purpose and then eaten by the community or the family after making the sacrifice. It is the blood or the life force along with the symbolic action itself that are considered necessary. One Greek myth even tells the story of why the Gods get the fat and bones while humanity gets the meat for itself.[277]

One of the primary functions of sacrifice in Indo-European cultures is the renewal of the cosmos. In mythic imagining, the world is literally the sundered body of a cosmic being. This living identity emphasizes the sacred nature of the land upon which we live and the importance of the body's symbolic links with the world in which we exist. Microcosm reflects macrocosm and the repeated ritual of sacrifice at regular intervals ensures the continuity of and re-infuses life into the world. The ritual reiteration of the world as a divine body resonates spiritually and offers manifold reasons for the preservation and reverence of the planet and all within its living field.

In Norse myth, the giant Ymir is killed and his body is cut into pieces; Ymir's skull becomes the vault of the sky, his bones the mountains, and his blood the sea.[278] This is paralleled in Hindu cosmology, where the sacrifice by the Brahmins reenacts the death of Purusha, a divine, cosmic being whose body creates the cosmos.[279] Although we do not have a Celtic creation myth preserved in the corpus of written and oral materials, in the *Táin Bó Cúailnge* one of the bulls is sundered and his body becomes the landmark features of the Irish landscape.[280] The process of this sundering resonates with older meaning.

Semitic cultures also had the concept of cosmological sacrifice, as related in the ancient Akkadian epic *Enûma Eliš*, the cuneiform text that describes how the god Marduk killed the sea-being Tiamat and created the land from her dismembered body.[281] The tale was written on clay tablets in about the 18th century BCE.

---

277. Carl Kerényi, *Prometheus: Archetypal Image of Human Existence* (Princeton: Princeton University Press, 1991), p. 43. Prometheus tricks Zeus into choosing the fat and bones of the sacrifice as the share of the Gods while men were given most of the meat and entrails.

278. Patricia Terry, *Poems of the Elder Edda* (Philadelphia: University of Pennsylvania Press, 1990), p. 39, "The Lay of Vafthrudnir," stanzas 21-22.

279. Ralph T. Griffith, *Hinduism: The Rig Veda* (New York: Quality Paperback Book Club, 1992), Book X, Hymn 90, pp. 602-603. Not only is the world composed from his body, so are the castes of humanity, birds, animals, hymns, spells, and charms.

280. Cecile O'Rahilly, *Táin Bó Cúailnge Rescension I* (Dublin: Dublin Institute for Advanced Studies, 1976), p. 237.

281. James B. Pritchard, *The Ancient Near East: An Anthology of Texts and Pictures* (Princeton: Princeton University Press, 1958), pp. 35-36.

If a theology of creation requires death and dismemberment to occur, then it would follow that only the sacrifice of something living would do to fulfill the cosmological purpose of its renewal. Life in this sense could not derive from non-living matter. In these mythologies the living world is created from sundered living flesh. Flesh and life are not created from inert stone or clay as they are in some mythologies where the bodies of the first humans are created from earth with life breathed into them by deity.

This is not to say that monetary and other sacrifices were not made under other circumstances. They obviously were and this method is still being used in our communities, although it is usually in the context of a gift to the Gods rather than of cosmic renewal. Mauss would say that this sort of sacrificial gift creates a mutual relationship between the Gods and the human community that requires a reciprocal gift from the Gods of continued food, shelter, and other necessary survival substances.[282] But, as I've said, these gift exchanges do not serve to renew the cosmos in a theological sense, nor is it their intent. They serve instead to renew community bonds. This is, in itself, and important ritual task.

Some anthropologists and historians have speculated that the sacrifice of animals followed a period of the sacrifice of humans as the vehicle of cosmic renewal. We do know that some Celtic peoples sacrificed prisoners of war[283] and occasionally other humans in some rituals,[284] so they had not left that type of sacrifice behind them entirely before the incursion of Christianity. In the case of the sacrifice of war prisoners, it is possible that what we are looking at are gifts to the Gods or an exchange of life for life on the battlefield. We have no written records from the Celtic peoples themselves regarding this practice so anything we can say would only be speculation.

Other human sacrifices may serve as messengers to the Gods, carrying requests and information that might need to be conveyed by a human carrier. A human sacrifice, particularly as a foundation sacrifice, may serve as a spiritual guardian for the structure being built.[285] Ultimately, at some point, animal sacrifice was apparently

---

282. Marcel Mauss, *The Gift: The Form and Reason for Exchange in Archaic Societies* (New York: W. W. Norton, 1990), pp. 15-17.
283. Bruce Lincoln, *Death, War, and Sacrifice: Studies in Ideology and Practice* (Chicago: University of Chicago Press, 1991), p.183.
284. Ralph Merrifield, *The Archaeology of Ritual and Magic* (New York: New Amsterdam Books, 1987), pp. 24, 43.
285. *Ibid*, pp. 50-51.

substituted for human sacrifice in cosmic renewal ceremonies, as well as in other kinds of sacrifice and divination, so there would seem to be historical precedent for considered changes in this type of ritual.

Reconstructionists make these kinds of considered changes in practice regularly, at least in part because of changes in society that render many rituals illegal, distasteful, or impossible. With these considerations in mind we can see that an animal sacrifice where the animal is later consumed would not necessarily be an act that is either illegal or considered immoral by most people who consume meat. When properly performed, an animal sacrifice can be meaningful to the spiritual community and moving for those in attendance, as well as returning needed food to the community on these occasions. This, of course, leaves aside any arguments based on a theological position of vegetarianism.

We are not, then, looking for an excuse to stop performing the sacrifice due to matters of legality. In the State of Washington, and presumably in any state where kosher and halal slaughter is permitted, the ritual slaughter of animals is specifically defined as legal and humane under freedom of religion statutes.[286]

For some people, a theologically valid way to transform the ideal of sacrifice while maintaining its focus and import, as was done in the alleged transition from human to animal sacrifice, would hold great appeal. To those who are vegetarians, sacrificial rituals that did not involve animals would obviously be infinitely preferable for a variety of reasons. I believe that we can argue for a theologically valid plant-based substitute for the body and soul of an animal.

We know from the story of Miach and Airmed that herbs are associated with different parts of the body -- three hundred sixty five herbs, symbolically for every joint and sinew.[287] We can demonstrate that a suitable sacrificial body may be ritually created, built of herbs. Blodeuedd, the flower-woman, is a Welsh mythological example of a living human being with volition and consciousness who was magically created from herbs.[288] We know that she has mind and agency because she acts against the intentions

---

286. RCW § 16.50.150, retrieved May 8, 2009 from

http://law.onecle.com/washington/animals-and-livestock/16.50.150.html.

287. Elizabeth A. Gray, *Cath Maige Tuired* (London: Irish Texts Society, 1982), pp. 32-33.

288. Patrick K. Ford, *The Mabinogi and Other Medieval Welsh Tales* (Berkeley: University of California Press, 1977), p. 103.

of her creators, exercising her own preferences and planning for her own success independent of any potential programming instilled at her creation.[289] Such a being is no mere mindless golem of plant matter.

We also know from a Welsh medieval medical text, and from Irish tradition, that the body is related to the cosmos in insular Celtic thought. The eyes are stars, sun the face, breath the wind, stone as bones, water as blood, soil as flesh, and so on.[290] I would argue that through these associations, a living "human" body could be created of ritually appropriate plants to serve as the vehicle of cosmic renewal. In this way, the death and dismemberment of the "herbal body" would serve as the living force that is the source of cosmic creation and its renewal during ceremonies with that intent.

The sacrifice of plants is not invalid as a sacrifice of spiritual efficacy. In an animist theology, plants have sentient spirits no less than humans or animals. I would argue that plants are in fact more important than humans or animals in a biological sense, for without plants, the energy of the sun cannot be transformed into food and oxygen, and no life would exist without them. Plants can exist without us, but without them there is no possibility of independent animal life. The life force of a plant can, therefore, be considered just as pure and acceptable for sacrifice as would the life of a cow or a human being. From the point of view of primacy, it might even be considered more acceptable, more pure, as these beings are closer to the primal source of solar energy than we. Individual plants lack only the social construct of the complete human body to be an acceptable substitute for the human being. But as we have seen, this can be attained through symbolic ritual.

The question then becomes, what plants would be appropriate as sacrifices? How many, and what must they symbolize? There are several ways we can approach this question. Lists of sacred plants like the listing of woods for a sacred fire found in the *Carmina Gadelica* might be a place to start for Gaelic Reconstructionists.[291]

---

289. *Ibid*, pp. 104-105.

290. See Whitley Stokes, " Mythological Notes VI: Man octipartite," *Revue Celtique* I (1870–1872), pp. 261–62; J. M. Evans, "Microcosmia Adam," *Medium Ævum* XXXV (1966), pp. 38–42; Hildegard Tristram, "Der homo octopartitus in der irischen und altenglischen Literatur," *Zeitschrift für Celtische Philologie* XXXIV (1975), pp. 119–53.

291. Alexander Carmichael, *Carmina Gadelica*, 6 vols. (Edinburgh: Scottish Academic Press, 1978), Vol. 4, pp. 102-103.

Another approach we can use for choosing appropriate plants is to look at their functions. As an example, plants are used for food (oats), for medicines (foxglove), for fiber (flax), for fuel (alder), and for their entheogenic properties (belladonna). We could examine the herbal lore of the Celtic peoples and choose plants from these categories that also represent the various parts of the body to use as the sacrifice. Plants used as entheogens seem quite appropriate for use to symbolize the soul of the cosmic being, for instance, or to symbolize the head which is the seat of the soul and the vault of the heavens. Food plants might symbolize the flesh. Medicines can serve to symbolize many different parts of the body, as they are used to treat the different organs and body systems. Fiber plants might symbolize hair or the skin covering the body. Fuel plants might represent the spark of life, but they would also be used to burn the sacrifice during the ritual, so they would not be necessary to the construction of the herbal body. Magico-medical sources using the medieval doctrine of signatures would also be a way to determine suitable plants for the different parts of the body.[292]

In doing this kind of a sacrifice, I would argue the plants would have to be fresh. The life force would have to still be within them in order for the sacrifice to be useful or valid in a theological sense, as a living substitute. Going out and buying dried roots and leaves would not hold the same energies as growing or wildcrafting the appropriate plants. It is not a sacrifice of life and spirit if the spirit and the power of the living green left the plants six months ago. Lack of spirit invalidates a sacrifice as a meaningful ritual, meant to connect us with the necessity of an immediate and felt death in preparation for cosmic re-creation. There is little emotional impact in burning the dried dust of leaves, while the burning of freshly harvested plants would connect us with the death of the green being. The sap of life should still run through them, preferably having been harvested in a ritual manner shortly in advance of the sacrifice. According to the ideals of cosmological sacrifice, the plants used would have to be free of blemish so that the world when renewed would be likewise perfect in body and potential.

Although Celtic lore regarding plant associations with the body is essential knowledge, I believe that we also have to consider the implications of attempting to sacrifice plants not grown in native soil, aside from the difficulty of obtaining fresh non-native plant

---

292. John Lust, *The Herb Book* (New York, NY: Bantam, 1974) p. 599.

materials. What local plants carry the same symbolic significance as the ritual plants of Celtic Europe? As modern Celtic Reconstructionists, scattered all over the globe and born of many different ethnic backgrounds, I believe we must renew the local cosmos through the use of locally grown plants for this kind of sacrifice. This would necessitate close observation of local plant lore, and the development of relationships with local plant spirits so that we begin to understand how they fit into the herbal body. Blodeuedd's creation would be different in Minnesota than it was in Wales, different again in Sydney or Vladivostok. If our spirituality includes a deep and true connection with the land on which we live, we must take these things into consideration and develop a theology of place and of what Gary Snyder refers to as reinhabitation.[293] The essence of the soil where we live must enter us physically and spiritually, must link us with the spirits of the place.

Some ritual would need to be devised to take the chosen diverse plants and "birth" them together as one living being, whole in the sense of a cosmic and divine body. It would have to transform them from a group of separate plant-beings into the divine body of the sacrifice, to unify their spirits into one perfect soul. This, of course, is not necessary in the case of animals or humans, because they are already a single, discrete life force and body. The spell that created Blodeuedd must be spoken, as it were. From that point, the sacrifice could proceed as the ritual of death and dismemberment, with the burning of the plants to release the spirit-body and its component parts in the act of cosmic renewal.

The next question is, who deals with this kind of sacrifice? In Celtic societies, Druids claimed that they created the universe and, through this form of cosmogonic sacrifice, it could be said that they indeed did so. Druids acted as sacrificing priests, according to the Greeks and Romans who encountered them in Gaul,[294] and were capable of excommunicating people from sacrifice if they violated the laws of the tribe.[295] Among the Hindus, it is the Brahmins who perform these sacrifices.

Given this evidence, is cosmological sacrifice really something that can be performed in an egalitarian fashion, with any celebrant in a group capable of playing the part of sacrificing Druid?

---

293. Gary Snyder, "Reinhabitation" in *A Place in Space: Ethics, Aesthetics, and Watersheds* (Washington, D.C.: Counterpoint, 1995), pp. 183-191.

294. John T. Koch and John Carey (eds.), *The Celtic Heroic Age*, Fourth Edition (Aberystwyth and Andover: Celtic Studies Publications, 2003), p. 14.

295. *Ibid.*, p. 21.

Will anyone who has been ritually purified be acceptable as the sacrificer? Should the sacrificer be one who has not killed in battle? One who has not violated certain laws of the land?

If people could be excommunicated from participation in the sacrifice as observers, it would stand to reason that some crimes would disqualify people from actually making the sacrifice. If these things are important, should the one who performs the sacrifice be required to be someone who identifies as a Druid or, rather, someone whom a community acclaims as its Druid? Should it be someone who has studied Celtic lore and theology enough to understand the implications of sacrifice and renewal? I maintain that a baseline of appropriate knowledge and of ritual purity within a given community's guidelines is necessary for the sacrifice to be valid.

If it is an animal rather than an herbal sacrifice, it is essential that the sacrificer be skilled in the humane killing of animals so that the sacrificed creature does not suffer unnecessarily. A botched sacrifice would be, at the very least, an extremely ill omen, as well as being pointlessly cruel. If the animal struggles and dies badly, this reflects badly on the sacrificer and the community and imperils the entire purpose of the ritual itself, as well as simply being cruel. It seems obvious that some training would be required for the effective sacrifice of an animal and that previous experience on a farm with the slaughter of food animals would be a bare minimum requirement.

What should be the ritual state of mind required of the sacrificer? Obviously there is more going on internally than just going through the motions of a slaughter. To perform the ritual without the proper intent and the proper state of spiritual purity would be more sacrilege than sacrifice. To attain the proper intent and the proper state of purity would likely be the work of a great deal of training and meditation, along with a certain amount of ascetic practice. At a minimum, one would have to be able to perform the ritual while maintaining the required state of mind and visualizations without falling prey to distractions. The outer form of the ritual would also have to be done flawlessly for the cosmological renewal to be perfect. The intent and focus of the assistants and witnesses to the ritual must likewise be pure, although perhaps not as flawless as the state of the one who must physically perform the sacrifice. If we follow the logic of the ritual itself, anything less endangers the very renewal of the cosmos. In taking this seriously, these considerations argue against the idea that anyone who feels like it can perform a cosmological sacrifice, whether animal or herbal, without first intensively practicing both the outer and inner techniques and understanding the theological implications.

I believe that animal or herbal-being sacrifice for purposes other than cosmological renewal can be a valid practice for groups that have the resources and can afford to honor the deities in this way. Sacrifice for the foundation of a home or a sacred grove, for example, might be a festive and meaningful occasion resulting in a feast shared with the entire local community. Regardless, such practices require a great deal of thought and both self- and group-examination before enactment. The ethical implications should be considered, as should the humane treatment of any animal chosen for the role of sacrifice. The officiant should have experience with animals and a solid background in the lore and theologies that form the basis for the ritual and its justifications.

In a world whose ecosystems are collapsing, whose animal life is dying in massive extinctions, and whose people are indiscriminately slaughtering each other in acts of war and genocide it might be reasonable to consider the option of cosmic renewal sacrifices. Our communities talk about acts of magic as social activism. Rituals are held to "heal the earth" at many festivals throughout the Western Pagan world. Perhaps it is time to consider cosmic renewal sacrifices as another tool to renew the lost balance.

Queering the Flame: Brigit, Flamekeeping, and Gender in Celtic Reconstructionist Pagan Communities

I began tending Brigit's flame in 1993, at the founding of Daughters of the Flame, a women-only order of flamekeepers based in Vancouver, Canada. To this day, with more-or-less steady regularity, I light her flame upon an altar in my home every twenty days and keep it burning for twenty-four hours. I attempt to remain mindful of this Goddess and to dedicate my creativity and my work on these days to her. This practice has been a deeply significant part of my spiritual life for over twenty years.

Flametending has been a rhythmic, almost tidal support to my spiritual and creative life. The regular presence of the flame on the altar near my writing desk is a tangible reminder of Brigit and of her patronage of poets, of the accessibility of inspiration, and of the dedication necessary to nurture a life as a poet and writer. Each time I light the flame, I renew my devotion to creativity as a deep and necessary part of my spiritual path.

In 2006, Brigid's Irregulars, a Celtic Reconstructionist (CR) focused mixed-gender order of Brigit devotees and flamekeepers was founded, its advent marked by a great deal of controversy within the CR community. I was one of several individuals involved in the founding of Brigid's Irregulars. Critics of the group said that flamekeeping had traditionally been a woman's prerogative and to allow men to do so was unacceptable; it was even called "blasphemy" when the concept was under discussion.

Brigid's Irregulars was by no means the first mixed-gender flamekeeping order; that distinction belongs to Ord Brigideach, founded by a former member of the Daughters of the Flame in 1998. Brigid's Irregulars was the only specifically CR flamekeeping group that I'm aware of, as both the Daughters of the Flame and Ord Brigidheach are open to people of any faith. Over the last decade a number of other groups, both women-only and mixed-gender, have come and gone, demonstrating a need in the community that some groups have been able to hook into and support.

Women in the CR movement, and in western society generally, are fighting for a release from restrictive traditional gender roles and an expansion of the rights of women and the gender-variant. We take on employment and social roles that were traditionally reserved for men and strive for the freedom to define ourselves as we will. We point to rare historical and mythic examples of women breaking gender roles in Irish and other Celtic cultures, even when there is little evidence that actual living women did these things regularly. We assert that the past should inspire us, not chain us. Yet in this one thing, some members of the CR community argue that gender should be the absolute defining factor. Why?

What would make the act of tending a perpetual flame in the name of a particular Goddess problematic or contentious? What are the theological assumptions at work, and why is gender such a central issue within some of those assumptions? More importantly for this essay, what does queerness have to do with it?

To address these issues, we need to look at the person and place of Brigit as Goddess and saint, the practice of flamekeeping generally, and the ritual traditions that surround this act. Sacred perpetual flames are not unheard-of in the context of Pagan religions, though they are by no means a universal feature of such. Both the Greek deities Athene and Hephaistos had perpetual flames; while the flame in the temple of Athene was tended by a married priestess, the flame at the temple of Hephaistos was, presumably, tended by a man.[296] The Prytanaeon in Athens housed a perpetual flame dedicated to Hestia, as well.[297]

The most famous perpetual flame of the ancient world was that of the temple of Vesta in Rome, which was tended by the Vestal Virgins, a group of women who served for thirty years and were constrained to virginity during that time, on pain of death by whipping and burial alive.[298] While they had a great deal of stature within Roman society, their activities and sphere of influence were extremely restricted.

In early Ireland, Brigit's flame was not the only perpetual flame being tended in a sacred context. Three other perpetual flames were mentioned in the historical record, all kept at Christian monasteries and tended by men. The church of St. Molaise, called *Teach-na-Teinedh* or "Church of the Flame," located on the island of

---

296. Karl Kerenyi, *Athene: Virgin and Mother in Greek Religion*, Spring Publications (Woodstock, 1978), p. 78

297. John M. Camp, *The Archaeology of Athens*, Yale University Press (New Haven, 2001), p. 27

298. John X.W.P. Corcoran, "Roman Mythology," in *New Larousse Encyclopedia of Mythology*, Prometheus Press (New York, 1968), pp. 204-205

Inishmurray off the Sligo coast, was one of these.[299] All three are briefly described in a passage from the *Life of St. Magnenn of Kilmainham*.

> This is then my counsel to thee, holy bishop. Farther yet: to thy successors' see great prerogatives shall belong, and in Ireland thy fire shall be the third on which privilege [of sanctity] shall be conferred, i.e. the fire of the elder Lianan of Kinvarra, the lively and perennial fire that is in Inishmurray [in Sligo bay] and bishop Magnenn's fire in Kilmainham.[300]

These sacred fires, both in Rome and in Ireland, were considered community hearthfires, regardless of the gender of the flamekeepers. Regional ritual fires were lit from the Irish flames, as were household flames on particular holy days, and if a household's flame were accidentally extinguished, it also would be relit from the sacred flame. The hearthstone at Inishmurray is specifically cited as a source for the relighting of household flames, even after the church itself was long-deserted and the physical flame extinguished:

> On this flag, or fire-stone, fire was always kept burning by the monks for the use of the islanders. In later times, when monks no longer inhabited the cashel, whenever a householder wanted kindling for the family fire, a sod of turf or a piece of wood deposited on this holy hearth ignited spontaneously.[301]

Brigit's perpetual flame is originally, and most famously, mentioned in the 12th century account of Gerald of Wales from the record of his travels in Ireland. It is in this text that we are told that the flame could not be approached by men.

---

299. W. G. Wood-Martin, *Traces of the Elder Faiths of Ireland*, Longmans, Green & Co. (London, 1902), pp. 278-279
300. Standish H. O'Grady, *Silva Gadelica: A collection of Tales in Irish with Extracts Illustrating Persons and Places* (vol 2), Williams and Norgate (London, 1892), p. 41 Bracketed comments added by O'Grady.
301. Wood-Martin, p. 279

This fire is circular and surrounded by a hedge made of withies, and which no male may cross. And if by chance one does dare enter – and some rash people have at times tried it – he does not escape the divine vengeance. Only women are allowed to blow the fire, and then not with the breath of their mouths but only with bellows or winnowing forks.[302]

Gerald tells us of two different men who are injured by the flame:

At Kildare an archer of the household of earl Richard crossed over the hedge and blew upon Brigid's fire. He jumped back immediately and went mad. Whomesoever he met, he blew upon his face and said: 'See! That is how I blew on Brigid's fire.'

And so he ran through all the houses of the whole settlement, and wherever he saw a fire he blew upon it using the same words. Eventually he was caught and bound by his companions, but asked to be brought to the nearest water. As soon as he was brought there, his mouth was so parched that he drank so much that, while still in their hands, he burst in the middle and died.

Another who, upon crossing over to the fire, had put one shin over the hedge, was hauled back and restrained by his companions. Nevertheless the foot that had crossed perished immediately with its shank. Ever afterwards, while he lived, he was lame and feeble as a consequence.[303]

In Gerald's account, it should be noted that both of these men take deliberate action to insult the flame itself or in some way violate its sanctity. Could it have been this violation that was supposed to have caused madness or injury to the man in question, rather than

---

302. Gerald of Wales, *The History and Topography of Ireland*, Penguin (New York, 1982), p. 82
303. *ibid*, p. 88

simply his gender? He does not say no man may see the flame, nor does he describe the height of the withy enclosure; it is likely that men could view the flame over the hedge, considering his descriptions of the apparent ease with which the hedge was climbed over. The physical hedge itself may have been a largely symbolic separation from the rest of the community.

It is also important to remember that Gerald of Wales, in his writings, was playing to a Norman audience, pointing out the allegedly superstitious, primitive, and uncivilized nature of the Irish in comparison to the supposedly more rational and civilized citizens of his own country. We do not know how reliable he was as a narrator, and many of his tales involve creatures and situations we know to be impossible, like most other extant ancient and Medieval travel accounts.

We find that the male-tended perpetual flame at *Teach-na-Teinnedh* also destroyed those who would desecrate it, even after the flame itself had been extinguished and only the hearthstone was left. Wood-Martin notes:

> Not many years ago, if dependence can be placed on oral tradition, a Scotchman had the profane assurance, whilst visiting the island, to desecrate the sacred firestone of St. Molaise. Though generally reputed to be of placid temperament, the insulted saint and patron of the island implored his God to work a miracle for the confusion of the impious miscreant, whereupon a supernatural flame, issuing from the "fire-stone," reduced the wretch to a cinder, and the islanders still point out his calcined bones, deposited on the site of the hearthstone, as a warning to unbelievers.[304]

Given this account, we can infer that it is, in fact, desecration rather than simply viewing or proximity that is the salient point in the destruction of the miscreant. It is not the gender of the flamekeepers here that is relevant, but the fact that the fire itself is sacred and has been desecrated. It is the fire's inherent sacrality that triggers disaster when it is defiled, if we consider that the results are the same, no matter which sacred fire is disturbed.

---

304. Wood-Martin, p. 279

Another account of the desecration of a sacred flame tells of the sacred fire at the monastery of Saigyr, extinguished by a young man from the company of Saint Ciaran:

A certain boy of the company of holy Kiaranus, called Crithir of Cluain (a boy of great wit, but hurtful and wanton) fled from Saint Kiaranus to the settlement of Saigyr, in the northern border of Mumonia, that is, the land of Hele, to the other Kiaranus, the most holy aged bishop. And that boy, sojourning for some days with the holy bishop, after his devilish manner took the drink of the brethren, and poured it over the fire; extinguishing thus the consecrated fire. Now Saint Kiaranus the elder would have no other fire in his monastery save the consecrated fire, maintained without being extinguished from Easter to Easter. When Saint Kiaranus the elder heard what the boy Crithir did, it greatly displeased him, and he said, "Let him be chastened for this of God in this life." When he heard that Saint Kiaranus the elder was angry with him, he went out from the settlement of Saigyr, and when he was gone a short space from the settlement, wolves met him and killed him; yet they did not touch his body after he was dead, after the likeness of that prophet who was killed by the lion.

Now when Saint Kiaranus the younger heard that his boy had been with Kiaranus the elder, he went to him; and on the day when the aforesaid things took place, he came to the settlement of Saigyr and was received with fitting honour by the holy bishop Kiaranus the elder. And the holy abbot Kiaranus the younger said to the holy bishop Kiaranus, "Restore to me, holy father, my disciple alive, who hath been slain while with thee." To him Saint Keranus the elder said, "First needs must your feet be washed, but we have no fire in the monastery, to warm the water for you; and ye know that it is because your disciple quenched our sacred fire. Wherefore beseech for us consecrated fire from God." Then the holy abbot Kieranus the younger, son of the wright, stretched his hands in prayer to God, and straightway fire from heaven came into his breast, and thence was the hearth kindled in the monastery.

But the holy bishop Kiaranus the elder prayed to God for that youth slain by wolves, and straightway he arose sound from a cruel death, with the scars of the wolf-bites visible upon him. And blessing them all, he took food and drink with the saints, and afterwards he lived many days.[305]

Unlike the other accounts, after this deliberate desecration of a sacred flame, the punishment inflicted on the miscreant was reversed, and the flame itself was miraculously rekindled. Crithir, still scarred with the bitemarks of wolves upon him, is raised from his grave and restored to life. It also seems noteworthy that the flame itself was not set apart from the group in any way. It appears to have been being used as a central hearth around which the monks and their guests sat as they were eating and drinking, easily available for a deliberate dousing by a "hurtful and wanton" young man. This strongly emphasizes the community hearth aspect of the sacred flame.

A second account of this incident specifies that the sacred flame was in the kitchen, which further emphasizes its accessibility.[306]

Carrying this theme from sacred fire to sacred water (in which flame dwells), we find similar prohibitions against desecration. In the *dindshenechas*, the place-name tales of Ireland, we read of the deaths of two women who approach sacred wells without authority or proper ritual protection in the tales of Siannan and Bóand. These wells, said to belong to Connla or Nechtán, were regarded as the otherworldly well of wisdom, with a fire or a light

---

305. R. A. Stewart-Macalister, *The Latin and Irish Lives of Ciaran*, The Society for Promoting Christian Knowledge (New York, 1921) pp. 36-37 The First Latin Life of St Ciaran manuscript dates to the late 15th century.
306. *Ibid* p. 93 The Irish Life also dates to a late 15th century manuscript, but Macalister suggests the material dates to perhaps the 11th century, with some segments being of earlier provenance. (see pp. 4 and 7)

representing sacred, poetic knowledge (*imbas*) at their hearts.[307] In both cases, the woman approaching the sacred spring is pursued by the holy water within and rent asunder, leaving a river in her wake – in the case of Sinann, the Shannon,[308] and of Bóand, the Boyne.[309] We can see here that it is not solely men who are at risk in approaching sacred sites without permission or with the wrong attitude. The account of Bóand states explicitly that she went to challenge the power of the well:

Hither came on a day white Bóand
(her noble pride uplifted her),
to the never-failing well
to make trial of its power.

As thrice she walked around
about the well heedlessly,
three waves burst from it,
whence came the death of Bóand.[310]

Sinann's challenge is made even more explicit:

One night this lovely maiden,
this sweet, full-mouthed woman,
thought she had nearly everything,
only the imbas she was lacking.

So one day, this shapely beauty
came to the river to see;
she saw, indeed couldn't miss,
the glorious bubbles of imbas.

The girl, proud as she was,
leapt in to seize the bubbles;
but the effort came to naught there
for she drowned; and thus the Shannon river.[311]

---

307. Patrick Ford, "The Well of Nechtan and 'La Gloire Lumineuse'" in *Myth in Indo-European Antiquity*, ed. Gerald James Larson, University of California Press (Berkeley, 1974), pp. 67-74

308. Edward Gwynn (trans), *Metrical Dindshenechas*, (1905), Sinann I and Sinnan II, pp. 288-298 (poems 53 & 54)

309. *ibid*, Boand I and Boand II, pp. 28-39 (poems 2 & 3)

310. *ibid*, p. 31

Brigit's association with multiple holy wells in Ireland offers some resonance to these *dindshenechas* tales. Patrick Logan lists fifteen different wells dedicated to her in his short study, *The Holy Wells of Ireland*.[312] I do not doubt that there are more than he lists. Holy wells are associated with particular rituals that must be adhered to in approaching them in order to gain the benefit of the well's power. These rituals included circumambulations and prayers that must be performed in specific ways. Brigit's status as a goddess or patron of poets offers an interesting link to the idea of the power of the otherworldly wells of Connla and Nechtán, both of which were approached for access to poetic inspiration and arcane wisdom. Nechtán's well at the source of the Boyne is said to physically exist as what is now called Trinity Well near Carbury. It is, perhaps significantly, found in county Kildare, which is the seat of the Christian cult of Saint Brigit.[313]

Saint Brigit's abbey at Cill Dara, known today as Kildare, was a site where both men and women were cloistered. While Gerald says that only nuns tended the flame, the compound itself was not solely restricted to women. Indeed, when Saint Brigit died, she was buried next to the bishop Conlaed, who was also her smith, though the altar was kept between them. It is therefore possible that the female-only character of the flame's enclosure was simply part of the function of this double monastery's regular separation of the sexes by a partition in the body of the church -- a normal occurrence at all mixed monasteries -- and might not have been a theological position regarding either the flame itself or any holdover of attitudes regarding Brigit as a Goddess. Lisa M. Bitel notes:

> The segregation of sexes had a firm [Christian] theological foundation. Eighth-century canonists decreed that no women were to enter the holiest space of the enclosure, its sanctuary. Even when they came to church with men, women were socially segregated by their need to maintain the strictest of Pauline silences. The principle on which canonists based gender segregation is not hard to detect: the equation of women with sexual sin,

---

311. Patrick K. Ford, *The Celtic Poets: Songs and Tales from Early Ireland and Wales*, Ford & Bailie (Belmont, 1999), p. 45

312. Patrick Logan, *The Holy Wells of Ireland*, Colin Smythe Ltd. (Gerrards Cross, 1980)

313. *ibid*, p.48

which we have already encountered. Keeping women apart from men and confining them together seemed safer than turning them loose within the churchyard. At Christian sites, theologically informed misogyny was as strong a force as legal restriction or economic utility in pushing women into social spaces shared with other women, not men.[314]

There is no mention of a perpetual flame in Cogitosus's 7th century *Life of St. Brigit*. Lacking mention in such a detailed description of the site, it is very likely that the perpetual flame was lit sometime after about 650 CE when Cogitosus wrote; in the 12th century, when Gerald traveled, the flame had already been in existence for a long time. The flame was briefly extinguished in 1220, so had obviously been an established part of Brigidine tradition by the 13th century, some six centuries after Cogitosus. We do not know if Brigit's flame genuinely dates back to the Pagan period. There is no physical evidence of a pre-Christian perpetual flame at Kildare. Of course, given that there are no Pagan written records, we have no way of knowing what was happening before Christianity's arrival; all records of Brigit and her flame must be seen as part of a Christian context unless further evidence comes to light.

The name of the site itself – Cill Dara, a specifically Christian place-name -- argues fairly strongly against a pre-Christian origin of the flame and the practice. There are no known *dindshenechas* regarding the origins of Kildare, and *cill* place-names are of specifically Christian origin.[315] Had the site been spiritually significant to the indigenous Pagan population, it – like so many others – would certainly have rated a tale in either the poetic or prose *dindshenechas*, though it may have been described under some other, original name. These tales are, in a sense, the genealogy of the land as it passed from Pagan to Christian political power.

Another interesting point is the role of fire in the struggle between Paganism and Christianity as exemplified by Saint Patrick's lighting of a "Passover" (Easter) fire on the hill of Tara.

---

314. Lisa M. Bitel, *Land of Women: Tales of Sex and Gender from Early Ireland*, Cornell University Press (Cornell, 1996), p. 155

315. *Cill* means, specifically, a church or an ecclesiastical or monastic settlement. DIL s.v. *cell*. A place-name with such an element, and no previous name or lore connected with it, must by definition be of Christian origin.

Muirchú's 7th century *Life of Patrick* describes the reaction of the druids when the fire is seen by king Loíguire:

> The wise men answered: "'O king, live forever!'
> This fire, which we see lit this night before the fire
> of your own house, must be quenched this night.
> Indeed, if it is not put out tonight, it will never be
> extinguished! You should know that it will keep
> rising up and supplant all the fires of our own
> religion. The one who lit it, and the kingdom he is
> bringing upon us this night, will overcome us all —
> both you and us — by leading away everyone in
> your kingdom. All the kingdoms will fall down
> before it, and it will fill the whole country and it
> 'shall reign forever and ever.'"[316]

It is extremely unlikely that this legendary Pagan fire was lit on Easter, as no native Irish festival takes place at that time of year. It is more likely that the supposed event occurred on Bealtaine, when all the fires of the countryside were traditionally doused and then relit from sacred bonfires on the hilltops.[317] I believe this sheds a different and distinctly Christian light on the idea of a perpetual flame, as opposed to the annually extinguished fires of Irish Pagan society; the idea that Patrick's flame would perpetually rule over Ireland seems a reasonable argument for the keeping of symbolic perpetual flames in Christian monastic communities.

Regarding the subject of the Christian Saint Brigit and the virginal status of those who tended her flame, Brigit herself was aggressively virginal, going as far as putting out one of her eyes in order to remain unmarried and unmolested. The life of Brigit known as *Bethu Brigte* says:

> Her brothers were grieved at her depriving them
> of the bride-price. There were poor people living
> close to Dubthach's house. She went one day
> carrying a small load for them. Her brothers, her
> father's sons, who had come from Mag Lifi, met
> her. Some of them were laughing at her; others

---

316. "The Life of Patrick by Muirchú," in Oliver Davies (trans. & ed.) *Celtic Spirituality*, Paulist Press (New York 1999), p. 100
317. Wood-Martin, pp. 261-262

were not pleased with her, namely Bacéne, who said: 'The beautiful eye which is in your head will be betrothed to a man though you like it or not.' Thereupon she immediately thrusts her finger into her eye. 'Here is that beautiful eye for you', said Brigit. 'I deem it unlikely', said she, 'that anyone will ask you for a blind girl.' Her brothers rush about her at once save that there was no water near them to wash the wound. 'Put', said she, 'my staff about this sod in front of you.' That was done. A stream gushed forth from the earth. And she cursed Bacéne and his descendants, and said: 'Soon your two eyes will burst in your head.' And it happened thus.[318]

The Goddess Brigit, on the other hand, is known to have been married twice and has four named sons.[319] Given this difference, it is reasonable to suppose that virginity would not be required of Brigit's Pagan priestesses, presuming that there was a perpetual flame kept in her honor before the founding of the abbey at Kildare.

It is also worth pointing out that when we examine the place of Brigit (possibly as Brigantia) in insular Celtic society, it is Minerva to whom she is compared, not Vesta.[320] If we follow this connection through its links to the Greek Athene, we find another perpetual flame, previously mentioned, this one tended by married women. Brigit is associated not strictly with hearth fires, but also with the usually "masculine" occupations of smithcraft and poetry. She may also be associated with warriors,[321] as Brig Ambue, lending further resonance to the thought that a Pagan perpetual flame (if the Kildare flame was not actually Christian in origin) might not have been "vestal" in character, nor might it have been restricted only to women.

In looking at gender in conjunction with Brigit in Irish folk practice, we find instances where gender is deliberately confused or obfuscated. In Imbolc processions, cross-dressing is practiced in

---

318. Donncha Ó hAodha, *Bethu Brigte*, Dublin Institute for Advanced Studies (Dublin, 1978), p. 23
319. Peter Berresford Ellis, *A Dictionary of Irish Mythology*, Oxford University Press (Oxford 1991), p. 50
320. Proinsias MacCana, *Celtic Mythology*, Hamlyn (New York, 1970) pp. 34-35
321. Phillip A. Bernhardt-House, "Imbolc: A New Interpretation," *Cosmos* 18 (2002), pp. 57-66

several locations. This cross-dressing is not the strict property of one gender. Both males and females engage in this behaviour in a variety of regions.[322] Séamas Ó Catháin quotes a report of this ritual cross-dressing:

> The *Brídeog* procession from house to house was and still is held on the eve of the feast. Both boys and girls took part and there are sometimes two or three (or more) groups, each group out for itself in an area of a square mile according as the district is thickly populated or not. Sometimes during the last week in January the young people who may be of any age up to twenty years, gather at a certain house in the kitchen or barn of which the rehearsals take place. Boys dress in girls' clothes as a rule and vice versa.[323]

This same account further states:

> ...Priests; were always against girls taking part in the processions and whenever they met them, they were sure to take the disguises off the *Brídeogs* to find out if there were girls among them. Should a girl be found, she was severely reprimanded by the priest and sent home. Boys were allowed to carry on.[324]

This priestly disapproval certainly points to something transgressive and possibly pagan in origin, if it isn't simply Christian misogyny in action. A county Kerry account of a *Brídeog* procession implies that it originally was undertaken by young girls, but that boys were eventually allowed to join this procession as well:

> On St. Brigid's Day, people still go out in the *Brideog* in this area. Long ago it was the girls up to fourteen years of age or thereabouts who used to

---

322. Seán Ó Duinn,*The Rites of Brigid, Goddess and Saint*, Columba Press (Dublin, 2005), p. 85, men cross-dressing
323. Séamas Ó Catháin, *The Festival of Brigit: Celtic Goddess & Holy Woman*, DBA Publications (Dublin, 1995), p. 10
324. *ibid*, p. 11

go around but nowadays young boys go around as
well.[325]

This demonstrates that traditions have changed in regard to the
procession carrying the image of the saint – or the Goddess. If this
traditional gender restriction was lifted over time in regards to folk
practices surrounding Brigit and her rituals, the implications for the
ways we approach flametending are significant.

Other times of year had elements of cross-dressing as well.
Bealtaine's May Queen, in some districts, was a cross-dressed
male.[326] It is possible that the liminality of these quarter days was
important, and that cross-dressing expressed the ambiguity of a
time and place where Otherworldly powers could break through
into the mundane world.

In the debate regarding the sanctity of the flame and the
necessity of its isolation from the male gaze, modern Irish practice
should be mentioned. CR places a great deal of importance upon
living Celtic cultures, stating that respect is a necessary component,
even if what we are doing is not the same. Great importance has
been placed, in Ireland, on giving Brigit's flame to the world as a
symbol of peacemaking and unity. It was initially kindled in 1993 in
the Kildare Market Square by Sister Mary Teresa Cullen, in full view
of the public, indicating the original intent of the Brigidine sisters to
make Brigit's flame available to everyone in modern times.

This is particularly relevant given that, on Imbolc of 2006,
Brigit's flame was specifically and deliberately given to the world,
being lit in the town square of Kildare by the then-president of
Ireland, Mary McAleese. The flame is kept publicly in a sculpture
commissioned for that purpose, visible and accessible to everyone.
Her flame is passed to anyone who asks by the Brigidine sisters at
Solas Bhríde, and the altar at their shrine is open to men and women
equally, though only the sisters currently tend the flame housed
there.

Most arguments for women-only flamekeeping in the CR
community fall into one of the following categories:

1.   Brigit's flame is theologically similar to the Vestal flame
and male presence defiles it. Only women kept Brigit's flame at the
abbey: it is traditional and we cannot change this tradition.

---

325. Ó Duinn (2004), p. 85
326. Kevin Danaher, *The Year in Ireland*, Mercier Press (Minneapolis, 1972), p. 103

2.   Hearth fires are a female prerogative and men cannot be involved in this feminine mystery.

3.   Being in the presence of Brigit's flame is hazardous to men.

4.   Women's space is critically important to women's spirituality and autonomy and therefore no men should be allowed to appropriate or participate in this woman-specific spiritual practice.

Many people arguing from the position that the flame is similar or equivalent to the Vestal flame in Rome are not aware of the Greek perpetual flame of Athena, kept by married women. This practice does not follow the requirements of the Vestals. If we argue that the flame must only be kept by women because we are following the Vestal model, not only are we ignoring evidence of male-tended flames and flames tended by married women, we are placing ourselves in a slippery slope position where we may eventually find ourselves arguing that, like the Vestal flame or the flame at the abbey at Kildare, it must then be kept by unmarried, childless, sexually chaste virgins who live apart from society in cloister, and whose virginity must be kept at all costs. If this were a requirement, not many people would be tending Brigit's flame today. Very few adult Pagan women could likely fulfill these qualifications, even if they were lesbians. It is possible that even Saint Brigit herself didn't fill this Vestal level of qualification.[327]

This necessity for virginity within the cloister was such an imperative that rape was used to depose at least one abbess at Kildare. In 1132, men under the orders of Diarmait mac Murchada committed rape against the sitting abbess in order to disqualify her from her position, and mac Murchada subsequently installed one of his own relatives as the new abbess so as to appropriate Kildare's political and religious power in the region.[328] I would not like to believe that women who have been sexually assaulted would be barred from being flamekeepers and participating in what can be a profoundly healing spiritual practice.

---

327. Some authors suggest that Brigit's relationship with her successor, Darlugdacha, was a lesbian relationship. They are said to have shared a bed, and sexual relationships between women were certainly not unknown in early Ireland. Peter Berresford Ellis, *Celtic Women: Women in Celtic Society and Literature*, Wm. B. Eerdmans Publishing (Grand Rapids, 1995), pp. 125-126, p. 149

328. Lisa M. Bitel, *Land of Women: Tales of Sex and Gender from Early Ireland*, Cornell University Press (Cornell 1996) p. 224

If we argue that hearth fires are purely a woman's prerogative and that men cannot partake in this particular activity, we need to account for the existence of male-tended sacred perpetual flames at monasteries in Ireland, like the one on Inishmurray. This flamekeeping practice was so ingrained in custom that, long after the monastery itself had fallen into disrepair, the hearthstone at *Teach-na-Teinnedh* was said to magically light a sod of turf or a piece of wood laid upon it, even without the presence of the monks.

The tales of Gerald of Wales regarding the madness and death of men who came in contact with Brigit's flame are, as noted above, accounts of men who deliberately acted to defile the flame's sanctity. We also find this theme at the male-tended hearth of Inishmurray and the flame at the monastery of Ciaran at Saigyr. The approach itself may not have been the key factor, but rather the intent of the man to violate the flame or the hearthstone. It seems likely that, had a woman approached the flame with an intent to desecrate it, a similar fate might have befallen her.

Likewise, as noted above, the women approaching the wells of Connla and Nechtán were punished for their transgressions against this manifestation of fire-in-water associated with poetry and wisdom. Brigit's patronage of poetry certainly seems relevant in this regard; women who approach a source of the inspiration that Brigit provides without the proper rituals and with the intent to challenge the power of these sources are punished just as are men who have defiled the sacred flames.

It should be noted that Irish Pagan religiosity was much more associated with natural features than enclosures, and the majority of worship appeared to take place in natural settings, not within buildings. The apparent Pagan emphasis on fire-in-water in the form of sacred wells, rather than fire alone as a permanent sacred feature, might argue for the idea that holy wells were more closely associated with Brigit the Goddess than the saint's fire within the monastery.

An additional argument against Brigit's flame being somehow hazardous to men is the continuous flamekeeping practice of men in Ord Brigidheach. Certainly none of these men has been driven mad or died from their ritual tending of Brigit's flame, as might be expected if Gerald were correct and gender was the defining factor of appropriateness in Irish flamekeeping rituals. There are also men participating in flamekeeping with Brigid's Irregulars, as practitioners of CR Pagan spirituality, performing the same liturgy as the women, who report having a fulfilling, moving spiritual practice as flametenders. This living experience cannot and should not be discounted.

A desire for women-only space is understandable for some women, and can be a very meaningful experience. It is a perfectly legitimate need. I am, myself, a member of Daughters of the Flame, a women-only flametending order. Yet the need for such groups doesn't mean that men should be excluded from all CR flamekeeping orders, or that they would not find the practice equally valuable. Our respect for the past does not mean we must be utterly bound by it, particularly if there are compelling reasons to allow a broadening of participation. Women in Paganism generally, and in CR in particular, argue against the exclusion of women from traditionally male roles on a regular basis. This is fair and right, and it seems unfair to exclude men who feel particularly called to Brigit's service as flamekeepers, even if Christian tradition demands it.

Gender equality is an important tenet of CR Paganism.[329] Many of the founders of the modern CR Pagan movement identify as queer, bi, lesbian, gay, or transgendered. Women are not excluded from any role or function within the CR community, nor is sexual discrimination tolerated. Women claim roles as clergy, as warriors, as poets, craftspeople, and leaders, despite the well-documented fact that women in most of these roles in early Celtic societies were extremely rare exceptions to strongly defined gender roles. The ancient socially mandated sexual dimorphism of Iron Age Celtic cultures is one of the aspects of tradition most strongly rejected by modern CR practitioners. Our intention is not to recreate the Iron Age, but to imagine Celtic spiritualities as they might have evolved were they uninterrupted by fifteen hundred years of Christian rule. Many Christians today support the ordination of women called to priesthood despite the fact that they were traditionally excluded from this office. Should we be more conservative about gender roles than Christianity?

With this general attitude of openness in the CR community, it is difficult to understand why, in this one case, a gender-based tradition must take precedence over the right of an individual to respond to the call of service to deity. In addition, restricting the tending of the flame by the criteria of whether or not one possesses

---

329. http://paganachd.com/faq/ethics.html#queerqueerqueer accessed 16 July 2011

a penis entirely dodges modern understandings of the construction of gender, and the issues posed by transgendered individuals who are living as their appropriate gender either with or without transitional surgery.

By this criteria, a trans man who has not had genital surgery would be able to tend the flame due to his alleged "female" sex, while a trans woman in a similar situation would not, despite being and living as the "appropriate" sex for this ritual duty. Intersexed individuals, whose genitalia are often ambiguous for the purposes of determining a physical sex, would be forever barred from the practice of flamekeeping, regardless of their gender identification or the lives they live. No spiritual community should be in the position of policing its practices based on the presumed contents of an individual member's trousers. The CR community is not the arbiter of its members' sex, gender, or gender presentation. Even "ability to give birth" is not a true indicator of female gender, given how many women are infertile for one reason or another, whether deliberately or by accident of health or life circumstance. Trans men have also given birth, further blurring the boundaries of traditional binary concepts of gender and sexuality.

It should also be noted that CR Paganism is not specifically "women's spirituality." It is a path based on the spiritual beliefs and practices of entire communities: women, children, men, and the gender-variant, as individuals and in community.

Cross-dressing activities associated with Imbolc, Brigit's specific holy day, further blur the distinctions between man and woman. These are deliberate boundary-breakings, removing gender from a firm binary and placing it on a spectrum of performed behaviors within a ritual and social context associated with Brigit. The cross-dressed individual is in a liminal state, and this liminality is a vital concept within Celtic spiritualities. It is the place where the otherworlds touch the world of humanity, where mundane reality blends and blurs with the spiritual. These liminal places, times, and activities are confluences of power.

Brigit, in her role as saint, deliberately degendered herself when she refused her expected social role of wife and mother and entered the church. Lisa Bitel's work offers a strong argument that cloistered women within the church, and saints in particular, were considered "ersatz men" rather than women under the definitions of society at the time. In a discussion of the complexities of gender within the Christian clerical context, Bitel reports:

...most women were guided into traditional roles
of wife and mother, and Christian theology limited
its female professionals to chaste imitations of
these real-life roles; yet the most admirable and
saintly nuns were not real women at all, at least by
early Irish standards, but ersatz men.[330]

Religious women were granted a number of the rights of men that
were unavailable to women in secular society. They participated, if
in limited ways, in the political sphere and sometimes controlled
property. A very few had authority over men, which was almost
unheard-of in Irish society. Bitel says that religious women were
"the exception to every unspoken rule about men and woman in
early Ireland."[331] This "ersatz" masculinity, or perhaps even
transgenderedness, is highlighted in the life of Saint Moninne.

Moninne herself was as much man as woman,
going beyond imitation to take "a man's spirit in a
woman's body." Moninne severely lectured her
own right-hand woman on the sinful weaknesses
of the female sex, which was more vulnerable to
demons than men because "a little thing can upset
a woman."[332]

Significantly, Brigit was, if "accidentally," masculinised when she
was ordained a bishop instead of a nun by Mel, the bishop
performing the ceremony, in this 9th century account:

The bishop being intoxicated with the grace of God
there did not recognize what he was reciting from
his book, for he consecrated Brigit with the orders
of a bishop. 'This virgin alone in Ireland,' said Mel,
'will hold the episcopal ordination.' While she was
being consecrated a fiery column ascended from
her head.[333]

---

330. Bitel (1996), p. 192
331. *ibid*, p. 168
332. *ibid*, p. 200
333. Donncha Ó hAodha, *Bethu Brigte*, Dublin Institute for Advanced Studies
(Dublin, 1978), p. 24

Women were restricted from assuming such positions of authority within the church, and it is unlikely that this event actually occurred. The event is not mentioned in the 7th century Cogitosus account. It is in fact unlikely that any woman was ever genuinely ordained as a bishop, but the statement itself is a powerful one. Christian women's power was seen as having masculine attributes, even when they were regarded as "brides of Christ."

This does not present a useful model for Pagan women's spirituality. The deep misogyny at the heart of this theology is problematic. It does, however, play havoc with the notion that men could not, by their nature, be entrusted with the flame. If the women tending it were, themselves, seen as in some way masculinised, as (in Bitel's words) "ersatz men," then gender roles and boundaries may in many ways be regarded as fluid or perhaps even arbitrary for our purposes.

When this conceptual ontology is combined with the multiplicity of male-tended perpetual and sacred flames, we cannot see the role of flametender as the particular domain of a single gender. It then becomes possible to suggest that the tending of Brigit's flame might have been restricted to women, not because men were somehow inherently unfit to tend a flame, but rather because it was housed at an abbey administered by a woman rather than a monastery administered by a man. At the very least, we are forced to make a much more nuanced argument for the complete exclusion of men from keeping Brigit's flame.

The need for women-only sacred space is not an unimportant concern. Part of the difficulty of defining this space, however, is found in the difficulty of defining "women." Even if a suitable definition of "woman" could be achieved, no one is arguing against women-only groups. Instead, alongside the desire for women-only groups, there is a desire for additional groups that also admit men and other genders.

Further complicating the issue is the idea of male appropriation of women's spirituality. If we look at this through the lens of early Irish thought, we find ourselves challenged by their assumptions of gender and power. While we see occasional women acting in traditional men's roles and assuming men's power, for a man to take on a woman's role would be seen as a failure of his masculinity. Bitel offers the following commentary:

> The sagas were full of references to the feminine
> counterparts of male professionals: *ban-file*, female

poet; *ban-láech*, female warrior; *ban-saer*, female craftsman; *ban-liaig*, female physician. But since no categories existed for women other than in relation to men, and since they had no formal identity except their gender function alone, no masculine counterparts to the "female-man" existed. What is more, these were exceptional women, not everyday wives and neighbors. Ordinary women were no more likely to take up doctoring or soldiering than they were to shift shapes or hop a chariot to the otherworld.

The wisdom texts, narratives, and secular and ecclesiastical laws all suggested that men needed to know about women to avoid becoming like them. To become like women was also to become socially inferior, beastly, otherworldly. ... When extraordinary women crossed gender boundaries, they became better humans, but for men, the crossing could only be disastrous, a demotion, and completely taboo.[334]

There is, fairly explicitly, no power for men to appropriate within this context. For a man to strive to be a keeper of Brigit's flame in the company of women, in early Irish terms, would have been a degendering: this practice would rob him of what made him a man. Only those who were (or are) truly dedicated to Brigit without regard to social consequences would have desired such a thing.

There is a reflection of this in the gendering of male poets in Irish society; poets frequently wrote of themselves as the spouse or – presumably submissive – sexual partner of their male patrons. Given that Brigit was regarded as the patron or Goddess of poets,[335] this gender construction is telling. Men under Brigit's patronage were symbolically feminized, taking on a woman's role as spouse or widow of the political patron. The most skilled poets are, paradoxically, also regarded as being of extremely high status and possessed of great magical power.

---

334. Bitel (1996), p. 37
335. John O'Donovan (trans), *Sanas Chormaic: Cormac's Glossary*, Irish Archaeological and Celtic Society (Calcutta, 1868), p. 23

Poets are liminal figures in Irish society and mythology, filled with otherworldly power and able to see and shape deeper realities. They cross the boundaries between insider and outsider in Irish culture.[336] Their potential for blessing and cursing is dangerous and insulting or angering them, like insulting the sacred flame itself, is fraught with danger, for poets can maim, transform, or kill with a verse.[337] Gender ambiguity may well be a part of this overarching theme of liminality; it could also be a signifier of Brigit herself in her role as patron of "masculine" occupations.

Poetry, when personified, is also a shape- and gender-shifting entity. In a tale called "The Spirit of Poetry" we find the personification of poetry first as a hideously ugly young man:

> Truly, if anyone pushed on his forehead with his finger, a gush of putrid matter would spurt out and run down to the base of his neck. A rough membrane covered his head right down to his shoulder blades; it looked as though the grey matter of his brains had burst through his skull.[338]

The description continues for some time in gory detail. After the youth engages in a poetic contest with a woman poet and successfully completes her quatrains, he is revealed as the spirit of poetry itself and becomes beautiful:

> As they drew near to Ireland, they looked at the lad we spoke of before. What they saw was a radiant, regal, great, broad-eyed, valorous youth. His curly hair was yellowish-gold, like gold thread, wavy as the spine of a small harp. ... ['and he was never seen from that time on. Therefore there is no doubt that he was the spirit of Poetry.'][339]

Yet, in an Old Irish poem, "Ode to Poetry," this spirit is described as female:

Hail poetry,

---

336. Ford, (1999), pp. xxii-xxv
337. *ibid*, pp. xxix-xx
338. *ibid*, pp. 39-40
339. *ibid*, p. 42

Daughter of wisdom,
Sister of reason,
Daughter of prudence,
Noble, revered![340]

Poetry walks the boundary between genders as it transcends the terrain between worlds and the balance between fire and water. It is neither one thing nor another, ambiguity itself. Its power is transformative, for both good and ill, and its practice was highly regulated in Irish society. There was, in fact, an entire volume of law texts regarding the status and regulation of poets, called *Uraicecht na Riar*.[341] Poetry, while highly desirable and useful, was also dangerous and required regulation, much like women in early Irish society.

One fascinating detail is the equation of poetic grades with the well that is the source of poetic inspiration, lending a certain mythic resonance to the idea of both well and poet wreaking destruction on those who challenge their power. The *Uraicecht* tells us:

> As for a man who has splendid poetry, and splendid poetic standing, where neither his father nor grandfather of his has, what is the name of that grade? Not difficult; a well. And his son, what name? Not difficult; a spring. And his son who has splendid poetry and splendid poetic standing, what name? Not difficult; a splendid stream, i.e. an *ánsruith*; each of them having splendid learning and splendid poetry.[342]

The poet, therefore, is explicitly the well of wisdom, the source of fire-in-water.

Smiths, along with poets, were also considered uncanny, dangerous, and filled with supernatural power. One of the prayers of Saint Patrick contains this section:

Around me today I gather all these powers:

---

340. Calvert Watkins (trans), quoted in Morton W. Bloomfield & Charles W. Dunn, *The Role of the Poet in Early Societies*, D. S. Brewer, (Rochester, 1989), p. 47
341. Liam Breatnach, *Uraicecht na Riar: The Poetic Grades in Early Irish Law*, Dublin Institute for Advanced Studies, (Dublin, 1987)
342. *ibid*, p. 115

against every cruel and merciless force
to attack my body and soul,
against the charms of false prophets,
the black laws of paganism,
the false laws of heretics,
the deceptions of idolatry,
against spells cast by women, smiths, and druids,
and all unlawful knowledge
that harms the body and soul.[343]

Smiths and druids – many of whom were also poets – are specifically classed with women in this prayer. Where Brigit is in some sense given a masculinized identity, those men who fall under her tutelage are classified by Patrick with women, sharing in their dangerous, otherworldly powers and, presumably, in their lowly status in Patrick's estimation.

What does all this mean? Ultimately, form and gender are mutable entities where they intersect with the sacred, making a strict definition of "woman" difficult. Gender is now understood to be a complex multiplicity, not the simple binary that modern Western society has generally presumed. It is defined as much by action as by physical form. There are a number of instances surrounding Brigit where gender is deliberately blurred, whether through ontological structuring or through the use of disguise. Brigit as a saint transcends socially constructed gender roles, as do the various devotees of Brigit the Goddess. We cannot demonstrate that the keeping of sacred flames in Ireland was the sole provenance of women, however we decide to define that term. We also cannot prove that, had a woman approached Brigit's flame with the intent to desecrate it, she would not also have been injured or killed by its magical power; the danger of violating the flame is most likely not solely restricted to men. The absence of tales demonstrating the consequences of women violating the flame are made up for in the incidents of Sianann and Bóand at the wells of Connla and Nechtán; in these, we do not see men punished for violating the wells, but we can imagine they might have been.

Given all this, there seems no compelling reason to deny people of any gender or gender expression the opportunity to tend Brigit's flame, even within a CR context. This does not mean that women-only orders (however one wishes to define women) should

---

343. Davies (1999), p. 119

not exist. It is simply an acknowledgement that Brigit's flame is a true community hearth, welcoming all who seek it. When any person is called to tend Brigit's flame, it should be the strength of that call, not the gender of the person, that determines their suitability for the role.

Chapter 2
Interviews

Edge of the Circle
with Raven Branch-Butler (2008)

I'm delighted to be able to present this interview with Celtic Reconstructionist author and Fili, Erynn Rowan Laurie. She's not only a walking compendium of all things Celtic, but also a dear friend.

Erynn Rowan Laurie (author) (The Cauldron of Poesy, A Circle of Stones: Journeys and Meditations for Modern Celts, Not Your Mama's Tree Ogam) presents a much broader, deeper view of ogam.

EOTC: Happy Imbolc to you, Erynn! Congrats on your new book, Ogam: Weaving Word Wisdom.

ERL: Thanks, Raven, and a blessed Imbolc to you as well. I'm very excited about the ogam book – I'd been working on it for years. This was actually the fourth version of the book. I started over three times from scratch, throwing out everything I'd done before and rewriting everything. I'm very pleased with the end result, though.

EOTC: You're one of the Founders of Celtic Reconstructionism. How did that happen?

ERL: Wow, that's quite the question. The "how" probably just has to do with me being stubborn and really bookish and being in the right place at the right time. When I started learning about Celtic mythology, Wicca was being presented as "Celtic" and it was nigh unto heresy to suggest that it wasn't. The more I read, though, the more I realized that early Celtic religion looked nothing like Wicca at all. Eventually the idea started to gain more acceptance in the Pagan community, and I connected with others who were saying the same things.

I think I ended up as one of the founders just because I write a lot. I founded several online forums for the exploration of Celtic Paganism and it snowballed from there. It's always been something of a surprise to me to see how much influence that I and a few friends have had in the community over the years.

EOTC: How has Celtic Reconstruction grown and changed over the years?

ERL: These days it's no longer heresy to say that Wicca isn't of Celtic origin, or to find people pointing to better books and resources for folks who are interested in exploring Celtic paths. There's a lot more good material available and much more easily. Folks like Robert have helped that along, by carrying some of the more scholarly stuff for folks like myself in their shops and that's been a great resource. Thanks, Robert![344]

When I started out on this, there were no books at all on CR. Now there are a couple, and more folks working on new texts about ritual and personal experience, as well as writing on Celtic Pagan theologies. There are actually a lot of folks locally who are working on CR ritual and community, though we're all coming at it from different angles. One old friend of mine is working hard on the warrior tradition and has been a student of Gaelic swordsmanship and other similar esoteric topics. There are more ways into the community now than there were at the beginning, and it's easier to find information of all kinds. More people are talking about CR in more places, and we've been mentioned in books now along side other types of Paganism.

There's more of an awareness of Celtic cosmologies and deities than there was, more of an acceptance of genuine polytheism rather than the duotheism you find in a lot of Wicca and general Paganism. People are exploring different aspects of the Celtic paths and while there aren't any large CR organizations, I think local communities are actually starting to come together finally. I think this is a more important step than trying to found national or international organizations or start up training programs. Until there are communities to serve, there's not really that much call for clergy training!

There's a lot going on in online forums, particularly on LiveJournal, and more people are expressing interest all the time. It's pretty exciting. In my experience, a lot of the newer folks are hesitant to speak up in online forums because they feel intimidated by the amount of knowledge that the folks who have been around for a while have.

Everyone starts somewhere, and asking questions is important – this is why several of the elders in the community put together the CR FAQ project. It was over 150 pages online and is now available as a book. It doesn't tell you how to do CR or give ritual scripts, but it does offer some really good suggestions for places to start. I'd love to see more of these folks speaking up and participating. Just because you don't know that much right now

---

[344] Robert Anderson, owner and proprietor of Edge of the Circle Books in Seattle.

doesn't mean you can't have a personal practice or talk about what you're learning and working on.

EOTC: Do you see this form of spirituality growing in the next decade? Where do you think it's going to go? Where would you like to see it go?

ERL: My hope is that local communities will continue to develop in much the same way that Heathen hearth groups started. I think there are going to be quite a few more books coming out on different aspects of CR, from theology to ritual to devotionals for different deities. I think there will be regional CR gatherings at some point, and I'd also love to see more interfaith work between different reconstructionist traditions, as we have many of the same approaches and issues in our communities and in our concepts of theology and interactions with the larger Pagan community.

I'd love to see other people in the CR communities writing books. I have at least two more in my head, and I know other folks are working on other aspects of CR ritual and practice. My personal practice focuses on the Irish and Scottish material, but others are interested in other Celtic cultures, and I'd love to see more variety with that as well.

Right now, CR tends toward solitary practice, and I think for some of the more mystical forms it will likely remain so. There are household-based forms, though, and people will be developing groups around holy day and household practices as time goes by. A lot of the CR founders don't have children, but many people who practice at home do have kids, and it will be wonderful to see how that develops and how families with kids can be a part of the movement as a whole. We need them as the practice develops, because without the kids, this can never be a living Pagan culture.

My personal preference is to see CR as a balance between historical study and personal inspiration, each informed by the other. Sometimes we get people who believe that reconstructionist Pagans don't have an actual spiritual practice, but that's really not true. We do, but we try to back it up with things we can learn from history and from the scholarly sources. The way I put it when I founded the Nemeton list back in the early 90s was *"aisling* and archaeology" -- inspiration and study together, hand in hand. Leaning too far in either direction can lead to spiritual dead ends.

EOTC: Books on Ogam are rare, so it's wonderful to see yours on our shelves. "Ogam" is a departure from the standard fare that one commonly sees in the bookstores. How does you book differ from others?

ERL: Pretty much every other ogam book out there deals with the ogam strictly or primarily as a tree alphabet. The truth is so much broader. My approach has been to work from the actual meanings of the names of each letter, and from the *briatharogam* or "word ogams" associated with each letter. I've found this to be a much more accessible and varied system, more like Norse runes than what's usually presented.

I also deal a lot with the misconceptions surrounding ogam, like the idea that it's a "Celtic tree calendar" or that it has anything to do with the recently-created "Celtic astrology." Part of the original tradition was that people created their own ogam lists and I talk about how, when, and why you might do things like that. It's not so much a table of correspondences as a web of connections, and I think it's limiting to see things in rows and columns when dealing with such an organic system.

I also talk about the use of ogam in ritual and how to make your own set of ogam. I don't give ritual scripts, but rather talk about how and why to choose individual ogam *feda* or letters to use for your personal needs.

My approach to the whole thing is that my readers are intelligent people and they don't need to have their hands held through the process. They know the kinds of rituals they need and what they want to accomplish spiritually and magically, so they're intelligent and mature enough to use the resources I've laid out and create those things for themselves.

EOTC: You use a term to describe yourself and your practice: Filidecht. What does a Fili do?

ERL: *Filidecht* is the practice of poetic nature mysticism in the Gaelic tradition. As a *fili*, I do divination, otherworld work that includes vision-seeking and healing, and I also do a lot of work out in the wild. I get out into the wilderness whenever I can, because this particular type of path demands contact with the wild world, even if you live in the city. Some types of Paganism are perfectly comfortable as urban paths, but *filidecht* really needs contact with the outdoors and with the land spirits in order to get deeply into it.

Part of my devotional work involves writing, both prose and poetry. I do my best to work through those knotty philosophical and theological questions and to share what I know with others. Music is also a part of the path, though "bard" and "*fili*" are not the same thing – originally in Gaelic, a bard was an untrained poet, while a *fili* was one who had gone through years of strict training in many fields, from history to genealogy to philosophy and natural history.

EOTC: How is that different from a Druid?

ERL: That's a very complicated question – much more than it appears on the surface. The easy answer would be to say that the druids were more concerned with questions of public ritual and sacrifice than the *filid*. Because of the fact that everything we know about the druids and the *filid* come from either later Christians or from outsiders to the Celtic cultures, there are a lot of questions we need to ask. It would appear that the *filid* and the druids originally had rather different functions but when Christianity arrived, the *filid* took over many druidic functions within the Christianized society.

Technically speaking, what we know about the *filid* and druids all comes from what the *filid* were doing. We know very little about the druids per se. It's much easier to reconstruct an authentic and traditionally-based practice of *filidecht* than of *draíocht*, to be honest.

EOTC: What do most seekers expect from you, and how does that differ from reality?

ERL: I've had a lot of people approach me thinking I know all the answers. I really don't. I'm just another student on the path with more years of study under my belt. I do my best to share what I know

EOTC: The month of February brings the Gaelic holiday, Imbolc. Do you have any special ways of celebrating it, according to your tradition?

ERL: Imbolc traditions include putting the *brat Bríd* or cloak of Brigid – any cloth or piece of clothing will do, traditionally – out over night to collect the dew at dawn and receive the blessing and touch of Brigid's hand. Brigid's crosses are often woven, and that's a great thing that kids can do for fun. Brigid's beds are also prepared, usually in the fireplace, and in the morning traces of her presence might be seen in the ashes around the bed.

Imbolc is also a festival very likely associated with the *fianna* or outsider warriors, much like the Roman Lupercalia festival. It was likely a time when the outsiders were reintegrated into the tribe after they'd spent their time in the wilds. In Scotland, Imbolc is said to be the time when serpents come out of the ground and it's the beginning of spring in the Gaelic tradition.

I celebrate with a fire in the fireplace part of the night, candles on her altar, laying out the *brat Bríd*, making offerings of food and mead, and by keeping a vigil until dawn.

EOTC: You're hosting a discussion group at our store. What's it about?

ERL: It's partly a discussion group, partly a group to develop community, and partly a ritual group. We'll be having our Imbolc of Bríg Ambue ritual on Monday the 11th at Edge, between 7-9 pm. Bríg Ambue is Brigid of the Cowless Warrior, basically the patron of the outsider warriors, and the ritual will be about incorporating outsiders into society. It's my hope that the group will foster the growth of the CR community locally, and that folks will be interested in studying the path and doing ritual and other work together.

EOTC: Anything else you'd like to add?

ERL: I'll be down in California at PantheaCon later this month, doing workshops and the Bríg Ambue ritual down there.[345] I've been to the con several times and I always have a great time. If anyone is going down there, by all means, look me up! It would be great to see some of the locals down by the Bay.

Locally, I do ogam readings and I sometimes teach classes and workshops. Interested folks can get in touch with me through email.

EOTC: Erynn, it's been a real pleasure. Blessings, and happy Imbolc.

---

[345] The Bríg Ambue ritual was performed by several members of Brigid's Irregulars.

Ogam and Otherworlds:
Interview by Rebecca Buchanan of Sequential Tart (2008)

I first met Erynn Rowan Laurie on the Reconstructionist Interfaith list several years ago. I found her to be an invaluable source of information on Celtic Reconstructionism. It turns out that she is also an author and incredibly talented poet. She took a few moments to answer some questions for ST about CR, ogam and the importance of owning up to your own creativity.

Sequential Tart: *There are many misperceptions about Paganism. If you could correct one, what would it be?*

Erynn Rowan Laurie: I think the biggest misconception that I run into constantly is that all forms of Paganism look like Wicca. In truth, there are so many different types and paradigms of Paganism out there that you can't even characterize Paganism as a single religion. Not everyone casts circles, uses four elements, or calls upon The God and The Goddess.

There are a large number of reconstructionist Paganisms that have nothing to do with these worldviews and that don't find those cosmological constructions useful or even valid within the culture being reconstructed. Even if I can see the validity of those approaches within Wicca and more generic modern Paganism as it arose from medieval Ceremonial Magic, it doesn't mean that it has to apply to everyone else's work or worship. Our differences don't invalidate our different paths any more than Hinduism invalidates Christianity. This, I think, is one of the beauties of genuine polytheism — that multiple things can be simultaneously true.

ST: *While Wicca is fairly well-known (if misunderstood), most people are unfamiliar with Celtic Reconstructionism. What is CR? And how did it get its (modern) start?*

ERL: CR is a movement very much in flux. Some will say it's a methodology applied to Pagan Celtic religion, while others will say it is a spiritual path in itself. Generally speaking, CR can be understood as a way to approach pre-Christian Celtic spiritualities in an attempt to use history, folklore, mythology, and modern understandings of the world to create different types of Celtic spiritual paths firmly based on historical practices but with relevance to modern life.

Some people have, I think, the mistaken impression that CR is either some kind of historical recreation society, like the Society for Creative Anachronism, or that it is just a bunch of dry research by wannabe academics that don't have a spiritual bone in their body. Neither of these is true. History is important to us, but we also embrace and enjoy things like running water, modern medicine, and social liberties that didn't exist two thousand years ago. We also must recognize that there are many things the early Celtic peoples did that we don't find ethical these days — human sacrifice, divination by the death-throes of prisoners of war, counting our wealth by the number of female slaves we own. In these ways, we have to recognize that we can't have and don't even want a pure historical reconstruction of Celtic tribal societies. I certainly don't want to live in a slave-keeping society that slaughters people for the sake of divination, nor do I want to live under a tribal petty king whose word is law.

The spirituality of CR is based on the work of many poets, mystics, and dreamers for whom reconstructionist work and historical and literary research are foundations for spiritual exploration and growth. There are lost or partially understood sources of spiritual techniques including sweat houses, breathwork, meditation, internal energy systems, purifications, and prayers that we can focus on and bring into our daily or seasonal ritual lives to produce a very rich spirituality that is true to its Celtic origins while still being viable and meaningful today. It takes a great deal of work and dedication to find the facts and a lot of spiritual understanding and processing to put what we find into a meaningful context for practitioners today.

CR got its start out of issues arising in the mid- to late-1980s, with quite a few people getting fed up with the claims of many Pagans that Wicca was the ancient religion of the Celtic peoples. The more we researched and looked into it, the more patently obvious it was that this wasn't the case, and so we decided to try to understand what those Celtic religions originally looked like in different times and places. There's a lengthy discussion of the origins of CR at the CR FAQ website.

There were a lot of people involved in the beginnings of the movement, some of whom have moved on to other things. People who were formative to the movement in different ways include Kathryn NicDhána, Kym ni Dhoireann, Gordon Cooper, John

Machate, Francine Nicholson, Seán Ó Túathail, myself, and many others. Over time, some agreements in the community were arrived at, and eventually the CR FAQ was written by a colloquy of different long-time members of the CR movement. It's not a be-all and end-all statement about the movement and shouldn't be seen as dogma or used to beat people into some semblance of orthodoxy, but it's an important historical document that describes some broad issues for the community as well as being a snapshot of some of the internal politics of the movement when it was written.

I believe that CR has a long way to go and that it will develop and evolve as time goes by. More sources will be translated, and more people will be actively practicing with localized groups. I would much prefer to see development through working groups than through online organizations where the focus is on bylaws and tax-exempt status. There simply aren't enough of us to worry about that kind of bureaucracy before we actually develop face-to-face community. Long distance discussion can be fruitful for theoretical work, but when it comes to practicalities, what you do in your own home and what you do with others you work with personally in local communities is where the important growth and innovation lies. More books by CR authors on CR topics will be very important to that development, and the growth of the movement and its various traditions.

ST: *What does a typical CR ceremony or festival look like (assuming there is a typical one)?*

ERL: There really isn't a "typical" CR ceremony or festival at this point. Considering that we are inspired by and using sources from all over the ancient Celtic world, and that each tribe was going to have its own rites and deities, it would be impossible to have homogeneity anyway. Because we have cultures spread as far apart as modern Turkey, Spain, Ireland and Iceland to consider and time periods ranging from the proto-Celtic Urnfield cultures of about 1200 BCE up to modern Celtic folk practices, again we're going to have a vast variety of things to draw upon. None of these is going to be inherently more correct or appropriate than the others.

That said, modern CR focuses on spiritual and ritual interaction with deities, ancestors and land spirits, acknowledging that these categories blend and overlap. Much of CR ritual is based in making offerings to those beings into fire, water, or pits in the earth. We also bring in things as fun and diverse as storytelling around the fire, feasts for the ancestors, mumming plays, divinatory work by various methods, and healing with traditional herbal medicines and verbal charms. The look and feel of a ritual is going to reflect the deities and the land where any local CR practitioner lives, and this is as it should be. I don't think it would be right for us to even try to enforce an across-the-board uniformity of practice, cosmology, or theology beyond going back to the original Celtic cultures and weeding out modern Neopagan assumptions about Celtic deity and rituals.

My own rituals tend more toward the animist, with a heavy emphasis on talking to spirits, divination work, incubatory ritual for vision-seeking, and on vigil work in the wilderness. I've done several three-day rituals structured around growing closer to my chosen deities and spirits as I've been camped out in the rainforest or on the coast, usually backpacking in to help with isolation from crowds and other kinds of interference. I describe one of my vigil rituals in my book *Ogam: Weaving Word Wisdom*, where I backpacked out to the wild coast of Washington with a friend and spent three days doing work with the ogam and getting more in touch with Manannán Mac Lir. I also facilitated a similar three-day retreat for a friend on the California coast two summers ago as she prepared for a very important ritual of her own.

ST: *In your book* Ogam: Weaving Word Wisdom *you explore the history and uses of the old Celtic alphabet. Why a book about ogam?*

ERL: Well, first, the ogam is Irish Gaelic, not generically Celtic, so it's important to keep that in mind. It arose in Ireland, even though it has been used a bit in Scotland, Wales, and the Isle of Man. It was carried there by Irish speakers and was created by them for their own language.

For me the book was a personal project. I was fascinated with ogam when I first met it, but the more Celtic scholarship and historical source material I read, the more I realized that the books generally available were filled with flaws and errors. People are even claiming that there are ogams in North America which is, unfortunately, patently untrue. Unless you actually read Old Irish or had access to academic texts, it was very hard to find good, solid, truthful information about the system.

It was then that I realized nobody else seemed to be doing the kind of work I was with the ogam. Everyone was fixated on the tree ogam and on Robert Graves's fictitious tree calendar when there was a much more easily understandable and accessible way to use the system for divination and magic in the original Irish sources. I felt it was important to let people know that there were other ways to approach the ogam and that, even if it wasn't originally created by druids for divination and magic, it could certainly be used that way today, once a proper understanding of context and meaning was outlined.

ST: *In Ogam, you associate each letter with a tree, keyword, color, bird, even musical note and planet. How did you determine these associations? Through research? Personal experience? Both?*

ERL: This was a combination of both. The historical sources give a great number of associations with each letter — dozens of them. Most of them, however, aren't really of much use to people not living in Ireland, as they're lists of things like Irish rivers and fortresses. Others are really only linked by the first letter of their name in Irish. Yet with things like trees, birds, and colors, there are mythological associations that can be useful.

The keywords are my own, based on my work with the actual meanings of the names of each letter and the associations that they brought up for me. It makes a huge difference in dealing with the letter Tinne, for instance, when you know it refers to a bar of metal rather than just a holly tree, and that metal/iron was both a means of exchange and a thing from which weapons are made.

The musical notes were derived from the work of Seán O'Boyle, a Celticist who was suggesting that the ogam might have been a harp tabulature, and I felt that this would be interesting to folks who use music in their spiritual work. The planets was my own modern system developed to show people what could be done with things from outside of a strictly Irish context and give a feel for how ogam can be a tool in modern magic.

One of the things I feel it's important to point out, given the amount of chicanery being written about the ogam these days, is that the whole "Celtic tree astrology" thing was invented in the 1980s, based on Robert Graves. I don't see any particular issues in working with it, but anyone claiming it's ancient and druidic in origin has no genuine understanding of either the ogam or of Celtic history and culture. Remember that it doesn't have to be ancient to be valid, so if the so-called "Celtic tree astrology" system works for you, fine — just call it what it is instead of propping it up with fake history.

As I've always said, I have far more respect for people who innovate and own their creativity than for people who lie about that same act of creativity in an attempt to give it more spooky mystical weight. Let's be honest — honesty is one of the virtues of CR.

ST: *You reference a number of myths in* Ogam. *Why do you consider them important? What can those old myths tell us about ourselves today, in the 21st century?*

ERL: People don't really change all that much. No matter when in history you look at us, we need food and water, we need relationships with other people, we deal with strangers and friends, we try to explain the world around us, and we explore its mysteries. Mythology talks about the ways we find to relate to each other and the world. It offers tales that tell us things about the ways we conceive of deity and each other. It gives us metaphors to help us understand the spiritual origins of things and their relationships. It illustrates both positive and problematic ways of dealing with life and the universe, giving us object lessons for ethical and spiritual contemplation and action.

Do I believe any mythology is literally, physically true? No. I do believe that it describes, to a certain extent, existing spiritual beings and energies and it helps illuminate our relationships to that reality. I believe that it gives us a glimpse into the realities of the Otherworlds through the visions of poets and mystics. I also believe that such things can be interpreted in many ways and that the interpretation of myth can give us keys for opening the doors to the Otherworlds and learning how to work within them.

Mythology doesn't just illuminate the past for us. It helps us discover ourselves and examine the implications of what we do for the future. Celtic mythologies tackle issues of truth, good judgment, generosity, kindness and courage. They offer us examples of failure so that we can learn by them and try to avoid the same problems. They give us hints to mysteries that could not be preserved more directly in a culture that was already massively changing under the conversion to Christianity. I don't mean that the myths are hidden druidic mysteries that the monks were writing down; rather I mean that the attitudes and many of the symbols were so ingrained in the culture at that time that even institutionalized Christianity could not entirely eradicate them. And I believe mythology is important to us today because if we don't understand the past, will inevitably repeat its errors. Myths are a rich source for us to learn from because myth is the language our dreams speak. Without them, how will we translate that deepest core of ourselves?

ST: *What kind of research went into writing* Ogam? *Were you surprised by any unexpected or interesting historical tidbits?*

ERL: I went into it expecting to find what Robert Graves had been asserting — that the ogam was druidic, that it was all about the trees, and that the Gaels had a tree calendar. So that was my first eye-opening experience with my research: everything I knew was wrong. When I hit that realization I knew I couldn't just turn my back on it and take the easy route. The challenge of it was very stimulating and exciting and my own pursuit of the ogam and of CR has been a gradual process of growth and integration.

As I grew more interested in the historical realities, I found myself really needing to learn Irish in order to pursue the matter more thoroughly. I actually took a quarter of Old Irish at the University of Washington to help my understanding of the source materials and so that I could at least attempt to do some of my own translating, to sort through the different biases in both the Pagan and the scholarly communities. I've never been what anyone could consider fluent, but with the help of dictionaries and grammars, I can sit down and do a rough translation and get the gist of a passage, a poem, or a myth.

In following the trail of ogam, I found an immense number of places where modern popular Paganism was wrong about Gaelic and other Celtic cultures: cosmology, deity concepts, language, holy days. Those discoveries really challenged me, as I was a more or less traditionalist Wiccan in an Alexandrian coven while I was doing some of this research. Yet the Irish deities had a strong grip on my spirit and by following the threads of ogam, I found a home for my heart. It's been a difficult path sometimes, but I'm so much happier doing this work than I was working within the Wiccan paradigm.

In my work, I've studied mythology, cosmology, history, law, literature, folklore, herbalism, poetry and rhetoric. I've had to make side-trips through medieval Christianity, the lives of saints, journal articles in French and German (neither of which I actually speak), and tackled passages in Latin and Greek. As it is, even distilling that research down into my ogam book left a pretty dense text. All I can say is that I do truly hope some of it is accessible!

ST: *You published* Ogam *through Megalithica. Why that publisher, and would you recommend them to other authors?*

ERL: I love Megalithica! I had offers from a couple of other presses before I signed a contract with them, but they offered me a chance to write the book I truly wanted to rather than a watered-down popular press version. While I was working on this book, one of my dear friends was working on a book on numerology for Dummies press. He ran into incredible frustration and opposition at every turn. He feels that numerology is the king of occult sciences, and the Dummies press folks wanted a book that teenage girls could "giggle over at a slumber party." There was an incredible disconnect between the writer and the publisher there that was ultimately unresolved and the book was never published.

Taylor and Lupa, my editors at Megalithica, are fantastic to work with and I would recommend them to any serious, innovative author, without reservation. They ask great questions when issues come up and they're very good about working out the best way for both the author and the publisher to be pleased with the finished book. Megalithica is determined to publish cutting edge occult and Pagan books on intermediate to advanced topics and they're not afraid to challenge the community with tough issues. Right now, there are anthologies in the works (and that I'm writing for) that deal with controversial issues like cultural appropriation and animal sacrifice in Pagan communities.

I would not have been able to publish a book anywhere near as in-depth at any other occult press that I know. Their editing was hands-on and responsive. The press may be small, but I believe Megalithica is going to be seen as one of the most influential occult presses of the early 21st century, and I don't say that lightly.

ST: *What is* A Circle of Stones *about, and where can interested readers find a copy?*

ERL: *A Circle of Stones: Journeys* and *Meditations for Modern Celts* was my first book and it was the first one that dealt entirely with the idea of Pagan prayer beads. It describes a round of prayers and meditations based on insular Celtic cosmology, taking poetry and fragments from traditional Irish and Scottish sources to describe and evoke different parts of the cosmology, from the three realms of land, sea and sky, to the winds of the primary directions. It was groundbreaking for its time and for a long time was the only book written by a CR practitioner for other CR practitioners.

Today I'd say that the work is deeply flawed, and I've learned a lot in the over ten years since its publication. It has been out of print for a long time and only available at highway-robbery prices used. I felt that was terribly unfair to people who wanted a copy but weren't able to pay the $60 to $200 I've seen it going for in different places. It's now back in print from Megalithica[346] for a much more reasonable price. As long as you realize that it's an historical document that shows where I was when I was writing it in the early 90s and that it isn't a manifesto on modern CR, you might find it of use. I know that a lot of people were grateful when I finally made it available again.

ST: *Just writing can be an intimidating exercise, let along publishing. Do you have any advice for authors hoping to publish?*

ERL: Keep working at it. Have people other than your best friends read your writing and offer constructive criticism on things like your grammar, your spelling, and your style. Learn from those critiques. Spell-check is only your friend sometimes — learn to tell when it's your enemy. If you're working on a Pagan book, please don't write yet another basic introduction to Wicca! There are hundreds of them out there, all of them rehashing what's already been said dozens of times before. I want to read something different.

Don't be afraid to do original research. You can avoid a lot of problems later if you're willing to spend some time at the library looking at sources other than recently published Pagan books. If you're innovating, claim that creativity and please, don't say it's an ancient family or cultural tradition if it isn't. Let us know your sources so that we can judge the material for ourselves. You'll respect yourself and your readers will respect you as well.

Haunt the history and mythology sections of the bookshop. Read about comparative religions and theology. Look at books on anthropology and archaeology. Look at art and listen to music related to the topic you're writing on. Immerse yourself. Understand your biases. Meet people who are doing what you're writing about. Listen to them and get to know them. If a culture

---

[346] Erynn Rowan Laurie, *A Circle of Stones: Journeys and Meditations for Modern Celts*, Megalithica Books, Stafford (2012)

you're interested in speaks another language, learn that language. Not everything you want to know is in English.

And don't get discouraged. All writers get rejection letters. I've had my share. Most writers could paper their walls with them. If you're good and you're persistent, you will get published. Let your friends be your cheerleaders and help pick you up when you're feeling discouraged, but don't listen only to them. All-positive feedback is no more realistic than all-negative feedback. The truth is almost always somewhere in between.

You have to work at writing consistently. If you don't actually sit down at the keyboard, it won't get done. Talking about writing never wrote a book. But don't let writing be the only thing you do. Walk in the woods. Work at your altar. Play games and read books and articles for your pleasure, not just for research.

Have fun!

ST: *Which resources would you recommend (websites, email lists, books, journals) to someone interested in Celtic Reconstructionism and ogam?*

ERL: Wow, that's a big question that covers a lot of territory. I'll try to keep it down to a few places and publications that I think are the most useful, though they may not always be the most introductory.

There's the CR FAQ project, which also is in a print edition. Information on both can be found on the CR FAQ website. The FAQ has several lists of books on different Celtic topics. Another CR project was edited by the late Francine Nicholson, titled *Land, Sea and Sky*,[347] and it's available online.

An excellent source for books on all Celtic topics is Books for Scholars, an online shop.

The most active online forum for CR I'm aware of at the moment is the LiveJournal CR community.

The Imbas email list is usually fairly active, though I'm not a member.

I have a number of articles, rituals, and other resources up on my own website, The Preserving Shrine.[348]

Damien McManus, *A Guide to Ogam* (An Sagart) Maynooth 1991 — This book covers all the known ogam stones, a translation of the characteristically brief texts on them, and a discussion of what is known about the names of the ogam letters. Not for the faint of

---

[347] http://homepage.eircom.net/~shae/contents.htm accessed March 15, 2015
[348] http://www.seanet.com/~inisglas/ accessed March 15, 2015

heart. Almost everything else that's useful is out of print and often only available through inter-library loan.

For Irish texts with translations, an indispensable resource is the Irish Texts archive at CELT. Not everything on this page is translated, but many things are and they are well worth perusing.[349]

The number of recommendations I could make is pretty much endless, but these are all good places to start and will lead you to new discoveries on your own!

ST: *What other projects are you working on?*

ERL: I have two essays coming out in *Talking About the Elephant: An Anthology of Neopagan Perspectives on Cultural Appropriation*, due out in November 2008 from Megalithica. Both essays deal with aspects of CR and issues of cultural appropriation.

Engaging the Spirit World: Shamanism, Totemism and Other Animistic Practices, another Megalithica anthology, will have an essay from me on animist aspects of CR practice, both historical and modern. That anthology should be out by mid-2009 if all goes well.

I've also got an essay in progress for the Megalithica anthology *Digging Up the Ostrich's Head: Animal Sacrifice in Modern Pagan Practices*. That essay had its genesis in a Nemeton email list post many years ago, but there's a lot to say on this topic and it's definitely one that causes a lot of kneejerk reactions within the Pagan community.

I'm hard at work on my next book, in the research and outlining phase. It will be about the *geilta*, a phenomenon of sacred or poetic madness that is personified in mythic and poetic figures like Suibhne Geilt, Mís, and Myrddin. Its manifestations in Gaelic and Welsh myth bear many resemblances to Post Traumatic Stress Disorder, and I've found the *geilt* paradigm a very striking one for looking at healing through trauma within a CR context. It deals with spirituality, the environment, poetry, and psychology as interconnected aspects of a poetic path.

The work I've put into this has been coming together over many, many years of personal experience, discussion with others who have suffered trauma, and literary and historical research. Much of what I learned in my research on ogam and on *filidecht* (the Gaelic poetic tradition) also comes into play in this book, so it should be a great project.

---

[349] http://www.ucc.ie/celt/ accessed March 15, 2015

I'm also working on a more private project that I'm blogging about on my LiveJournal, putting together an incubation chamber for exploring meditative and vision-seeking techniques based on what we can piece together about the practices of the early *filid* or poets of Ireland and Scotland. It has involved clearing out the closet in my room and equipping it as a meditation chamber that can be isolated from as much light and sound as possible to assist with sensory deprivation-based meditations. Some of this work will touch on entheogens as a part of the exploration and I look forward to seeing what works and what doesn't, and where that research will lead. Some of it will no doubt influence the writing I do for the *geilt* book and a later book on *filidecht*.

ST: *Which book fairs, conventions or other events will you be attending in the near future?*

ERL: I don't actually get out all that much, though in November I'll be in Phoenix, Arizona, speaking at the Irish Cultural Center on November 15th, presenting the following workshops:

The Irish Cultural Center
1106 North Central Ave,
Phoenix, AZ
7pm - 8:30pm

"Ogam: Past and Present" — A talk on the history and development of the Irish ogam alphabet, the earliest form of written Irish. We'll cover theories of origin, linguistic roots of the letter names, common misconceptions about the character and uses of the ogam alphabet and modern developments in the use of ogam in different forms of Celtic spirituality.

"Poetry and Satire in Irish Culture" — The poet has been one of the most respected — and feared — figures in Irish folk culture. Descendants of the druids, it was said that poets had the power to curse or to bless, to ruin or to raise a name to immortality. Praise and satire were among their functions and in this talk we'll examine some of the ways that poetry and satire were used by different kinds of poets in early Irish culture.

I'll be going to PantheaCon in February 2009 down in San Jose, California. I've been presenting workshops there for the past several years and having a wonderful time. I haven't heard back from them yet about which of the several proposals, if any, they've accepted, but I do expect to be pretty busy there.

In Seattle, we have a monthly CR Schmooze on the second Monday of every month at Edge of the Circle Books. We get together monthly for discussion and building community and we also have dinner together afterwards at a local restaurant, so that's a lot of fun. We're also doing ritual together several times a year aside from those monthly meetings. The group is open so if anyone will be in town, you're welcome to drop by and visit with us.

I try to keep folks posted on my random appearances on my LiveJournal and on my website, The Preserving Shrine, so that's always a good place to check. I'm also open to traveling around if folks want me to speak locally, so feel free to contact me to arrange it if you're so inclined.

Interview for *Talking to the Spirits* by Raven Kaldera and Kenaz Filan (2008)[350]

1. What's your current religious tradition? What religious tradition were you raised?

My primary tradition is Celtic Reconstructionist (CR) *Filidecht*, the practice of sacred poetics within a CR framework. A *fili* is, at least in part, a sacred poet and nature mystic within the Gaelic spiritual and literary tradition. The *filid* have links with the *draoi* or druids, though they are apparently not and never were identical with them. The emphasis in *filidecht* is on verbal magic, poetry, music, and inner work toward spiritual transformation and visionary insight. Animism and polytheism are both important strands within this path. Otherworld work, visionary practices, and mantic and divinatory work are all part of the thread.

I often describe myself as a professional madwoman and identify in large part with the *geilta* of Gaelic tradition -- those who have been made "mad" by their experiences yet attempt to place their difficulties and challenges firmly within a spiritual context, using them to generate poetry and spiritual/mystical experience as ways of healing and of normalizing life after intense trauma. It could be said that one major difference between a *fili* and a *geilt* is that the *fili* usually works within society while a *geilt* is at its margins; one is socially sanctioned while the other is not.

I am also a member of the local Shinto shrine, a Mystes of the Ekklesía Antínoou, and a member of the Neos Alexandria group. I hold initiations in Witchcraft and Wiccan traditions and have studied Siberian shamanism with an Ulchi woman in some depth. I no longer practice Wicca. I do feel that Buddhism, Taoism, and Hinduism all have some small influence on my approach to many of my personal practices.

I was raised in a fairly generic, conservative Protestant Christianity. My father is an atheist who was raised Catholic. My mother is a dedicated but somewhat agnostic Protestant who believes that religion should be a personal choice between an individual and their deity. Most of my other relatives are or were either Polish Catholics or fundamentalist Protestants.

---

[350] Kenaz Filan and Raven Kaldera, *Talking to the Spirits: Personal Gnosis in Pagan Religion*, Destiny Books, Rochester, 2013

2. How do you define the terms: gnosis? Personal gnosis? Unverified personal gnosis? Peer-corroborated personal gnosis?

My definition of gnosis is, simply, spiritual or ritual knowledge and insight. This knowledge or insight may be about the self, the nature of spirit/deity, the world, ritual, or other topics within the purview of one's personal or group spirituality and practices.

Personal gnosis is knowledge and insight that one achieves through their own work and spiritual practices. Such gnosis is not a matter of information or training passed on from one person to another -- this is why it is "personal". It may, however, be the result of meditation on or ritual work with knowledge that has been passed on from someone else. Personal gnosis, in my opinion, is a form of insight that is primarily or solely applicable to one's personal practice and may not have any meaning to a greater community.

UPG is personal gnosis that hasn't been verified by authentic or historical sources.

Peer-corroborated gnosis is a form personal gnosis that is discovered or intuited, usually prior to discussion about a particular topic, by several people arriving at that knowledge or insight independently. It may or may not have any relevance to historical information about a tradition but may be something that new ideas and practices within a given group are then based upon.

3. How do you feel about personal gnosis?

I feel that personal gnosis can be very important to personal practice, and even sometimes to communities, but that caution is necessary in approaching it. We as individuals, and as communities, need to have ways of discerning genuine spiritual knowledge from self-delusion so that our practices don't become pure fantasy. Not everything that we get is going to be either true or useful and it's best to acknowledge that up front rather than kidding ourselves about how we're special little snowflakes whose every subconscious whim has to be followed.

My feeling is that as long as personal gnosis is marked as such within the community, there's nothing wrong with it. When it is falsely touted as "traditional" practice or belief I believe that a line has been crossed from personally valid practice into fraud. Within reconstructionist traditions, sources should be cited -- including personal gnosis as a source -- so that individuals can judge for themselves how to proceed and how much weight to give to each source or practice.

4. How does the religious tradition that you are now a member of feel about it? (If applicable.) How do they judge what is valid and what is not? What does "valid" mean to them - objectively and provably true, intuitively true, or whether it's applicable and useful to them?

Within the larger CR community, personal gnosis is often entirely disregarded in favor of scholarly sources, whether literary or archaeological. This is not always the case, but in some ways I do believe we err a bit too much on the side of caution. CR tends to prefer things that are historically verifiable, though there is often not much to go on within the source material that is authentically Pagan in origin.

I think it's important to point out that there is a difference between "validity" and "authenticity" -- a practice can be valid because it works, but inauthentic in any historical or cultural sense. Chanting "awen" in an OBOD circle is a valid practice in that it works for the group doing it, but it's not culturally authentic for any pre-Christian Druids I'm aware of.

Something might conversely be culturally authentic, but not particularly valid as a modern practice. Human sacrifices are certainly culturally authentic in some places, complete with archaeological remains of said sacrifices, but they're not exactly a valid modern spiritual practice!

CR is often so preoccupied with debates about "what is Celtic" that it's difficult for newcomers to feel welcome or even competent to engage in a beginning practice. While it is an important question, it's certainly not the only one, nor should it be the sole focus of the movement as a whole.

CR traditions generally demand a comparing of personal gnosis against scholarship within Celtic studies and the historical record. Folklore and folk practice are considered important sources as well. Personal gnosis that falls too far from the patterns established in such sources is usually discarded or disregarded. In some more extreme cases, any personal gnosis at all tends to be rejected. The struggle to balance cultural authenticity and modern spiritual needs is a large current within CR debate.

As an example of the necessity for personal gnosis, we know for a fact that the Irish and other Celtic cultures had sweat traditions. We know almost nothing about how those traditions operated and nothing at all about the words of any rituals that may have been performed in those sweat houses. Unless we explore ideas that we get through our own personal gnosis and do some actual experimentation with our own bodies, we will not be able to in any way reconstruct sweat practices for modern use. Research, meditation, and experimentation are all necessary if we are going to develop this into something that any practitioner with the necessary physical resources can use. To dismiss personal gnosis regarding this work simply because it can't be proved through historical sources at this point would be to dismiss any possibility of creating a workable tradition. That is, very simply, not a useful answer.

5. How do you judge it? According to what criteria? What standards do you think should be applied to it?

I believe in a moderate approach. Certainly I think that both cultural and scholarly sources should be used as an important standard for authenticity. I also think that if we are to have genuine mysticism and a living practice, at some point those sources will have to be transcended and some innovations -- usually based on somebody's personal gnosis -- need to be introduced into the tradition so that CR becomes practical in our lives and for our emotional and spiritual needs.

From my earliest involvement in what was to become CR, I have been an advocate of "*aisling* (dream/vision) and archaeology" -- a balance between gnosis and history. Today I would add to that to make a triad with "argumentation", meaning not that we should be having rows over our practices but that both our innovations and our history should be open to civil discussion and thorough debate about what is meaningful and useful for us today within a Celtic context. Without all three of these elements I do not believe we can develop a full and meaningful living practice.

6. Have you had any conflicts with people over your personal gnosis? Please describe.

Oh, definitely. Some of my personal practices have come under fire from people in the community even though I have never said they had anything at all to do with my CR practices. Despite the fact that I had agonized over and examined the idea of engaging in these practices for over twenty years and had consulted with people who I felt were authentic authorities on the practices before doing anything at all about them, I was publicly accused of cultural theft and of mixing non-Celtic practices with CR.

I have been told that because I practice other paths along with CR, I can't actually be CR. I've been the subject of public attacks by some in the CR community and have lost friends due to these attacks. I am, naturally, saddened by this but there's really nothing I can do about it except remain true to myself and to the practices that I follow and the spirits whom I honor. I refuse to engage in public shouting matches about who's right. I don't see any point to it.

7. Have you ever felt ashamed or afraid to share your personal gnosis for fear of being attacked?

I think ashamed is the wrong word, but I have certainly been hesitant to talk about some things because of incidents like the one described above. I went as far as writing an essay for my LiveJournal that was later edited and published in an anthology on cultural appropriation and Paganism that deals with this kind of intimidation in reconstructionist Pagan communities titled *Work and Fear*. In a lot of reconstructionist communities, intimidation is heavily used to keep people inside some fairly strict lines of "cultural purity" that may never have historically existed as these traditions promulgate them.

I agree that discussion and close examination of personal gnosis and shared gnosis is vital within reconstructionist communities. These insights may be useful for the community, or they may have nothing whatsoever to do with it. They may later be found to be firmly within the tradition when further research is undertaken, and that corroboration is a very exciting feeling.

I do not, however, think that people should be shouted down and silenced for expressing opinions that fall outside of a tradition's mainstream. Mystics are always outside the mainstream of a tradition; there is no religion that I'm aware of where every member was a mystic. Outlying voices have almost always been regarded with suspicion because of their potential challenge to established authority and orthodoxy.

If people are not comfortable discussing the results of their meditations and their visionary work they are not likely to be able to connect with others getting the same or similar results. Nor is it likely that they'll just stumble across corroborating facts from the scholarly end of the tradition. I see discussions about personal gnosis as a necessary part of collaboration within a community and a way of sorting the wheat from the chaff. I see it as a necessary part of the growth and maturation of a community. Without these discussions, the community can only stagnate. The CR community already has a widespread reputation for stifling discussion and being more interested in books than in spiritual practice that I don't think is entirely deserved.

8. Have you ever seen something accepted as personal gnosis by a group that then went horribly wrong? Please describe.

With the strong tendency of the CR mainstream to reject any personal gnosis at all, it's difficult to cite any instances of an acceptance that went bad. At best, some things just haven't panned out very well in small local groups. There haven't been any community-sized disasters that I'm aware of, thankfully.

9. Have you seen the addition of personal gnosis handled well by a group? Please describe.

At an earlier point in the CR community, a number of people working separately were given the sense that moss agate has resonances with the Irish Goddess Airmed, who is an herbal healer. It seems to work well in my personal experience, and for those who have shared that insight.

There's nothing in the historical materials that suggests such a thing was a part of Gaelic tradition -- there is very little to suggest much work with stones and crystals at all -- yet many people are getting good results with this particular bit of information. We don't label it as part of the traditional lore, but it does get discussed as a part of CR as a modern development and I do think it's been helpful for some folks pursuing healing work within a CR context.

10. Please describe what personal gnosis comes to you. Do you experience it as a direct message from the Gods, or something more subtle?

Personal gnosis comes to me in a variety of ways. I do a lot of dreamwork and meditation on different aspects of my personal practice and lately I've been doing incubatory work as well. Sometimes I do feel like I get insights from the deities and spirits I work with, though I check on those just as thoroughly as I do the ones that come through more standard meditative practices or through divination.

My feeling is that different individuals receive their personal gnosis through sources and methods that resonate most with their personalities and the practices they employ in their daily lives. Some folks are more prone to getting insights through divination, for instance, while others get profound insights through dreamwork or through journaling practices. In my experience, it very rarely comes through full-blown in a flash of ecstatic light. A lot of my insights also tend to come when I'm deep in discussion with others, triggering associations by what's being said.

11. Who, in a group, gets to decide whose personal gnosis is valid? By what authority?

Within CR, I think that Celtic scholarly sources, folk material, and archaeology are the final authorities, depending of course on their individual reliability. If personal gnosis directly conflicts with those sources then it is going to be rejected outright, end of story. We have to deal regularly with ludicrous assertions like "the early Irish worshipped a potato Goddess" and "the Druids made pumpkin-blossom soup for their winter solstice celebrations" that are absolutely, patently false and provably so. Graves's "tree calendar" and its even more modern bastard offspring "Celtic astrology" is another example of something that might work for individuals but which is rejected by CR practitioners as being entirely inauthentic. It's only right that such stupidity should be shot down in flames.

If personal gnosis doesn't conflict with or if it can be confirmed by widely accepted sources, then it is likely to be discussed in more depth and even embraced by a working group or a larger community. I've had insights through different sources that have later proved to be documented parts of the historical tradition that were subsequently taken into larger community practice. Those instances have never been anything earth-shattering, but they've been personally important. Others in the community have had this experience as well.

12. How should disagreements over personal gnosis be mediated in a group? Is there any social engineering that can be done in a group's culture to better prepare people to be able to handle the process of discrimination?

Ultimately I think we should be polite and civil to one another as much as possible. Things that are demonstrably wrong should be pointed out, kindly at first, but with greater insistence if falsehoods are deliberately promulgated. People who publicly and knowingly publish lies as facts should certainly be taken to task publicly and exposed as liars.

In cases where something can't be demonstrated, but it makes sense in the context of the tradition, then it should be up to each individual to decide whether or not they wish to incorporate those things into their practice. Such things should be labeled as personal or shared gnosis so that others can judge its usefulness and veracity for themselves without mistaking such insights for objective historical truths of the tradition.

When personal gnosis matches up with sources regarded as authoritative, then they can be cited as part of the tradition and the corroborating sources should be given. I think these insights should be celebrated within the community as cases where someone has connected well enough with the tradition's roots as to be able to intuit a part of it through their own practices and meditations.

13. How trustworthy do you find ancient texts/primary sources?

I think that depends greatly upon the individual text or source, and what its provenance is. I certainly do not regard any written source from the Irish tradition as infallible. I'm not a literalist in any sense when it comes to medieval pseudo-histories or the mythologies. Everything within the Gaelic literary tradition was written down after the conversion of the Gaels to Christianity and must be viewed through that lens at the very least. All written sources need to be regarded with some skepticism and examined thoroughly for their biases, the influences on them from other cultures, and their assumptions.

With this said, I do think that a thorough knowledge of the major texts is important in any tradition where there is a literary corpus. "Lore" should be regarded as an important guide, and one with potential veto power, but not as defining the absolute limits of all knowledge regarding personal practice within any given tradition. Given the vast amount of territory and time-depth that "Celtic" encompasses, what holds true in County Mayo in the fifth century may have nothing whatsoever to do with Celtiberian practices on the Portuguese coast seven hundred years earlier.

It's important to recognize regional differences and to acknowledge that they will develop within modern reconstructionist paths just as they did in the original cultures. CR practice in New England is going to be very different than CR practice in the Pacific Northwest for reasons ranging from land spirits and weather patterns to the temperament of the inhabitants of those regions. Emphases on different deities will arise, holy days will be celebrated somewhat differently due to seasonal changes and local vegetation, and the flavor of ritual will depend on the cultural preferences of individual groups. All of these factors are also going to influence the nature of the personal gnosis experienced by individuals living in these diverse places.

14. How important is personal gnosis to your personal path? Does it define everything you do? Is it not really a big deal? Is it something you keep private? Could you be part of a group that didn't accept it - or are you now? Would you give up everything for it? How many life decisions do you make based on this?

Personal gnosis is extremely important to me in my work, but it is not the sole defining aspect of my practice. Some parts of my gnosis I do keep private, but other aspects of it are things I happily share with the community in hopes of getting more insight or finding potential corroborating information. I'm well aware that I don't know everything so it is important to me to check in with the community on a regular basis to compare notes and see if anyone else has a source or an insight that might prove useful.

The local group I'm part of is fairly open to personal gnosis at this point, for which I am grateful. I think I would be very uncomfortable in a group that refused or negated all personal gnosis of any sort. I doubt I would stay long. I would like to think that we support each other in our personal explorations and help to keep one another on track when we get too far afield while encouraging each other when insights tend to be supported by currents within the folk and scholarly traditions.

I don't know that I would "give up everything" for my personal gnosis. I do know that I have sometimes given up important things for it, including important friendships. It would depend a lot on the content of that insight and what I felt its source was. It would also depend on how strongly I felt it was corroborated by other sources. I've had discussions with my counselor at the Veterans Administration Hospital about some of my personal gnosis and how it affects my practice, and her feeling is that so long as following the advice of those voices or intuitions isn't causing harm, there's no reason not to pursue them. In many cases

I've found following up on some of my insights and personal gnosis, whether within or outside of the framework of CR, to be very healing for me or helpful for others.

There have been some serious life-decisions I've made based on my personal gnosis experiences. I have sometimes suffered for them in my community but have usually felt the rewards were worth the difficulties. I do believe that sometimes it's possible or even necessary to tell the Gods "no" for reasons ranging from physical impossibility to general impracticality or illegality.

Ultimately, I feel that so long as personal gnosis is labeled as such and it's not patently false, people should do as they please in their personal spiritual practices. If you want to stand on your head chanting "woooo" while rubbing blue clay into your navel, more power to you -- just don't call it Celtic.

The Druidic Dawn Q & A[351] (2009)

DD: Hello Erynn. First of all I'd like to thank you for taking the time to answer some of the community's questions. Welcome!

ERL: Hi Jenn, and greetings to everyone at *Aontacht* and *Druidic Dawn*! Thanks for giving me the opportunity to talk with you all.

DD: How did you first get involved in the Celtic tradition, and the Reconstructionist movement?

ERL: I first got actively involved in Paganism back in 1984. At the time the only thing I knew about out there was Wicca, so that was where I started, like so many others at the time. Reading Celtic mythologies and learning about ogam was what really sparked my interest in finding a Celtic path that was meaningful to me. The more I looked at the history and the archaeology and traditions of the various Celtic peoples, the more I realized that Wicca didn't fit the patterns I was seeing and so I gradually moved closer to a reconstructionist approach and attitude.

DD: Would you like to share some of your journey as an encouragement to the readers of Aontacht?

ERL: At the time when I was seeking, there wasn't an internet as we now know it. There were a few commercial online services like GEnie or CompuServe, with some Usenet access and email listservs if you were lucky. There were also Pagan bulletin board services like PODSnet, which was run on a FIDO model, so communication was slower and less far-reaching.

Because I wasn't really finding anyone who was doing what I was doing, I started talking about my research and my experiences on Celtic-L and founded the PODS Celtic echo in hopes of finding like-minded others. Back then it was practically heresy to suggest that Wicca wasn't Celtic, though it's become much more accepted and understood now. The folks on Celtic-L mostly wanted to talk about sports and current events; discussion of mythology, non-Christian spirituality, and anything hinting of Druids tended to be discouraged, sometimes harshly. Because of this I founded the

---

351. From Aontacht: vol 2 #3

Nemeton email list, giving those of us who were interested in the spiritual end of things a safe place for discussion. From Nemeton, other groups and email lists developed and the ideas and ideals of Celtic Reconstructionist Paganism began to expand on the web.

I never much intended to become a "leader" in the community but, as has been said, history is made by those who show up. I was one of the many folks who showed up and did the work. We're all still doing the work today. CR is far from highly developed at this point, though it has been finding its bearings and branching into a rich and multifaceted movement.

People find themselves inspired by different Celtic cultures and languages, interested in and touched by many different Celtic deities, and working on and reconstructing a number of approaches to ritual, devotion, household worship, magic, and divination. This is really as it should be, because "the Celts" were never a monolithic cultural structure. It's only to be expected that different groups and locations will develop different responses to the stories, the research, the deities, and their own land.

We're at the beginning of a movement. Anyone who gets involved can help to shape it and bring forth constructive and meaningful dialogue and ritual. All it takes is a sense of devotion that evolves into action and to sharing with the rest of the community.

DD: What are some common misunderstandings and misrepresentations of Celtic Reconstructionism amongst other members of the Celtic Pagan community?

ERL: There are a considerable number, and some of us addressed these in the CR FAQ, which can be found at http://www.paganachd.com/faq/. While it's important to remember that this document was written by committee, a good deal of it applies fairly broadly.

Some of the big misconceptions include the idea that CRs are all druids (only a few of us use that title), that we're Celtic shamans (I think we all uniformly shudder the idea), that we're hostile to Wiccans (some are but most of us just want folks to know we're not the same thing), that we're big meanies (okay, some CRs are obnoxious, but you get that in every community), and that we're all about intellectual pursuits to the detriment of our actual spiritual practices.

Like many misunderstandings and stereotypes, there's some small grain of truth to some aspects of these. For the most part, though, misunderstandings are just that. They may not always be helpfully dealt with by some in the community but there are those of us who are happy to engage with the rest of the Pagan community and to discuss the issues openly.

DD: What advice would you give the readers on how to address and overcome those misunderstandings?

ERL: Talking to folks in the CR movement is helpful if you're not familiar with us; unfortunately some of the folks on the CR lists tend to be very off-putting to new folks and those perceived as "outsiders". These folks make it harder for the rest of us. Just plain politeness from people speaking from the CR movement would go a long way to dealing with most of the problems. It's really hard for someone new to get an accurate look at the movement as a whole when a few loud people are monopolizing the discourse. The fact that we identify with a complex of cultures where warriors and honor were important doesn't give anyone an excuse to go off on people, which is something I've seen all too often.

The idea that CRs are only about intellectual debate and citing sources isn't helped by the dominance of that discourse in public. Very few CRs actually talk about their personal and group practices in public. The fact is that behind all the discussion there's a lot going on both ritually and as personal daily lifestyle practice, like living cultural virtues. Part of the problem is that people are hesitant to talk about their personal work because they're afraid they'll be told they're doing it wrong or they're not "Celtic enough." Many people feel they don't know enough to participate in the conversation and that restricts the types of discussions that are had in public forums. Remember that every one of us had to start somewhere and that we're all learning day by day.

Part of this is based in the misconception that there's only one "real" CR way of doing things. The fact is that the Celtic peoples were never a monolithic culture any more than Native Americans are one monolithic culture. Each tribe was doing different things than the tribe down the road a bit, and those things also changed with the passing generations. We need to understand and accept localization and regional variations within the movement, and to encourage discussions of what people are actually doing while listening with reasonable attention and respect. This doesn't mean that misconceptions shouldn't be corrected -- we're always going to correct someone if they start talking about ogams in North America, for instance -- but corrections need to be done in a way that encourages people to learn rather than shutting them down and shutting them out of conversation.

In the end analysis, courtesy and openness about who we are and what we do would solve a lot of problems.

DD: What originally inspired you to write a book on the Irish ogam? What do you think is the book's overall message or relevance?

ERL: When I first ran into the ogam system I was quite interested because it was something Gaelic. I picked up what books and materials were available at the time, but the more I read and the more research I did, the more I realized that what was being put out in the Pagan community wasn't actually true. There was no tree calendar. There was no tree astrology. Some of the letter names being used were entirely wrong, historically speaking. So I went searching for a more accurate historical perspective.

Eventually I realized that a non-tree-based system made a lot more sense to me and seemed more historically authentic, but nobody outside of academia was talking about it at all. This was what pushed me to actually write my book. I got four false starts on it over a period of about 18 years and threw them out entirely. Eventually I got a booklet together for a class at PantheaCon in San Jose that became the core of my ogam book. From there it was a matter of further research, refinement of the system, and expanding on the booklet to include other aspects of my use of the system.

As to the book's message and relevance, I think it's important for people to understand the origins of systems they're using. Tree astrology may work for some people, but no one should be claiming it as an "Ancient Druidic Astrology System." To make that claim is fraud. I think it goes back to individual creativity: if you create a system that works for you, own that creativity rather than trying to give it a fake historical cachet. The important thing is that it works! Honesty helps all of us in the community, and to acknowledge our own creativity is important. I would have far less quarrel with "Celtic tree astrology" if people weren't claiming the ancient Druids did it.

I'd like to think that my discussion of my rituals and experiences with the ogam is relevant to the community as an example of what can be done with the system, and that it will inspire others to further the research and the work. I think it's also an important book because it was written from a specifically CR perspective; there's not much of that out there as yet. There's a good deal of interest, but the movement tends not to be very accessible for a variety of reasons. I hope to make it more accessible through my work and to demonstrate that CR is not just spiritless academic discussion.

DD: Is there a particular ogam symbol or tree that speaks to you more than others? Is the 'Rowan' in your name connected to this?

ERL: Coll and nGétal are both very important symbols to me. Coll is the hazel tree and a symbol of poetry and deep wisdom. It's a quality that I work toward integrating and embodying in my life. It's an ideal I aspire to. NGétal is a *fid* that addresses wounding and healing; it's both the wound inflicted and the work of healing the wound. As a disabled veteran, this is a really important concept to me; I've been working for years on bringing myself back to health and, while it's happening, it moves slowly. This *fid* or letter is a reminder of my goals and one I use for much of my healing work. While the rowan tree was certainly the inspiration for my middle name, it wasn't specifically connected to the ogam.

DD: How are you progressing with your book about the healing potential of the Ogam?

ERL: It's going very slowly. I have about four books that I want to write at the moment, in addition to all the essays I've been doing for anthologies in the past year or so. I'm kind of overwhelmed with the amount of writing that I need to do and, as someone working with fibromyalgia, I only have a limited amount of energy to give to any one project at a time. I use the techniques I want to talk about, and they do often help me, but I still have a long way to go.

DD: Besides the ogam and Irish Gaelic Reconstructionism, what are some of your other major interests, areas of study and hobbies?

ERL: Wow, that's a huge question! I actually have a lot of different interests outside of ogam and CR.

Spiritually speaking, I'm a member of the local Shinto shrine and I do participate in occasional Hindu pujas when the opportunity arises. I do quite a bit of not-specifically-Celtic animist work. I've done a good bit of interfaith activism as well, though I'm certainly not on the level of the folks who are going to the Parliament of World Religions. My work has primarily been local on that front.

Sometimes when I want a break from working on intensive non-fiction writing I'll write some fanfic for fun and to clear out the cobwebs in my brain. I love to read, as well, though primarily nonfiction in the humanities and social sciences.

I really enjoy traveling when I'm able. This past summer I went on a three-week road trip to teach at an ADF camp-out and then visit many friends in California. It was a fantastic experience. It involved camping and hiking, which I love, as well as stops in San Francisco and Los Angeles.

Cooking is a lot of fun for me, and when I have the energy I really love cooking for friends. I keep a blog at LiveJournal where I talk about the ins and outs of my daily life, and I'll often post some foodporn about whatever I've been cooking lately. I love food from different cultures, particularly Asian, Middle Eastern and North African.

Musically I've always loved singing. For several years I was performing with Seirm, Seattle's Scottish Gaelic choir, though that's not the only public performance group I've been a part of over the years. I've studied gamelan, which is an Indonesian percussion orchestra, as well as playing many other kinds of percussion. I used to play guitar, though too much pain in the hands put a stop to that years ago. I love to go to live concerts, though, in many genres of music. Lately there's been a lot of steampunk music in my area, and quite a few of my friends are musicians of varying types, from medieval a cappella vocals to gothic industrial bands and I love to support them when I can afford to go to their shows.

I'm also a big fan of weird, obscure, and foreign film. I get a lot of really fascinating stuff online to watch when I'm in the mood. I find stuff by Werner Herzog and Jan Švankmajer to be really interesting and fun. I also love bad, cheesy science fiction movies!

On a more serious note, I do a lot of information activism around women veterans' issues like military sexual trauma, and am a member of Veterans for Peace. Peace activism, feminism, and environmental activism are important to me, particularly as they interact with human rights issues. A few years ago I was interviewed on the local National Public Radio station with one of the psychiatrists from the Veterans Administration about military sexual trauma, and I spoke on a panel to a regional Veterans

Administration health care professionals conference on spirituality and post-traumatic stress disorder. The local CR group I work with is also doing a lot around ritual work for warriors in terms of rites for people going off to war, and for folks returning from military service. We had a panel last year at PantheaCon on the warrior ritual for sending someone out and will be doing a similar one this year on our warrior return ritual. One of our folks recently returned from Iraq and we'll be doing his ritual in January. One important bit of this is that one of the chaplains from the local Veterans Administration Hospital will be coming to participate in the ritual, which I think is a really groundbreaking thing. I've been talking about the ritual and this aspect of it on my blog, as well as my experiences with my own warrior return ritual twenty-six years after leaving the military.

DD: What is your stance on other spiritual traditions, and what are your methods to avoid cultural appropriation?

ERL: I think it's important to learn about and understand other traditions, and to work on building bridges between spiritual communities. Attending the rituals or services of other religions offers not just an opportunity to learn, but an opportunity to show respect for those traditions by participating when it's appropriate. I really believe that we're less likely to be suspicious of or to offend people of other religions if we have seen or experienced what they do and learn about their traditions. And they, conversely, are less likely to be suspicious of or to offend us if they know us as individual human beings whose path is simply different than theirs. One thing I've learned is that when you're polite and you're doing your best to understand, most folks are happy to have you attend a ritual or a service and tell you about their tradition.

As to cultural appropriation, that's an immense and difficult topic. I did a couple of essays for an anthology on Paganism and cultural appropriation that came out last year, titled *Talking About the Elephant*, from Immanion/Megalithica Press. Because no culture exists in a vacuum, it's impossible for cultures not to influence one another. Respectful interaction is key. Knowing the sources of things and how they relate to one another is also vitally important. It's also very easy to read "cultural appropriation" into things that are not appropriation. Some Native American groups express the belief that any non-Native sweat practice is appropriation of Native tradition. The truth is, sweat rituals and practices are found in cultures around the globe. From Finnish sauna to Gaulish stone sweat-houses, there are models that exist and that do not in any way steal from Native American cultures.

One can legitimately be studying and trying to reconstruct an Irish sweat tradition without appropriating, for example, Lakota sweat ritual. The fact that most of the Irish tradition regarding this is lost means we have to look at other cultures to try to understand what might have been done, but that doesn't mean we can do a Lakota ritual and claim it's Irish. Honesty about our sources cannot be over-emphasized.

DD: What would you say is the predominant Celtic Reconstructionist view on topics like reincarnation, animism, ecological activism, meditation, etc?

ERL: I don't think there is one. The wide variety of personalities, locations, and cultural emphases in the movement means that all of these things are tackled as matters of individual conscience and personal practice.

DD: Do you mind briefly sharing your own personal opinions on the above topics?

ERL: I tend to believe in reincarnation as a transmigration of souls, that we come back in many different forms many different times. I think this view is supported by Irish and Welsh poetry where the poet identifies with many different kinds of animate and "inanimate" objects, and by a number of tales that tell of a venerable ancient who returns again and again in different forms.

Surviving evidence of beliefs does suggest that Celtic cultures experienced their religions as animist, with spirits, deities, or various other entities occupying landscape features like mountains or wells. It's how I approach my own personal practice. I think of pretty much everything as ensouled in some way.

As far as ecological activism, whether or not such a thing can be supported by lore, I think it's imperative. Without immediate, rapid movement on issues like global climate change and overpopulation, there's not going to be an environment left that will support human life. It's a matter of survival rather than theology or ideology. We're killing ourselves and we should stop that.

Meditation is a part of my personal practice, but I also know folks who don't really get anything out of it, or who have a lot of trouble settling into it. I don't think it's something everyone absolutely has to do. I think incorporating your spirituality into your daily life as a given that permeates everything, rather than as big formal ritual, is more useful and important. Living the various traditional virtues like generosity and hospitality has more practical value than trying to clear your mind for ten minutes if all you're going to do is get frustrated because you feel like you're not making any progress. Absolutely, keep up with some sort of practice, but don't keep it separate from everything else you do and are.

DD: Is it possible to have a "general Reconstructionist opinion" on any single given topic (ie is the Reconstructionist group cohesive enough to have an agreed stance)?

ERL: No. At best you're going to get a "most CRs think this is important" rather than "this is what all CRs believe or do".

DD: How do you make the historical, academic side of Celtic Reconstructionism into a well-rounded but active, every-day practice?

ERL: Study, research, learning, and communicating what has been learned has always been a traditional part of Celtic cultures. It was incredibly highly respected and encouraged. In the most traditional sense, one cannot be a Druid or a *Fili* without it. In the original cultures, people would spend years or decades studying and learning in order to fulfill their responsibilities to their tribe or clan.

For me, the research is usually fun, and I find wonderful things to integrate into my personal and group practices, often in the most unexpected places. Law texts have been as much a rich source for me as traditional mythological tales and folklore. Excerpts from source texts often make it into rituals or deeply influence the way I work. Language study is important because it allows participation in a worldview that can otherwise only be seen from outside. To understand what words mean and where they come from helps contextualize practice.

As a poet and a devotee of Brigid, study and history give me a rich field of myth and symbol that influences my writing and poetry. There's no part of my spiritual life that doesn't incorporate something from the historical and academic aspects of CR. The plants I use, the words I choose, the way I conceive of cosmology -- all of it is deeply influenced by the reading and study I've been doing over the years, and what people in the movement are sharing with each other face to face or in correspondence with one another.

Trying to separate the "academic" from the "spiritual" would be impossible for me.

It's the academic work that tells me about the deities I worship. Their sobriquets and their names have meanings, which we can't really know unless we understand something about the Celtic languages. It makes a huge difference knowing that Daghda's epithet *"Ollathair"* means "great-father", not "all-father," for instance. Without looking at a wide variety of sometimes difficult-to-find sources, I wouldn't have found the protective prayer that invokes the "silver warrior who has not died, who will not die" and the "seven daughters of the sea". Research taught me that juniper smoke was used for purification. Commentary on early Irish law texts gave me the image of the preserving shrine and of the connecting thread of poetry in all things. Archaeology has given us images of deities like Nehalennia and Coventina, of Ogmios and Taranis. This is the stuff of my daily practice. Without this, we would have nothing upon which to base our practices. Working with this material is also a reflection of the Gaelic preoccupation with truth or *fir*. Without knowing what's true, how can we practice at all? The study of history and Celtic cultures helps us find and recognize truth. It helps us separate the real from the fraudulent. Armed with truth, we can recognize when people are trying to scam us with fake "Celtic Bibles," Atlantean origin stories, and similar impossible claims. If Atlantis works for you as a metaphor, more power to you, just don't try to tell anyone that the Druids really came from Atlantis or that your granny left you a previously-unknown Old Irish text that you only have the German translation for.

The other thing it's important to recognize is that scholarship continues to move. What we thought was the truth twenty years ago is quite different now. New archaeology opens up new possibilities, uncovers the names of new deities, and sheds new light on historical practice. New translations of texts correct misinterpretations or offer up manuscripts that have never previously been available outside of their native languages, and these can influence ritual and practice very deeply. The interplay of history, academic work, and practice is a complex, ever-shifting dance. We can't remain static in the face of this ever-changing tapestry. These are good for examining the connection of spirituality and poetry with ecological sensibility and the process of connecting with the land.

DD: If you could recommend any authors or books to us, which would be, say your top five or top ten on that list, in no particular order?

ERL: This will be a rather idiosyncratic list, given my focus and interests. Always understand that other folks would recommend other books and authors. These are primarily recommended for folks interested in the path of the *fili* or sacred poet.

Joseph F. Nagy, *The Wisdom of the Outlaw: The Boyhood Deeds of Finn in Gaelic Narrative Tradition*
John Gregorson Campbell, *The Gaelic Otherworld*
John T. Koch & John Carey, *The Celtic Heroic Age: Literary Sources for Ancient Celtic Europe & Early Ireland & Wales (4th edition)*
J. G. O'Keefe, *Buile Suibhne: The Frenzy of Suibhne*
Robin Skelton, *Spellcraft*
Robin Skelton, *Samhain and other poems in Irish meters of the Eighth to the Sixteenth Century*
Jane Hirschfield, *Nine Gates: Entering the Mind of Poetry*

These deal with aspects of poetry, metrics, translation, and poetry as magic.

Gary Snyder, *The Practice of the Wild*
Jason Kirkey, *The Salmon in the Spring: The Ecology of Celtic Spirituality*

These are good for examining the connection of spirituality and poetry with ecological sensibility and the process of connecting with the land.

DD: What are your future plans, both personally and professionally?

ERL: I intend to keep writing as much as I can, though it does go more slowly than I'd like. There's a lot to say and to explore and there are so many things yet to contribute to the community to help it grow and mature. Definitely expect more anthology essays from me as well as new books in the coming years. More immediately, I'll be heading down to PantheaCon again in February of 2010, so if you're going, look me up! I go every year and usually do a class or two.

For the most part, I'm in a pretty good place with my life. I love the Pacific Northwest, I've got a good local community to work with, and I love having friends come visit me from all over. Most of my networking takes place over the internet, through my website and my LiveJournal. I'm always open to discussion with new people, though I don't always have as much time to talk with folks as I'd like.

At some point I'd love to go visit Scotland and the Isle of Man and experience the land there. I was blessed with the gift of ten days in Ireland some years back and had a fantastic time there. I think it's important to travel to the places that are important in our myths and stories so that we have a deeper understanding of the roots of this path. Those of you who live there already are very lucky to have that kind of connection with the land.

Mostly, I just want to keep practicing the fine art of being human. Someday I might even get it right!

DD: How do you see the future of Celtic Reconstructionism and Druidry developing in the 21st Century? How can we make them relevant for our present world crises and challenges?

ERL: I think that the ecological sensibilities of the Druidic movement are already relevant to the current situation. The ideal of our connection with the spirits of the land that we find in CR and the interest that many groups have in localizing that sense of the sacred follow the same spiritual logic. I believe that helping people move away from mono-vision is one potential role for these paths; to see the world through polytheistic eyes opens vast new possibilities. There's less of a sense that there can only be one truth or one solution to a problem.

I believe it will be important to recognize that there are important ways that we can never and would never want to recreate the past. CR needs to adapt and be open to change if it is going to be relevant in the 21st century. We can learn many valuable lessons from the past, but we can't remain stuck in it. Regionalizing and localizing are going to be important forces in the movement. Recognizing local climate, local ecology, and local sensibilities will, I think, become increasingly necessary. What works for Seattle, Washington isn't going to work for Phoenix, Arizona. The land is different and so are the people and the energies. We can't expect to do everything exactly the same way someone in 2nd century Ulster or 1st century Gaul would; for one thing, we just don't know the exact details. Our technologies are different, as are our social expectations. I do believe that CR and Druidism can offer a model for more sustainable living with the land.

The development of a virtue-based ethic is important within CR and could have a strong and lasting impact on the world at large if it's whole-heartedly embraced. I don't know what the future will bring. I just hope that we regain our collective sanity before we manage to wipe ourselves off the planet.

DD: Do you have any closing words or advice you would like to leave with us?

ERL: Live in the world like a poet. See the world through lovers' eyes. Practice compassion. Be kind to yourselves. Be excellent to each other.

PantheaCon Newsletter Interview (2009)

PCon: Tell us a little about what you'll be presenting at PantheaCon this year.

ERL: This year I'm a part of six different sessions. I'm presenting two workshops, speaking on three panels, and am a ritualist in one ritual.

My workshops will be focused on experiential material. Advanced Topics in Ogam will deal with some specific magical and healing techniques, while Meditation Techniques of *Filidecht* will be focusing on both modern Celtic Reconstructionist cosmological meditations and on some techniques that are hinted at or discussed in older sources.

The panels I'll be doing are one on a CR warrior ritual that our local group did for a member who is now in Iraq, one on mysticism in reconstructionist religions that I think will be really fascinating, and a panel with authors from Immanion/Megalithica, discussing Pagan small press issues and writing for small presses.

The ritual I'm participating in is the Ekklesía Antínoou Lupercalia. I participated in this ritual two years ago as one of the Luperci and had a great time.

PCon: Are there any PantheaCon events that you're excited about as an attendee rather than as a presenter?

ERL: For me much of the fun of PantheaCon is seeing old friends and meeting folks I've known online but haven't yet met face to face. It's a wonderful opportunity to say thank you to folks who have been influences on me in years past. Seeing everyone is one of my favorite parts of the con!

PCon: What challenges does the Celtic reconstruction movement face in bringing ancient practices into modern life?

ERL: Modern society is nothing like any Pagan Celtic society, so finding ways to bring those ideals and some of those practices into our time in relevant ways is a distinct challenge. Because the sources are so spotty on actual rituals, we must acknowledge that most things we do are based on ancient ideas but the words and many of the actions are going to be modern. To do this with respect for the ancient cultures and the deities is the biggest challenge of any reconstructionist path. Doing it without falling into hardline fundamentalism is problematic for many reconstructionist paths.

PCon: How do you incorporate Filidecht, or poetry, into your spiritual practice?

ERL: *Filidecht* itself is broader than just poetry but I regularly use writing and research as a devotional practice. I incorporate meditative and magical techniques that I've developed from early sources on the *filid* into my daily work as well. I'll be covering some of this in my *filidecht* workshop this year.

PCon: It seems to me that a lot of the neopagans practicing Celtic paths congregate in certain areas of the U.S., for example, in the Northwest. Do you think that there is a connection between physical location and spiritual practice?

ERL: I think there's always a connection between one's physical location and one's spiritual practice. The land we live on will always shape our perceptions of the divine. That said, I know Celtic Pagans in the desert southwest who seem to be doing very well there, so I don't think it's simply a matter of the Northwest environment being similar to Ireland and Scotland that influences us as Celtic Pagans or CRs. What this says to me is that we carry the deities in our hearts and adapt ourselves to the lands upon which we live and the spirits we find there.

PCon: You also work with Siberian Shamanic practices. Do you incorporate those with your Celtic practice or do you keep them separate?

ERL: I originally studied Siberian shamanism to determine for myself whether or not what I knew of Celtic spirituality actually was "shamanism." I really don't think it is. My Otherworld work isn't based on Siberian technique and, for the most part, I keep the two separate. The only real exception is when I'm doing healing work. For that, I think it's important to use what works for the situation regardless of its origins and so I may use ogam techniques and also call on Siberian spirits, but I make no claims that my healing work is anything but personal and syncretic.

PCon: What one piece of advice would you give someone interested in Celtic reconstructionism?

ERL: It's important to remember that CR, while rooted in history, is also modern. We need archaeology, but we also need *aisling* -- vision -- and a certain amount of argumentation. By that I don't mean shouting matches, but critical examination of evidence and of individual claims about practices and sources. No culture arose in a vacuum; CR cannot exist in a vacuum either. Beyond that, find practices and deities that appeal to you and work with them to make them an integral part of your life.

PCon: Do you have any new books out that people should know about? New projects that you're working on?

ERL: My most recent publications are two essays in *Talking About the Elephant: An Anthology of Neopagan Perspectives on Cultural Appropriation* from Megalithica.

I've got one finished for their upcoming anthology on animism and have been asked to write a second for that collection. I've also got an essay in progress for their anthology on sacrifice.

Another essay I'm working on is for another press on Pagan coming out experiences. I'm also preparing a response to an article that just came out in *Thorn* magazine about ogam.

As for books, I'm currently working on the *geilt* figure -- the sacred madman/madwoman in Celtic cultures, and may also be doing a paper on that topic for an academic anthology on disability and world religions. The *geilt* material plays into the book I'll be doing on CR *filidecht*. The two topics are closely related, but *filidecht* deals with someone who is integrated into society, while the *geilta* are marginal, outsider figures and in some ways can be considered an example of what can happen when something goes wrong with the initiatory process or when a person is dealing spiritually with deep trauma.

Poet On Fire: Erynn Rowan Laurie on Celtic Paganism (2010)[352]

"My spiritual life has been a meandering path . . . it helps broaden my understanding of how other people and other cultures approach the world and the sacredness of life."

When it comes to Celtic Reconstructionism, ogam, military Pagans, and the poetic arts of ancient Ireland, Erynn Rowan Laurie reminds me I have a lot to learn. Author and contributor to several books and blogs on Celtic and Pagan spirituality, Erynn was named the "Shining Star" of Polytheist Reconstructionists in Jason Pitzl-Waters' article on the most influential Pagans in *PanGaia* magazine. She is active in the Seattle Celtic Reconstructionist community and has been a speaker at the PantheaCon Pagan conference in San Jose.

SF: My first burning question is about PantheaCon: Did you ever find your hat?

ERL: Sadly, no. I'm still a little bummed over the whole thing. Thirty years is a long time to have anything of that nature, but so it goes. I've replaced the old fisherman's cap with a really spiffy trilby. The guy at the hat shop handed me a frequent customer card -- buy ten, get one free. I told him my last hat had lasted me for thirty years. He laughed and said, "Then I'll see you in thirty years!" I actually have several hats that I like, but that fisherman's cap was tough and it served me very well, whether I was out backpacking or running around in the Seattle rain. I'll probably get another one at some point because they're so functional, and black goes with pretty much everything.

SF: You're a pioneer of the Celtic Reconstructionist (CR) movement, but that wasn't always your path. I understand you're also an Alexandrian initiate. How did you find your way to Paganism initially?

ERL: I was interested in tarot and astrology as a kid, psychic phenomena and the like. When I was 12 or 13 I read a story in the

---

[352] interview by Star Foster on the Patheos website
http://www.patheos.com/Resources/Additional-Resources/Poet-On-Fire-Erynn-Rowan-Laurie.html accessed March 15, 2015

local paper about some witches and thought that made a lot more sense than the Christianity I was raised in, but it wasn't until I was about 23, back in 1984, that I actually met folks who were practicing, read some decent books on the topic, and started getting involved in the Pagan community in the Pacific Northwest. I talk about the whole thing in a little more depth in my essay in *Out of the Broom Closet: 50 True Stories of Witches Who Found and Embraced the Craft*, edited by Arin Murphy-Hiscock, who asked me if I would contribute to the anthology.

My Alexandrian initiation came about after I moved to Seattle, through Greenleaf Coven, which has lineage from both Alex and Maxine Sanders, though I'm not a practicing Wiccan anymore. I was elevated to second degree but never wanted to run an Alexandrian coven, so I didn't go on to get a third. I enjoyed the community and the friendships I found through that group, but British Trad Wicca never really moved me in the same way the Irish deities have. I found that the cosmology didn't appeal to me that much after I began looking into other options. Like most people, I got involved with the groups that were available to me at the time I was looking. Before my Alexandrian initiation, I was the priestess of an eclectic Pagan coven down in the Willamette Valley; we were really into percussion and trance dance.

My spiritual life has been a meandering path and I've explored a lot of things over the years. These days I'm very interested in Shinto and am a member of the local Shinto shrine, one of the few outside of Japan. We're very lucky to have such a resource so nearby, and it's been fascinating exploring it and experiencing the ceremonies. I've never had a problem with practicing more than one spiritual path at the same time; I don't feel that they contradict one another in any significant ways. I do feel that such exploration informs my thought on other aspects of my spiritual life and helps broaden my understanding of how other people and other cultures approach the world and the sacredness of life. I don't think that being a part of a Reconstructionist spirituality means that I have to give up my interests or connections in other traditions. With the BBC reporting about taiko drummers at a Bealtaine celebration in Scotland, I don't think I have much to worry about.

SF: You describe yourself as an animist and I know many people who follow Reconstructionist paths describe themselves as hard polytheists. Some Wiccan groups are focusing more on praxis to encompass different theological beliefs. How important do you think theological stance is to practicing CR?

ERL: To be honest, I think it's considerably more important to have a practice of some kind than to worry about the exact theological details of what we believe. Animism works for me, as does a semi-squishy polytheism, and I approach my spiritual life informed by both of these philosophies. I do think that theological discussion is important, particularly as it arises from our experiences and informs our daily lives. Yet when I'm at a Samhain vigil with a dozen people, I'm not going to vet them on the way in the door to ask if they believe the same things I do; ultimately we're all there to honor our ancestors and celebrate together. Whether they're hard polytheists or monists or atheists doesn't matter at that point. We're all there for the ritual.

I know there are people out there who say I'm a hard polytheist, though if it's defined as "each and every deity out there is always a separate entity" I can't quite agree. I do think that there are deities out there who are the same deity, like Thor and Thunor, for instance, who really are the same but whose name is being spoken in different languages and whose details are being appreciated from a slightly different angle. Yet that deity is not the same as Odin, nor Yemaya, nor Lug, nor Amaterasu Omikami. That's what I mean by "semi-squishy" polytheism. We're never going to prove anything about the nature of deity by any objective, scientific means, so I can only speak from my experiences of deity and the spirit world when I talk about these things.

SF: I've heard a lot of what we think of as Celtic Reconstructionism today sprang from just a handful of folks talking to each other and digging deeper into Celtic lore. Can you tell us a bit about how this process evolved? Did you have a goal to create a new religious tradition?

ERL: Before any of it went online, I think most of the face-to-face stuff was happening on the east coast, and I wasn't privy to any of it because I live in the Pacific Northwest, so I can't really speak to that from my own experience. There are better people to ask, who were actually present at those discussions and the festivals where some of them took place. I hope that doesn't sound like I'm ducking the question — I honestly don't know the details. I do know that Murtagh's late-1980s talk on what "Celtic shamanism" might look like if it had actually existed was a seminal event for many people, and I've talked to him about it several times since I first met him. He's a fascinating guy and really sweet, and I know he's very happy and excited about all that's happened in the years since that presentation. He feels like it's a vindication of much of what he had been saying for so long.

Once we did get online, things moved a little more quickly, or at least made networking more possible. It was always a joy to share sources and insights with others who were working toward the same goals, even if we weren't all doing exactly the same thing. We talked about what we were reading and suggested books and articles to each other, along with talking about Celtic languages and cultures and how to sort through things to arrive at tentative conclusions about what we could know of ritual and beliefs in pre-Christian Celtic religions. We also had a very uphill fight to convince the larger Pagan community that Wicca was not actually Celtic; happily, that work has paid off and we don't see too many people making that claim anymore. I think people who are interested in Celtic Paganisms have become somewhat more discerning over the years.

I do think that, overall, there was a specific consciousness of working toward creating a new religious tradition from what we could discover about the past. When you're working with a spiritual tradition that left very little of its actual ritual materials to future generations, you do need to start some things anew and it wouldn't be accurate to say that CR is exactly what any of the previous cultures were doing. In my opinion, it's a reconstruction because we don't have a lot of pre-Christian material to fall back on and revive, and we're having to fill in the often very large gaps with what we find in other related cultures and from what works for us now, as a post-modern society with global communications.

We as individuals wanted at some point to have groups to work with, rituals to work with, and some general ideas of what CR actually encompassed as opposed to what it did not. Those ideas and opinions have been evolving over time, as people add more to the base of knowledge that we're working from. It's been good to see people finally working on writing material with a CR community in mind. I know we'll be seeing more of it in coming years, as CR gets more exposure in the larger Pagan community and material becomes more easily available for people to just pick up and work with as opposed to having to do it all yourself from scratch. The *CR FAQ* project was a major effort and has, I think, helped somewhat with folks moving in that direction. I still see people who have read it, though, and come away thinking that we're monolithic and that it has to be absolutely traditional with nothing at all modern in it. I don't know any group or individual anywhere who's doing CR with absolutely nothing modern in it; I'd be extremely skeptical of anyone who claimed they were.

In starting up the online discussion groups of PODS Celtic in the Fido BBS days, and Nemeton in the very early days of what subsequently became the web, I was actually looking for my peers or, even better, for people who might know more than I did, rather than trying to deliberately start a tradition. I eventually realized that if I couldn't find them, I'd have to then share what I knew so that people could examine the material for themselves and become my peers. I really did feel inadequate to the task, and I often still do, because there's just so much still to learn and I'm only grasping a fragment of what's out there. There were a few people at the time who were on a similar level of knowledge -- a little more or a little less than I had -- and that was a great joy to discover. We could help each other grow. It meant I no longer felt I was talking into a vacuum, and these resources gave us ways to encourage each other and allowed others into the dialogue who would never have had the chance if it had remained a localized offline process. Ultimately, I think the process has been a success, because now there are a lot of good, intelligent folks who are pursuing the path and who are contributing to the community who wouldn't be out there if we hadn't laid the groundwork in the late-80s and early-90s.

SF: You talk about the desire for Celtic Reconstructionist groups to begin to form local communities in the same way Heathen hearths have sprung up. Are you seeing more local groups form? Is there a networking initiative underway in the CR community to help facilitate this?

ERL: I'm certainly seeing more signs of local groups out there, though I'm not nearly as wired into the larger CR community as I was in years past. That said, the community's pretty fragmented and there's no central forum like Nemeton used to be, so I can't say there's any kind of networking initiative at the moment. The IMBAS organization was an early attempt at creating a larger organizational framework for CR, but I think it was just too early for an international organization. There weren't nearly enough people who were interested and committed enough to make a project like that work. These days there are a few smaller organizations around, and I know there are an immense number of individuals who are doing their own work. I think growth of this sort will be slow because of the community's fragmentation.

Locally, we have a small group that's been meeting for a couple of years now, though we have a long way to go before we have a stable set of rituals for the year or anything that we're able to just sit down with someone and say "this is what our group does and how we do it." I think a lot of this is the result of the fact that we're building it by committee rather than having someone come down with a fait and saying, "we're doing it this way." There are advantages to either option, and doing it as a group is the slower path.

What I do see are individuals who are taking what they find online and working with it when they feel it suits their needs. I'm also seeing people translating extant CR materials into other languages. Pieces that I've written or been involved in writing have been translated into several languages. I've seen stuff out there in Portuguese, Spanish, German, Russian, and French so far; I know there are some active folks in Brazil who have been doing quite a bit of work on translations for their community. That really excites me.

SF: I first encountered your writing through A Circle of Stones: Journeys and Meditations for Modern Celts *over ten years ago. It had a huge impact on my personal practice. What was the inspiration for the book? Why use meditation beads?*

ERL: My inspiration for the beads was really from some local Welsh Trad friends of mine who were working with beads in that way, built around their own tradition. It seemed to me that this would be a fairly easy way to introduce some of the cosmological concepts that I'd been finding into a personal practice, immersing the user in a way of thinking, particularly because almost everything I was using for the meditations themselves was from traditional Irish or Scottish Gaelic language sources. I would do it very differently now than I did then, because I've learned so much in all those years, but I'm always surprised and heartened to hear that people continue to find that work valuable or inspirational, so thank you for that.

Beads are a pretty easy and concrete way to have a personal practice. The idea of having this little ritual you can perform whenever you need a connection to your sacred cosmology or your deities, rather than needing something elaborate like a feast for the ancestors or passing between two bonfires for blessings is appealing to a lot of folks, I think. It can be a solitary pursuit, so it doesn't depend on finding other people to help you carry it off in the same way you need three or four or a dozen people and a large room or an outdoor space to do a more complex ritual. It's really just a ritual you can put in your pocket and take with you anywhere. It's a reminder of our place in the greater pattern of things.

SF: You've also written a book on ogam, the Irish Gaelic alphabet. I understand you work with ogam differently from other authors on the subject. How is your book, Ogam: Weaving Word Wisdom, *different from other books on the subject, and why is that difference important?*

ERL: Most of the books on ogam that have been available in the Pagan community have come at the system from a tradition that identifies each letter with a tree. They tend not to go any farther than that, even though there's this immense, rich tapestry of material available on the topic. A lot of the material that most -- but not all -- of these books rely on for their source meaning is the reading that Robert Graves proposed in his *The White Goddess*, which is really a deeply flawed work that has more to do with Graves's imagination than with Celtic spirituality or the ogam alphabet and its origins.

The tree ogam is certainly a valid way of coming at the system, but I was never really quite able to fall into that as a meaningful symbol set for myself, and I saw contradictions in some of the Pagan resources I was reading, so I looked into it more deeply, going as far as taking a university class in Old Irish language to help my understanding. What I found was quite surprising, in that the meanings of the names of the ogam weren't, as I had always been told, all trees. They were really conceptually much more like the Norse runes, where the names translated to objects or concepts, only some of which were trees. Once I found that out, suddenly ogam became a much more useful and accessible system to me. I was able to actually touch it and turn it around in my mind as a workable system for both magic and divination.

There are literally dozens of different ogam lists that people could work with in the source material, and limiting one's understanding to just trees robs the system of much of its beauty and depth, in my opinion. My book opens out the system to let people explore the other aspects of ogam, beyond the trees and their mythic and folkloric associations. It also helps people get an understanding of *filidecht*, or the craft of sacred poetry, in the Irish tradition, because the ogam material is embedded in the poet's craft as metaphor and allusion. I also point out that the ogam didn't have a druidic origin, which is a deeply-held myth in the Pagan community; its origin is several centuries after Christianity arrived in Ireland, and was a part of the monastic literary tradition, but this doesn't mean we can't use it in ways that are meaningful to us as Pagans. To call ogam a druidic alphabet is misleading if one is referring to its history rather than its use by some contemporary druids.

SF: There are several Druidic traditions that have been around for a while and delve into the myths and practices of the ancient Celts. Where does Celtic Reconstructionism merge and diverge from those traditions?

ERL: When we're talking about groups like the Order of Bards, Ovates, and Druids (OBOD), there's really not much overlap or commonality at all in terms of theology or practice. OBOD and some of the other older druid groups come out of the magical lodge tradition and have more to do with groups like the Masons or the Odd Fellows than they do with Celtic spirituality. It's a long and valuable tradition, but it doesn't really have anything to do with what CR does. I know that some OBOD material has incorporated more actual Celtic sources into it in the last decade or so, but they're very clear that what they're doing is in the western magical current, and that OBOD is a philosophy rather than a religion per se.

Groups like Ár nDraíocht Féin: A Druid Fellowship (ADF) are certainly much closer to CR in terms of methodology and some aspects of theology, though I've always rather twitched when ADF refers to groups within its organization that practice with Greek or Norse or Lithuanian deities as "druids." To me, that's a complete non sequitur and I've had to just say, "Okay, they mean ADF druids, not druids in the original cultural sense" and back away slowly. They do emphasize research and scholarship, and we certainly have that in common. Their cosmology is more similar to what CRs are generally doing than is the cosmology of Wicca. I have some great friends and colleagues who are ADF members and whom I respect very much, even though we're not doing the same things.

Last year I went to ADF's regional Eight Winds festival and had a fantastic time; I'll be going back again this summer and one of the things I'll be doing there as part of the workshops program is having an open dialogue with Skip Ellison, who wrote a book on tree ogam, to discuss our differing perspectives. That should be a great conversation and it's one we're both looking forward to. Eight Winds runs over the summer solstice weekend and this year, 2010, it's in Washington state -- last year's was in northern California -- so I'll be driving down to see everyone again.

Overall, CR focuses primarily on Celtic cultures and deities, and looks to what we can know about what was done historically in building our practice. Our ritual formats are usually quite different than either the OBOD style groups or than ADF's ritual framework.

SF: At PantheaCon you spoke about the need for rituals to honor the leaving and returning of our soldiers. That seems like such an ancient thing, yet I hadn't encountered talk of it among modern Pagans before. Is this something Pagan military chaplains are active in, or is this something you feel is lacking in Pagan ritual on military bases?

ERL: First, there are no Pagan chaplains in the U.S. military at all that I'm aware of. There are Pagan lay leaders and there are, I believe, some enlisted chaplaincy assistants who are Pagan, but the chaplaincy itself is a particular designation within the military officers ranks and the vast majority of military chaplains are from fairly conservative Protestant Christian denominations. Issues regarding Pagans in the military are becoming more visible, primarily because there are more out Pagans serving these days than there were twenty or thirty years ago. It can be difficult and sometimes even dangerous to be an out Pagan in the military, even now.

When it comes to ritual for deploying or returning Pagan military personnel, these things are being dealt with in local communities if they're being touched on at all, and that's pretty rare. There are a few resources out there for military Pagans, but it's still very thin on the ground. Most of what I've seen happening tends to be in Reconstructionist Pagan communities, because we're the traditions with a strong warrior current, if you will. A lot of Wicca and other more general modern Paganism tends to regard "warrior" as more of a spiritual than a physical role, or to reject the idea altogether.

The local CR group's warrior rituals sprang from the fact that one of our people was being deployed to Iraq and had requested a ritual before he left. We had to do a lot of hard thinking about what we were going to do before we came up with that ritual. The return ritual arose under similar circumstances, though I was the person who was the recipient of that first return ritual, almost thirty years after I'd been discharged. It's very powerful stuff, going through a vigil like that as a reintegration to the civilian community, and there's far too much to say about all of it for an interview like this. All I can say in brief is that I found it a very profound experience and that it has a very deep influence upon my life.

I think one thing that needs to be said is that not all people in military service are "soldiers" — neither the Air Force nor the Navy designate their people that way; we're airmen and sailors, not soldiers, and that doesn't mean that people in those branches never see combat. Another thing that I think is very important is that combat veterans are not the only ones who need these rituals. Just because we're not being shot at by an enemy doesn't mean we aren't dealing with serious issues of our own. From military sexual trauma to the stresses of dealing with the possibility of having to fire nuclear weapons on a daily basis, there are a lot of things going on in the military that service members need to be able to process when they're discharged or when they return from deployment. Some of us have always been military — I was born in a Navy hospital and have been associated with the military, whether I've wanted to be or not, for my entire life. That kind of family and personal history leaves a very deep mark, because military culture is very different than civilian culture on so many levels.

SF: You served in the Navy in Hawaii from 1979 to 1982. As a devotee to the seafaring "Uncle Manny" myself, I have to wonder if you have an affinity for Manannán Mac Lir?

ERL: I was only in Hawaii for part of that time. I spent a good chunk of my enlistment at the Bangor submarine base on Puget Sound as well, which is how I came to live out here in the first place.

Manannán is a very large part of my personal spiritual practice. I've done several large-scale rituals for or with him over the years, including spending three days in vigil out camping on the Washington coast seeking his aid. Every year near the summer solstice I do a ritual of paying rent to Manannán, which is a Manx tradition that's mentioned in the Manx Traditionary Ballad.

I work with him as a gatekeeper and, in some ways, as a psychopomp within the Gaelic tradition. He has affiliations with but is apparently not strictly a part of the Tuatha Dé Danann, and I've found him a really fascinating figure. He's one of the deities who has his own altar in my home, rather than having to share his space with someone else. His guidance has had a huge influence on my work and my practice. There's a very nice website out there called the Temple of Manannán Mac Lir[353] that has a good bit of material on him, including artwork, links to articles, and rituals.

SF: You're participating in a Military Pagan blog project being put together by Jason Pitzl-Waters of The Wild Hunt. Can you tell us a bit about that?

ERL: The new blog started up very recently and is called Warriors and Kin, and it's a part of the Pagan Newswire Collective project. Jason has been really good about finding people from different parts of military culture to write as bloggers. We have family members, active duty, and retired members, as well as folks from different parts of the political spectrum. All of us have different perspectives on military service and what it means to or has done to us. It's just finding its feet, but I think it will be a really interesting project, looking at different aspects of military life and warrior traditions from a Pagan perspective.

Jason spoke to me about the project back in February when we met at PantheaCon. He's very interested in exploring all different aspects of Pagan culture, from the arts to politics to news of import to Pagans and their friends and allies. I'm quite excited about participating. My personal focus has been on issues of women veterans and service members, as this has been my own personal experience. I'm also interested in the Veterans Administration system and disabled veterans, looking at what services are available and how being a Pagan may affect our interactions with that system. I'm seeing some interesting changes in the last couple of years, particularly in the area of the VA addressing spirituality in its counseling programs, as well as an increasing awareness of military sexual trauma. The VA has a very long way to go yet, but they're making some moves in the right direction, at least in places like Seattle. I know that rural VA hospitals and clinics still have very antiquated attitudes and equipment and some real difficulties in actually serving the needs of veterans, particularly women veterans.

SF: I understand you're working on a book about "poetic madness." It's a common thread in Celtic myth that brilliance in poetry, divination, and riddles is the product of an encounter with madness. My favorite example of this is the portrayal of Nimue in Bernard Cornwell's Arthurian trilogy.

---

[353] http://www.manannan.net/ accessed March 15, 2015

Why is encountering madness so important in poetry? "Fire in the head" sounds profound, but isn't it also dangerous? Didn't we invent Prozac to prevent that sort of thing?

ERL: I wouldn't say that brilliance in poetry and such are strictly the product of an encounter with madness. The tradition says that when one wishes to become a poet, the search may result in poetry, madness, or death. Madness in this context is, in a lot of ways, a partial failure of the poet to fully integrate their experience. Seeking poetry is a search for an initiatory experience and sometimes that experience is traumatic and results in an inability to cope with society in normative ways. In an essay I recently wrote, I discussed the *"geilta,"* the mad poets like Suibhne and Myrddin, as being similar to those who suffer from post-traumatic stress disorder. Poetry can become a coping mechanism, a healing path, or simply an expression of the experiences one has in the depths of this kind of suffering. Yet it isn't the madness that brings about the poetry. The spark has to be there beforehand or there's no art to it at all. The poetry that happens here is a result of an attempt to cope creatively rather than entirely succumbing to despair and dying of it.

The book I'm working on deals with *geiltadecht* as one way to look at poetry as a healing path within the CR tradition. For many years I've wanted to write a book on *filidecht*, but I found that I really needed to write about this aspect of *filidecht* before I could address the more normative poetic tradition. *Geiltadecht* is a part of *filidecht* that deals with a lot of the exceptions to the usual rules, so I think it's important to discuss that in some depth because those exceptions are important.

I've had people walk away from workshops I've taught on *filidecht*, thinking you had to be broken or crazy as an occupational requirement, and that has never been what I've said. It's really a misinterpretation of the message. Becoming a *geilt* is a side effect that sometimes happens, or it's a way in which a really damaged person may find their way into the poetic tradition in an attempt to work on their healing. In discussing the *geilta*, I can then go on to the *filidecht* book and say "this is what the socially-sanctioned part of the tradition looks like" as opposed to what I'm often doing, which is the personal healing work that was being attempted by people who were marginalized and unable to be a fully functional part of mainstream society.

There is definitely an idea in the Gaelic tradition that poetry is dangerous. Anything powerful can be dangerous, particularly if it's misused. Any initiatory experience has the potential to go wrong and damage rather than initiate the recipient; I think that's an issue that gets far too little attention in our communities. Yet the fire that burns down buildings is the same basic fire that warms us and cooks our food. The key is learning responsibility and control, which reduce the chances of accidents happening. It's important to understand that, even under the best of circumstances and with the utmost care, an accident can still happen and people can be hurt or killed because of it. Spirituality that doesn't address danger and failure doesn't address the whole of human experience.

I do think it's possible that overmedicating people can destroy or seriously mute their creative impulses, but I believe the same thing about overworking people so that their lives consist only of working, eating, sleeping, and going back to work. There has to be a certain amount of room in society and in individual lives for creativity, for time to think, for time to learn and explore. Looking at madness as necessary for the creation of poetry is like looking at breaking your leg as necessary for taking a day off of work. They can certainly bring those results, but it's not the most desirable way to go about getting there. I work with what I have, which means I deal with *filidecht* through the lens of the *geilt* most of the time. It can often be as much a hindrance as a help, but it does make me work harder at my art to try to make things communicable to others.

Interview with Marc Sommerhalder
(bachelor thesis) (2012)

1. What do you think about myths in general: Do they have a meaning, purpose or function?

I think, overall, most of the recorded Irish myths have a fairly heavy Christian influence to them, but that they are useful to reconstructionist Pagans anyway. I suspect they served the purpose of keeping some connection of the Irish Christians with their ancestors, but they would also have served for entertainment, and as an illustration of some of the virtues and values the Irish tribes found in their ancestral past.

2. How can myths be used in a religion/in religious practice?

I believe myth can serve as a useful resource for ritual drama and for personal spiritual and meditative practices. They can be used to gain some understanding of how different deific or heroic figures were seen at the time the tales were written down. They can give some idea of what a particular deity or hero might respond to in a ritual situation, and offer epithets for invocation, among other things.

3. What do you think about Celtic myths (tales of the Mabinogi, Irish mythological cycle) in particular (do they differ? Do you prefer some and why?)?

I enjoy the myths and tales a great deal. While I have some familiarity with the Welsh material, my primary interest is and has always been in the Irish. So very little is known of Gaulish and most other Celtic mythologies, so for the most part I have tended to stick with the Irish because there's a vast amount of material there. I definitely see an Irish influence on Welsh myth, so there is certainly a use for knowing about more than one Celtic culture/language's mythologies and literary tales. Comparisons can be extremely useful and informative.

4. How can Celtic myths be used to reconstruct Celtic belief?

I think, at best, they offer a window into how the Christian scribes understood their Pagan past. They really need to be read with other Indo-European mythologies with an eye to similarities and differences. The archaeology and folklore of a given culture also need to be considered when looking at the reconstruction of belief and practice. Literary sources must always be approached with caution and with an eye for the influences on those who wrote them down, and their purposes and audience. I also find a knowledge of the Irish legal and poetic texts and literary gloss texts (rough medieval dictionaries) to be of a great deal of importance, as many mythological and pseudo-historical tales are found in them; they are a deeply important source.

5. How do you personally use myths in your religious practice?

I use the myths as inspiration. I use them as resources for my research in working out how to approach my personal practice, and in construction of personal rituals. Information in them may or may not be terribly accurate, but it can certainly give useful references for names and epithets of deities and heroic/folkloric figures, it can provide associations of deities/heroes with regions, rivers, landscape, animals, plants, birds, and other things, it can show rough sketches of ritual or divinatory techniques, and can provide inspiration on the various moral and ethical stances of the people who shared these texts.

The myths and other texts provide not only positive inspirations, but also negative examples of warning against the violation of different virtues or strictures within a society. The texts point out the importance of virtues like truth, generosity, eloquence, good judgment, and kindness. They also provide passages from which to draw liturgical text for rituals and ceremonies, they offer hints about beliefs regarding the Otherworlds, the nature of the inhabitants of those Otherworlds, what afterlife beliefs may have consisted of, and how the origins of the landscape were conceived.

I have found the texts important enough to my practice that I have studied Old Irish and have done translations of a few primary texts for myself, to better understand both the texts themselves, and what might have been the underlying ideas. Some concepts are difficult or impossible to translate fully into English, so it's important to have a grasp of the original language and a working vocabulary of technical terms in order to properly understand the background and philosophies of the spiritualities expressed in the texts.

6. Which are your own influences (religious traditions, authors, sources etc.)? Do you see yourself as part of a religious tradition?

I'm going to stick solely to Celtic and primarily Irish and Scottish sources here, as that's where I draw the majority of my practice from. One of the most important texts for my practice is the so-called *Cauldron of Poesy* poem, which is one of the texts I've translated for myself. It deals with the training and work of the poet in Irish society from a mystical and internal point of view, rather than dealing with the grammatical and metrical aspects of poetic training. This is an extremely important text for my practice of *filidecht*, the magico-poetic tradition of Ireland.

The Suibhne Geilt text, the story of the Frenzy of Suibhne, is also an important source for me in my study of the phenomenon of the *geilt* or sacred mad figure. Many of these people were poets, but what primarily interests me about them is that so much of the material surrounding them appears to describe a manifestation of post-traumatic stress disorder. As a military veteran, this is something that directly concerns me, and I find the models of the *geilta*, both those who recover from the madness and those who do not, a fascinating and informative source for ways to deal with my own psychological issues in a spiritual and artistic manner.

The usual Irish sources, from the various versions of the *Book of Invasions* to the *Voyage of Bran* all have interesting material in them that has been very useful for me. I've used selections from *Cormac's Glossary* for some of my work as well, particularly as it relates to the practice of *imbas forosnai*, which appears to be an incubatory ritual for communication with Otherworldly powers. I've done a lot of study of the *Auraicept na n-Éces* or *Scholar's Primer* in my research on the ogam alphabet and ogam divination.

From the Scottish material, the *Carmina Gadelica* is an important text that offers source material for prayers, spells, and charms as were current in Scotland in the 18th and 19th centuries; some of this material was in use until the early- to mid-20th century as well. The author Martin Martin discusses Highland and Island practices including poetic incubation and animal sacrifices in some of his books, written in the 18th century.

I use a wide variety of secondary sources that are too numerous to mention. I can't really list all of my sources, even my primary sources in translation, in this email as there are just too many of them.

As to whether I see myself as part of a religious tradition, I'd have to say yes. I am certainly a part of the Celtic Reconstructionist stream of spiritualities and my personal practice touches on *filidecht*, the craft of sacred poetry. A lot of my writing has been useful and perhaps inspirational to others who are a part of this spiritual community and I hope to continue producing material that will be of use to others in years to come. While I am by no means the only person doing work within the tradition, I'm one of the few authors who has published very much as yet, though it is my continual hope that other authors will write well-researched, well-written, and well-thought-out books on practice and theologies. My path as a *filid* is very much polytheist and animist and I see writing both prose and poetry as a part of my spiritual practice.

Author's Roundtable: Interview
by Jason Bourne (2013)[354]

JB: How long have you been writing? Has writing always been something you wanted to do?

ERL: I've been writing all my life, and getting published since I was in junior high school during the 1970s, in various venues from the school paper to the regional Mensa newsletter. I think the first time I got published in something with a national circulation was in the late 1980s, in a Pagan newsletter, *Circle Network News*, where I'd contributed a short piece. My first professional publication was an article in *SageWoman*, in 1994, another Pagan publication. I framed a copy of that first check and kept it on the wall for several years to remind myself that I was a "real" writer. It was a very exciting moment. Several of my articles and essays, and some of my poetry, have been translated into about half a dozen different languages over the years. My first book, *A Circle of Stones*, was published in 1995 and is going to be reprinted in a second edition to be released in May of 2012.

Writing is definitely something I always wanted to do, ever since I realized that every word in the books and stories and poems I had ever read had been *written* by another person. I was very young when I started reading – about three, according to my mom – and to me it seemed like magic. The ability to create worlds, to make music with language, to convey emotion and information and mystery, has always impressed me very deeply. There's something holy about creating like that; I think that to write well is to share in that power, to touch the heart of what it is to be human. Words well-used have the ability to change the world, and to change the hearts and minds of those who read or hear them.

JB: What books or stories have you written?

ERL: I have a fair list of publications out these days from various small publishers and have three more projects definitely due out this year, with a few more anthology pieces waiting for the editing process to finish. I enjoy working with small presses because it feels

---

[354]   https://jbournesblog.wordpress.com/2013/01/14/authors-roundtable-erynn-rowan-laurie/ accessed March 15, 2015

so much more personal, and because I think I have considerably more control over what the finished work looks and feels like. Small presses are, in my experience, much more willing to work with an author rather than dictating content. They don't pay as much, but I don't have to worry about making a living with my writing, so I'm content with what comes.

My work is mostly non-fiction, with a fair bit of poetry as well. I write essays, articles, and books primarily on Celtic Pagan topics of interest. My biggest project so far has been my book on the early Irish ogam alphabet, *Ogam: Weaving Word Wisdom*. People use it for divination and magic, and I spent about eighteen years doing the research and writing for it before it was finally released in 2007. Part of what took so long was the fact that I'd had to throw everything out and start over entirely, four times. It was very frustrating, but I think the end result was much better for having done all that.

My approach is very much based on history and research, but the applications are as much influenced by practical modern use as by the historical context. I'm always very clear about what's history, what's conjecture, and what constitutes my own interpretations of the material, so that people can decide for themselves how they want to handle the material and what they want to do with it. I'm all about the footnotes; I tend to be a little obsessive about them, but it's largely because when I read, I want to know where things come from, so I'm giving my readers that same ability to chase down sources themselves if they want to.

My first fiction piece was published last year in a short story anthology. I was very excited about that. I enjoy writing fiction but don't particularly pursue publishing it at the moment because I feel like my non-fiction work is more important, both to me and to the community for whom I write. I write fiction largely as a way to relax and clear out the cobwebs between longer and more serious projects. It's possible I'll try writing a novel someday, but I'm not terribly motivated to do so right now. When it comes to writing outside of nonfiction and research-based work, I'm much more inclined toward poetry, and my first poetry collection, *Fireflies at Absolute Zero*, is due out in late October of 2012 from Hiraeth Press.

One of the works I'm proudest of is a piece in the academic anthology *Disability and Religious Diversity: Cross-Cultural and Interreligious Perspectives*. This was particularly significant for me because I don't have a degree. I've only taken a couple of spare college classes, and have never had the money or the focus to attempt to earn a degree. I live with post-traumatic stress disorder, fibromyalgia, anxiety disorders, and a variety of other issues that mean it's hard for me to keep to a consistent schedule, or to deal reliably with other people on a daily basis. Far too often, I have days when the idea of leaving the apartment is just overwhelming. I work very hard on having something like a normal life, but chronic pain and the effects of my other problems make it difficult.

My article for the anthology is about PTSD and the *geilta* or sacred mad figures in early Irish, Scottish, and Welsh literature and myth. These figures are usually presented as "going mad" after great trauma, either in battle or as the result of violence or the death of someone close to them. The ways in which they act out that madness reads as being very like the symptoms of PTSD. Yet most of these individuals are strongly associated with poetry, music, or prophecy, and I find the concept of seeking healing through poetry, art, and interaction with the sacred a very inspiring one. It has served me as a very useful model in my own personal work in dealing with PTSD and other issues in the context of my Celtic Pagan spirituality.

JB: What are some of the hardest things you've had to overcome as a writer, in order to be published?

ERL: Dealing with my body and the mental issues caused by the PTSD, the fibromyalgia, and my other problems is the hardest part. I've been in chronic pain for so long that I no longer remember what it feels like to not hurt. One of the symptoms of fibromyalgia is a sort of brain fog that makes it very hard to focus, and this can cause memory problems as well. When I have a migraine or when I'm having brain fog, I can't focus enough to even read, much less write a sentence. I've found myself sitting on the couch for hours, reading the same paragraph or sentence over and over again because I've forgotten that I read it just a moment ago, and that's incredibly frustrating. Some days just opening my eyes is agonizing because light hurts. It's hard to feel like I can accomplish anything at all when I hurt that much.

As you might imagine, this can make it very hard to put together a coherent sentence when I'm writing, as well. I have to try to take advantage of the days when things are a little clearer, or when I have enough energy to do anything at all, and sit at the keyboard with a lot of discipline and determination. I write even when I don't feel well, because sometimes just getting a hundred words in a file means I've done *something* that day. So often, I have to make a choice between writing and making something to eat, or writing and doing the laundry. Taking care of the basics of my daily life can be very challenging. I've had to let go of my expectations over the years and realize that this is what's normal for me and that I'm all right with the choices I make in order to research and write and finish up a project to send off to a publisher.

Not every day is like this. I have really good days where I don't hurt that much and the words flow and I feel inspired, but I take them as the blessing they are and don't imagine that every day will be a good one. I've also had to come to the understanding that I'm going to hurt whether I do anything or not, so I might as well do things I enjoy when I'm able to, and writing is one of the things I enjoy most in my life. It gives me an incredible sense of pleasure and accomplishment to finish a project, and to finally hold a book or a magazine in my hands that has my work in it. This feeling makes all the struggles and the pain worth the effort I've put into it. On days when I can't write, I feel restless and incomplete. All those writers who say that we write because we'll die otherwise, they're right. I can't refrain from writing. Something precious and irreplaceable in me would be extinguished.

JB: Is there any advice you have been given that you could give to a young up-and-coming writer?

ERL: Sit down every day and write something. It doesn't matter what – an email, a blog post, a poem, a paragraph in your diary – but write. It doesn't matter where or when, or whether anyone else ever sees a word of it. Every word you write is another word that makes you a writer.

Learn to accept constructive criticism and editing, because not every word you write is going to be a good one, or appropriate to the work. We all have an ego attachment to our work, because that's what writers do, but it's important to detach as much as you can and learn to be a better writer by working with an editor or a writing group, or even just a friend whose honesty you can count on and whose work you respect. Always hearing how wonderful you are is never going to improve your work. You need to hear where you've got weaknesses and where you misstep, then make an effort to work on those weaknesses, in order to grow and learn.

If you want to write nonfiction, learn to do research. Learn where to look for information, how to keep track of it, and how to share it effectively with others. Be in love with learning new things, and be willing to throw out or modify old theories when something comes along to change what you know. Write about things that spark your passion, because that passion will come through in your words. Flexibility and openness are so important to the process of writing.

Even when writing nonfiction – or perhaps especially when writing nonfiction – be awake to the music of language. Read your work out loud and listen to what it sounds like. Think about how it will sound to someone else's ears, and how it sounds to your own. Is your language clear? Does it really say what you intend to communicate to others? Does it flow and have beauty to it? Do the words bring you up short or take your breath away? If they do, you're on the right track.

JB: Do you think writing has any benefits, and if so what would they be?

ERL: Writing expands us. Every time we sit down to write, we learn something new about ourselves and about the world around us. Writing opens our souls to something larger than ourselves and allows us to share what we hold within. I've learned so much about life and people and the world through my writing, no matter what the genre.

It can be a healing art as well as a path of learning. Sometimes there are things in our lives that are difficult or impossible to talk about, to say out loud, or even to whisper in the presence of others, but the ability to write those words can crack us open and let that pain out and turn it into something manageable.

To sit silently with a keyboard, or a pen and paper, teaches us to quiet ourselves and listen, both to the world and to ourselves. I think, properly done, writing can be a deep and valuable spiritual practice, no matter what your religion or spirituality.

Through my writing, I've met so many absolutely incredible people. I've been given opportunities to travel, and to teach some of the things that I know, because of the things I've published. Every year I drive down to California to one of the major Pagan gatherings, PantheaCon, and speak there; I have a wonderful opportunity to talk with my readers, to offer new information that I haven't yet had a chance to write about, and to learn from other people who are involved in our communities. I've even, this summer, been given the amazing gift of being able to lead a pilgrimage to Ireland to teach poetry and writing as we explore sacred sites associated with Brigid, the goddess and saint, as the patron of poetry, smithcraft, and healing.

None of this would have happened if I had not taken a chance and submitted my writing to publishers and to magazines. I'm never going to be wealthy because of my writing, but my life has been so vastly enriched because of it. It has been the most amazing blessing imaginable.

JB: Has writing made you a better person? Was there a point in your life where writing helped you deal with something, a death or a problem relationship perhaps?

ERL: I like to think that it has. Writing has shown me how the process of growth is a slow one that happens a little at a time. It's shown me that it's okay to make mistakes, because we can go back and edit if we need to, we can change ourselves just as we change our words. It offers me a way to look back at where I was five or ten or twenty years ago and understand where I've moved forward and where I still have work to do and things to learn. Writing offers incredibly valuable perspective.

Poetry has been a deeply healing practice for me, and it was particularly useful for me when I was an inpatient in the PTSD ward at the veterans' hospital back in the late 1990s. Poetry allowed me, for the first time, to talk about things that I had never before dared to say out loud, and showed me that there was a path through the horror and the confusion. Ordering my words helped me to order the chaos of my mind and my emotions, and it gave me a handle with which to grasp the enormity of some of the things that had happened to me, and that are still happening in the world. It has allowed me to fight to right some of the things that are wrong in the world.

Writing allows me a constructive way to express rage and sorrow and fear so that it will not destroy me. It's given me strength to continue when I thought I had no path forward. And it's allowed me to express my deep gratitude and joy to friends and family and to the other powers at work in my life for all the great gifts I have received over the years as my life has improved.

Interview for *Tending Brigid's Flame* with Lunea Weatherstone

LW: Erynn, how did you come to know Brigid?

ERL: This might sound a bit unusual but I was introduced to her by another of my deities, Airmed, initially through their mutual interest in healing and herbcraft. I suspect most people, even those who might have heard of her, would consider Airmed an obscure deity, but she has been very important to me over the years and I am deeply grateful to her for introducing me to a deity who is central to my practice.

Brigid the healing deity was eventually subsumed by Brigid the patron of poets as we became better acquainted, and it is this Brigid who has made the deepest impression on my life. I have been interested in poetry since I was very young, and Brigid has led me to some very deep and worthwhile things in my poetic work, connecting that poetry to my spiritual work in a very direct way. Not long after this shift in focus from the healer to the poet, I began practicing the ritual of flamekeeping through Daughters of the Flame and my dear friend Casey Wolf, with whom I had been corresponding for several years in *Pagan APA* back in the mid-1980s.

Flamekeeping has been both one of the most profound and one of the most stable ritual practices I have undertaken in my life. Even when it has only been the act of lighting a candle with Brigid's name on my lips, it has been a central and necessary act of mindfulness. As I write this, I am in the middle of an international move and have been living out of a suitcase for the last few weeks. That will probably continue for a while longer, until I have my own apartment again, but one of my Brigid images and some of my flamekeeping ritual items are in boxes that I sent ahead of me me, ready to be set up as the first sacred thing in my new home. I'm not currently in a place where I can do a flamekeeping ritual with open flame, but I am still keeping my shift through meditation and focus until my altar can be erected again.

Coming to know Bríg Ambue, a Brigid associated with outsider warriors, has been part of the healing work I've done surrounding the PTSD that developed while I was serving in the Navy many years ago. That work has been deeply connected to my poetic work, and my work with the theme of the *geilt* or sacred mad figure of Celtic mythologies; there are many resonances to be found there with people suffering from PTSD, and many of these figures are also poets.

LW: *Tell us about filidecht and your practice of it.*

ERL: *Filidecht* is a Gaelic poetic tradition, which had both secular and sacred functions in early Gaelic societies. While the word means the craft of the poet in a literal sense, it carries larger connotations than the English words "poet" and "poetry" usually convey. The *filid* were professional poets who went through many years of education and training and it should be noted that in Ireland a *fili* is quite different from a bard, who was considered an untrained, amateur poet of less status and skill.

The *filid* distinguished themselves through the use of complex poetic meters, and through the use of magical and oracular arts, in addition to their composition of poetry for social and political purposes. They were required to be able to create extemporaneous poetry, but they also practiced incubatory rituals for inspiration and divination, and had prophetic functions in their communities. As satirists, they could curse those who acted against them or against the best interests of their communities, and the practice of satire was regulated by law. They were experts in the tales of their people and would have had deep and detailed knowledge of history, and of the genealogies of their patrons, as well.

Filidecht as I see it practiced by modern Celtic Pagans focuses primarily on the artistic, magical, and spiritual currents of poetic work. My own practice is centered around artistic creation that arises from the search for *imbas*, a word meaning poetic inspiration, but which carries connotations of an overwhelming spiritual ecstasy achieved and directed through techniques of poetic composition, incubatory ritual, and cultivation of the internal cauldrons spoken of in the poem referred to as the *Cauldron of Poesy*. Working with the cauldrons demands a deep engagement with our emotions, unlike many Eastern paths, which emphasize detachment. *Filidecht* is also a healing path for me, through the pursuit of my art.

I see the practice of modern *filidecht* as animist at its heart, and my own practice reflects this. My poetics have always been very much affected by the land on which I live, and the various spirits with whom I work, as well as by Brigid and some of the other deities that I worship. As such, I expect that my practice will be strongly affected by my move to Italy, and the process of becoming acquainted with the land and its spirits. Incubation and Otherworld work will be necessary, as well as finding a way to get out into the land here to go camping and hiking as I develop new connections and new relationships with this place.

Part of this process is learning the plants and animals, the seasonal and weather patterns, and the character of the land, which means getting outside as much as I'm able to observe and absorb the physical and spiritual environment. The complementary work is incubation and journeying to explore the spiritually resonant space that develops, and experience how the Otherworlds connect with this place. Poetry comes as part of the integration process, working through and learning to understand this matrix.

Poetic initiation in the Gaelic traditions was said to lead to one of three things – poetry, madness, or death. The *geilta* reflect the potential for madness in the poet, particularly through the experience of violence. Poetry becomes a way for someone so wounded to find a path to healing through confrontation of the experiences, and the transforming power of words and art. I have found the practice of *filidecht* to be immensely healing for me, bringing together Brigid the poet and Brigid the healer through the conduit of Brigid the warrior and outsider. Bríg Ambue has helped with my personal sense of reintegration after traumatic experience.

Because of an experience I had when I've done talks on *filidecht* and *geilt*, I feel it's necessary to expand a little on the concept of "madness" here. I use the word as a signifier for some kinds of mental illness, or for the emotionally damaging result of trauma that can twist and ravage a person's life, and I apply it to myself when I refer to myself as a professional madwoman. For me, it is a reclaiming of a certain amount of power over my circumstances, and what has happened to me over the course of my life. I also understand that sometimes, for other people, the word can be very problematic. It's an extremely imprecise word, and it's important to understand that in this context. I use it specifically because it appears in the context of poetic initiation in the traditional texts.

When I speak of madness, I do not mean that poets are "mad," or that you have to be mentally ill to be a good poet: I have had someone walk away from one of my talks having misinterpreted me in that manner even though I clearly stated during the talk that this was not what I meant. Nor am I saying that "madness" is going to make a person a good poet. It is what happens when something goes wrong in a biochemical, spiritual, or emotional sense, and poetry is one path of many that can help in stabilizing or healing from trauma and depression, or some other conditions, for some people. When one cultivates poetic skill, it is possible to express painful experience in a very artful manner that can be healing for the poet and for others who might read that work. It is also possible to write really bad poetry you could never show to anyone else – except maybe your therapist – that is still very healing for the writer because it allows the poet to speak of the otherwise unspeakable, to approach a state or an experience through a potentially less triggering back door of metaphor and allusion, or of mythic parallel. Poetry and the practice of *filidecht* can be a crack through which the light begins to shine into chaos and darkness.

LW: How do you personally experience Brigid in the creation of your poetry?

ERL: In Cormac's Glossary, Brigid is said to be three sisters: Brigit *be n-éces*, Brigit *be legis*, Brigit *be goibne* – Brigid the woman-poet, Brigid the woman-physician, Brigid the woman-smith. It is Brigit *be n-éces* that I most often approach in my poetic work.

She is a source of inspiration and understanding for me, as both a deity with a strong and specific personality, and a well of metaphor with which to work. I feel her presence sometimes when I'm writing, and her altar has always been near my desk so that I can spend time in contemplation and have that physical reminder of her presence in my work. When the flame is lit on her altar, it is filled with her vibrant energy rippling out through the room and into the world from that place.

Brigid is often a background to the Otherworld journeying and the dreamwork that I undertake, and she is one of the deities I call on when I go into these spaces. Sometimes she will go with me, or will meet me there. When I am there, I am sometimes gifted with images or experiences that I bring back with me, and craft into poetry.

I also feel that she helps with my process of refinement of the poetic work once it has been initially drafted. That editing and refinement process is as critical to the practice as the originating spark of inspiration, and can be much more demanding for the dedicated poet. The word *éces* signifies not just poet, but scholar, and this editing and refinement is the work of the scholar as well as the poetic artist, because it is diligent study that brings a wide vocabulary of both words and images with which to work. That scholarly aspect of the poet is also necessary for drawing connections, for understanding the linguistic and symbolic layers that manifest in deeply resonant poetry, and for making certain that all the essential senses of a thing are present in the poem, or for digging them out of the images themselves in order to create a poem that expresses as much of them as possible.

Brigid is present in the words, and in the hands that write. She is present as the bright spark of the mind, and the thread of memory. She is the water in the well of wisdom, and the salmon in the spring, consumed by the poet and bursting into poetry. Brigid is the song, and the signal-whistle at night, warning of the approach of danger. She is the string in the harp, resonant with magic, and the skill with which it is played.

She is the fertile darkness of the incubation chamber that gives birth to chanted poems. Her knowledge enlightens and inspires.

LW: Do you have a particular devotional practice connected to your creative process?

ERL: My central devotional practices are twofold.

First is the ritual of flamekeeping, which honors her and brings her visibly to mind as the spark in the well of wisdom. I keep the flame in company with others as part of the Daughters of the Flame, and of Brigid's Irregulars, which is a specifically reconstructionist-oriented group that has a shared liturgy. The flame is kept by groups of nineteen, each of whom tends the flame every twenty days in sequence. Brigid tends the flame herself on the twentieth day. The flame manifests Brigid's presence in the world, passed from hand to hand by members of the flamekeeping orders, even when we live scattered to the far corners of the world. Most often, I dedicate all of my creative work to Brigid on the days when I am keeping her flame on my altar.

My second devotional practice connected to my creative work is reading and research. As Brigid is a scholar, so I study as well. It is my joyful duty to learn and to understand the kinds of things that a traditional *fili* would have known. Myths and history, ogam and poetry, symbolism and ritual, law and folklore and language, are all a part of this body of knowledge. I have too often heard it said that practitioners of reconstructionist paths "don't have spirituality," only books, but I think the people who say this don't understand that the study itself is a devotional act, and that books are ritual tools for us. Without our study, without our knowledge of myth and folklore and history and custom, we would have very little upon which to base our personal spiritual work as contextualized in a particular culture. You can never know the joy of discovering that an inspired insight you're using in ritual has historical precedent if you're not doing research work.

Both of these processes contribute to the soil from which my poetry grows. Reading, when meditated upon, places mythic images and cultural knowledge into the subconscious, where it can be incubated and produce insight that connects things into patterns; these patterns can manifest themselves consciously as the insights upon which we base our creative and ritual work. This is one of the purposes of our study, not the random cataloguing of dead, empty lists of facts.

Another of the purposes of devotional reading and research is cultivating the understanding of what might be seen in dream and visionary work. If you find yourself in an Otherworld space and find yourself confronted by a Raven, it might be difficult to know which Raven you're dealing with. Ravens in Gaelic spiritualities are very different than Ravens in Pacific Northwest spiritualities. Their powers manifest differently, they are or represent different deities and spirits, and they carry extremely different messages. Not all Ravens are the same Raven, and it is important to be able to distinguish them, to discriminate in the positive sense of the word that is the ability to tell the difference between one thing and another – between water and hydrogen peroxide, or between edible and toxic mushrooms, for example.

Being widely read helps give range and understanding to the interpretation of dreams and visions, and it also allows for a much more interesting and artistic integration of these figures and images in one's poetic and other creative work. Study helps a person to understand the context of a thing, to know what fits and what doesn't in a particular culture or mythology. Part of the work of a poet is interpretation, and broad knowledge gives a better basis for that interpretation, which can be transformed into wisdom through discerning practice.

If I respect and honor Brigid, then I must also respect and honor what she does, and one of the things she does, one of the things she is, is the work of the scholar. If I wish to devote myself to her and become more like her, I must cultivate that scholarly aspect of myself and develop the talents of discernment and synthesis. One of the goals of devotional work is to become more like what one has devoted oneself to, and to bring those qualities into our lives. If I am to live authentically as a devotee of Brigit *be n-éces*, then I must devote myself to learning and to the poetic arts, and I must cultivate the pursuit of wisdom.

LW: In an article on your website, I love that you say: "Celtic Pagans must be poets, even if they aren't great poets." Can you expand on this a bit? And how would you suggest a devotee of Brigid access this poetical part of herself?

ERL: An early Irish law text says that all things are connected by a thread of poetry. In that sense, all of us have some spark of poetry within us, something that links us to one another, and to everything else that exists.

On the surface, my statement can be read as a call for everyone practicing a Celtic Pagan path to try to have some skill with words, to be an artist with them and to use them as tools of beauty and magic. I do think that this is important, and it's obvious that we all have to start somewhere in learning those skills. Very few people outside of myths begin with the fire of *imbas* burning on their tongues. Not everyone is going to be a great poet, or even a good one, but we can attempt to make our speech artful, to bring beauty to our expression, and to practice the poetic art as a spiritual path of learning and devotion.

Beneath the surface of the words, poetry is about how we live in the world, about who we are as human beings. Do we strive for truth and beauty and compassion? Do we work on ourselves to become better human beings, and to leave the world a better and more just place for our having existed? The thread of poetry here is the art of being human, of manifesting whatever gifts or arts we have within us as an integral part of our souls. We speak of dancers or athletes as being "poetry in motion" and this is a part of what I meant by the statement as well – living our lives as poetry.

We must be willing to take risks and to make mistakes if we are to learn and to cultivate our humanity. We must be willing to look at our mistakes and to analyze them if we are going to learn from them and move on to new and more interesting mistakes and eventually, with a good dose of determination and practice, to the skillful application of what we have been learning.

We must become poems, become words of power, become moments of beauty in the world. Even our roughest and most painful experiences, our sharpest edges, our night terrors, can be used to bring forth something profound and poetic if we are willing to do the work. This takes looking at ourselves with honesty and knowing that we will never be perfect, and understanding that we can still at least attempt to act with grace when we have a choice.

For those who wish to practice poetry as an art as well as a metaphor for life, tapping into those experiences, the things that generate the most powerful emotions, is a place to begin. Learning to put those things into words that are both strong and artful takes time and a great deal of work, but it is rewarding, and there is deep and powerful transformational magic in the process.

Sitting down and putting words on paper, or on a screen, is a fundamental part of the process. If someone is serious about poetry and practicing the art of poetry, it's very useful to try composing different kinds of poems, whether they have specific types of rhyme and meter, or they are attempting to achieve a particular artistic or emotional effect. Over the years I've read and worked with dozens of books on writing and poetry, playing with exercises and trying new things. I've studied with other poets. I've also read hundreds of volumes of other people's poetry, both translated from other languages and by poets writing in English. I've done some reading and translation of poems from other languages myself. We need the examples of both good and bad poetry in order to understand what works when we're dealing with the rhythms and sounds of language. Every good poet I've ever read has been a wide reader of poetry. It takes exposure to art to refine our own art.

In a spiritual sense, I think it's necessary to find something to devote ourselves to and to immerse ourselves in it. If there is no particular passion in your life, look to Brigid for a spark of inspiration, look to the land around you, reach into history and myth and see what presents itself. Carry a notebook and scribble down thoughts and images and overheard scraps of conversation. Record dreams. Read everything. Look at works of art. Listen to music. Walk with your eyes and your heart open, and observe the vast world around you. Look deeply into your own heart and explore the things that you love, and the things that ache and tremble with your pain. Breathe slow and deep.

Now write.

Bríg Ambue

if you believe I am the comforting mother
        you are wrong
if you believe only in the creation of my forge
        you are wrong
if you believe my songs are only to praise
        you are wrong

I am the *cainte*
        singing curses on my enemies
I am the destroying flame
I am the wolf
        who lays low the tyrant
I am wrath and fury blazing
I am the brown swan rising from the lake
I am the torch in the hand of every *díberg*
I am the poison of satire and pain
I am the anger that calls to justice
I am the foot that treads upon evil
I am the fear in the hearts of oppressors
I am the shield against every attack
I am the courage that streams in your veins
I am the death of every illusion

my children shatter every binding chain

Literary Magpie Interview
by Jory Mickelson (2014)[355]

Jory Mickelson: How do you see your role as a poet? Is it to generate work that expresses your feelings/thoughts or is there something deeper there?

Erynn Rowan Laurie: That's actually a tricky question to answer. I see the role of a poet, of myself as a poet, as something multivalent and polymorphous. Certainly I write poems that explore my thoughts and feelings, but that's rarely the entirety of what's going on in a given poem.

For me, the creation of a poem is a sacred act. I intend the poem and its composition to connect me to something outside of myself, as well as reaching very deeply into the core of my being to draw out something essential about my experience of life and of the world around me. Poetry is something I regard as a devotional act, as well, and many of my poems address deities and spirits, speak with their voices, or tell their tales. I've also done a lot of poetry steeped in dream imagery and the feeling of being in a dreaming state, with a sense of the surreal to them.

In addressing the role of myself as poet, rather than the types of poetry I tend to write, I am trying to follow the ancient traditions that place poets as seers and spiritual figures, and to touch the wellspring of that inspiration in a search for wisdom. This is as much an embodied, sensual wisdom of the flesh as it is of literary tradition and knowledge, or of the types of spiritual wisdom expressed in myth and folklore. I see my poetic purpose as, in part, burrowing into mystery and finding meaning in physical and spiritual experience.

In finding ways to experience and understand mystery, I also see my role as delineating a poetic healing path through the experience of trauma and finding ways to integrate that experience into a more functional life. There are poems that I write strictly for my own personal work on my issues, poems that don't ever see publication because they are too personal and they're not meant so much as art as they are intended as medicine in an Asclepian, magical, dreamwork sense. Some of this poetry may be nearly as artful and polished as the work I present for publication, but a lot of

---

[355] http://jorymickelson.blogspot.it/2014/08/interview-with-poet-erynn-rowan-laurie.html accessed March 15, 2015

it is very rough-hewn and visceral, intended primarily to begin the work of speaking about unspeakable topics, bringing them into consciousness in a more-or-less safe manner so that I can work through them without having to voice them to other people before I'm ready.

Ultimately I see my poetic work as a way to speak deep truths into the world, and myself as a keeper of the sorcery of words. Words are incredibly powerful things and can be wielded in so many ways – as weapons, as tools, as seduction, as art, as glamour and illusion, as healing, as the making of ardent wishes. All of these things are revelations of truths of different sorts, or concealments of truth in ways that highlight the deepest roots of a thing.

Jory: That is quite a first answer! One thing a reader first notices about your poems is that they tend to be all lowercase and mostly without punctuation. Did this style develop naturally? Was it something that happened with revision? Can you talk a little bit about your decision to move away from typical grammatical structures?

ERL: There are a couple of reasons for that style. One of my favorite poets as a child was e.e. cummings, whose work usually lacks capitalization and has non-traditional structures. Later influences on my work include the Surrealists, and the Beat poets, all of whom have tended toward non-traditional structures, less emphasis on formal grammar, and lowercase typography, though each of those poetic traditions approaches their subject matter quite differently.

I also find that giving less attention to capitalization and punctuation leaves the work with a more stream of consciousness feel and can foster a more dreamlike atmosphere, which is important to some of the types of poems I write. Ambiguity can arise when the reader finds a lack of punctuation in some of the poems, allowing more room for idiosyncratic interpretations by the reader, and for multiple possible layers of meaning.

In German, nouns are all capitalized, and that lends a very different emotional weight to texts in that language than English has. If you look at the work of Rilke in German, your eye is drawn to the capitalization and to the nouns where, in English, that visual emphasis is absent. I think this gives German poetry a different sort of rhythm than poetry in English, and illustrates what I'm getting at to some degree.

Rather than a focus on traditional English language punctuation and capitalization, I prefer to work with sound and flow, with how things feel in the mouth, the vibration of sound in my chest or the air passing between my lips, and the various regular and irregular rhythms that can be generated through line or stanza length, or word spacing and breaks. Consonance and assonance within a line or a stanza or an entire poem can encourage particular emotional resonances, feelings of warmth or distance, or evoke feelings of connection with particular times or places. Some sounds are bright and sharp, while others are rounder and deeper, more resonant.

I think that some of this may be the result of my having spent years as a vocalist with different choral groups from the time I was a child until well into my adulthood. To me, language is very musical, and its sonic qualities are important. I can also liken certain types of sounds to various types of musical instruments in a poetic context, and strive to create poems that are reminiscent of different types of music. Some poems are percussive, with the driving depth of timpani or the complexity of a gamelan ensemble, while others are more like strings, or woodwinds.

If we consider poetry a form of sorcery, then sound sets the mood and pattern for the spells being woven and the realities being created. Some poems have a feeling of breathlessness and a rush to them, while others build slowly, layering on their power with repetition and emphasis. In these poems, capitalization can signal a shift in the power being touched and directed, the choice of a line or stanza break might place a breath as effectively as any comma or period.

In translations of the *Greek Magical Papyri*, there are words capitalized as *voces magicae*, as words of power, that stand out from the text in an emphasis of their potency, and these words or strings of sounds might be recited or chanted in ways distinct from the rest of the text, lending them a particular sense of uncanniness. My poem on Abraxas[356] borrows a couple of those words – ARAI, LAILAM – and in the recitation of that poem, those sounds seem to come out of an abyss of magical vibration. Sometimes, when the sounds and the words are just right, I can feel the hair on my arms rise when I recite them aloud. For me, there is a liquidity in non-traditional structures that's very appealing, and I find it easier to tap into that electricity, that potency, when I use those techniques.

---

[356] Erynn Rowan Laurie, *Fireflies at Absolute Zero*, Hiraeth Press, Danvers, 2012, p. 27

I've done some work with traditional poetic forms and, as a prose writer, I'm very conscious of proper capitalization, grammar, and punctuation. Even in my prose work, though, I try to have a poetic consciousness as I approach the page. Nonfiction can absolutely have a flow and a feeling of artfulness to it that is, sadly, often neglected, particularly in academic writing. It's possible to be factual and clear while still having a sense of the beauty of words or the resonance of sound, and to bring a poetic turn to the phrasing. Language should not have to be angular and utilitarian any more than architecture must. I think there's a difference between clean lines and sheer, boring ugliness, but appreciating that and bringing out those differences can lead one to walk a delicate balance. How do you get your point across quickly and easily while still allowing breath and life to flow through the words? How do you engage the reader if your goal is clarity of communication?

I honestly think most prose writers would be well-served by studying poetry and poetic technique, and that it would help bring something deeper to their work.

Jory: I would say that your poetry is lodged in landscape. Deeply. Do you find, now that you have moved to Italy from the Pacific Northwest, that your work is changing because of it?

ERL: The separation from a place that's been so important to me for so long feels strange, but I've always been something of a wanderer. I miss the place, but am quite happy where I ended up. I've been spending so much time attending to the purely physical aspects of moving from one continent to another and establishing a new place to live that I've not yet had a lot of time to settle into the spiritual aspects of it until very recently.

Because of the physical demands of transplanting my whole life to a place so very far away, I've honestly not had that much time or energy to write, though I've done a few poems for an anthology recently. The anthology was a themed one, so it wasn't really a chance to dig down into the place where I'm living now. I'm taking up the challenge of learning a new language, finding new friends, and trying to navigate a new city that's not laid out in ways I'm used to. I'm slowly growing acquainted with the streets and alleys, the waterfront, and the green spaces of Trieste, where James Joyce and Italo Svevo and Umberto Saba lived and wrote. I'm finding a new pace for my life and developing new rhythms and habits.

Certainly, I think that being in a place so different is going to affect my poetry and my prose writing, once I'm able to get more comfortably back into that mental and emotional space. With the Adriatic Sea and the hills of the Carso surrounding me, there is a certain familiarity to the landscape, like the waters and mountains surrounding Seattle, but the entire atmosphere of the place is still alien in a lot of ways. I haven't lived in a place with this much sun since Hawaii, back in 1980. I always felt like the rain and the mist of the Salish Sea helped cultivate a certain amount of my poetry, bringing forth particular themes. The weather in Trieste is very different—more humid, hotter, windier, and with vastly more thunderstorms. The levels of history here—Istrian, Celtic, Roman, Austrian, Slovenian, Italian—it's a fascinating border mix and a brilliant weave of new things for me to explore. It's all very exciting.

Jory: Writers, over the course of their work, tend to accumulate a set of repeated images. This is sometimes called their symbol horde. What symbols do you see reoccurring in your own work? Also, what would you say is the one animal that keeps appearing in your poems? Why do you think that is?

ERL: I think things that recur in my work tend to be oceanic themes - waves and mist and things in and associated with the sea, for instance. Water, generally, but the sea in specific, and the Well of Wisdom from Irish mythology -- the salmon of wisdom that lives there and migrates there from the ocean. Birds of many kinds appear, over and over, as messengers or as a mask of the poet or as sentient beings whose actions have meaning in an oracular or visionary sense. In the same way, plants are sentient spirits here as well. They all, to me, have mythic resonances and symbolic meanings, whether it's the cedar that is central to Pacific Northwest cultures, or the hazel tree that dispenses wisdom in Irish lore.

If I were to consider which animal or animals keep showing up, I would say birds, as a class, tend to be what I see most often. They are filled with so much meaning, whether as symbols of freedom and independence, as in "Sugaring," where the poet becomes the fledgeling and grows feathers to fly, or as spiritual relations in "My Feathers Grow Out at Night." They are hidden, otherworldly beings with human speech and nations in "their secret," sitting around their fires at night when humans are not observing.

Birds fascinate me, and I've shared my home with many over the years. Birds have an uncanniness to them, able to speak in a literal sense and to converse with humans, but their ability to fly is central, and I think it touches on the poet as a shamanistic figure, flying on the wings of words. For centuries, pens were feather quills, filled with ink, carrying meaning in the trail of color left on the page. Birds are omens, they're harbingers of birth or death, they consume the bodies of the dead, their cries evoke intense emotions of fear or delight or sensuality. We speak of writing as "chickenscratch" or think of the footprints of birds as letter-like symbols. Robert Graves spoke of how the flight of cranes, to him, symbolized the origins of the alphabet in shapes across the sky. The native songs and cries of different birds can sound like words of human speech, language echoing in a deserted landscape.

Look at what Wallace Stevens does in "Thirteen Ways of Looking at a Blackbird," how he manipulates image and emotion through the use of that one symbolic creature. The poem is simple but so deeply layered. There is attention to the tiny shimmer of movement that is the blackbird's eye in a vast, mountainous landscape; to the flight of a flock of blackbirds as a larger motion that takes up the sky; and even just the implication of blackbirds through a mistakenly-imagined shadow. There's a fleetness there, an ability to mistake one thing for another when birds are involved, because they are, in so many ways, so alien to our experience.

I think birds are mysteries, and this is why poets so often bring their presence into poems.

Jory: Do you find any other kind of art influencing your own work? Would you say that an art form outside of literature has helped to shape your work or specific poems and if so, what is the poet's relationship to other kinds of artistic expression?

ERL: It's funny you should ask this question because I just got back from Turin last week, where I attended a talk and panel discussion by Daniel Albright, a Harvard professor of literature and music, who was talking about his most recent book, *Panaesthetics: On the Unity and Diversity of the Arts* (Yale, 2014). He and a group of Italian academics discussed the intersections and unities of the various arts – poetry, music, sculpture, painting, literature – and it certainly both gave me a lot to think about, and affirmed many of my own thoughts on the topic.

I've always been influenced and informed by other arts in my poetry. One of my poems, "Duchamp's Bride,"[357] came entirely out of a dream. I wrote it down when I woke that morning, almost exactly as spoken by the dream-woman who represented the bride from Marcel Duchamp's surrealist painting, "The Bride Stripped Bare by Her Bachelors, Even." I had been recently listening to a musical album by Black Tape for a Blue Girl, "The Scavenger Bride," which was likewise inspired by the visual and literary works of Duchamp and Kafka, and the "Bride" in particular. The visual and the musical both came together in that dream state to produce a poem.

The Surrealists, I think, were particularly good at taking inspiration from and offering criticism of other art forms in their poetic works, whether literary, visual, or musical. Because they were reacting against perceived constraints of form and function, I think they were able to cross these lines quite consciously as they created their different works and interacted in their movement. André Breton, in his *Second Manifesto of Surrealism*, says, "The problem of social action ... is only one of the forms of a more general problem which Surrealism set out to deal with, and that is *the problem of human expression in all its forms*."[358] Everything was gathered together through the medium of dream, and of other forms of randomization or symbolization – divination methods like tarot, or tools like automatic writing, for instance – then filtered into their poetic, literary, and visual work to produce art that retains something of that dream state.

In this sense, I'm inspired by occult art and symbol systems, by Siberian and Northwest Native sculptural forms, by petroglyphs, by architectural forms. Music speaks to me, and painting, and the Zen forms of Japanese gardens and bonsai. I'm sometimes inspired by images or characters in movies and television, as well. Is there anyone who doesn't have a visceral reaction to the image of the false Maria, transforming in arcs of lightning and those Saturnian electric rings from machine to flesh, when her blazing robotic heart begins to beat, in the Fritz Lang film, *Metropolis*? How can these things not be given form in words? How can they not inspire poetic works?

Jory: Good questions indeed! Thank you for this wide-ranging talk on poems, poetry, and place!

---

[357] ibid, p. 95

[358] André Breton, *Manifestoes of Surrealism*, trans. Richard Seaver and Helen R. Lane, University of Michigan Press, Ann Arbor 1972, p. 151

Chapter 3
Responses and Reviews

Life, the Deities, and Everything

In a private entry on a friend's LiveJournal a week or two ago, she asked about how others deal with the idea of synchronicity in magic, commenting as well about her views of deity, and I responded:

I tend to believe in deities as external to "us" but not to the universe itself. I don't think anything is outside the universe, really. That said, when it comes to synchronicity, I try to just surf that synchronic wave and let things take their course. In that sense I suppose that some of my practice is deeply influenced by Taoism and the concept of *wu-wei* -- doing by not doing, or just letting things be once a particular magical act is set in motion. I've found that the less I interfere, the better things will tend to go for me.

She asked in response:

"Yes, I suppose nothing would really be external to the universe, would it?"

"You work with deity quite a bit, though, yes? How do you conceive of them and your relationship to them? No small question there. "

After getting her permission to respond here, rather than at length in comments on her LJ, I've been giving some thought to her questions. I work with deities constantly in my practice. They're ever-present to me and much of my worldview depends on their reality on some level. They are, to me, guides and guardians and mentors and the bearers of challenge and change.

I'm undisturbed by atheism and can appreciate to some extent those who view deities as archetype or strictly internal to the human mind, though it's not my personal worldview by any means. For me, the reality of deities is in their action and that action appears to me to be external to my own mind and being. As always, with things spiritual, your mileage may vary.

The larger question is how I conceive of deities and my relationship to them. It's a complex matter and probably self-contradictory in many ways. I experience deities and spirits in a variety of ways and my primary feeling is that the human mind isn't really capable at this point of categorizing such entities easily and conveniently, hence the inherent contradictions in how even one single individual might experience them in the course of a day or a lifetime. As Whitman said,

306

Do I contradict myself?
Very well then I contradict myself,
(I am large, I contain multitudes.)

For me, deities exist on a larger continuum that includes pretty much all types of spiritual beings, including humans. We have the capacity to become divine through our efforts and actions, or through the efforts and actions of others. Ancestors, land spirits, spirits of animals or birds or trees -- all of these are in that vast spectrum of spiritual beings that are, or potentially can be, divine. In some ways, I suppose, I see deities as older, respected relations -- elder siblings, aunts and uncles, great-grandparents, if you will. We are all of the same stuff; some of us are just possessed of more power, experience, and knowledge than others. I don't believe in omnipotent, all-knowing, perfect deities as proposed by monotheism.

My relationships generally are those of respect and even reverence, but I don't see that reverence as being any kind of groveling, nor do I see myself as a mindless automaton in their service. I know several folks who consider themselves Godslaves, who have essentially given over the responsibility for their lives and their actions to the deity or deities they serve. I can see why people might be willing to do this, but it's not really a relationship that would work for me. In my own life, I see my understanding as too flawed to be certain that what instructions I was getting would be clear enough to follow to guide my entire life's work and all my decisions. I spend a lot of time evaluating what I do get and deciding whether or not it seems viable on my path and in my relationships with them.

As a polytheist, my relationship with an individual deity or spirit depends on that entity and its larger or smaller place in my life. My relationship with Antinous is different from my relationship with Airmed or with Brigid, for instance. My relationships with the animal spirits are as deep as those I have with my deities, but of a different kind. Brigid and Manannán are very active in my life, as are several non-deific spirits of animals. Some of those animal spirits are much more important to me than many of the deities I work with and revere.

There are deities and spirits whom I honor because I live in their territory and I prefer to have cordial relationships if possible. It's not good to ignore or have hostilities with the house spirits or the spirits of the land you live on. That sort of thing can only lead to trouble. Even if all I have is a nodding acquaintance with most of them, it's still polite to greet them when I see them and to make offerings when it feels appropriate to do so. Being at peace with one's neighbors is just good policy, whether those neighbors are physical or spiritual.

There are deities and spirits who are daily presences in my life, appearing in dreams or tapping me on the shoulder with something they want me to know. Many of them have active altar space in my home, with frequent offerings made of everything from water and incense to food. Brigid, particularly, has a dedicated altar where I keep my flamekeeping shifts as I have for many years. At the altar in my bedroom, where Manannán shares some space with the other spirits that are a large presence in my life, I make an offering of fire and purifying incense every day, with a brief prayer of thanks and a request for guidance and protection through my day.

My relationships with deities and spirits are reciprocal; we give each other gifts of time and attention. They ask things of me, but I also ask things of them, so I feel the exchange is reasonably well-balanced. And I've found my work with them to be very helpful and healing, aiding me in getting my head together and in keeping things like my physical pain under control not just through meditative techniques, breathwork and the like, but through focusing past that pain and confusion into devotion and ritual. My work is not unquestioning; everything has to be examined. That, though, is at the root of how my relationships with them work. Examination, testing and experimentation have led to my best results. This isn't about a lack of trust, for I do trust them. It's about working to understand as much as possible and to filter for my own potential misinterpretations.

Even when I'm working on understanding, much of the time I try to just let things flow. I do less active magic these days than I did when I first started out. Initially I needed to do magic to figure out how it worked, and to experience that set of skills and to sharpen them. As I grew into it I found that magic seemed to work its way into the fabric of my life until, in a sense, life became magical. I no longer needed to push for things as much. I found myself in a flow where, even if things sometimes go wrong or are hard for me, my life overall is moving in a good direction. This, I think, is from the influence of my relationships with the spirits. I don't expect my life to be perfect any more than I expect deities to be perfect, so it just blends into an organic whole, flaws and all.

I look to my deities and spirits for inspiration and, more often than not, it seems to me that they help me find it.

Thoughts on Interfaith Dialogue

Jason Pitzl-Waters over on the Wild Hunt blog has recently had a couple of posts about Christian-Pagan dialogue, and Gus diZerega's book, *Beyond the Burning Times: a Pagan and Christian in Dialogue*.[359] The first of these posts dealt with non-Christian perspectives on marriage equality and the newer one deals with Pagan pessimism surrounding Christian-Pagan dialogues and interfaith work.

Most folks who know me or who have been reading here for a while know that I've been involved with some interfaith work. Nothing like the intensity and length of time that Rowan Fairgrove and others have put into it, but still, I've got some experience in the field. I believe it's good and necessary work and that it has been making a difference in how people in other religions understand and experience interactions with the Pagans they meet. It has offered some concrete proof that we're not as we've been imagined and if, ultimately, it only ends up convincing people we're harmless I think that's a pretty good thing because with any luck it also means they'll leave us alone to do our own thing in peace.

Yet an underlying theme of much specifically Christian-Pagan dialogue is a general Christian desire to spread the faith. I know a lot of Christians and they're good folks and they don't give me any trouble about being Pagan nor do they try to convert me. But the fact remains that motives in Christian interfaith dialogue often tend to boil down to learning about other faiths so that arguments can be prepared for use in attempts at conversion. The reviewers of Gus's dialogue on the *Sacred Tribes Journal*, particularly William Stewart, take the object of the dialogue specifically as an exercise in understanding with an eye toward evangelism. Stewart says:

> Pagans are more often the objects of spiritual warfare rather than the subjects of apology and evangelism. Dialogue must not be a substitute for mission but I believe missional Christians will increasingly need to engage in this type of dialogue in order to gain a hearing in our multi-religious, post-Christendom world.

---

[359] Gus diZerega and Philip Johnson, *Beyond the Burning Times: a Pagan and Christian in Dialogue*, Lion Hudson, Oxford 2008

Given this attitude, I think it's only natural and right that Pagans should approach such dialogue with a certain amount of skepticism and even cynicism. I am by no means saying that we should not have these discussions. I do think they're vitally necessary in reducing inter-religious tensions and fostering understandings between communities. Yet I believe we need to go into these discussions with our eyes open, understanding that there are some very likely ulterior motives in many who would engage with us.

This takes me back to the interfaith discussion at the Gathering Grove a couple of weeks ago. The gentleman facilitating the discussion was a Jewish Unitarian Universalist pastor. A great deal of his discussion focused on how learning that not everyone sees God in the same way can undermine a person's entire worldview and shake their faith. The idea that there are multiple truths can be seen as threatening. Stephen is working hard at seeing the world as multivalent and multi-religious, yet he seems to believe that everyone around him is stuck in a particular sort of mono-think that, to my mind at least, arises from the very roots of monotheism and its concept that there can only be one truth and one right way of being in the world.

He rejects the idea that the question is as simple as monotheism vs. polytheism, yet I find it difficult to believe that the basic assumptions of these monotheistic worldviews -- one reality versus many realities -- is not somehow at the heart of the problem he describes. A polytheist might quite conceivably worship only one deity, yet that same polytheist would not likely insist that all other deities are false or evil or nonexistent. This, though, seems to be the root position of monotheism and a large part of the reason for that existentialist distress Stephen speaks of when he talks about losing oneself and having one's worldview shattered when one opens their mind to the possibility of multiple truths. To me, there's no reason not to allow a new truth into my life because that addition to my worldview is not going to destroy me; if anything it may expand my world considerably and make it a better, richer one. If it's a frightening truth, then it may expand my world by making me aware of new things to be cautious about and take precautions over. In my experience, it's only some monotheists who live in dread of new information that challenges their worldview because it could lead to an undermining of everything they've built their life upon.

For such people, threatened with fear for their lives and sanity by allowing a new viewpoint in, it seems like the only possible reason for engaging in interfaith dialogue is to convince others of the rightness of their own point of view. This is the fear that so many fundamentalists appear to live within, and why they seem to get so angry when their worldview is contradicted in any way. It is entirely possible to have a Christianity that doesn't feel it must impose itself upon the world. I know Christians who live within that Christian paradigm. I'm grateful for them in my life — they're excellent people who live what they believe and who work to expand the amount of love and kindness in the universe.

In my work on reconstructionist spirituality, I end up reading an awful lot of Christian theology and Christian texts, being as my focus is on insular Celtic mythology and spirituality. It's unavoidable that I have to read up on Christian worldviews and Christian assumptions because it was the Christians who wrote everything down. Some of it is fascinating, some of it is boring, and some of it is distasteful as a dried turd on a dinner plate. Pretty much all of it convinces me that no one answer will serve for everyone. I read because I want to understand, not so I can argue with Christians to try to convert them. I find some of the material useful for suggesting ways to deepen a Pagan practice, and for shedding light on some of the mythological texts recorded by the Irish monks, as I dig through looking for fragments of Pagan insight. If I go to a Christian friend for a deeper explanation of what I've read regarding their religion's theologies and practices, I don't want them trying to use that dialogue as an excuse to advocate for my conversion, it just means I want to understand what certain things mean, as clearly as possible, and to make sure I'm not misinterpreting.

In the same way, when I engage in interfaith dialogue in more formal settings, I'm interested in learning about other religions to satisfy an intellectual and spiritual curiosity, not because I'm thinking of becoming a Christian or a Sufi or a Jew. And I don't expect people who ask me questions to become a CR Pagan; I answer questions because I value knowledge and am pleased that other people value it as well. Understanding can foster respect, and this should be the broad goal of interfaith dialogues. To go into such a dialogue with the ulterior motive of conversion is to undermine the process and to misrepresent the dialogue itself.

Hyperlinks or Hype:
A Response to Edwin Chapman[360]

Any article that states Robert Graves "was one of the first reconstructionist NeoPagans" is not only guaranteed to make me twitch, it also makes me question the author's definition of "reconstructionist." The article in question is Edwin Chapman's "The Ogam Alphabet: Hyperlinks of the Gods" in a recent issue of *Thorn* magazine. It's not the only assertion in the article that made me sit back and go "huh?"

Let's examine Robert Graves for a moment. The man was the grandson of Charles Graves, a preeminent late 19th century Celticist and the acknowledged expert on ogam of his generation. Robert completely ignored his grandfather's work on the ogam. When Robert wrote to the Celticists working during his own era with his theories, he was told in no uncertain terms that he was wrong, yet he persisted in his mangling of the system, complaining that no current Celticist would give him the time of day. I find this unsurprising, considering his blithe dismissal of his grandfather's work and his ignoring whoever disagreed with him.

It's vaguely possible to argue that Graves was "NeoPagan" by some stretched definition of the word, but he was in no way a reconstructionist. His misstatements have done an incredible disservice to modern Pagan ogam scholarship and created some of the most persistent errors that would-be ogam students will find in writings about ogam and Celtic mythology. I would argue that *The White Goddess*, even generously reckoned, is more than "somewhat flawed." It is, in fact, absolutely worthless as an ogam resource. The only reason I would ever recommend it to ogam students is to show them where things went so badly wrong in modern Paganism's adaptation of the system.

Chapman says that Graves's system is "off the wall, and yet perfectly in keeping with what the ancient Druids did with it." This is wrong on two counts. First, the ancient Druids were not using the ogam alphabet. It was created after the arrival of Christianity and there are no existing ogams earlier than that arrival. Secondly, while the *filid* did in fact create their own ogam correspondences, they did

---

360. A response to "The Ogham Alphabet: Hyperlinks of the Gods" by Edwin Chapman, Thorn vol 1 no 1, December 2008, pp 38-40

not arbitrarily discard the entire tradition surrounding it in favor of their personal fixations.

The ogam alphabet is, at its root, a specifically Irish alphabet, and a system of mnemonic devices. In Old Irish its name might be pronounced "aw-gum" and in Modern Irish the gh in ogham elides to become "oh-um", but it's never pronounced "oh-gum" in either variant of Irish. He posits its name as possibly derived from the word *"ghuaim"* (which he alleges means "bardic wisdom"), but the only similar Irish word I can find is *guaim*, which means "regulation" or "self-restraint." In Scots Gaelic the same word means "economy" or "thrift." The Online Etymological Dictionary suggests[361], instead, that "ogham" may be derived from PIE *og-mo*, "furrow" or "track," with a possible metaphorical indication of "incised line," which I suspect is far more likely, and less of a folk etymology based on sound and similarity of spelling.

The ogam alphabet is not a pan-Celtic system, and should be referred to as an Irish alphabet, not "Celtic runes." Although ogam stones have been found in Wales, the Isle of Man, and Scotland, in all cases the language of the inscriptions is Irish, with a few parallel inscriptions in Latin.

The names of each letter are, contrary to Chapman's assertion, not kennings. "Kenning" is a word that refers to a poetic phrasing, not a simple translation. In an Icelandic poem, for instance, the ocean is referred to as "the whale road." This is a kenning; it's a poetic phrase referring to a particular word or item. The word "terror" is a translation of the name *h-úath*, not a kenning. The *briatharogam* or "word ogams" would more properly be referred to as kennings when it comes to the ogam system. In this case, the kennings for *h-úath* would include "a pack of wolves" or "most difficult at night."

Chapman refers to the use of ogam staves tossed for divinatory interpretation as *"coelbreni."* In fact, *"coelbren"* is nothing more or less than a Welsh alphabet invented by the infamous forger Iolo Morganwg and has nothing to do with ogam or the Irish language. Graphically, it is an alphabet styled after the Norse runes and completely unrelated to the ogam. Referring to the divinatory use of an Irish alphabet by the name of a fake Welsh alphabet is, at best, a culturally-muddled misunderstanding of both sources. The ogam letters themselves are not "fews" -- a phrase that seems to

---

361. http://www.etymonline.com/index.php?term=ogham accessed September 17, 2014

have originated with Edred Thorsson. An individual ogam letter is a *fid*, pronounced pretty much as it looks. In the plural, they are *feda*, also pronounced pretty much as it looks. A variant spelling is *fiodh*, which can be approximately pronounced as "few"-- likely where the problem arose.

It is indeed true that there are literary references to the ogam being used for divination. Yet we cannot conclude that these are realistic portrayals of the pre-Christian use of ogam. As noted above, the ogam did not exist prior to Christianity's introduction to Ireland. More importantly, the tales are Christian imaginings of what druids and other Pagans might have done. They can't be considered historical evidence, which is part of why reconstructing Celtic Paganism using medieval literary sources can be so problematic. The use of ogam for magic in the modern era, at least, is proved by the use of the amber bead mentioned in a passage from Macalister's late 19th century volume on ogam inscriptions, which Chapman mistitles *Ogam*. The title is actually the ponderous Latin *Corpus Inscriptionum Insularum Celticarum*. Personally, I'd want to use a shorter, more memorable title myself!

Chapman's central argument -- that the ogam can be used in a variety of ways to create a web of meanings by an individual practitioner -- is correct. Unfortunately, his article is riddled with historical and factual errors. Those mentioned here are only the most egregious. To enumerate all of them would be pedantic and probably more rude than useful for the average ogam student. The Celtic corpus is not nearly as mysterious and obscure as people seem to want to paint it. When Celtic material is portrayed as impossibly difficult it leads to an atmosphere wherein ludicrous assertions such as those of Robert Graves, D.J. Conway, Edain McCoy, and Douglas Monroe are accepted as the only accessible materials available. This just isn't true. Even popularizers such as Miranda Green and Peter Berresford Ellis, with all their various flaws, are a far better choice.

Avoiding books on Celtic myth and religion by occult authors and going to actual scholarly sources is probably the best way to dispel that impression. Better yet, a trip to the library if you can't afford more expensive and more reliable works is always an excellent option — interlibrary loan is easy and usually free! Ultimately, the best advice to any would-be student of the ogam is: question everything, and always check your sources. You'll be glad you did.

Aisling, Ársaíocht, agus Agallamh:
A Modern CR Triad

Several new blogs have appeared in the past few months that would likely be of interest to folks who have read my (admittedly and shamefully infrequent) posts here on *Searching for Imbas*. These include *The Presence of the Past* by Disirdottir, *A Wolf-Man, Not a Wolf in Man's Clothing* by Faoladh, and *Finnchuill's Mast* by Finnchuill.

Each of these individuals, all of whom I know and who are friends of mine, are approaching reconstructionist religions and, usually, Celtic Reconstructionist religions, as an enterprise that requires as much flexibility and attention to intuition and mysticism as it does to history and archaeology. Some people would argue that intuition has no place in reconstructionist religions, or that anyone who is researching or (horrors!) practicing more than one path can't be a "real" reconstructionist, but I would argue that the ancient world was filled with both of these ways of living and that a search for a pure, non-intuitive indigenous Pagan religion is unlikely ever to turn one up. People worshipping deities from multiple cultures happened all over the world without being the "dirty word" sort of eclecticism that some reconstructionists appear to hate, and it still occurs in many places, including in many modern reconstructionist Pagan households.

Pretty much anyone who has ever read my work knows that I am as much in favor of a mystic approach as I have been of an approach incorporating a necessary understanding of history, folklore, and the archaeological record. I proposed this when I originally founded the Nemeton email list as *"aisling* and archaeology." It's a phrase that still comes up from time to time in discourse with in the CR community, and I'm pleased that there are still some who remember that the concept is there.

In a conversation on Finnchuill's blog, on the post *Revisiting the R Word*[362], it was noted that an expansion of this duality needed to be brought forth and what needed to be included was "argumentation," not in the form of fighting about viewpoints, but in terms of discourse between people who might disagree but who still treat one another with respect for their knowledge and ability, as we see in *The Colloquy of the Two Sages* from the Irish literary

---

362. http://finnchuillsmast.wordpress.com/2011/04/03/revisiting-the-r-word-toward-an-experimental-reconstructionism/ accessed September 17, 2014

tradition. In this text, two *filid* fight it out for who will be the supreme poet. They each strive to gain that position, yet their discourse was a respectful one that acknowledged both parties, and that they were both worthy to contend for the position. The conversation in the comments on Finnchuill's post is well worth exploring.

The triadic construction that was arrived at for the concepts we are discussing was *Aisling, Ársaíocht, agus Agallamh.*

Aisling is the power of vision. It's a word that means "dream" and is also one of the classes of tales memorized by the *filid* in their studies. This, in the context of CR, could be classified as unverified personal gnosis, or UPG, though *aisling* is a term recognized within Gaelic culture, where the term "UPG" is not. Dream, vision, Otherworld work and journeying, and oracular work all fit here. All of them were recognized and, in fact, necessary aspects of the original cultures and spiritualities of the larger Celtic world. Prophets, oracles, dreams, and diviners were an immensely important part of public life in Celtic cultures and, in fact, in all ancient cultures.

Ársaíocht is "antiquarianism" and fills in for "archaeology" in the original dyad; it stresses the importance of the past, of the physical record, of the textual, and the problems of the textual within the tradition. It signifies history and tradition. It also explicitly implies (given the nature of "antiquarianism") that our knowledge of history and tradition is incomplete and ever-evolving as new discoveries are made and new theories in scholarship are proposed. Our understanding of the past is not static. When new information is brought forth, we must decide whether, or how, we are going to readjust our understandings and our practices.

Agallamh is the word used for a colloquy: a conversation, a discussion, a debate between those with knowledge that serves to generate a process of critical discernment wherein the other aspects of tradition and practice are brewed. Without learned discourse within the tradition, little can be learned and nothing can be fruitfully passed on to a new generation. This is the place where history and mysticism meet, where the insights of *imbas* are brought into practice, where ideas are examined critically and with respect for both the past, and the needs of the present and the future.

All of these aspects must balance one another. Mysticism, history, and discussion are all important in the rediscovery and reconstruction of oral traditions like those of the Celtic peoples. If we lack one or more, we risk falling into different types of dogmas that can solidify into fundamentalisms. This is an undesirable place for us to be, as anyone can plainly see just by looking at everything happening in the world today.

Pagan literalist fundamentalisms are as appalling as any Christian or Islamic literalist fundamentalisms, even if we're not lobbing bombs at one another over it. We have to remember that "the lore says" is often just another form of "the Bible says," and remind ourselves that a phrase frequently found in that same Irish "lore" was, "and other versions say..."[363] The texts are no more flawless in their revelations of the Pagan past than are the various interpretations of archaeological sites that have fallen in and out of fashion over the decades.

It's obviously possible to fall too far into the idea that what we get from our practices of *aisling* and *imbas* should apply universally, but this is where *agallamh* will serve to curb the worst excesses and bring one back to balance. Individual practice has a lot more space in it for these things, but public and community practice can both be deeply enriched by inspiration. The answer is not to crush any and all manifestations of mysticism within reconstructionist religions because there is a risk that one might be wrong (by far the most common response I have seen), but to examine these manifestations both critically and *respectfully* in light of what is known, then make a decision.

Talk without action, study without practice, leads only to spiritual masturbation that, generally speaking, isn't pretty and should only be done in your own space with those who have consented to be present. Debate simply for the sake of debate, or argument just to stir people up, is useless and annoys nearly everyone. It certainly doesn't contribute to building either community or practice. If you're only going to stand there arguing, get out of the way while the rest of us do the work.

In the end, the practice of *filidecht requires* mysticism, the study of history, and discourse. A *fili* who was unable to access the Otherworldly spark of *imbas* was no *fili* at all.

---

[363] Frequently pointed out by P. Sufenus Virius Lupus on many occasions and in many places both online and off.

What's the Point?

A couple of weeks ago, Teo Bishop wrote a blog post entitled *What is the Point of Your Religion?*[364] over on Patheos. He asks the questions:

> Why do we do what we do? What does our tradition provide us in the way of making the world we live in, the communities we build, the people that we care for, better? More importantly, how does it inform our capacity to love, our ability to experience joy, or, for that matter, our willingness to stand with the full spectrum of human experience? Is our religion pacifying us, or challenging us to go deeper?

He states a belief that "there *has* to be a greater purpose to our religious traditions than providing us with a sense of security, comfort, and personal or cultural validation." Further along, he continues with the questions:

> What is the point of your religion? What tools does it provide to you? Does it equip you for defense or for outreach? Does it lead you to question, or does it encourage you to rest in your knowing?

I suspect that most people are seeking purpose and connection. Most people walking a spiritual path will tend to use that path as a tool, possibly one of many, in that search. As always, I can only speak for myself, as a person who strives to practice *filidecht* within a CR community, and as someone who identifies very much with the *geilt* as the wounded outsider poet, seeking healing through art and isolation. In this context, community and isolation are not mutually exclusive states. The *geilta* pass from isolation into community and back into isolation, responding to need and circumstance.

Community and culture make connections possible. Within a reconstructionist movement, history is a centering point and the

---

364. http://www.bishopinthegrove.com/what-is-the-point-of-your-religion/ accessed September 17, 2014. Teo is no longer a practicing Pagan but has moved on to Christianity.

recovery of polytheist culture is a creative and expansive activity. Done properly — in my opinion, at least — a reconstructionist path recognizes and celebrates diversity without, as Teo suggests, a "need to squabble about whose deity is best, whose laws are true, and whose cosmology is most relevant." I fail to see how the acknowledgement of difference must perforce result in such struggles. Polytheism as a theology acknowledges multivalent realities, multiple deities, and the fact that different people will have relationships with different deities. A "need to squabble about whose deity is best" seems to me to be a remnant of the monotheism that so many of us grew up in, and which permeates western culture with the attitude that there can only be one "true" or "best" anything. We see it in monotheism, we see it in the belief in a singular soul-mate or "one true love," we see it in the idea that there is only one "right" model for family or for gender or for sexuality. It's a hard set of beliefs to shake off, but people do, to greater or lesser extents.

When I look at what the traditions I practice bring to the table in the way of helping make the world, our communities, and the people around me "better," I look at the effect art has. The *fili* has a duty to speak, to create poetry and to use words as praise and satire in an effort to bring things into balance, to correct flaws, to praise what is praiseworthy. The *fili*'s work is to encourage the practice of virtuous behavior within the context of the good of the community, the improvement of the world, and the improvement of individual human lives. It is to acknowledge the beauty of sacred things. It is to call out violations of virtues when harm is done. As a path that is, as one of its roots, animist, community includes far more than just the human element; the environment and everything in it participates in that community. Particular places are sacred, associated with deities or expressing something numinous that may well be beyond human comprehension.

The *geilt* recognizes that culture and community can also harm. Humans in groups can be cruel and petty, and can harm and kill those who are more vulnerable. That cruelty and pettiness can destroy more than just other human beings - it can destroy ecosystems, cultures, species. Culture can be a nurturing parent, or it can be a selfish, bullying child, and it us up to all of us to see to it that culture is a nurturer, not a destroyer. *Geilta* use art as a tool to salvage remnants of a damaged self after culture and community have destroyed something in their souls.

The paths of the *fili* and the *geilt* urge us to look beyond the surface of things, to understand the weight of symbol and image. The idea of passing through the mist, of walking between worlds, is one of mental, emotional, and spiritual expansion. It enables a perception of links without having to perceive everything as undifferentiated. Language as poetry is a very powerful tool for conveying mysteries, for articulating what's wrong with the world, and discussing approaches to reparations and healing. Poetry allows language to approach things obliquely, to treat them with subtlety, to envision something new growing from the roots of something ancient.

Why do I do what I do? I think any artist would understand the sense of compulsion that drives creativity. So many writers and poets have spoken of the *need* to write, or they will die. Rilke, in *Letters to a Young Poet*, wrote, "Find out the reason that commands you to write; see whether it has spread its roots into the very depth of your heart; confess to yourself you would have to die if you were forbidden to write." This is why I do what I do, because I will die if I do not. I will vanish into a nothingness from which there is no possible escape. That my writing serves a community is a wonderful result of responding to that need, but it is the need itself that is at the heart of everything.

When we are doing what is right for us, doing that thing that our soul will wither and die without, it is likely that our community and our world will benefit from that in some way.

For you, Teo, I offer this quote, from the same source:

> Be patient toward all that is unsolved in your heart and try to love the questions themselves, like locked rooms and like books that are now written in a very foreign tongue. Do not now seek the answers, which cannot be given you because you would not be able to live them. And the point is, to live everything. Live the questions now. Perhaps you will then gradually, without noticing it, live along some distant day into the answer.

I think it's important to recognize that the experience of comfort is not necessarily complacency. It may in fact be a necessary component of healing and of cooperation. I've lived in an absolute uncertainty of where I would be sleeping on any given night and not knowing where my next meal would come from - it is not particularly conducive to spiritual practice unless that uncertainty is deliberately chosen and embraced. Being forced into it by circumstance can destroy a person. Having enough safety and comfort to keep body and soul together is important. It isn't the only thing, but it is necessary. In a place where we feel some safety, we can learn and grow, we can be compassionate to ourselves, and thus develop our compassion for others. Different cultures and different spiritual paths may express these things in diverse ways, but unless we know there is the possibility of safety and comfort, most people cannot find it in themselves to go deeper. There must be a place of returning so that the risk is worthwhile.

As in all things, this is a process. It unfolds slowly, only rarely emerging in that flash of brilliant light. Even then, there has often been some subterranean motion that has led to that moment of *imbas* - the *filid* trained for up to twenty years to be able to experience it, to give them the ground from which to grow, the spring from which to draw water, and the techniques used in the process of incubation.

Reviews: *A World Full of Gods:*
An Inquiry into Polytheism and Pagan Theology:
Paganism as a World Religion

I just finished John Michael Greer's theology book, *A World Full of Gods: An Inquiry into Polytheism* from ADF Publishing.[365] I'll be talking about that one, and Michael York's *Pagan Theology: Paganism as a World Religion*.[366]

I could probably say a lot about this book, but I really don't think I need to. I found a lot to agree with in John Michael's material, and have very few complaints about it— actually only one real technical complaint at all, concerning his characterization of the *Audacht Morainn* as a Pagan text when all the written texts of Ireland are from the Christian period and bear its influence.

He shows the major arguments for monotheism as "better than" polytheism for the straw men they are, and argues that real world evidence suggests polytheism as a logical explanation for the vast variety of human spiritual experiences. John Michael deals with the whole "all religions are really talking about the same thing" argument the same way I do — they aren't. We're not all climbing to the same mountaintop. In fact, we may not all be looking to climb mountains at all, and that's just fine.

I think that monotheists of all stripes are going to come away from this book feeling very uncomfortable, but considering the death-grip that monotheism has had on Western theology for the past 1500 or so years, it's good to have that complacency poked and disabused. John Michael argues that polytheism's inclusiveness is its strength, and a more accurate reflection of reality than the exclusivity of monotheism with its warring "exclusively true" texts that contradict one another in their generalities and their specifics. Greer manages to show how monotheism chokes on its own circular logic, and that isn't going to sit well with mainstream religions at all. At the same time, I think it's essential for Pagans doing interfaith work to have this information and these arguments in their arsenal, and it would probably be a good idea to share it with your

---

[365] John Michael Greer, *A World Full of Gods: An Inquiry into Polytheism*, ADF Publishing Tucson 2005
[366] Michael York, *Pagan Theology: Paganism as a World Religion*, New York University Press, New York 2003

monotheist colleagues to show them just how *different* our worldviews really are from their own.

He presents polytheistic deity as differing in kind and quality from monotheistic deity, and argues that deity does not by definition require omnipotence, omnipresence or omnibenevolence to be deity. In fact, many of his arguments are those I've used over the years, though rather less eloquently than him. I think this is an essential book for Pagan theologians who want to reach beyond the "we're all one" rhetoric of interfaith work and the shadow of monotheism that continues to envelop most theological inquiry, despite Paganism's inherent polytheism. It's a potent reminder for newer Pagans that we're not playing in the same field as the monotheistic religions so many of us have left behind us in our spiritual search.

I think that any quibbles I might have with details in this book are far overshadowed by its importance in dealing with the usual arguments assembled against polytheism and Paganism by the adherents of the major monotheist religions of the world. It addresses differences between polytheist paths rather better than Michael York's *Pagan Theology* simply because John Michael's not trying to squish every Pagan religion into one particular overarching theological pattern. Greer allows for differences where York attempts to find unity in his presentation. Both books are valuable, but Greer's approach allows for the differences between the reconstructionist paths and the Wiccan-based Paganisms where York's approach doesn't.

York's definition of Neopaganism (which includes, for him, reconstructionists and pretty much anyone not a member of a tribal or indigenous religion) is the following:

> Neopaganism may be broadly defined by its calendar of eight sabbats, or festivals; its ceremonial circle; its peculiar identity of the directions and elements; its ritual paraphernalia and invocations, chants, and songs; and, above all, its bigendered or bitheistic notion of deity.[367]

I don't know about all you folks reading this, but the only thing CR fits in that list is that we have ritual invocations, chants and songs. We accept deity as being more than one gender, but we are by no

---

[367] York, p. 61

means "bitheistic". This is the great lack in York's work on Pagan theology — its narrowing of Neopaganism to one particular definition rather than dealing with Greer's much broader category of polytheistic religions — all of which are Pagan either by their own or by others' definitions.

That said, York's book lays some excellent groundwork and I think it's absolutely necessary for Pagan theologians but, in the end, Greer's book is, I think, more generally accurate and addresses more of what is actually of concern to Pagan theologians. It offers a direct challenge to monotheist assumptions, while York often seems to buy into the "we're all on different paths up the same mountain" monotheist paradigm.

York's work, whatever its other worth, really serves as a good reason for reconstructionist Pagans to differentiate themselves from Neopaganism and its definitions. If Neopaganism embraces York's definition in its entirety then reconstructionists, by that definition, are not and cannot be Neopagans. We have to define ourselves entirely differently, and our beliefs and practices do fall closer to York's definitions of tribal and localized Paganisms. He uses the word "recopaganism" but nowhere does he actually attempt a definition of the sort he's put onto Neopaganism.

Review: *The Deities Are Many* by Jordan Paper

The Deities Are Many: A Polytheistic Theology by Jordan Paper[368] is one man's encounter with polytheism through Native American cultures and through the polytheism of his Chinese wife and her family. He's also studied Afro-diasporic traditions to some degree, and has written on feminist theology in the past.

This book, in my opinion, falls somewhere between Michael York's *Pagan Theology* and John Michael Greer's *A World Full of Gods: An Inquiry Into Polytheism* in usefulness and relevance to the Pagan community. Paper doesn't really touch on Paganism per se in his book, but does delve into the problems of western and monotheistic attempts to discuss polytheism and Pagan theologies. He addresses deities, culture heroes, ancestors, and other classes of divine and semi-divine beings in a more in-depth way than Greer has, giving an interesting feel for various categories of the sacred. His chapter on semi-divine beings also addresses creation myths, and he makes an important point that I've often felt is overlooked in Pagan theological discussion. Paper reports that there are, in fact, many societies in the world that do not have "creation myths" as such — no singular creation of the world — until after they've been in contact with monotheistic societies, and that most of these creation myths were imposed by outsiders rather than being an organic part of the cultures in question.

In cultures with cyclic rather than linear concepts of time, there is no need for a creation myth, for "creation" and the world were already here. They have, instead, re-creations after periodic catastrophes, or localized creations of features, pretty much exactly as we see in the Irish *Dindshenechas*. I've always maintained that we don't have an Irish "creation myth" because there probably wasn't one. The world was here, and various deities defined its features. The migrations incorporated into the *Book of Invasions* are as much a product of Paganism as of Christianity, and migration myths are apparently quite common as "origin mythology" in polytheistic societies, which are more concerned with how we got here than with whether the world had one singular beginning and/or ending.

Paper also offers a critique in several places about York's work, and how it is steeped in his own monotheistic, western

---

[368] Jordan Paper, *The Deities are Many: A Polytheistic Theology*, State University of New York Press, Albany 2005

academic worldview. In fact, it was York's attempt to homogenize Pagan "theology" into one overarching system that grated on me most. I still think that Greer has a better handle on modern western Pagan polytheism, but Paper gets the global stuff where Greer has less experience. Paper also insists, along with many Reconstructionist traditions, that language is the key to understanding a culture's worldview, and says that without learning the language a religion is expressed in, it will be impossible to truly get into that religion's headspace. On the down side, he generally insists on sky/solar deities being male and earth/lunar deities being female, though he does acknowledge there are exceptions. He talks about the difference between mythology as theology, and mythology as ritual, stating that in most polytheist societies, mythology and ritual don't necessarily have anything to do with one another, whereas in monotheism, mythology is enacted in ritual far more often.

Paper states frankly and openly from the outset that his book is a personal take on polytheistic theology, rather than a strictly scholarly approach. With that in mind, there are no footnotes or endnotes, though he does offer reading suggestions for each chapter. He speaks candidly of his own experiences with deity and numinous beings, and carefully does not mention particular entities by name in respect for the traditions in which he was trained. He points out, rightfully, that most books about Native American religions are written by Native elders raised in Christianity and instilled with that theology forcibly, overlaying a monotheistic gloss over an originally polytheistic system, pointing out when and where "the Creator" and "the Great Spirit" were absorbed into those cultures and mythologies.

His final chapters, 6, 7 and 8 are, in my opinion, the strongest and most generally useful for modern Pagan polytheists, in which he addresses culture heroes and tricksters, the misconceptions of monotheism, and the general tolerance of polytheism as a worldview. I'd highly recommend this book for those chapters alone.

Four and a half numinous beings out of five.

Review: *Druid, Shaman, Priest: Metaphors of Celtic Paganism* by Leslie Ellen Jones[369]

I was lucky to snag this book for $12 at a Canadian used book shop in Vancouver last time I was up there, which was very nice as it goes for about $40. I have heard rumor that there's a paperback edition available in the UK but haven't actually seen one anywhere.

Jones's basic premise in the book is that "druids" are reconstructed by each generation as they are wished for, rather than as they were. She traces the history of the perception of druids from the classical writers through the antiquarian period and into the post-modern Neopagan movement, with useful and interesting insights along the way. Her discussion of the sources that most neo-Druids use — including the reprints collected with such enthusiasm by John and Caitlin Matthews — is a valuable look at how most of the older material is flawed, and how even modern scholarship draws upon and interprets sources in accordance with fashions rather than offering sound fact in most cases.

Particularly interesting is the central section of the book, where she argues that if there were shamans among the Celts, they were not the druids at all, but rather the poet-warriors. Druids, she says, were never really shown traveling in the otherworlds, never shown doing that much divination, and really didn't seem to have much of a magical aspect to them. Yet poet-warriors like Fionn mac Cumhaill and Owein ap Urien can be shown to have a much closer link to shamanic otherworld travel and transformation than the literary tradition's druids. Other figures, like Taliesin, also make a strong showing, but it is the complex surrounding the poet-warriors that holds the strongest hints of anything that might have been actual shamanism. I find the argument a fairly good one, to be honest.

Her discussion of modern druidism deals with Neopaganism as well as with druids in fiction and film. She concludes that we can't really ever know what the druids were or what they did and so, in that way at least, anyone who wants the druids is essentially entitled to them. She is not actively hostile to modern Druidism, though she does regard it with more amusement than seriousness, as so often happens in the field.

---

[369] Leslie Ellen Jones, *Druid, Shaman, Priest: Metaphors of Celtic Paganism*, Hisarlik Press, Middlesex 1998

Her concluding section of the book says:

> Carrying around the weight of two millennia of theories about the druids is a heavy burden. No one theory can account for it all. The lived reality of the druids of Iron Age Britain and Gaul is irrecoverable, but that does not invalidate recreations of druidism as systems in and of themselves. The belief that there is a pre-Christian religious system underlying the literatures of the medieval Celtic countries is one tool for reading those literatures, but not the only one. This book has only begun to scratch the surface of druidic representation. Contemporary neo-druidism deserves to be studied in its own right, rather than dismissed as fringe lunacy. The references to druids in the medieval Irish secular and hagiographical texts should be collated and studied in depth. Are there patterns there which have been missed? The efflorescence of eighteenth-century druidism deserves a volume in and of itself, preferably by someone more qualified than I to see its connections with the philosophical, literary, and religious trends of the day.

Overall, the book is well worth reading and contemplating. It is not particularly negative about modern Pagans but neither does it ignore the flaws that many neo-Druidic groups have in their perceptions of druids and of the past. I'll give this one four Atlantean Druids out of five.

Review: Religion in the US Military: Comforts and Controversies

Bill of Rights: Amendment I

Congress shall make no law respecting an establishment of religion, or prohibiting the free exercise thereof; or abridging the freedom of speech, or of the press; or the right of the people peaceably to assemble, and to petition the Government for a redress of grievances.

Chaplains Under Fire[370] is a documentary by Lee Lawrence and Terry Nichelson exploring the nature of the chaplaincy in the US military. Its makers wanted to approach the controversies surrounding military chaplaincy in an increasingly diverse population, exploring issues of freedom of speech, free exercise of religion, and the mandate that the US government shall not establish any religion as favored above the others. In order to do this, they followed several chaplains living on the front lines in Iraq and Afghanistan, as well as individual service members, officials in the chaplaincy, former chaplains, secularists, and first amendment and non-establishment activists. This documentary is difficult viewing. Some scenes are shot in operating rooms with emergency surgery taking place, others illustrate the open and normative day to day sexism of the military experience that has helped create an atmosphere where sexual harassment and rape are common occurrences. Some scenes follow service members into the homes of Afghanis and Iraqis as they look for weapons or signs of dissent, and the tensions and fears of both sides are very evident.

To understand what the chaplaincy is, it is necessary to see what it does and what individual chaplains do in war zones, in military hospitals, interacting with Islamic clergy in-country, and the work they do at home in the US, counseling military families about the loss of a parent, a child, a sibling, or a spouse. Most of the chaplains interviewed were white, Christian, and male. This is in large part because most of the people volunteering to serve in this capacity are in that demographic. Most of these Christians are also from conservative independent evangelical churches with a strong mandate to spread their faith, as more moderate Christian denominations began to actively distance themselves from the

---

370. http://chaplainsunderfire.com/ accessed September 17, 2014

military during and after the Viet Nam war. As Charles Haynes, Ph.D., of the First Amendment Center states, military chaplains are "both a violation and a living example of the best" of the military's efforts to observe conflicting first amendment rights against establishment and for the free exercise of religion among service members.

It's apparent that many chaplains are providing a vital service to at least a segment of the military population that cannot be served by military mental health personnel due to differing privacy and reporting requirements. Taking problems to mental health is risky because the records of doctors and counselors can be subpoenaed, while the chaplaincy is not required to surrender records. Going to mental health is widely regarded as weakness and opens people to harassment and denigration by their fellow service members, as well as potentially exposing them to losing their jobs. The chaplaincy has confidentiality requirements in place that make the chaplain's office one of the few safe spaces for service members to talk about what's troubling them and to seek aid without worrying about those concerns getting back to the command or their coworkers.

It is also quite apparent that, in some cases at least, the chaplaincy is – or comes very close to – an establishment of a particular religion within the structure of the US military. This problem has been particularly blatant in the US Air Force Academy in recent years, brought to light primarily by activist Mikey Weinstein of the Military Religious Freedom Foundation. The documentary offers footage of chaplain Pat McLaughlin instructing military officers that, while they cannot attempt to convert the local populace in a war zone to Christianity, "there is a mission for you every single day on base," and that mission is clearly stated to be evangelizing those under their command. A conservative Christian military is presented as the only moral military. Due to the efforts of Weinstein and others, these offenses are being called into question and some policies have been changing, though official orders and the actions of the people receiving those orders are sometimes at odds. Some of these chaplains believe their religious certainties trump the constitutional rights of non-Christians.

Individual chaplains approach the conflicts between their own faith and the need to serve others of different faiths from different perspectives. It's clear that some chaplains are genuinely doing their best to look beyond their sectarian faith and offer real advice, comfort, and a sympathetic ear to anyone who walks through the door. The levels of their success will, naturally, vary depending on the empathy and the understanding of other religions that any individual chaplain may possess. For others, there seemed to be an assumption that an invocation in "the name of the one who died for our sins" is religiously neutral when, in fact, it does not address the religious views or needs of Jews, Muslims, Buddhists, Pagans, traditionalist Native Americans, or other minority and non-monotheist faiths. Such language is often an attempt on the part of the chaplain to get around regulations concerning what is and is not permissible at functions where attendance is mandatory, such as change of command ceremonies, retirements, and other functions were service members are ordered to attend, or face disciplinary action. This language is exclusionary, as is the attitude, and there is an overarching assumption that secularists, agnostics, and atheists have no place at the table at all. These underlying assumptions can make it less likely that people who are not of the same faith as the chaplain will walk through that door at all.

It is a fact that the current majority of the US military is Christian, whether by actual professed faith or by default. Yet there are growing minorities of Jews, Buddhists, Muslims, Pagans, and others within the ranks. A few Jewish, Muslim, and even Buddhist chaplains do exist in the system, but they are a comparative rarity. Military regulations regarding such concerns as facial hair and other uniform requirements can make it extremely difficult for Sikhs or conservative Jews, among others, to qualify for a chaplaincy without violating the tenets of their religions. Within this system, many Christians, both Protestant and Catholic, can find the support and service they need, but it becomes difficult for those of other faiths whose practices are considered less mainstream.

One interview illustrated the difficulties faced by non-Christians quite clearly. Rev. Billy Baughaum of the International Conference of Evangelical Chaplain Endorsers, a retired military chaplain, verbally and physically expressed absolute disgust and revulsion for the Wiccan faith, openly mocking it. At one point in his interview, he said, "I think the Wicca religion is repulsive, however if there's a Wicca [sic] chaplain who comes, I will swallow my grimace, but I believe the first amendment, he has a right or she has a right to pray to the horned god of the north. ... Although I think it's a bunch of baloney personally ... if that's what they want to pray to I will put on my greens again and get in a foxhole and I'll support their right to do that." A statement that he believes in first amendment rights is not a commitment to neutrality in actually helping service members in need of spiritual counsel. How genuinely can someone serve another spiritually when they are attempting to "swallow my grimace" and disguise hatred and contempt for the person seeking help? I cannot imagine feeling comfortable in the office of a chaplain who openly and publicly states that other religions are false and that they find them repulsive; that hatred cannot help but transfer over to the individual practicing the hated faith.

It is individuals like this, and like those in the Air Force Academy who urge officers to attempt to convert their subordinates, who create the difficulties that highlight first amendment and establishment clause issues within the military. The immense sense of privilege and righteous indignation these people express at the idea that other religions deserve an equal place at the table is appalling. They illustrate the reasons why so many people argue that the military should not be employing chaplains at all because they create a pervasive atmosphere of officialized Christianity within the Pentagon and the entire military command structure from the top on down to the lowest-ranked enlisted person in the field. This pervasiveness harms morale and alienates non-Christian service members; it can be demoralizing when someone from a minority faith has no one to turn to but a chaplain who hates the religion they practice, in a time when they most need spiritual or emotional support. It also leads to an atmosphere where harassment has been commonplace and where non-Christians are passed over for promotion because of their religion or lack thereof.

The chaplains themselves also suffer under the system. Many of them struggle with the dissonance created between their own views on religious truth and the requirement to serve others who do not agree with them. When a Christian chaplain believes that an "unsaved" individual will go to hell, what do they tell the friends of the dead person when they ask about the state of their dead friend's soul? A senior command non-commissioned officer told the friends of a man who committed suicide that their friend was now "burning in hell." The chaplain, when those friends came to him for advice, said, "Ultimately, God is [his] judge." This answer, while accurate from one particular Christian point of view, may have nothing at all to do with the religion and beliefs of the person who has died, or even of those asking for comfort.

First amendment issues regarding freedom of speech are also argued around public invocations. Some churches insist that a chaplain has a right to pray and counsel according to their individual beliefs, even if those beliefs do not serve the person coming for counseling. When a Buddhist comes to a Christian chaplain for help, being told that they have to pray to Jesus is a violation of the rights and dignity of that Buddhist under the establishment clause that states the US government cannot establish any particular religion as favored. Weinstein reports on receiving complaints from military personnel who said they were told by their chaplain, "Be born again a second time or I cannot help you."

Chaplains often have no one else to talk to, yet they bear the brunt of other people's tragedies and crises on a day-to-day basis. Chaplains are as much subject to developing post-traumatic stress disorder as any of the service members they counsel. While they might be able talk to one another for aid, assuming other chaplains are stationed close enough to do so, there may be no outlet for them at all. People in helping professions are notoriously subject to burnout, and this is even more of a risk for people in a war zone. Some of these chaplains end up committing suicide because of the unrelenting and unrelieved stresses, traumas, and responsibilities of their position. I can't help but think that the dissonance some of these chaplains feel between their own absolutist faiths and the need for neutrality in serving others would aggravate the problems they experience under the stresses of combat, where nothing is certain and death may strike at any moment. They express feelings of guilt over services not provided, or for being unable to help when someone has asked. They experience the same anxieties and fears around separation from their families, risks of injury and death, and the extreme contrasts between long stretches of boredom and sudden danger that every other service member experiences in a war zone.

Although this is a difficult 90 minutes of film, it offers some very important perspectives for anyone who is interested in issues of freedom of religion, free exercise of minority faiths, and religion in a military context. Pagans are mentioned at several points, and segments from the funeral of a Pagan serviceman, Stephen Snowberger, are shown; Pagans are a growing segment of the military and our demands for equality in both the military and the Veterans Administration are helping advance the cause of other minority religions in the US military. If you want to understand what spiritual issues are being faced by service members and by those who would protect the rights of minority religions within the military, this is an excellent place to start.

War and the Soul: Healing Our Nation's Veterans from Post-Traumatic Stress Disorder
by Edward Tick, Ph.D.[371] — A Pagan ReView

As a veteran with post-traumatic stress disorder (PTSD), I'm always interested in people's spiritual approaches to healing in this field. Edward Tick, from the title of the book onward, tackles PTSD as a spiritual problem of moral trauma, soul-loss and soul-wounding. His approach is Jungian and New Age, with all the advantages and flaws inherent in those methods. His language is monist and he treats all spiritual entities as archetypes, which is not a problem if one takes spirituality as a psychological complex rather than, as many Pagans do, a complex series of relationships with deities, ancestors, or other spiritual beings.

Tick postulates the problem of PTSD as a failed warrior initiation. This failure is not entirely the fault of the veteran but, he says, of society as a whole. It is the fault of the technological changes in warfare that have stripped war of its mythologized meanings and resonances. In treating PTSD as the potential result of a warrior initiation, he specifically positions it as the result of a male adulthood rite gone wrong. Of course, this framing ignores women's service entirely. In framing PTSD as a "failure" he, perhaps inadvertently, places blame on men and women who are already struggling with issues of responsibility, reintegration, and physical and emotional traumas. In his own words:

> Post-traumatic stress disorder is a constellation of fixated experience, delayed growth, devastated character, interrupted initiation, and unsupported recovery. Many veterans who cannot get on with life are boy-men stuck in the psychic war zone, lost in an incomplete and horrific rite of passage. ... Many of their symptoms – lack of impulse control, confused sexuality, drug and alcohol abuse, intimacy and employment problems, emotional explosiveness, mistrust of authority, alienation – characterize adolescence in our culture. Many veterans with PTSD are, psychically, shell-shocked

---

[371] Edward Tick, *War and the Soul: Healing Our Nation's Veterans from Post-Traumatic Stress Disorder*, Quest Books, Wheaton 2005

teenagers unable to enter adulthood with its demands and rules.[372]

In one sense, some of this is true. PTSD is certainly aggravated by "unsupported recovery," though the Veterans Administration is slowly beginning to deal with this problem. Unfortunately, even now, a great number of veterans are deliberately misdiagnosed with underlying "personality disorders" and brushed off so that the government, which has damaged us in the first place, is absolved of the expense of treatment, compensation, pensions, and rehabilitation. Civilian society has a long way to go in dealing with its damaged veterans and rarely even knows where to start. One important thing Tick ignores is the different patterns that women's PTSD often takes, which include the turning of anger and violence inward to oneself. This is particularly prevalent in women suffering military sexual trauma (MST), who usually have further levels of difficulty in even believing they deserve help, or that they can get it if they do go seeking it. Stories of women blamed for being raped or assaulted are familiar enough to be a devastating cliché in both the military and civilian worlds. It doesn't help at all that he takes an almost dismissive attitude about PTSD in the face of ritual. He says, "When the survivor can accomplish this [initiatory] work, post-traumatic stress as a soul wound evaporates."[373]

"Evaporates." Think about that for a minute. He's claiming that after an initiation, there will be no more nightmares, no more flashbacks, no more physical symptoms. I'm a firm believer in the efficacy of ritual, but there's only so far ritual can take us. I certainly believe ritual can also help with PTSD, with reframing our traumatic experiences, and with self-understanding. I also believe that such profound transformations take time to root and grow. We have to remember that an initiation is, technically speaking, a beginning. It's a place to start and a finger pointing along the path. It is not the path in itself.

In this book, the author's primary focus is on combat veterans, specifically Viet Nam era vets. While there is nothing wrong with this relatively narrow focus, it is problematic in that he claims his theories and approaches are universal, that his work applies not just to combat vets, but to non-combat veterans, women veterans who experienced MST, genocide survivors, draft resisters,

---

[372] Tick, pp. 107-108
[373] Tick, p. 7

peace activists, and members of military families and the civilian community as well. Certainly he offers a few stories from people in several of these categories, but within a sentence or two, these experiences and stories are left behind and the book carries on with its theme of Viet Nam combat vets, presumably because these men constitute the bulk of his counseling practice.

Tick's suggestion of a solution to the problem of PTSD is the ritualization of going out and returning from military service. I certainly agree that this is a good idea and have done work in my own community around precisely this issue. Because he is operating from within a Jungian, monist worldview, he does not have a great deal to fall back upon in his envisioning of these rituals; in fact, he advocates (generic) "Native American" sweat lodge practices as a cathartic purification upon return from service. I find this a somewhat problematic suggestion for a variety of reasons, not the least of which are the assumption that just anyone can participate in this ritual if they are spiritually "ready" for this purification, and the political and spiritual issues surrounding cultural appropriation, particularly in the shadow of the October 2009 deaths in an Arizona non-Native sweat led by James Arthur Ray.

This is not to say that purificatory ritual is unnecessary. I think it's obvious that such things are desperately needed, particularly (but not solely) for veterans who have seen combat and who have killed during their service. Being in the military separates us from the usual rules of civilized life and makes killing an imperative, something to be commended; returning from that world and leaving behind that necessity can be a terrible struggle with a constant state of hyper-alertness and inappropriate responses to situations most civilians would regard as harmless and safe. Our own bodies are instruments tuned to destruction, to fight or flight, to the instant assessment of threat levels and vulnerabilities. A significant marker of purification and the return to civilian society is, in my opinion, imperative as a first step.

One significant component of Tick's approach to the treatment of PTSD in combat veterans is a return to the place where the war occurred. While this can be possible for some Viet Nam vets, and vets from other wars now over – those who can afford plane fare, obviously – it is problematic for veterans of the ongoing conflicts in Iraq and Afganistan today. It is also problematic for those of us who served during the Cold War era. When one's service consisted of maintaining readiness for the Mutually Assured Destruction of the planetary population in a potential nuclear holocaust, to whom do we make restitution? Where do we return? When PTSD is the result of sexual harassment, rape, or assault, particularly by fellow service members, what then?

Fortunately, Tick also addresses in lesser detail the ideas of art and storytelling as potential paths to healing, and these are much more broadly applicable tools. When we are able to express our experiences, to speak of what happened, of what we did and of what was done to us, and when we are able to do so in the presence of those who have never been through such experiences, the acknowledgment of these things can be profoundly transformative. Yet none of these are a one-time cure. The causes and symptoms of PTSD are complex and multilayered; the treatment of such things is also complex and multilayered. It's not as simple as embracing an identity as a "warrior" rather than a soldier, sailor, airman or marine. Nor is it as simple as going through a gateway ritual upon our return from deployment or separation from service. We are prepared for military service through eight weeks or more of what is essentially brainwashing and indoctrination; it takes more than an hour's ritual, an overnight vigil, or a weekend retreat to undo what has been burned into us by this deliberate change. Even those small, inadequate things, however, are more than the military gives us upon our discharge – an exit interview and a DD-214.

Tick does call for civilian society to take up a moral responsibility for its service members and veterans and notes, in my opinion accurately, that much of society regards veterans as scapegoats for the responsibility of war. Military members go where they are sent and follow the orders they are given, frequently even if those orders are immoral, because disobeying orders is made as difficult as possible. Given that US society passes for a representational democracy, warfare is waged in the name of each of us and the military serves US governmental goals and agendas; we the people are as much responsible as any service member firing a missile, but we are so insulated from the realities of war that we can, if we choose, entirely ignore what is going on in our names.

I suspect that if society took more responsibility for acts committed in our name and under our flag, the return from service would be somewhat easier and war would be much more rare. It isn't enough for someone to say "thank you for your service." It's hard to hear those words if you believe that what you were doing was wrong or immoral, or if it put you in a situation of being assaulted by your co-workers.

All these things said, Tick's book does raise some excellent questions about the nature of modern warfare and of PTSD. Many of his suggestions will be thought-provoking for Pagans both in the military and in the larger community who interact with military Pagans and Pagan vets. As Pagans, we have a significantly larger tool set for dealing with ritualizing the going out and return of our service members, and for dealing with the psychic, physical, and emotional wounds that service members so often suffer during their service. Those of us practicing reconstructionist paths, which often have an honored place for the warrior within their social and spiritual structures, are perhaps best equipped to deal with these situations and to offer models of departure, purification, and return to the larger Pagan community.

What I found particularly moving and useful about the book were the stories of the veterans themselves. There were a number of points where I found myself in tears because these stories resonated so strongly with my own emotions around military service and PTSD. Each of these people were engaged in struggles with isolation, guilt, anger, and a constellation of other emotions with which I'm intimately familiar, even though our individual stories are very different. Each of us deals with trauma and its results in very different ways. There are many ways to heal from trauma; it's important to recognize spiritual work as one of those paths without implying that it will work for everyone in exactly the same ways.

Chapter 4
Short Essays

Following a Celtic Path

What elements are required to make a path true to the Celtic spirit?

I think that there are several. The more of them you have, the closer you get, in my opinion.

First is reverence for Celtic deities. This is easy, and pretty widespread, even among groups that are not really Celtic in focus. Lots of purely Wiccan groups, for instance, revere Celtic Gods and Goddesses, without fulfilling any of the other possible criteria.

Second, connection with ancestors and land spirits. This one is pretty generic and needs to be taken in combination with several other things, because ancestor worship and reverence for land spirits happens in most old Pagan cultures. I would suggest that this connection and reverence must happen in a style not unlike that shown in Evans-Wentz's *The Fairy Faith in Celtic Countries* for it to be seen as a continuation of the Celtic spirit. We can carry it forward into a modern Celtic spirit by having a general love and reverence for the earth and its creatures. A deep appreciation of nature is revealed in early Celtic nature poetry from Ireland and Wales.

Third, poetry as intrinsic to the structure of magic. Lorax[374] and I have done a number of rants on poetry here.[375] We're not talking about lame moon/June/tune rhymes, but about the kind of poetry that stirs up fire in the soul, the kind that speaks power in its descriptions and its focus. The sort of poetry that sucks you in and churns your guts. Although we often get clinical in our writing, we also try hard to make much of our writing lyrical in that sense. I hope that we sometimes succeed. In addition to poetry as magic, there was also respect for poetry as a social mechanism; it offered praise for those who were worthy, and satire and scorn for those who were not. It isn't just the reading of poetry, but the making of poetry that is important. Celtic Pagans must be poets, even if they aren't great poets.

Fourth, a connection with the past. The Celts had a reverence for history, and that reverence is a part of the Celtic spirit, I believe. For some, this connection comes through physical ancestry. For others, it comes through study of history. Some people get it through connecting with the feeling of the myths. Other folks get it in other ways. I think that this is why we have such heated debates

---

[374] Gordon Cooper, my husband at the time.
[375] "Here" being the Nemeton email list.

here about the importance (or lack thereof) of sticking to historical fact. We all recognize that something from the past is speaking to us strongly, but we disagree about the methods of judging its veracity and usefulness.

Fifth, a sense of early Celtic cosmology; doing things in terms of three realms rather than the classical Greek four elements, using Celtic symbols like triskeles and spirals rather than pentagrams, celebrating Celtic holidays rather than (or more deeply than) the holidays of other religions, threes and nines as ritually important, use of a sacred/cosmic tree and well combination. Much of this cosmology has had to be painstakingly reconstructed from fragmentary hints, and it goes back again to the argument that historical research is important to learning about and preserving the Celtic spirit.

Sixth, I think that inclusiveness is important. We can't rely on genealogy or geography to determine who is Celtic. The historical Celts roamed all over Europe, and lands beyond. Anyone worthy might be taken into the tribe through marriage or adoption. The Celts are roaming still, moving to America, Australia, and other widely diverse lands. And they're still taking people in through marriage and adoption.

Seventh, respect for women was a definite part of the Celtic spirit. While Celtic women didn't have it perfect, they were far better off than their Greek and Roman counterparts. Likewise, respect for and acceptance of gays and lesbians seems important. There is certainly text evidence for men loving men in early Celtic society. Women were not as often written about, but I think it is safe to assume that women had similar choices open to them.

Eighth, an appreciation of the complex and intricate. This is found in Celtic art, law, myth and poetry. The classical historians noted that the Celts spoke in riddles and loved to obfuscate. Wordplay and veiled reference were common.

Ninth, personal responsibility and a deep sense of self are a part of the Celtic spirit. Boasting and personal pride are evident in every Celtic tale. Sometimes it went overboard, so of course, like some other things (head hunting, etc), we have to be careful not to get too deeply into it. I think that some of us do act on this Celtic instinct, and that's why we often have heated debate on this list. So long as it doesn't get out of hand, I find it encouraging and a growth-oriented activity. Spirited argument was a part of the poet's duty, and was one of the ways in which the younger poets learned from the older. Along with this, I would say that the Celtic spirit includes a strong sense of ethics about what is right and what is wrong. The Celts were not an "anything goes" kind of people. They had a very complex body of laws governing what was appropriate and what was not. Celtic Pagans need both a strong sense of personal responsibility and a code of personal and social ethics in order to carry the Celtic spirit forward.

Creideamh Sí and Celtic Reconstruction[376]

One thing that people have been debating in CR for a long time is what do we call ourselves? What do we call what we do? After my sojourn to Ireland, I've had a few thoughts on that.

I've always acknowledged that "Celtic Reconstruction" is a very awkward and not terribly appealing term. Different people have tried using different words or phrases for it over the years, some of which have stuck for individual groups and organizations, though most have fallen by the wayside. We describe ourselves in so many ways -- *filid*, *draoi*, warrior, mystic, *bo áire*, *aes dána*.

One thing I've realized recently is that what most of us are doing, in one way or another, is practicing some form of what Evans-Wentz referred to as the Fairy Faith, and what the clergyman Seán Ó Duinn calls *creideamh sí*. The *aes sídhe* are not just the gods, not just the ancestors, but all the spirits. Those of us who are animist and mystical in orientation work with each of these differently, and each Celtic culture approaches them somewhat differently and by different names, but each of these strands is woven into a larger plaid that is, in essence, reaching for the same root.

The blessing and curse of thinking of CR as part of the *creideamh sí* is that "fairy faith" is an immense, broad tapestry. Each time we leave an offering at the base of a tree or pour it into a river or a lake or the sea, we are continuing that long tradition. Each time we tie a rag to a tree or take water from a sacred well, we participate in that strand. When we pray to the old gods or sing a traditional song at the closing of the day as we turn out the lights, we are leaving our own traces in the weave of that pattern. Because the *creideamh sí* has so many expressions, and changes with the generations, it is my belief that we can legitimately claim to be a part of that so long as we preserve the central tenets of its animistic source — respect for the land and the *aes sídhe*, telling the old tales, singing the old songs, honoring the ancestors and making the offerings.

This is a fairy fort just down the hill from Poll na Brón ("hole of the quern"), a portal tomb in the Burren, which is a largely barren limestone area of the west of Ireland. These places are still largely undisturbed due to respect for the *aes sídhe*, and now due also to conservation and heritage laws.

---

376. erynn999.livejournal.com/81508.html

Because so many of us live outside of the traditional "Celtic" territories, we have to make do with what is mobile about the tradition. In this, though, we are still following tradition, because the Celtic peoples did exactly this in their travels — they adapted to the spirits and territories to which they moved. And if the spirits with whom we speak are sometimes the Native spirits of North America or Australia or New Zealand, it doesn't negate the fact that we are still doing essentially what those early Celts were doing. We shift and change as they did, speaking new tongues, and integrating new knowledge and new places into our experiences.

What we find within the land and what is numinous is *neart* — "power" or "strength." So many of us practice as solitaries, following that impulse to isolate and interact with the world of spirits just as the *geilta* and the early Irish Christian monastics did. Is it the path itself that pulls us this way? Is this how it is meant to be on the path of the *creideamh sí*? I've asked this question before, and do feel that it is a part of the strand of what makes CR what it is. It's not just a lack of critical mass for groups, but a larger impulse, I think. To walk the rounds of a holy well, even in the company of others, is a solitary occupation fraught with individual prayers and requests. The larger celebrations are less "ritual" in nature than social, with races, games, and feasting. Offerings made, even by groups, are still done as individuals sharing space with each other and the *aes sídhe*.

When we study Celtic languages and lifeways, we are attempting to make a deeper connection to the spirits that call us. Twenty years ago, when I was first called to Celtic deities, before I was even formally a Wiccan, one of the deities who would become a tutelary Goddess came to me and said, "I want to hear the old tongue spoken again." After all my years of walking a Pagan path, I have been moving in that direction. I phrase prayers in Irish and Scots Gaelic. I try to do what those before me have done, and to give offerings that would be recognized as similar or the same. I have stood by the water on the proper days and called out the old names.

I am a *fili*. I follow the *creideamh sí* as best I can. The deities and spirits press me in these directions, lead me along these ways, and when I look at the world around me, I see wonder and am filled with that *neart*, that power, that flows through all things.

Who but I am filled with holy fire?

Geiltadecht

One word you'll find me using frequently here and in other places is *geilt*. It is translated as "one who goes mad from terror, a panic-stricken fugitive from battle, a crazy person living in the woods and supposed to be endowed with the power of levitation, a lunatic." It may also be the name of some kind of bird or it might mean "grazing." The title I'm using here, *geiltadecht*, is a neologism to describe the practice of the *geilta*.

In the *Buile Suibhne*, the eponymous Suibhne goes mad in battle as the result of a saint's curse. The symptoms he displays are very akin to what we could today interpret as post-traumatic stress disorder. He flees from the place of battle and ends up hiding out in the forest, running from phantoms and spirits, unable to tolerate the company of others, eating only plants. Eventually he was said to have grown feathers, and flown from treetop to treetop like a bird. He is not the only *geilt* described in the literary tradition, and there is even a valley where the *geilta*, the madmen, were believed to gather until their sanity was restored.

But along with this madness came poetry. The body of nature poems attributed to Suibhne Geilt is impressive and the images are striking and powerful. His visions and terrors evolved into poignant laments and strange dialogues with trees and beasts. Whether the Irish writers believed that Suibhne was actually in communication with such spirits is an open question, but the story can certainly be read in Pagan and animist ways. Suibhne himself was described as a Pagan who attempted to kill the "saint" who cursed him, presumably attempting to preserve the old order in his kingdom rather than give his power over to the church.

Other "madmen" in the Celtic literary tradition, including Myrddin and Lailoken, were regarded as prophets — seers and possessors of a certain "crazy wisdom." Sacred madness is a current in many spiritual traditions around the world. It's found in many Native American tribes, and within Hindu and Buddhist practice, as well as in Islam and Christianity. Such traditions have their gifts and their difficulties. As someone who lives on disability with a diagnosis (one among many) of post-traumatic stress, I've looked at these roles and potentials and seen them as models for my own life in much the same way that many individuals in Siberian cultures deal with healing spirit-sicknesses by falling into the spiritual world and coming out again transformed.

By pursuing poetry as a spiritual practice I've managed to find my way to a certain amount of healing and sanity. It has exorcised many of the figurative demons that made my life a misery. In seeing Suibhne's madness as a metaphor for my own experience, I've embraced the idea of the professional madwoman and claimed the title of *geilt* as a badge of honor for what I've gone through. I think that poetry can take suffering and illness and turn them into art and a potential for healing and growth. It's not that poetry by itself will do this — I've done a lot of years of therapy and medication as well — but the work of poetry can give a spiritual focus and purpose to what feels like continual chaos and destruction. In this sense, the task of the *geilt* is to refuse to succumb to the pain, and to work through the mists to transcend that condition, in order to bring something useful out of the fear and the misery.

Working with the arts of the *fili* or sacred poet, the experiences of the *geilt* can be mediated and expressed. Expression often helps to clarify and understand what is happening, aiding the person to get to the root of the problems and issues, whether they are physical, spiritual, emotional, or socio-political. Techniques that help to communicate with spirits and deities, as well as journeying work, can help with clarity and understanding, as can acts of divination through seeking oracles or finding omens. Rituals to embrace the madness as a part of working through it can be effective, reinforcing positive patterns and activities and drawing the mind out of the obsessive circles it may fall prey to without such focus.

That said, the nature of the *geilt* means that control is often an illusion. Interpretation and acceptance is a more fruitful path for one with these proclivities. This is not in any way suggesting "giving up" but merely a statement that the world and the Otherworlds are vaster than we can understand and we, mere humans, have very little power over some things that happen. That isn't necessarily a bad thing, though our culture values control, or the illusion of it, very highly. It can be a relief for guilt and anxiety to let go of inappropriate responsibility.

Sometimes I joke with friends that I'm only responsible for the decay rate of the hydrogen atom, hence I don't have to deal with anything else in the universe. Obviously, that's not the case, but it does serve as a reminder to me to only claim what I'm genuinely responsible for — and as a *geilt*, my own sanity and spiritual work is high up on that list. There are other priorities as well, but a *geilt* is an outsider, someone who lurks on the boundaries of groups and societies. That inclination to solitude is part of what marks someone as *geilt* but can also be a part of what helps to heal the terror and the insanity of those who have been through violent experiences, through abuse, through battle or rape or overwhelming environmental events that have destroyed their ordinary daily lives.

Within the experience of *geiltadecht*, madness and destruction are foundations for transformation.

Skin Deep:
Beauty and *Filidecht* in the Gaelic Tradition

One of the persistent themes of *filidecht*, the Gaelic tradition of poetic mysticism, is the dichotomy of beauty and ugliness. Within this tradition, and in the Brythonic tradition of Wales, we find stories where figures of power and knowledge are perceived first as ugly and then as radiant or beautiful.

It is not the external state of these figures that is important. The wisdom, or the lack of it, of the observer makes a difference in how the figure is perceived. The beauty of their true nature is only revealed when understanding opens the eyes. It is only when the surface ugliness is embraced, kissed, loved for itself, that the beauty within becomes manifest.

The world of *filidecht* is one in which loathly ladies grant sovereignty, hideous children conceal poetic eloquence, and terrible monsters bestow gifts of power. The art of poetry is practiced in forms beautiful and terrifying; praise poetry raises a name to immortality while satires raise physical blemishes that destroy the outer beauty of an ugly soul.

One of the great poets of Ireland, Senchán Torpéist, was so named because the spirit of poetry traveled with him in search of the daughter of Ua Dulsaine, herself a powerful poet. This spirit is embodied as a young boy who is described at first as having an "unnatural" appearance.

> Indeed, when anyone would put his finger upon his forehead, a gush of putrid matter would flow down to his neck. His rough *congris* (a caul?) over his head to his shoulder blades. Anyone who would see it would think that it was the *cáib* of his brains that had burst through his skull. As bulging as a blackbird's egg his two eyes. As quick as a wild animal, as black as death. As yellow as gold the ends of his teeth; as green as the trunk of a holly tree his backside. Bare and skinny his two shins. Two pointy, black-speckled heels under him. If the rag he had on were removed, it were not unlikely that it would set out on its own, unless a

rock were placed upon it, because of the multitude of vermin.[377]

Senchán got the name Torpéist because the word *péist* in Irish means "beast" or "monster", and it was at his invitation that the loathly lad entered his coracle to join him on his search. When the hideous child speaks for Senchán, answering the challenging verses of the satirist daughter of Ua Dulsaine, he shows his true nature as the spirit of poetry and is revealed as a thing of beauty.

> ...for he was a radiant, royal, mighty, wide-eyed, valorous youth, with yellow-gold, curly hair, like gold thread, wavy as the spine of a small harp. He was dressed in a beautiful royal cloak secured with a golden brooch. In his left hand he held a purple embossed shield, four-edged, full of carbuncles and precious stones and pearls and crystal and sapphires; in his right, a straight-edged sword with a reddish-gold hilt. A silver diadem with a crown of gold was around his head. The most noble and radiant appearance that was ever on man was on him.[378]

We find poetry is transformative in the other direction as well, when it comes to the work of the *geilt* or madman of Irish tradition. Suibhne, a king among the Dal Riada, is cursed and flies from battle in the midst of madness. He is transformed from a sovereign figure who must be unblemished and physically perfect into a naked and destitute feathered creature, flying from treetop to treetop as he creates his poetry — the only thing of beauty left to him. In this state he praises wild nature as the epitome of beauty, in sharp contrast to the hollow manmade sounds of bronze bells and stone monasteries. His perception is radically altered and with that alteration comes an eloquence and a beauty of words that is rarely matched in the Gaelic poetic corpus.

Ugliness and beauty are so often only clever illusions in Celtic tales. The surface never tells the entire story. In a complex dance of not-this, not-that, the shapeshifters and the places between are both

---

[377] Patrick K. Ford, *The Celtic Poets: Songs and Tales from Early Ireland and Wales*, Ford & Bailie, Belmont 1999, pp. 39-40
[378] Ford, p. 42

hideous and beautiful. It is this transitory nature, the shifting forms of beauty and ugliness, which reflect an underlying truth, and the only way to find genuine discernment is through the cultivation of wisdom.

Uncertainty

One of the things that I encounter a lot in my practice is uncertainty. *Filidecht* as a formal modern CR practice is still being created, and the hints about its place as a mystic and magical practice in the past are few and far between. We have bits and pieces, but those pieces need to be examined pretty carefully as, even though we can see some of the ways the *filid* operated, we can't be certain of exactly how rituals were done or what was said.

With material like the Cauldron of Poesy text, we have some statements about cauldrons in the body and what they do, and we can infer where they were situated. But when it comes to actual operations and getting those cauldrons to do what they're supposed to, the only thing we can really do is look at comparable systems from other cultures and do some experimentation. Will what I come up with be exactly what the pre-Christian practitioners of the art were doing? No. Will it have the same or similar results? Well, if it results in *imbas* as an upwelling of poetic inspiration and magical and spiritual power or enlightenment, then yes, I think the results are similar to what was intended. And if it works, then this is the direction in which we should be moving.

Within CR there are a lot of branches that people find of interest. Within any given culture you're going to find householder paths, warrior paths, magical paths, healing paths, storytelling paths, and more. And each of the various Celtic cultures adds another layer onto that complexity. You're much more in luck if, for instance, your interest lies in Irish material about household traditions than if it lies in the deities and practices of Gaul. It will be much harder to understand and reconstruct Gaulish practices because of the lack of easily available material. There is no extant Gaulish literature that describes deities and myths. Most of what is known is from archaeological sources, with a few inscriptions on altars or on spell tablets. A little more is added from references to Gaulish people by Greek or Roman writings.

A lot of Irish household tradition has survived into modern folk practice, though very much changed and buried within Christianity. It is by no means a fully realized polytheistic Pagan practice at this point, but it's a good and necessary basis to grow from. For Irish Pagan mystical and spiritual practices the material is rather less plentiful and so more has to be reconstructed or created by reference to other things. It's regrettable, but it's how things are.

So what's a person without a lot of sources to do? Here's where our uncertainties lie, and this is where a lot of people get discouraged. But comparative work helps in many cases. Nearby cultures can be examined, of course, and the field of Indo-European studies has a lot of useful material. Offerings are a practice common to every culture I've ever heard of, so that's always a good place to start. The archaeological record often provides fairly good material on what kinds of objects and foods were offered by any individual culture, or people in a given area.

But ultimately the words of our practice will always need to be our own. We can base them on material in sources like the *Carmina Gadelica*, but that text, wonderful as it is, doesn't cover all contingencies or address every circumstance for which we might need a ritual text. And if *filidecht* is about the creation of poetry, then always using someone else's words is a violation of that tradition.

We know that the *tarbhfeis* ritual of Ireland involved a *fili* who was surrounded by four people chanting truth spells, but we have no idea what the words of those spells were. We don't know if the same one was used each time, or if they were extemporaneous compositions created by each of the chanters. *Imbas* is what helps us to create appropriate words for situations like these and experimentation can tell us if those words work or not. We can't know until we try it.

Practice is about what works. We can theorize all we want, but until we commit something to physical ritual, until we commit words to speech, theory is all that we'll have. Uncertainty can be frightening, but it can also be fertile. In a practice involving extemporaneous poetry we won't know the words until we speak them. Without the uncertainty there's no room for spontaneity, which is the heart of poetry created in the moment. The words come out on our breath — *anáil* — and vanish into the universe. We look at what happens to see if there is an effect. And we note what happens (or what doesn't) and try again.

There's no escape from uncertainty, but we can embrace it and make it a friend.

Failures

Last month I set out to do another session in the incubation chamber. I've done a few now, mostly meditation but a couple of vision-seeking/journeywork sessions as well. I had high hopes when I set out, as I'd been wanting to work with some *psilocybe* and *amanita muscaria* I'd had on hand.

I set up the space, invoked the spirits and deities, went through all the processes I go through to set the stage for the work, and waited.

There was an immense sense of presence. It was so strong it woke my roommate, who had been sleeping in eir[379] room. I felt a sense of the incubation chamber breathing around me. I waited more. I sang and prayed and watched.

Yet beyond that sense of presence and breath, "nothing" happened.

I've worked with LSD a couple of times before and had some very powerful experiences with it. One I would even describe as profound. I've had some very good success with smoking *salvia divinorum*, though that was an entirely different quality of experience than the LSD had been. After all the accounts I'd heard and read about different types of fungal entheogens, I'd been expecting something big and consuming.

Sometimes, things don't work. They flop for whatever reason. Maybe the dried fungi were too old. Perhaps they weren't going to work with my body chemistry. Maybe there was nothing the deities or spirits wanted me to do that day beyond spend four hours in meditation and ritual. Maybe I was expecting the wrong things and was too focused on what I'd been told, rather than on being in the experience.

Yet our failures teach us just as our successes do. The lessons of failure can be very valuable if we are willing to accept them and work with them. When I posted about the issue in my LJ later that day, I got several responses from folks who were glad to hear that they were not alone in having rituals that didn't work out as planned.

When ritual fails, you're not alone. It happens to all of us, from the veriest noob to the grizzled grey elder. I can't think of

---

[379] a metagender pronoun appropriate to my roommate, https://aediculaantinoi.wordpress.com/a-note-on-pronouns/ accessed March 16, 2015

anyone who has never in their entire life had a ritual poop out on them at least once; some have even been spectacular in their failure. Failure, though, is a part of the human condition. We all experience it sometimes, and how we deal with it is important.

In failure, we learn that the universe isn't all about us. The spirit world isn't a giant wish-granting machine where you put in your ritual and out pops the result you wanted. Life, the universe, and everything is a big place and we're just tiny motes within it. We have our roles to play, but that doesn't mean we're at center stage.

We learn a certain amount of humility in our failures. We may do everything right and still not get the result we wanted. Approaching the spirit realms with humility and knowing that we're only a part of the greater whole is important. Pride may be a value of CR Paganism, but it should be properly placed pride and not hubris.

Failure encourages us to be resilient, to be creative, and to keep on trying. If we don't get it right the first time, perhaps something needs to be changed. Maybe we need to readjust our expectations. Maybe the conditions weren't right. Maybe we were using the wrong tools or the wrong symbol set. Maybe the spirits or deities were busy elsewhere. Some things have to be worked for much harder than others, and ritual is no exception to this general rule in life.

Patience comes with failure. Learning to bide our time until the next opportunity is an important lesson when dealing with not just the Otherworlds but this one as well. Planting a seed in midwinter is unlikely to be as successful as planting it in the spring, in its proper time and place.

Failure also teaches gratitude. Success won't feel like much when it's your only experience. Its value tends to decline emotionally in proportion to how routine it is. Failing shows us that success is a possibility, not a guarantee, and encourages us to make the most of success when it comes along.

When we examine the reasons for ritual failure we learn to think clearly and systematically about how we design ritual and how we understand its purposes. Taking things apart afterwards is a very helpful practice whether the ritual succeeded or not. Most of the folks I know who do public ritual have debriefings with the ritual team afterwards to discuss what went well, what didn't, and what could be improved. Examination, ideally, leads to growth.

In the wake of this particular experiment I've determined that I'd like to try again, but with fungi that are fresh rather than dried.

This may have some effect on the outcome. I know I have more luck with *salvia*, so I'll be doing more in-depth work with that in some of its forms other than dried, unenhanced leaf to see if that will change the ritual results.

I'll pay more attention to what is happening than what I wish for, as well. There were currents I could have ridden in that ritual that I failed to because of my preconceived expectations. Rather than doing the work, I expected to be carried along.

The session was a failure in terms of what I had hoped for, yet it taught me a number of things about myself and the process of the work I'm doing, and for that I'm very grateful.

Why Write About Entheogens?

In my earlier post about ritual failure, an anonymous person took it upon themself to suggest that "you don't need" entheogens and that I should look to the work of RJ Stewart and John and Caitlin Matthews for all the techniques of "the old bards" that I would ever need. Anonymous isn't opposed to entheogens per se, and I don't disagree with this. Yet there are reasons one might experiment with such things.

Kenneth talks in the comments about working with the spirit of the entheogenic plant or fungus as a part of the ritual. This is absolutely one good reason why someone might work with entheogens. It is, in fact, one of the reasons that I do so, as well. Touching the living spirit of such a powerful being is a profound experience when it works. And yes, once you've got to that state, you may or may not ever need to actually use the entheogen again to re-experience it or to have a good, solid contact with that spirit.

This, though, was immaterial to the point I was trying to make in that post. My point there was that failure of ritual can help us learn a lot of different and useful lessons. Failing means retooling the work and trying again, or repeating the experiment to see if something about the set and setting were problematic. Failing means reevaluating where you are and where you're headed. Failing means dealing with disappointment and losing the sense of being a special snowflake whose every action is fraught with spiritual significance. Failing means recognizing we're human and that we make mistakes, or that even if we haven't made a mistake, sometimes things just don't work the way we expect them to. Failure offers us chances to grow and mature.

What really rather gripes me, though, is anonymous's assumption that I've never read either anything by Stewart or the Matthews, or anything from the original Gaelic and Welsh source material. I've read a lot of sources on Gaelic pre-Christian religion and culture. I've read a lot of the medieval manuscripts in translation. I've even done translations of materials from Old Irish myself, for my own understanding. Hell, I've had my translation of the *Cauldron of Poesy* published at least twice. A lot of my work has been translated into other languages.

Much of what the Matthews reprint is 19th century scholarship, outdated in the mid- to late-20th century. While there are occasional useful nuggets in their reprints, I've already read the vast majority of what they're offering. And I disagree with a lot of their interpretations and uses of the material. I don't find RJ Stewart's ceremonial magic approach to the materials very useful for my own work either. While the Matthews do a somewhat better job of dealing with Celtic spiritual materials than, say, DJ Conway, Edain McCoy, or Douglas Monroe, it doesn't mean they are presenting the source materials without their own particular filter — in their case, usually, Celtic "shamanism," which is a rant in and of itself.

Certainly neither the Matthews nor Stewart talk about deity in any polytheistic fashion. The Matthews, in their *Western Mystery Tradition* books, refer to the Celtic deities as "unregenerate godforms," whatever the hell that's supposed to mean, and warn against working with them. Perhaps this is their way of saying the deities are dangerous. If that's the case, so is fire. So is the sea. So is walking out your door every morning to go to work. Should we stop heating our houses, cooking our food, and going outside because it might be dangerous? People are dangerous, too. Even our closest friends and the people we love might hurt us from time to time. Do we stop having friends and family because of this, or do we learn to deal with their rough edges and accept them for who they are?

Ultimately, I write about entheogens because I find them useful in some ritual circumstances. I write about them to show that there are many ways to define and practice rituals. I discuss my experiences, both successful and failed, in order to demonstrate that effects vary and that not everything is going to work every time. In modern US culture it's hard to find people openly discussing that kind of work. Discussions go on in closed fora and between friends in private. There are books out there, but the good ones can be hard to find. And to neglect such an ancient source of access to ritual states of consciousness, and such powerful potential spiritual allies, is to cut oneself off from the potential for powerful learning and spiritual experiences.

Yes, there are dangers inherent in the path. People have averse reactions to entheogens just as they do to any other substance they may put in their bodies. For some people, being in the vicinity of onions is a life-threatening experience. Strawberries have killed people.

Important things to remember are to research thoroughly, to exercise due caution, and to understand that these things will not always work as advertised. Sure, you don't "need" to use entheogens in a spiritual practice. One doesn't "need" a lot of things that are or can be useful. It doesn't mean they should never be used by responsible adults. And it doesn't mean that non-entheogenic practices can't get you where you want to go as well, depending on your goals. Humans are curious creatures. We are interested in new experiences and are prone to experimentation in all fields of life. Ritual is like sex, in the end analysis. Different things work for different people and my kink may not be your cuppa. The important thing is that we all try to get to our goal, by whatever pathway pleases us best.

Thoughts on Ritual and Homecoming

On July 18th (2009) the local CR schmooze held a ritual. The focus of this rite was a vigil of return for a warrior who has returned from duty. As most of you probably know, I was enlisted in the US Navy from 1979-1982. I was 17 when I enlisted. After leaving the service, I tried to pick up the pieces of my shattered life. It was hard and, while I've been dealing with things as best I can, I'm living on a veteran's disability pension due to what happened to me during my service and afterwards. That pension is how I can write books and articles and still keep a roof over my head.

Because I was thrown out of the Navy (I tried for almost three years before they actually did it, so that was my intention), I'm not the kind of vet the military likes to talk about. Not only am I queer, I was a "disciplinary problem" and stood for captain's mast (non-judicial punishment) three times in my enlistment, as well as once being court martialed. Needless to say, there was no recognition of my service and no one to welcome me home despite the fact that I'd given a goodly chunk of what passed for my sanity to the service of my country.

Over the last year our local group has been working with one of our members who is an active duty military man, currently serving in Iraq. We sent him off with a ritual last August and will welcome him home this August when he arrives. We've talked with the larger Pagan community at PantheaCon about the sending out ritual. This, the companion ritual, is a vigil for the warrior's return. For me, the ritual was a profound experience of welcome into a community that I have never had before. For Arlen, we hope to give him a welcome to the same community he left and hope that he won't have the same kinds of problems reintegrating with the civilian community that I've had over the years.

Our experiences of the military are very different. Arlen intends to re-enlist for another five-year hitch with an eye toward becoming a warrant officer. I hated my time in service and tried desperately to get out. Yet both of us have served, both of us have done what had to be done under the circumstances — me during the nuclear terror of the Cold War, him under fire in battle.

This is my account of the vigil.

Dusk came slowly that day, as it does so often at this time of year. I'd set up my tent in tall grass beyond the back gate. Last time I'd done a vigil there, I'd been eaten by mosquitos — over 20 bites all over my body, even through thick jeans and a sweater. The tent was a blessing because there would be no fire.

After I was sent out to take my place beyond the hedge, the night was filled with loud, thumping, percussive music, punctuated by occasional cheering. Somewhere nearby, there was a concert. It continued until late into the night, but was distant enough to be little more than background to my thoughts. I'd have preferred silence but, when one does vigil ritual in the burbs, even the heavily-wooded burbs of semi-rural Redmond, one has neighbors to consider.

The questions came at small intervals, presented by people who were attempting to affect floating, disembodied heads. Dark clothing, lit features. Between the focus of my headspace in ritual and their sometimes awkward attempts, it was effective enough. At one point P.S.V. Lupus looked like eir eyes were glowing. I'm told that at several points I didn't look much of anything like myself, either; a strange silhouette armed with spear and sword, leaning forward, overshadowed by something Other.

I felt that overshadowing. Each time I rose to exit the tent, alert and armed, it covered me. There was a hyperawareness, a sense of stretching beyond the boundaries of my body to encompass the area surrounding me, knowing where everything was despite the darkness. I was on guard, taking care of the community I'd sworn so many years ago to protect.

Thirty years ago, I took an oath. I swore to protect and defend the people and constitution of the United States of America. Twenty-six years ago, I "came home." Since that time I have lived on the edges of my ability, broken by my experiences in the military. I had been thrown out, by my own design. There were no ceremonies, no welcomes, barely a word beyond "thank god that's over." I don't remember the exit interview, I only know I had to sign my DD-214, which read that I was discharged under "General, Other Than Honorable" conditions. I walked away, too numb to try to make sense of it all.

I'm not the sort of veteran the services are proud of. I fought the whole time I was in. I hated it desperately and passionately. Nobody wants to hear about the broken ones, especially the ones who were broken between shooting wars, the ones that could never fit in to begin with. The ones who weren't properly military enough. I was good at what I did — good enough that they didn't want to get rid of me until I'd made myself such a nuisance that they had no other choice. The few times I was working in conditions I found tolerable, with people who would give me a chance, I was moved to new conditions within weeks. My reputation for trouble preceded me.

During the vigil I sat with questions that brought me face to face with who and what I am, what I did, and what it all meant. There are not adequate words for most of it. I wrote a couple of notebook pages for most of the questions. One particularly stuck with me, because it had a two-sentence answer:

What will you do if you don't get what you want?

Keep trying, just like I always have. The alternative is death.

In so many ways, this sums up my relationship to the military and to the Veterans Administration. *Keep trying, or die.* When they beat you down, stand back up. When they refuse you, return with a new set of forms. When they ignore you, shout down the walls. When they break you, pick up the pieces. To do otherwise is to suffer annihilation.

In my life, I have rarely gotten what I want. Often I've had to be content with other things but, in most contexts, that's okay. When it has come to the military, even the idea of compromise has been deadly to my soul. There are some things that cannot be accepted. They must be struggled for, even if that becomes the defining theme of a life.

One of the things I've struggled for all these years has been community and acceptance. I've tried to understand my place in the context of others as groups and individuals. I've stood outside so much of my life, even before I formally signed my enlistment contract. Its part of that *kshatriya*[380] thing I was talking about last week — the military displaces families. We don't belong anywhere because we don't stay long enough and when we do try to stay, we have tall barriers to surmount: being the new kid (eternally), being an unknown factor (because no one bothers to get to know you), being different (by background and by temperament).

In a small group of people last week, I found community. I am no longer outside the fence. I may walk the edge and be able to traverse it and live in the wild but I also, for once, belong inside. Welcomed in and given a place of honor, my history and my

---

[380] The *kshatriya* are the warrior caste of Vedic India. Not everyone within that caste, obviously, was a warrior, but they lived and breathed a warrior ethic regardless of gender or other social station. People born and raised in military families in the US have a similar type of separate cultural identity from the rest of US culture.

differences were accepted for what they are rather than rejected as a mark of unacceptable severance.

Good ritual changes something inside you. Those changes may not be obvious for a long time afterwards. I can feel them moving, though. This acceptance was very different than the superficial "thank you for your service" that I sometimes get these days when I note that I'm a veteran. I've never really known how to cope with that phrase. It brings too much back, and in a bad way. To be brought inside the gate, to be cooled and tempered in the waters and purified in the smoke of holy herbs, and to be placed at the head of the table for the feast in a place of honor is a distinctly different thing.

Sleep-deprived after a long night of intense focus and meditation, I was in a very different space than I usually am. Doing a vigil ritual brings it home much more deeply than a ritual that might take an hour or so, even if the content is essentially identical. The time and the effort involved intensify the effect. They separate us from the mundane much more fully. They emphasize the importance of what is happening.

Do I still identify with the *geilta*? Oh, yes. Yet I know I'm welcome inside the gates. My skills and talents are valued and I am valued, despite the problems I still, and may always, have.

Am I "cured" of my PTSD, my nightmares, my triggers? Not by a long shot. But I know how far I've come along that road, and I know that I can go further. I have friends and a community who have demonstrated with their efforts and their bodies that what has happened may have marked me, but I am capable of change.

Twenty six years after the fact, I've come home.

Polypraxy: A Multitudinous Future

Here's my wisdom for your use, as I learned it when the moose
And the reindeer roared where Paris roars to-night:
— There are nine and sixty ways of constructing tribal lays,
And — every — single — one — of — them — is — right!
~Rudyard Kipling, "In the Neolithic Age"

A lot of folks talk about Paganism in its varying manifestations as being not a religion of belief, but one of practice. Generally speaking, I agree with this assessment. Belief is all well and good. I believe in spirits and deities and that magic works. But when the rubber hits the road, practice is where things really happen in spiritual and ethical communities. You can believe all kinds of wonderful things, but if you never act on them, you might as well not believe either.

In monotheistic religions we see manifestations of orthodoxy (correctness of belief) and in many of them we see orthopraxy (correctness of practice) as well. The ortho- element in the words is defined in the 1913 edition of Webster's Dictionary as "A combining form signifying straight, right, upright, correct, regular." With this concept, far too often, comes the idea that there is only one correct belief or practice.

Calling various types of Paganism, including Celtic reconstructionist Paganisms, religions of practice doesn't point to uniformity, though. In the multiple Celtic cultures encompassing centuries of time and thousands of miles of place, practices varied from village to village and era to era, so it's hard to claim an orthopraxy in any meaningful sense. In Gardnerian Wiccan circles, you can usually expect to get something that doesn't vary a whole lot from group to group. There is a certain orthopraxy beneath the varied personal practices. A Gardnerian can, generally, expect their initiation rituals to be the same from group to group in a particular lineage.

The same can't be said in Celtic reconstructionist religions for the simple reason that we don't have handed down texts of rituals to work from. We can all look at the same source texts of poetry and tales and history and come away with different interpretations and different ways of ritualizing the content of those texts. Individuals in a community may influence one another's interpretations and practices, but even within a small local community like the Seattle

CR schmooze group that I'm a member of, we have different approaches, different interests, and different types of focus on the material. We have folks who are interested in Irish or Scottish materials and folks interested in Welsh materials. We experiment with different types of ritual based on the sources to see what happens and how it all works — if it does at all.

And so what we see in the Pagan community at large, and within many reconstructionist communities as subgroups of the Pagan community, is what can really only be called polypraxy; a multiplicity of practices based on variations in source materials, interpretations, and localized bioregional expressions, much as P. Sufenus Virius Lupus notes in eis essay on Niche Religions.[381]

Polypraxy still happens in Ireland, where the festivals for Lá Fhéill Bríde (Imbolc) vary from one town to another in the same county. In CR approaches to the same holy day, localized manifestations are going to be a feature of the movement by the very nature of human spiritual experience and its interpretation. One group might focus on the weaving of Brigid's crosses and putting out the Brat Bríd, while another looks at ways to bring in aspects of the cross-dressing Biddy Boys traditions and public processional, and a third deals with Bríg Ambue and the purification of outsiders who are then welcomed into the community as full participants.

None of these approaches are incorrect, nor does any group have to have all of them to be a "real" CR group celebrating a culturally appropriate festival. It's possible to have a philosophy of polypraxy within a movement and be very much true to the originating culture, the source texts, and the spiritual impetus of the individuals who make up the modern movement, without any of it being inauthentic. Each of these rituals addresses different needs in the particular community where the rituals occur, and all of them are based on traditional literary sources or folk practices.

There is another layer to this, though. Religion and spirituality are living things. They change with each generation and with each movement from place to place. Texts are reinterpreted within these new contexts of time and geography. Other cultures and religions are encountered, and their philosophies and practices are observed, discussed, studied, and even experienced. People add new practices to their lives. New non-spiritual philosophies are

---

381. http://www.patheos.com/Resources/Additional-Resources/Niche-Religions-Your-Own-Personal-Paganism.html accessed September 17, 2014

encountered as well – feminism, post-modernism, egalitarianism. Old ways are modified to accommodate the need for equality of gender and social class and, often, old exclusionary rules are discarded or modified. Women take their place as ritualists, teachers, warriors. Men take up tending Brigid's flame. These may not have been part of the original cultures, but they reflect our needs today, and the ways in which culture and spirituality are changing in response to our needs and the needs of generations to come.

People who consider themselves primary practitioners of one path often add secondary practices like Buddhist meditation, or attendance at an Umbanda house, or supporting dancers in local Native communities, or puja at a local Hindu temple to their personal spiritual work without seeing this as a source of conflict or a betrayal of their primary allegiance. We can still be CR or Asatru or Wiccan and have other practices and other altars in our hearts and our homes. Given the global nature of modern culture, I see this as a welcome step toward cooperation and understanding, not a dilution or a betrayal of tradition. It is an addition, not a subtraction, and it is one that fosters understanding between groups, between religions, and between cultures.

The ideal of polypraxy, of Kipling's nine and sixty ways of constructing tribal lays, is one that has always been a part of the human condition. Large orthodoxies have tried repeatedly to muffle or destroy this human urge, but it continues under the surface, even in the most conservative spiritual communities. In my work with a Siberian teacher from the Ulchi tribe, I was told that there are very firm rules for what kinds of things may be offered to the spirits, but if a particular spirit asks for something that is considered a violation of those rules, you listen to the spirit. Traditional ways are guidelines that preserve the culture, but even in traditional cultures, there are exceptions, there are changes, there are drifts. There are places outside the mainstream, and modern Paganism swims in these waters. Polypraxy is important to our future as a multifaceted constellation of spiritual communities.

And every single one of them is right.

On the Use of Juniper for Purification

I've been asked a few times recently about why I use juniper, why do a purification at all before doing ritual, and whether this is some sort of Christian influence on the tradition.

I'll address the last question first. A lot of non-Christian (and, in fact, uninfluenced by Christianity) traditions do purifications before they do ritual. Siberian shamans (Ulchi, Nanai, etc) purify with smoke. Lakota people purify with smoke. Shinto purifies with water. Many other traditions do purifications of varying kinds. They do them for a lot of different reasons.

Purifications like this don't imply that we are evil or sin-filled or unfit to stand before the Gods. A pre-ritual purification can be viewed in the same way as wiping your feet before you walk into someone's house or taking off your shoes at the door -- sometimes we carry stuff with us that we don't want to bring into a ritual space on our bodies or our clothing. It's not a value judgment about us as human beings, it's just a way to remove any unwanted influences before we enter ritual space, however we are defining that.

The reason I use juniper in particular is because it was historically used in Scotland. We don't know if they did this every time anyone did ritual, but for a lot of people, doing something like this before ritual is a comforting thing, or a signal that we are entering ritual space. In Scotland, juniper was burned on New Years morning in enough quantity to fill the entire house or byre. I don't want to suffocate my whole house and make all the smoke alarms go off, so using a little of it at the beginning of a ritual was something I considered a reasonable adaptation of the tradition. It was also burned on the quarter days (Imbolc, Beltaine, Lughnassadh, Samhain) for the same reasons.

Here is a quote from F. Marian McNeill's *The Silver Bough* regarding that tradition:

> Juniper, or the mountain yew, was burned by the Highlanders both in the house and in the byre as a purification rite on New Year's morning. Like all magical plants, it had to be pulled in a particular manner. The Druids, as we have seen, had considerable medical skill. They knew all that was known of botany and chemistry, and to them fell the selection of the herbs for the mystic cauldron.

These were gathered at certain phases of the moon. Magical rites were employed in the culling; sexual abstinence, silence, a certain method of uprooting, and occasionally sacrifice were necessary. Long after the disappearance of the Druids, herbs found by sacred streams were used to cure wounds and bruises and other ills, and traces of the rites and runes linger in folk tradition. Juniper, for instance, to be effective, had to be pulled by the roots, with its branches made into four bundles and taken between the five fingers, whilst the incantation was repeated:

I will pull the bounteous yew,
Through the five bent ribs of Christ,
In the name of the Father, the Son, and the Holy Ghost,
Against drowning, danger, and confusion.[382]

As with so many Gaelic prayers, we can take the form and consider which of the Pagan deities would suit the situation. Miach seems a very reasonable deity for the second line here, given that all of the healing herbs were said to grow from his cairn. The third line might work well with Dían Cécht, Miach, and Airmed, if you are so inclined.

John Gregorson Campbell, in several places in *The Gaelic Otherworld*, says:

> Juniper (*iubhar-beinne, aiteal*), pulled in a particular manner, was burned before cattle and put in cows' tails.

> Juniper (*Iubhar-Beinne*, literally Mountain Yew): This plant is a protection by land and sea, and no house in which it is will take fire.

> Shrovetide [the Tuesday before Lent] was one of the great days for 'saining' cattle, juniper being burned before them, while other superstitious

---

[382] F. Marian McNeill, *The Silver Bough* vol 1, Cannongate Classics, Edinburgh 1989, p. 80

precautions were taken to keep them free from harm.[383]

The *Carmina Gadelica* offers:

> *Iubhar beinne* [juniper] and *caorran*, mountain ash or rowan, were burnt on the doorstep of the byre on the first day of the quarter, on Beltaine Day and Hallowmas. The byre lintel was sprinkled with wine, or failing wine, with human urine. ... This was done to safeguard the cattle from mischance, mishap, and each other's horns.

Milliken and Bridgewater, in *Flora Celtica: Plants and People in Scotland* say:

> Juniper is another tree whose branches were sometimes hung above the doors and windows on auspicious days, or burned in the fire. Juniper burning, which formed part of the New Year rituals in some parts of the country, seemed to have a dual purpose. Not only was it supposed to ward off witches and evil spirits but, at a more practical level, it cleansed the house of pests and diseases. The branches were dried beside the fire the night before, and when all the windows and doors were shut, fires were lit in each room until the whole house was full of their acrid smoke. When the coughing and sputtering inhabitants could stand it no longer, the windows were opened and the process was repeated in the stables. Interestingly, the smoke of burning juniper is also used for spiritual cleansing in Nepal, where it plays a key part in puja ceremonies such as those held before attempts to climb Mount Everest.[384]

I don't have any particular investment in warding off witches, given that a lot of my friends fall into that category, but warding off evil

---

[383] John Gregorson Campbell, *The Gaelic Otherworld*, Birlinn, Edinburgh 2005, pp. 177, 231, 546
[384] William Milliken and Sam Bridgewater, *Flora Celtica: Plants and People in Scotland*, Birlinn, Edinburgh 2004, p. 156

spirits, bad luck, illness, danger, fires, and general klutziness seems like a pretty good reason to follow this tradition. Besides, juniper smells wonderful, and it grows abundantly around here, just as it does in the Highlands of Scotland.

Juniper was also known in Irish and Gaelic as *aiteal*. An Irish gardening website claims:

> The stems and branches which provide support for the tree's foliage and berries are covered in rich, brownish red bark, which can be seen to shred, curl and peel away in strips from the mature tree. Under the bark, you will find the pinkish white water-filled sapwood similarly aromatic to the pungent foliage. The interior brown heartwood is quite soft and has few if any wood working uses, apart from veneering; instead, it was used for burning because of its scent. The ancient Celts burned the wood of the Juniper at their autumn (Samhain) festival for purification, as an aid to allow contact with the dead.[385]

I haven't seen other references to the Irish or Scottish use of juniper for contact with the spirits of the dead, but this may well come from traditions in other parts of the world and have been attached to "ancient Celtic" uses for the plant, given that it was burned at the quarter days, one of which is Samhain. If anyone has further information about where this particular reference might have come from, please let me know. I'd be interested to see the sources on it!

---

[385] http://www.gardenplansireland.com/forum/about749.html

Muirgeilt[386]

She was Lí Bán once, before the flooding of Lough Neagh.

She tended a sacred well, keeping the door to its enclosure locked to prevent the waters from rising. The well she guarded had been magically created by the hooves of a horse given to Eochaidh, her father, by Oengus mac ind Óg. Eochaidh had been warned that if the horse ever stopped moving, destruction was sure to follow, and Eochaidh knew that the well was dangerous because it flowed forth from where the horse had stopped.

The story says that Lí Bán one day forgot to lock the door, and the waters of the well rose and flooded the countryside, creating Lough Neagh and sweeping everyone away, killing almost everyone but Lí Bán herself, and her lapdog. She took shelter in the enclosure that had guarded the well and remained there for a year, safe beneath the waves. At the end of the year, and the end of her rope, Lí Bán uttered a wish that she might be a salmon, so that she could swim with the fish outside in the water; she was transformed into a salmon with a woman's head and shoulders, and her lapdog became an otter.

After three hundred years, Beoan, a disciple of St. Comgall, was traveling along the coast with his company and heard the voice of a woman chanting. He looked down from his boat into the water and asked who was singing and Lí Bán responded to him. They conversed and, after he returned from his sojourn in Rome, he brought boats and nets and raised Lí Bán from the waters. They kept her in a boat filled with water and took her around the countryside. During these travels, her lapdog was killed and she fell into despair.

At the church of Beoan, Lí Bán was told she could either live a very long life there, or die and immediately be taken up into heaven. Tired of life and still grieving, she chose death, and was given the name Muirgeilt. Some sources translate it as "sea-wanderer" but, as we have seen before in our explorations of the *geilta* here and in some of my other writing, it can equally be translated as "sea-mad one." A saint on the Irish calendar, her feast day is January 27th.

---

[386] Standish H. O'Grady, *Silva Gadelica: A Collection of Tales in Irish*, Williams and Norgate, London 1892, vol 2, pp. 265-269

Like Suibhne, she is a poet, singing songs and chanting poems in her exile. Where Suibhne grew feathers during his years in the wilderness, Muirgeilt became part salmon, silver with scales. They were both profoundly alone in the world. None of her poems were recorded; we have only Beoan's report that she chanted and sang, the acts of a poet. She did not consume the salmon — she became the salmon. She embodied wild wisdom, originating from a sacred well.

Lí Bán shares a very similar name with Lí Ban, the sister of Fand, who is the wife of Manannán mac Lir, the sea god and the keeper of mists. We find her in the tale *The Sickbed of Cú Chulainn*, where she and Fand bring the warrior into the Otherworld to fight a battle for them. This Lí Ban is not known for her poetry, but she, like Fand, is another shapeshifter, appearing as a seabird. The intense liminality of shapeshifting, of taking on the partial form of a bird or a fish, or of total transformation into another species, is deeply resonant of the place of the *geilta* in early Irish society. They lurk at the edges of civilization, half-wild, steeped in creative power. They are unpredictable, taking on new shapes and redefining the human. They touch upon both human and animal nature, partaking of both.

Part of what I find fascinating about Muirgeilt is that, while her name contains the element *geilt*, she does not appear to be mad in the same sense that Suibhne is. They share an exile from their own people and the trauma of death all around them, but their isolation is different in quality. There is more desperation in Suibhne, and a certain sense of resignation in Muirgeilt. Both of them wander the wilderness — his of the forest and hers of the sea. Both of them are poets, even if we never see an example of Muirgeilt's work. There is a sad erasure of women's words here, but we can imagine her sea-songs and laments. We can imagine the wisdom she must have possessed. We can reclaim her salmon-human flesh from Christian sainthood and take her as a teacher from beyond the ninth wave.

I write about her today because of a friend's dream, where I showed up dressed in a feathered cloak that was shaped like a salmon, talking to them about the significance of the ogam letter *coll* — the hazel — and a cauldron filled with coals. They were unaware of the multiple layers of resonance that the image had for me. The feathered cloak is the *tugen*, the mark of the *fili*'s vocation. The *geilta*, after twenty years in the wilderness, begin growing feathers in a bird-transformation that bestows the *tugen* upon them by suffering rather than study.

The salmon shape of the cloak reminded me of Muirgeilt, and also of the strong presence of the salmon as a powerful spirit, who embodies wisdom ingested through the nuts that fall from the hazels that grow over the well of wisdom. The hazels themselves, as the subject of the dream-Erynn's discussion, are the root and source of wisdom and are a massively multi-layered symbol all on their own. Hazel is one of the nine traditional woods used for sacred fires, and fire is also a symbol of wisdom as *imbas*, the fire in the head of the poet.

The three cauldrons found within the body, discussed in the *Cauldron of Poesy* text, are echoed by the cauldron in the dream. My friend's cauldron contained embers that they could not allow to go out, an apt metaphor for some of the things happening in their life at the moment. In the dream, I instructed them to ask a mutual friend about the use of the cauldron. The image is a striking one and I will be trying to catch up with them for a chai to talk about the whole thing.

May your dreams be intriguing.

Airmed and Heapstown Cairn

Airmed was the first Celtic deity I ever had an experience with. She's been with me for pretty much the entire time I've been Pagan, though it took a couple of years to find out who she was and then figure out why she was with me, and what she was about. Even back when I was practicing a pretty generic Paganism based on eclectic Wicca, she was there. Her presence was earthy and expansive, but there was also something cosmic and overwhelming about her in some of my experiences.

Airmed was the one who told me she wanted to hear Gaelic spoken to her; I'm not very good at it, but I can manage a few phrases in prayers. I'm still working on it, but my foreign language skills aren't that great, so it takes time. She fostered my interest in healing work and herbs over the years, and I keep an altar dedicated to her in my home. The first piece of paid writing I ever did was an article on her for *SageWoman* magazine, in the Spring 1994 issue, called "Goddess of the Growing Green."

As a part of this summer's pilgrimage to Ireland (2012), our group visited Heapstown Cairn, a site associated with Airmed, Dian Cécht, Miach, and Octriuil, which is said to be the site of the healing well of Sláine that features in the Second Battle of Mag Tuired. The cairn is just at the northeast tip of Lough Arrow, in County Sligo and can be seen from the road, inside a large ring of trees.

This is a place I'd wanted to visit ever since I found out about it last year while researching sites for the pilgrimage. I'd been asked by Vyviane[387] if there were any Airmed sites in Ireland on behalf of a friend of hers and set out to see if there were. I hadn't been certain we'd be able to visit the place, given our schedule, but it turned out we were staying not far from there, just on the other side of the lake. I was determined at that point that we'd do an Airmed ritual there, and this was the place I wanted to dedicate the moss agate ogam *feda* that I'd made for her at the end of March this year.

Heapstown Cairn was our first stop of the day — later we would go to Knocknarea, to climb to Maeve's Cairn at the top of the hill. It was a grey day but not raining at that point. We crossed a verdant field to reach the cairn. As one does in Ireland, we had to watch where we walked to avoid stepping into the leavings of

---

[387] Vyviane Armstrong, of the Sisterhood of Avalon. She and the Sisterhood invited me to lead a Brigid-focused pilgrimage to Ireland in 2012.

cattle. Some of the ground was quite boggy, as you might expect near a lake when it's been raining a lot. Walking through the pastureland reminded me a lot of the fields I used to cross when I was growing up in New England, where my nearest neighbors were dairy farmers, and most of the places I wanted to play were in or across a pasture.

During our initial approach to the cairn, the group split and wandered, looking for a suitable place to hold our ritual. There were a couple of promising spots, but they weren't quite large enough for everyone. Eventually we settled on a little semicircular clearing on the southeast side of the cairn. As I walked, seeking the proper place, I was quietly singing a chant we'd written that morning as a part of our preparation for the ritual, based on traditional Gaelic healing lore, intertwined with singing Airmed's name.

Bone to bone
Flesh to flesh
Blood to Blood
Heal us now
Teach the herbs to us

The cairn has not, like Newgrange or Knowth, been excavated. There are kerbstones, but they are much overgrown and not visible, for the most part. No one knows if there are petroglyphs on them. The cairn itself is much reduced over the centuries. Local fences and other stone structures were built with some of the stones, and the pillar that once stood atop the cairn fell and was broken sometime in the last hundred years or so. We were told we shouldn't climb the cairn, to avoid destroying anything if stones were dislodged. I think it was also because people wanted to be sure nobody was going to be diminishing the cairn even further by taking stones away.

Most people interested in Irish mythology who know about Airmed will have heard the tale about Airmed and the healing herbs. In the first battle of Mag Tuired, the arm of Nuadha, the king of the Tuatha Dé Danann, was severed, making him ineligible to remain king. It was then replaced by a silver limb created by Dian Cécht. Having decided that this wasn't good enough, his son Miach replaced Nuadha's flesh arm by singing a charm much like the one above, and the use of the ashes of a wisp of burned straw to heal and regenerate the limb.

Dian Cécht, none too pleased by these proceedings, killed Miach, and he was buried under a cairn from which the 365 healing herbs grew. Miach's sister Airmed collected these herbs in her cloak, sorted by their properties and the parts of the body that they treated. Dian Cécht, not wanting the knowledge of this powerful healing to be available to everyone, scattered the herbs. Most people think of this as the end of the story.

It isn't.

During the second battle of Mag Tuired, Dian Cécht made a visit to the place called Lusmag, the Plain of Herbs, where he gathered up all the healing herbs in the land, and he brought them to the Well of Sláine, at Heapstown Cairn. The herbs were placed in the water and four healers chanted powerful spells over the well. Those four healers were Dian Cécht, Airmed, Octriuil her brother, and Miach. It makes sense to me that a god whose body became healing herbs would, like a plant, rise again and regenerate himself, reborn for healing work.

The Fomhoire, seeing that the warriors of the Tuatha Dé Danann would be wounded and rise up whole the next morning to battle once again, realized that the healing well was responsible for this. Indech's son, Octriallaig, disguised the warriors of the Fomhoire as the wounded of the Tuatha Dé Danann, and each warrior carried with him a stone, which he dropped into the well. So many were these warriors that a huge cairn rose over the well, sealing it off and making it inaccessible, removing some of the most powerful healing magic available at the battle.

Local lore says that the well is still under there and that it can be seen by crawling into a passage in the cairn. Our driver, Con, spoke to one of the local ladies while we were off doing ritual; she said that when she was young she'd heard about kids who had gone into the cairn and seen the well themselves. The passage was supposedly still accessible somewhere, but no one could find it.

For the ritual itself, I told the story of Airmed and the herbs, and of the well beneath the cairn. A cloth was laid out to represent her cloak, and a cauldron for incense and a bowl filled with water to symbolize the well were set in the center. Each person had been given a little packet containing an herb, and a slip of paper with the name of the herb and its properties listed on it. When we got to the part where Airmed was sorting the herbs from her brother's grave and laying them on the cloak, we each laid out our packet of herbs and described what the herb was and what it did.

When we heard the part of the tale where Dian Cécht brought the herbs from Lusmag and placed them in the well and the four healers stood around it chanting healing charms, we each put a bit of our herbs into the "well" and offered a pinch into the charcoal for an offering. Other offerings were made as well — whiskey was poured out, bits of food were offered, and herbs, and other personal things were given by those who had brought them. After we placed the herbs into the water, we sang the chant we'd created that morning, noted above, and took some time to do any personal workings we wanted to, whether communing with Airmed, meditating with the land, or asking for healing; this is where I did the dedication of my ogam feda.

After our workings, we heard the story of how the cairn itself was formed and the healing well buried. The ritual was closed, the water poured out, and the charcoal doused. The cloth representing the cloak still had bits of herbs clinging to it, and I shook it out into the wind, scattering the herbs as Dian Cécht had once done.

I know I'm not the only person in the group who felt that they had connected with Airmed in that place. I experienced a feeling of being very close to her, and of reaching into some essence of her spirit, her presence all around the edges of my perception. I felt her in the land and in the plants growing on and around the cairn, her blessings in the wind. I'm very thankful to have had the chance to visit this place and forge a deeper connection with my first Irish goddess.

The opportunity to do ritual in the landscape where these tales took place, where local lore has a connection to both history and the spiritual forces in the land, was profound for me. It cannot happen like that in the place where I live. The core myths of my spirituality take place in another country on the other side of the earth, and I bring what I can of it into my own place, but it feels very different here than it does in Ireland. The connection is easier and deeper but, at the same time, I can feel that Ireland isn't my place; mine is on the shores of the Salish Sea here in the Pacific Northwest. Much of the landscape is similar, the weather is very like, and many of the same plants and animals are found here, but their energies manifest differently.

Visiting Ireland, for me, wasn't like coming home. I know folks who have had that homecoming experience in Europe. For me it was like visiting the roots of something deep and significant, but it wasn't a return home. The act of pilgrimage is one of leaving home and familiar environs to make a holy visit to a sacred place, and then to return home once more, transformed. By its nature, the site visited is something set apart from one's daily life, whether it is visited once in a lifetime, once in a year, or even more often.

Pilgrimage offers us a way to approach a place in an altered frame of mind, with a heightened openness to certain types of experience of the numinous and the liminal. The places we visit on pilgrimage are, for us, threshold places where the Otherworlds bleed into our own.

On *Fireflies at Absolute Zero*

Experience is the soil in which the poet is buried, incubated like a seed.

In the Irish poetic tradition of *filidecht*, the practitioner is hidden away in darkness, and burial is an initiatory motif. In the ritual of the *tarbhfeis*, the Irish poets would wrap themselves in a fresh bull's hide, covering the eyes to seek inner vision, spoken in poetry. The Welsh poet Taliesin in his leather bag, at sea for forty years, or Aneirin, chained in a dungeon as he composed *Y Gododdin*, were wreathed in darkness as they composed. Students of oral poetry in Scotland would close themselves in darkened huts with their plaids over their heads, lying in an incubatory alembic as they labored over their poems.

So much of my poetry has arisen from darkness. The poem from which the title of this collection was taken is a phrase from a series of poems born in the darkness of dreaming. These poems address beauty and horror, myth and spirit, sound and image; they are the sparks that come out of darkness to burn in words on the page.

Fireflies at Absolute Zero[388] contains poems of time and place, from Navy piers to rutted dirt roads through the Berkshires, from the homes and hearths of friends to the snow that falls in the Northwestern rainforest, audible in the stillness, more quiet than breath. Some poems echo out of myth, with the voices of gods and spirits, while others speak of the bodies of lovers both real and imagined.

Poetry, for me, is a spiritual pursuit and a healing path. It allows me to enter the heart of things, to experience what it is to be deeply human, but its practice also allows me to reach into what it is to be something entirely outside of my small human existence. Over the years, I have used it to cope with the effects of trauma and loss, and to celebrate unexpected moments of great beauty or profound spiritual experience.

Writing is an act of devotion for me, whether I'm sitting in front of my computer in the small hours before dawn, or sipping chai at a friend's restaurant while scribbling in one of my notebooks. I carry them with me nearly everywhere, creating outlines, copying passages from research sources for my articles and books, recording

---

[388] Erynn Rowan Laurie, *Fireflies at Absolute Zero*, Hiraeth Press, Danvers 2012

likely phrases or bits of lines that might make it into a poem at some later point. I try to write every day, even if it's only a few lines, a few sentences. Eventually, something coalesces from these fragments.

Most of my writing and poetry has been the result of painstaking effort, cultivated with the patience of an ent, worried over and edited and shaped time and again. Now and then, though, something arises whole from the source, heard in a dream or striking suddenly, like a cobra. I won't deny that I love those moments of *imbas* – of the poetic fire within, sought by the early Irish poet-prophets – but it's the years of constant practice that have allowed these things to manifest, to flow out through my fingers in a frantic rush of ink. The ground requires preparation for seed to sprout, and that cultivated soil is experience and practice, patience and experimentation.

Part of that preparation has been reading poetry from many different times and places, from many languages and styles. It has been the *Epic of Gilgamesh*, and *Beowulf*, the haiku of Chiyo-ni, and the songs of Mirabai. Surrealists, Beat poets, the long, rambling lines of Whitman, and the mythic sensibility of Kathleen Raine have helped shape my work, along with the perception of poetry as magic expressed by Robin Skelton. The qualities of sound and of repetition seen in early Gaelic poetry and the Egyptian pyramid texts each bring something to my work, as does the wild, ecstatic work of Diane di Prima in *Loba*, and the sensual spirituality of Rumi.

Ultimately, like Tennyson's *Ulysses*, I have tried to use poetry as a way 'To follow knowledge like a sinking star / Beyond the utmost bound of human thought.' That work is never finished. I hope I have, at least, made a good start.

Author Bio

Erynn Rowan Laurie is a professional madwoman and the author of *Ogam: Weaving Word Wisdom* (Megalithica, 2007), *A Circle of Stones: Journeys and Meditations for Modern Celts* (Megalithica, 2012). Her poetry collection *Fireflies at Absolute Zero* (Hiraeth, 2012) won the Bisexual Books Award for poetry in 2012. She has been an active member of the Pagan and polytheist communities since 1984.